Based on the author's widely used earlier text *African Farm Management*, this account updates the economic analysis of tropical agriculture and broadens its perspective to include examples from all parts of the developing world. Writing in a clear, concise style, Professor Upton explains the essential theories of farm economics without numerous mathematical formulae. The text is completely revised, with increased emphasis on 'farm household economics', in which farms are seen as consumers as well as producers. Also included is a new chapter on the economics of irrigated agriculture.

This book provides an invaluable economic framework for better understanding the operation and management of farming systems in the tropics, and will be welcomed by students of tropical agriculture worldwide.

The economics of tropical farming systems

The economics of tropical farming systems

MARTIN UPTON

CAMBRIDGE
UNIVERSITY PRESS

Published by the Press Syndicate of the University of Cambridge
The Pitt Building, Trumpington Street, Cambridge CB2 1RP
40 West 20th Street, New York, NY 10011–4211, USA
10 Stamford Road, Oakleigh, Melbourne 3166, Australia

First published 1996

Printed in Great Britain at the University Press, Cambridge

A catalogue record for this book is available from the British Library

Library of Congress cataloguing in publication data

Upton, Martin.
  The economics of tropical farming systems / Martin Upton.
      p.   cm. – (Wye Studies in Agricultural and Rural Development)
  Includes index.
  ISBN 0 521 48289 5 (hardback). – ISBN 0 521 48340 9 (pbk.)
  1. Agriculture – Economic aspects – Africa. 2. Agriculture –
Economic aspects – Tropics. I Title. II. Series.
  HD2117.U68   1996
  338.1'0913–dc20   96–3040 CIP

ISBN 0 521 48289 5 hardback
ISBN 0 521 48340 9 paperback

SE

Contents

Preface

This book is based on my earlier text 'African Farm Management'; indeed the last six chapters are largely unchanged. However, since this version is to appear in the Wye Studies in Agriculture and Rural Development series, which is intended to serve all parts of the developing World, it seemed appropriate to broaden the scope to cover all the tropics. This required a complete revision of the early chapters, which are intended to set the broad framework of the ecological, social and economic environments within which tropical farming systems function.

At the suggestion of referees, who unfortunately remain anonymous so they cannot be thanked personally, more emphasis is placed on 'farm household economics'. This takes account of the fact that most tropical farm households are both producers and consumers, and provides a more realistic analysis than the traditional theory of production alone. For this reason the theoretical chapters have been completely rewritten from this broader viewpoint.

A difficult decision must be made regarding the use, or non-use, of mathematics to express and analyse theoretical, socio-economic relationships. For those who are happy with the use of mathematical formulae and models, this can greatly simplify and clarify analysis. However, for those who are less happy with this approach, it may confuse and obscure the theory. It also makes for 'dry' reading. In the event I have chosen to use a few mathematical equations, in support of largely verbal analysis. It is presented with apologies to my more numerate readers.

Another major change from the earlier text, is the introduction of a chapter on the economics of irrigated agriculture. This is really a huge subject area, which cannot be treated adequately in a single chapter. However, an attempt is made to summarize the main issues. Helpful comments, on the draft of this chapter, were received from Dr Mary Tiffen, who used to run the irrigation network of the Overseas Development Institute, London, and Dr Mario Falciai of the University of Florence, for which I am most grateful. Thanks are also due to Dr Jogesh Khatri of Cambridge University for helpful comments on Chapter 13.

Some may feel that, having used the term 'farming systems' in the title, more emphasis should have been placed on this approach and the associated methodologies, involving greater farmer participation. Some relevant ideas are discussed in Chapter 10. However, the main aim of this book is to expound the economic theories and methods which, I believe, provide the best framework for better understanding the operation and management of farming systems in the tropics.

Part I

Farm household economics

1

Farming systems in economic development

The farming population

This book is concerned with the analysis and planning of small-holder farming systems in the developing countries of the tropics and sub-tropics. Most of the low-income, and lower-middle-income, countries of Africa, Asia and Latin America (with Gross National Product *per capita* in 1992 of less than US$2,695) lie within these zones. In these countries, general economic development is heavily dependent on the performance of the large agricultural sector, made up mainly of semi-subsistence small-holder family farms.

The aims of this introductory chapter are to demonstrate the importance of the agricultural sector, to outline the domestic and international market environment, within which agricultural producers operate, to review the processes of change in this environment and finally to summarize the major characteristics of the smallholder farming systems.

In terms of the number of people employed, agriculture is the most important single industry in the world. The estimated agricultural population of nearly 2.5 billion, makes up about 44 per cent of the total. Although this proportion is decreasing, as a result of rural–urban migration, the absolute numbers engaged in agriculture are still growing. This pattern is repeated in the developing countries of Africa, Asia (Far East) and Latin America. Agricultural populations are only declining in the upper-middle and high-income countries, where they are already relatively small (see Table 1.1).

The figures given in this Table, and the remainder of this chapter, are derived from data collected from national statistical sources and published by FAO or the World Bank. There are many potential sources of errors and inconsistencies in these data. Hence, 'they should be construed only as indi-

3

Table 1.1. *Agricultural populations in developing regions*

	World	Developing countries			Developed countries
		Africa	Far East[a]	Latin America	
Agricultural population as % total	43.9	64.5	59.7	24.9	7.2
Growth rate agricultural population %	1.0	1.6	1.2	0.4	−3.4
Growth rate non-agricultural population %	3.5	7.2	5.7	3.2	0.9

Source: FAO 1994. Current statistics for 1993; growth rates annual average between 1980 and 1993.
[a] Far East includes South Asia

cating trends and characterizing major differences among economies rather than offering precise quantitative measures of those differences.' (World Bank 1994). This is the spirit in which they are presented here.

Consideration of these figures suggests three reasons why agricultural productivity growth is necessary for economic development and improvement of the general welfare of the populace. First, given that the agricultural population forms such a large proportion of the total, national average *per capita*, income must be strongly influenced by income levels in agriculture. Increases in farm incomes are automatically reflected in higher levels of national income *per capita*. Second, agricultural production must be increased in order to absorb the growing labour force even at the existing level of productivity per agricultural worker. Third a growing marketed surplus is needed to feed (and provide raw materials for) the growing non-agricultural populations.

Food and agriculture

The provision of food and fibre for the growing national population is another key role for agriculture. It is estimated that, for the whole world and for the developing countries of Africa, Asia and Latin America, the growth of agricultural production over the last decade has exceeded that of the population, so that agricultural production *per head* has increased. However, although food production per head increased substantially in Asia, it grew very little in Latin America, while it actually fell in Africa, where major famines occurred during the 1980s (see Table 1.2).

Table 1.2. *Food production* per caput *in developing countries*

		Developing countries			Developed countries
	World	Africa	Far East[a]	Latin America	
Growth in food production % 1980–92	2.1	2.9	3.8	2.4	0.7
Growth in *per caput* food production % 1980–92	0.3	−0.1	1.9	0.3	0
Growth in calorie consumption % 1980–89	0.5	0.2	0.9	0.1	0.4
Calories *per caput* per day 1989	2710	2224	2450	2732	3417

Source: FAO 1994.
[a] Far East includes South Asia

These trends in food production are reflected in changes in average dietary energy intakes, which improved significantly in Asia but which changed very little in Latin America. The mean daily calorie intake per head remained at a low level in Africa, but this was only maintained by increasing reliance on food imports. Over the 1980s the index of the volume of African food imports rose by 26 per cent to a level of 300 calories *per capita* per day (Alexandratos 1988).

The means for regional groups of countries hide large variations between and within individual populations. Using the methodology of the Fifth World Food Survey (FAO 1987) it is estimated that in 1983/5 over a fifth of the population of 89 developing countries, or 512 million people, were undernourished. (These estimates are based on the assumed threshold calorie level of 1.4 times the Basal Metabolic Rate: see FAO 1987.) Although well over half the undernourished people live in Asia, they represent a smaller proportion of the whole population than in Africa. Furthermore, both numerically and as a proportion of the total Asian population, they are predicted to fall. Elsewhere the numbers of undernourished people are expected to increase, although they will represent a smaller proportion of the total population (see Table 1.3).

It may be concluded from these statistics that agricultural growth and development is important to increase food supplies and improve the nutritional status of the people of Africa, Asia and Latin America. This is particularly true for Africa where food production per person actually fell over

Table 1.3. *Estimates of undernutrition*

	89 Developing countries	Developing countries		
		Afri :a	Asia[a]	Latin America
Number of persons 1983–85 (million)	512	142	291	55
Number of persons 2000 (million)	532	194	246	62
% of population 1983–85	21.5	35.2	21.8	14.2
% of population 2000	15.6	28.7	13.9	11.6

Source: Alexandratos 1988.
[a] Assumed to correspond with 'Far East including South Asia'

the last 20 years, but the argument may be extended to other parts of the 'tropical world'. Although hunger and famines may be attributed to poverty and lack of 'entitlements' it is none the less likely that increases in food production and supply will reduce relative food prices and allow general improvements in human nutrition. At the same time reduction of imports and greater self-sufficiency in food should yield benefits through import substitution and saving of scarce foreign exchange.

Agricultural trade and economic growth

During the process of economic development, and particularly under a strategy of 'primary export led growth' agriculture is expected to make a significant contribution to net foreign exchange earnings. However, for the developing tropical countries with which we are concerned, this is no longer occurring. Agricultural exports now make up only a small proportion of the total value of exports from each of the continental groups. In Latin America, where the proportion is highest, it still only amounts to about a quarter of the total. For the developing countries of the Far East, agricultural exports make up a smaller proportion of the total than in the developed countries. Furthermore, other than in Latin America, the cost of agricultural imports exceeds the revenue from agricultural exports, albeit by a small margin; thus the agricultural trade balance is negative (Table 1.4).

Even though for many countries it is no longer appropriate to treat agriculture as a leading export sector, there are appealing arguments for reduced dependency on food imports and greater national self-sufficiency.

Table 1.4. *Trade in agricultural products*

	World	Developing countries			Developed countries
		Africa	Far East[a]	Latin America	
Growth in agricultural exports %	2.6	2.0	5.5	1.9	2.2
Agric. exports % of total	9.3	14.9	8.2	26.1	8.8
$\dfrac{(X-M)}{(X+M)}$	−0.04	−0.05	−0.03	0.42	−0.06
Growth in agric. imports %	1.9	1.0	4.0	−1.0	1.5
Agric. imports % total	9.8	16.6	8.4	11.8	9.4

Source: FAO 1994. Current statistics for 1990; growth rates annual average between 1980 and 1990.
[a] Far East includes South Asia

In many cases the dependency on imports results from government policies, such as the maintenance of an overvalued currency, which have an adverse impact on the prices received by domestic producers. An important aim of structural adjustment programmes is to eliminate price distortions and provide incentives for increased home production and import substitution. Even where it really is currently cheaper to import than to produce domestically, the instability of world markets provides a motive for seeking greater self-sufficiency for security reasons. In any case, increases in the productivity of domestic agriculture should both increase food supplies and reduce the cost of production, relative to the price of imports.

Although the volume of agricultural imports grew over the 1980s, it should be noted that for Asia and Latin America agricultural exports grew faster; for Asia at a rate of six per cent annually. If this trend continues, Asia's negative agricultural trade balance should eventually be eliminated. The situation in Africa gives more cause for concern in that imports have grown while exports have stagnated. However, in all regions there are potential benefits to be derived from greater self-sufficiency and a reduction in import dependency provided that this can be achieved without any adverse impact on agricultural exports.

The contribution of agriculture to the national income is illustrated for individual countries (in Table 1.5), since comparable aggregate statistics are not available for the regional groups used earlier. In each case the selected country is reasonably typical of the whole group. Nigeria and India are

Table 1.5. *Contribution of agriculture to Gross Domestic Product in selected countries; 1992*

	Nigeria	India	Ecuador	Japan
GNP per caput US$	320	310	1070	28 190
Agric. GDP % of total	37	32	13	2
Agricultural labour-force % of total[1]	64.1 (3.0)	65.8 (4.1)	28.8 (2.7)	5.8 (3.0)
Growth agricultural GDP %[2]	3.6	3.2	4.7	0.7
Growth agricultural labour-force %[3]	2.4 (1.2)	1.5 (1.7)	0.6 (4.1)	−4.5 (5.4)
Growth total GDP %	2.3	5.2	2.3	4.1
Growth total labour-force %[3]	2.8 (−0.5)	2.0 (3.1)	3.0 (−0.7)	1.0 (3.1)

Source: FAO 1994 & World Bank 1994
1. In parentheses: labour productivity in non-agriculture, relative to that in agriculture, 1992.
2. All growth rates 1980–92
3. In parentheses: growth in productivity of labour-force.

low-income economies with about 60 per cent of the labour-force still employed in agriculture, in common with most countries of Africa and the Far East. Ecuador is a lower-middle-income economy like many other Latin American countries with about a quarter of the labour-force employed in agriculture. Japan is included, as a representative high-income economy for comparison.

First may be noted the huge differences in national income, *per capita*, between Nigeria and India on the one hand and Japan on the other. National income *per capita* is 90 times higher in the latter economy, and 28 times that of Ecuador. It may be inferred that there are similar differences in productivity per person. These differences may be accounted for, in part, by the relative size of the agricultural sector. In general, the larger is the Gross National Product per person, the smaller is the size of the agricultural sector in relation to the whole economy. It is also noteworthy that within each economy the contribution of agriculture to the Gross Domestic Product is only about half its contribution to employment. The implication of these statistics is that productivity per person employed in other non-agricultural sectors is much larger, apparently 3 to 4 times larger, than the productivity per person employed in agriculture.

Each member of the labour-force only receives a part of his or her product. Other inputs of land and capital assets, such as machinery and equipment, are also involved, and their costs must be met. Given that the average industrial employee uses substantially more capital equipment than an agricultural worker, the share of the total product received by the former is probably smaller than that of the latter. None the less the average net labour income in agriculture is generally markedly lower than that in manufacturing industry. Indeed, this 'wages gap' provides a major incentive for the rural–urban migration remarked upon earlier.

It might be inferred from these findings that real poverty is likely to be more prevalent in rural than in urban areas. This was in fact found to be the case in a study of trends in absolute poverty in developing countries, where the absolute poverty line was defined as that income level below which a nutritionally adequate diet and essential non-food items are not affordable (United Nations 1989). For all developing countries, 73.5 per cent of the poor lived in rural areas in 1985. For Asia (excluding China) the proportion was 77 per cent and for Africa it was 83 per cent. Only in Latin America did the numbers of urban poor exceed those in rural areas. These findings serve to emphasize the need for rapid rural development and increased agricultural productivity to combat rural poverty.

Some growth in agricultural production and labour productivity occurred over the 1980s in all these countries; indeed in Ecuador it was particularly rapid. In Nigeria and Ecuador this growth occurred despite a decline in overall economic productivity. Thus it appears that, although industrial and general economic development were retarded by the international economic recession of the 1980s, agriculture was less severely affected. In contrast the Indian economy, like many others in Asia, continued to grow faster than the agricultural sector throughout this period.

The much higher level of production per head, observed in non-agricultural occupations, provides support for the view that industrialization is the key to economic development. The evidence suggests that the smaller is the agricultural sector in relation to the rest of the economy, the larger is the overall Gross Domestic Product *per capita*. However there are limits to the rate at which non-agricultural industries and services can grow, set partly by the limited availability of new capital, and possibly the enterprise and skills needed to absorb this capital. In fact, there may be more scope for expanding productive employment in agriculture than in other industries.

Furthermore industrial growth may be retarded by the sluggish performance of agriculture. Where, as in sub-Saharan Africa, food production *per capita* is actually falling, it is very likely that food prices will rise, food shortages and poorer diets will result or food imports will increase; or a combination of all three will occur. Rising food prices create pressures for increased wages and thus reduce industrial margins; reduced dietary intakes have an adverse impact on labour productivity; while increased imports are a drain on scarce foreign exchange and compete with imports of equipment and other forms of capital needed for industrialization. Even if food production *per capita* is growing, the pace may be too slow to meet increases in demand associated with income growth. Thus problems may be created even in this situation. In addition, growth of agricultural incomes is necessary to provide an expanding market for the increased production of industrial consumer goods. These arguments for balanced growth of agriculture and non-agriculture are expanded upon below (also see Bhaduri 1993).

Market supply and demand for food

The majority of agricultural producers in the developing countries of the tropics are semi-subsistence farm households. Thus part of the total product is retained within the household for home consumption. The remainder, often referred to as the 'marketed surplus' is offered for sale. The total quantity of an agricultural commodity offered for sale in a given market (e.g. nationally) over a given period (e.g. a year) is influenced by the price of the commodity, the prices of alternative products and of purchased inputs, the size of the agricultural labour-force and the production technology.

Market supply is normally defined as the relationship between quantity offered and price of the commodity, with all other factors held constant. More precisely the supply curve, or schedule, relates amounts of the product that would be offered for sale in a market to the price prevailing during a particular period of time. Theoretical analysis, to be developed in later chapters of this book, suggests that this relationship is positive, so the curve slopes upward as shown in Figure 1.1. Many empirical studies of the supply response of tropical crop producers have confirmed this relationship (see Askari & Cummings 1976).

Changes in the other factors, such as the production technology, are assumed to cause the supply curve to shift. Over time, as new technology is introduced and the agricultural labour force increases, market supply is likely to increase and the unit cost of production is likely to fall. Note that an increase in productivity may be interpreted as an increase in the quantity of output for a given cost and price, or a reduction in the cost of producing a given level of output. Thus the supply curve shifts downwards and to the right as shown in Figure 1.1.

Effective consumer demand is reflected in a demand curve or schedule, relating the quantity that consumers are willing and able to purchase and the market price during a particular period of time. The slope of the demand curve is negative, since an increase in the price of the commodity is likely to persuade consumers to reduce their purchases and seek for cheaper substitutes. Here again, empirical evidence supports the theoretical assumption of a downward-sloping demand curve (curve *DD* in Figure 1.2). Other factors, such as consumer incomes and population growth, which may influence the quantity demanded are treated separately as causing shifts of the demand curve.

In a free market, with many buyers and sellers, the equilibrium price and quantity are determined by the intersection of the supply and demand curves (price P_1 and quantity Q_1 in Figure 1.2). Here the forces of supply and demand are precisely balanced; there is no unsold surplus and no unsatisfied demand. An increase in supply like that shown in Figure 1.2, with demand constant, must result in a fall in price as the point of intersection moves down the demand curve (quantity rises to Q_2 so price falls to P_2). Conversely a reduction in supply would result in a price increase. This is the basis for the suggestion made earlier that the decline in food production *per capita* in Africa would result in increasing food prices.

Figure 1.1   The supply response curve with a parallel shift

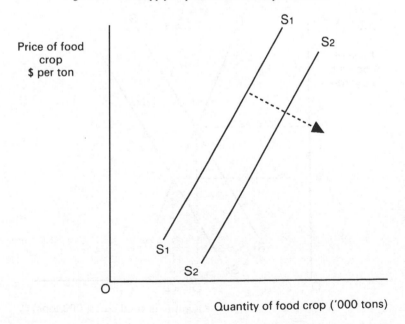

If the government attempted to raise producer incomes by imposing a minimum market price, which was higher than the equilibrium price (like P_x in Figure 1.3) then the quantity supplied would exceed the quantity demanded and there would be an unsold surplus (equal to Q_2-Q_1 in the Figure). In order to sell the surplus to private consumers, it would be necessary to reduce the price.

Alternatively, an export market may exist for the commodity. Given that the world market for the commodity is likely to be very much larger than the domestic market, it is safe to assume that the world (export parity) price is constant regardless of the amount that is exported from this one producing country. This is known as 'the small country assumption' for obvious reasons. If this export parity price is higher than the domestic equilibrium price, then production and sales can be increased by exporting the surplus over domestic needs. (In Figure 1.3, P_x is now assumed to represent the export parity price, quantity Q_2 is produced, quantity Q_1 is consumed domestically, while Q_2-Q_1 is exported.)

Similarly, an attempt to benefit consumers by holding the price below the equilibrium price (at P_m) would result in a supply deficit, or unsatisfied demand (equal to Q_2-Q_1). Parallel markets might develop and the price would be bid up to the equilibrium level. Alternatively if the import parity

Figure 1.2   Food prices fall with an increase in supply

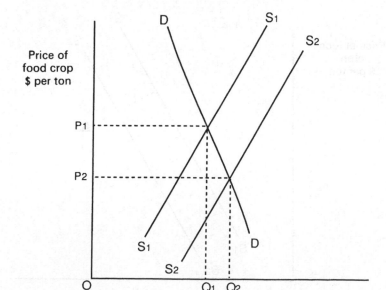

Quantity of food crop ('000 tons)

price was below the domestic equilibrium price, then the deficit could be made up by imports. (In Figure 1.3, P_m is now assumed to represent the import parity price, so quantity $Q_2–Q_1$ is imported.)

Actually this attempt to illustrate both import and export possibilities in one diagram is rather misleading since, in practice, the import parity price invariably exceeds the export parity price. The domestic equilibrium price for a staple food crop may well lie between the two. Exports only become feasible if the domestic equilibrium price falls to below export parity. Imports are only justified if the domestic price rises above import parity.

Growth and structural change

In order to analyse processes of change let us consider the supply and demand relationships for a staple food crop (e.g. rice or maize) in a national market. Initially we will ignore the effects of changing prices for traded inputs, and assume there are no substitute products. Thus the major remaining factors causing shifts in the supply curve are:

Figure 1.3   Price adjustment

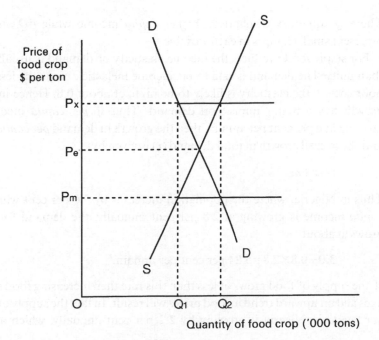

Quantity of food crop ('000 tons)

1. technological change and capital investment, and
2. changes in the size of the agricultural labour force.

Technological innovation and the associated capital investment are generally assumed to result in increases in productivity and a rightward shift in the supply curve. Given that the agricultural labour-force is still growing in Africa and Asia, and assuming that the additional labour contributes some extra production (that is the marginal product of labour is positive, see Chapter 3), this factor should also cause supply to increase. Note that even in Africa food supply increased over the last decade, but since the population growth rate was even faster, production per head fell.

The demand for food is also likely to increase over time as the population grows together with *per capita* incomes. If food consumption *per capita* remains constant then clearly an *x* per cent growth in population results in an *x* per cent growth in the total demand for food. However, if income *per capita* is also rising, then so too will the quantity of food demanded. The size of this effect is measured by the 'income elasticity of demand' (*n*), which is defined as the ratio of the proportionate change in the quantity demanded to the proportionate change in *per capita* income. Thus:

$$n = \frac{dQ/Q}{dY/Y} = \frac{dQ}{dY} \cdot \frac{Y}{Q}$$

where Q=quantity demanded, Y=*per capita* income while dQ and dY represent small changes in each variable.

For staple food products the income elasticity of demand is usually less than unity. The demand is said to be 'income inelastic'. None the less, in a poor society the elasticity is likely to be high, at about 0.8. Hence income growth has a major impact on demand. Thus if *per capita* income is growing at *g* per cent per annum, then the growth in demand *per capita* is *ng* and the overall growth in total demand (*r*) is given by:

$$r = x + ng.$$

Thus in Nigeria, where the population increases by 3.0 per cent while *per capita* income is growing at 2.8 per cent annually, the demand for food grows at about

$$3.0 + 0.8 \times 2.8 = 5.24 \text{ per cent per annum.}$$

If the supply of food grows at less than this rate then increasing food shortages and an upward trend in food prices will result. In fact the supply of food *per capita* in Nigeria is growing by 2.2 per cent annually, which almost matches the growth in demand of about 0.8×2.8=2.24 per cent. Thus the upward trend in food prices should be slight. However, this illustration should make clear that substantial growth in the supply of food is needed simply to keep pace with the growth in demand and avoid food price increases.

A hypothetical example is used to illustrate price changes in Figure 1.4 where the increase in supply of food over a given period, of a decade for example, is represented by the shift from S_1S_1 to S_2S_2. The corresponding growth in demand, over the same period, is shown by the shift from D_1D_1 to D_2D_2. Since the growth in demand exceeds the growth in supply, the price trend is upwards. It should be clear that if, on the contrary, the increase in supply exceeded the growth in demand then the price would fall over time.

A rise in the relative price of food, resulting from a failure to meet the growing demand, can have seriously adverse consequences for the general growth of the economy. Given that food accounts for a major part of the wages of industrial workers, a rise in the price of food must result in pressure for increased wages. This implies lower profit margins in industry, leading to reduced levels of employment and investment. Thus the rates of industrialization and economic growth are slowed down.

Alternatively, the growth in food demand may be met by increased

Figure 1.4   Food prices rise when demand grows faster than supply

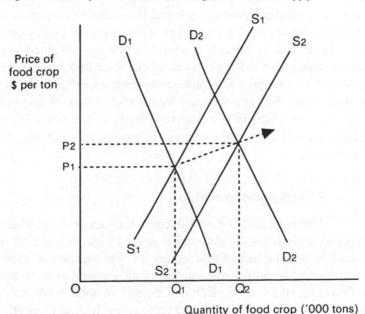

Quantity of food crop ('000 tons)

imports. However, unless they are matched by increases in exports or foreign aid, the result will be a growing current account deficit on the balance of payments. The ultimate effect must be to raise the effective prices of imported industrial inputs, and thereby reduce the rate of industrial growth. Thus in most developing countries, which have a relatively large agricultural sector, failure of growth in the supply of food and raw materials to keep pace with the growth in demand is likely to act as a serious brake on industrial expansion. Thus it may be concluded that growth and development of the agricultural sector is a necessary precondition for general economic development (also see Bhaduri 1993).

The effects of rising food prices will tend to correct the imbalance between the growth rates of supply and demand. Growth of demand will be slowed as the general rate of economic development is reduced; while rural–urban migration may slow down as agricultural prices, and incomes, rise in relation to those in other sectors. This effect, which is referred to as an improvement in agriculture's 'terms of trade' provides incentives for retaining resources in agriculture and increasing the supply of agricultural products.

The alternative scenario, where the growth in supply of food exceeds the growth in demand, is one where prices decline and the terms of trade move against food producers. This does not necessarily mean that agricultural incomes fall, since the decline in prices may be more than balanced by the growth in output per person employed. If producer incomes are adversely affected, however, while industrial growth occurs, the rate of rural–urban migration is likely to increase as a result of the widening income gap. This relative decrease in the agricultural labour force may bring about slower growth of food supply and a consequent improvement in the farmer's terms of trade. Thus there is a tendency for the rate of flow of resources out of agriculture to adjust in response to changes in the terms of trade and thereby stabilize the income differential between this and other sectors of the economy.

Changing product markets

Diversification into production for export is another possible response to declining domestic food prices or increasing food surpluses. Indeed for the first half of this century economic growth of most tropical countries was based upon expansion of agricultural exports. Since then, however, the share of agricultural exports in total trade has declined steadily from over 50 per cent in the 1950s to much lower proportions today as shown in Table 1.4. This reflects, in part, the industrialization and import substitution policies adopted and associated accelerated growth in domestic demand for agricultural commodities. For countries like Nigeria, Indonesia, Mexico and Venezuela with substantial mineral oil reserves, exports of this primary commodity grew to dominate foreign trade. Yet some major agricultural exporters remain in East Africa, Sri Lanka and Thailand, Argentina and Colombia for instance. As already noted, agricultural exports from Asia have grown quite rapidly over the last decade (Table 1.4).

There are three sets of factors that may limit the growth of agricultural exports: external demand constraints, market instability and internal restrictions. External demand constraints reflect the fact that the demand for agricultural export commodities on world markets tends to grow slower than supply, since income elasticities of demand are low and especially since synthetic substitutes are available for products such as fibres and rubber. Hence it is argued that there is a secular tendency for the terms of trade to decline for agricultural exporters (Singer 1987). This is exacerbated by restrictions on the imports of some tropical products, particularly in processed form, by high-income countries; and their exports of subsidized sugar, grain and dairy products which may depress world prices.

In addition world market prices are highly variable, as supplies and demands fluctuate. Attempts to stabilize domestic prices by high income countries may increase the price fluctuations on the international markets. For these reasons governments of developing tropical countries seek to reduce their reliance on world markets and adopt import substitution policies. Such policies have involved promotion of industrialization and effective taxation of agriculture. In the past many governments imposed taxes on agricultural exports to raise revenue for industrial development, although most of these were lifted in the early 1970s. More recently the maintenance of overvalued currencies, in many developing economies, has artificially depressed the prices received, for both exports and domestic food, by agricultural producers. Currency devaluation, as an element of structural reform, has eliminated such distortions in many cases, but the adverse impact on agricultural exports may have persisted.

In a growing economy the pattern of domestic demand for different agricultural commodities is likely to change. While the income elasticity of demand for staple food crops may be low, that for better quality or more convenient foodstuffs is generally higher. Thus although the income elasticities of demand for roots and tubers or coarse grains are generally below 0.25 or even negative, those for wheat, rice, sugar and livestock products often exceed unity. In the latter case a 10 per cent increase in *per capita* income is estimated to result in a more than 10 per cent increase in purchases of the commodity.

If there were no corresponding changes in farming systems and patterns of production, then the prices for the high elasticity commodities, for which demand was growing faster, would rise in relation to those of the more basic staples. In fact these changing prices provide incentives for farmers to change their patterns of production towards those commodities with the faster growing demand. Not only must total agricultural production expand, but also the types of crops and livestock produced must change in order to keep pace with the changing pattern of consumer demands.

The aim of the discussion so far has been to emphasize the continuing importance of the agricultural sector, its growth and development. Its importance lies in providing employment for a majority of the population in Africa and Asia, and about a quarter in Latin America, and in feeding the growing populations. Arguments have been presented to suggest that growth of the marketed surplus from agriculture is necessary to keep pace with growing demands for food and industrial raw materials to avoid imbalances and constraints on general economic development. At the same time changes in systems of production are necessary in the light of changing patterns of consumer demand.

The farm household

The bulk of agricultural output from the tropics and sub-tropics is produced by semi-subsistence smallholder family farms. There are some larger-scale commercial farms, estates and ranches in most tropical and sub-tropical countries, in some cases as remnants of a colonial past. However, they are far outweighed in importance by smallholder family farms not only numerically, but also in terms of land use and their contribution to total output. Even in Latin America, where there are large disparities in farm sizes, the numbers of very small farms (*minifundia*) generally exceed the numbers of large-scale, commercial farms (*latifundia*). Thus agricultural growth and development depends upon the decisions and actions of these farm households.

For such agricultural households, decisions about the management of the farm are closely linked with household decisions on what to eat or how to allocate time between farm work and other activities. The typical unit of production is a nuclear family comprising a man, his wife or wives and their unmarried children, although other relatives may be involved. Such a family may live in more than one dwelling, but all members generally 'share the same pot'. Female-headed farm households are common especially where there are employment opportunities for men in off-farm work. Agricultural pluri-activity is very common, and it is suggested that 25 to 30 per cent of the annual labour supply of rural households is spent in off-farm activities (see Eicher & Baker 1982). Remittances from family members living away also contribute to family income, and household decisions relate to both on-farm and off-farm activities (see Chapter 4).

Given that the household is the production unit, a farm may be defined as all the agricultural activities under the control of the household members. Within the household decision-making is shared in various ways. In some cases, decisions may be made jointly by all the family members, while in other cases there may be division of responsibility, for instance where subsistence crops are produced by women, while cash crops are tended by the men. Frequently individual members of the household may have independent control of some plots of land or groups of livestock. The allocation of resources and responsibility for decision-making within the household, and particularly the role of women, has important implications for the design of agricultural and rural development policies. Some progress has been made in recent years in researching this subject (for a summary see Ellis 1993, Chapter 9). None the less for much economic analysis, it is convenient to assume that there is a single decision-maker, 'the farmer', responsible for managing and controlling the household resources.

The productive resources under the managerial control of the farmer are conveniently classified under the headings of land, labour and capital. A typical tropical farm household cultivates a relatively small area of land, but frequently has user rights to a larger area which may be rotational fallow or grazed by livestock. In fact the term 'land' is generally assumed to include all 'natural resources' such as water, minerals, natural grazing, forests and other wild flora and fauna. All these are important to the farm household. The labour-force is mainly made up of family members, although some work may be done communally and some labour is hired.

Capital consists of everything else used in production, which is not a gift of nature but which has been produced in the past. It is frequently claimed that African smallholders use relatively little capital per person employed in comparison with large commercial schemes. Although this may be true in total cash value terms, the smallholder uses many kinds of capital including permanent crops, livestock, tools, equipment, buildings, land improvements and stocks of seed, fertilizer, animal feeds and agro-chemicals. The coffee, cocoa, tea, oil palm or rubber producer has a large amount of capital tied up in the standing crop, while a pastoralist similarly has a large amount represented by his/her herds and flocks.

It is useful to think of a farm as a system, or set of interrelated components. The components are the resources described above, the productive activities with their associated input–output relationships, and, in family farming, consumption and other household activities. Any system has a boundary which separates it from the larger systems which make up the environment. A farming system is under managerial control and the boundary represents the limits of that control.

'Farming systems analysis' is intended to improve our understanding of the interrelationships between the components, and the framework of farmer decision-making. Any programmes or policies aimed at accelerating the development of small farms should be based on an awareness of their relevance and likely impact. For instance, price policies to provide production incentives should take full account of costs of production and farmers' price responsiveness. Programmes for institutional change, aimed at making resources and new knowledge more readily available to farmers are doomed to failure if they are not guided by an understanding of existing institutions, current practices and farmers' attitudes. Above all, research and development of new technology should be directed towards meeting farmers' objectives and overcoming their constraints besides building on the indigenous technology already in use. Clearly this depends upon a knowledge of what farmers do and the grounds for their choices.

Such knowledge can only be obtained from the farmers themselves, so field studies and data collection are essential. Part III of this book is concerned with this topic. However, analysis of the findings requires a theoretical framework, which may be provided by the economics of production, consumption and resource use discussed in the remainder of Parts I and II. Finally Part IV describes some approaches to farm planning and evaluation of the impact of new technologies or policies.

Farming systems are complex; firstly because there are many fundamentally different components such as plants, animals, people, tools and wells, which means that a multi-disciplinary approach is needed to study them, and secondly there are many different ways in which the components can be combined. The disciplines needed obviously include crop and livestock sciences, but may also include soil science, hydrology, engineering, economics and sociology. However, to find our way through the complexity and improve our understanding we must simplify. This is achieved *either* by concentrating on particular sub-systems, such as the cereal-growing enterprise or an individual animal, or preferably by ignoring many interrelationships and concentrating on a few critical ones. Such a simplified, theoretical model of a farm may be represented diagrammatically as in Figure 1.5.

This diagram serves to illustrate that inputs of labour, natural resources and capital services are combined to yield farm products, and that these products may be consumed or invested. Investment simply means additions to the stock of capital, for instance when animals are retained for breeding,

Figure 1.5   A family farm system

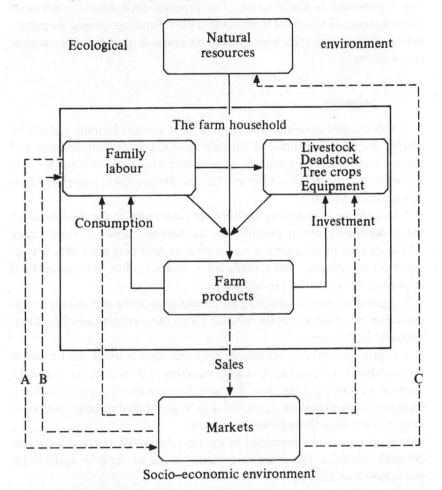

A = Off-farm work
B = Labour hire
C = Purchase or renting land

or yams are kept for planting sets. Other forms of capital, such as land improvements are created directly using farm labour, as shown by the arrow from labour to capital. The broken lines represent additional relationships for farmers engaged in the cash economy, which is the case throughout most of the tropics today. Then some products are sold and the proceeds may be used to buy consumer goods and items of capital, such as tools and machinery, or to hire labour and capital services or even land. Alternative off-farm uses of labour and capital, such as investment in education, are also represented in the diagram. The farming environment consists of larger systems, of which the farm is only a part. Farming systems are particularly influenced by (i) the ecological or natural and (ii) the socio-economic environment.

Summary

1 This chapter introduces the economics of tropical farming systems by emphasizing the importance of agriculture as a source of employment and means of survival for the majority of people in Africa and Asia and for over a quarter of those in Latin America. The absolute numbers engaged in agriculture are still rising.

2 In addition domestic agriculture provides most of the food needs of the fast-growing urban populations as well as those of rural areas. Although food production *per capita* grew in Asia over the 1980s, it stagnated in Latin America and actually fell in Africa, leading to increased food imports and many malnourished people.

3 Agriculture now represents only a small proportion of total exports of most tropical countries, whilst in value terms these exports are almost balanced by food imports.

4 Labour incomes in agriculture are considerably lower than those in urban industry. In Asia and Africa the numbers of rural poor far exceed the numbers of poor in urban areas. In Latin America the situation is reversed. However, agricultural development can make a major contribution to poverty alleviation throughout the tropics.

5 Food prices are determined by the intersection of market supply and demand schedules. Government policies to tax or support agricultural prices have a social cost.

6 Both the domestic supply (production) and effective demand (consumption) for food grow over time. If supply fails to keep pace with demand, then food prices, and/or imports, will rise. This in turn is likely to drive up industrial wages and cause inflation.

7 If supply growth exceeds that of demand, food prices may fall. However, this situation provides a sustainable basis for industrial growth and economic development, with scope for greater product diversification in rural areas.

8 The majority of those engaged in tropical agriculture are members of smallholder farm households, even in Latin America where there is wide variation in farm sizes and systems. Such households are engaged in both production and consumption of food, leisure and other goods.

9 The tropical farm household may be viewed as a system, operating within ecological, social and market environments and allocating limited natural resources, labour and capital between competing ends in pursuit of multiple objectives.

References

Askari, H. & J. T. Cummings (1976). *Agricultural Supply Response: A Survey of the Econometric Evidence*, New York, Praeger

Alexandratos, N. (ed.) (1988). *World Agriculture: Toward 2000. An FAO Study*, London, Belhaven Press

Bhaduri, A. (1993). 'Alternative development strategies and the rural. sector', in Singh, A. & H. Tabatabai (eds.), *Economic Crisis and Third World Agriculture*, Cambridge University Press

Ellis, F. (1993). *Peasant economics; Farm Households and Agrarian Development (2nd edn)*, Cambridge University Press

FAO (1987). *Fifth World Food Survey*, Rome, FAO

FAO (1994). *AGROSTAT* (Computerized Database), Rome, FAO

Singer, H. W. (1987). 'Terms of trade and economic development', in Eatwell, J., M. Milgate & P. Newman (eds.), *The New Palgrave: A Dictionary of Economics*, London & Basingstoke, Macmillan

United Nations (1989). *1989 Report on the World Social Situation*, Department of International Economic and Social Affairs, New York, United Nations

World Bank (1994). *World Development Report 1994: Infrastructure for Development*, Oxford University Press

2

The farmer's environment

The natural environment

Human societies have always exploited the natural environment to meet the necessities of life. In doing so the balance of nature, or ecological equilibrium is altered. Hunters and gatherers, by harvesting certain species of wild animals and plants, reduce the population, or biomass, of these species. By grazing the natural rangelands, pastoralists' herds may displace some of the natural fauna, and change the pasture composition. Cultivators modify the environment more drastically by clearing the natural vegetation, and growing new kinds of plants. Under irrigation, the amount of water available for plant growth is increased, thereby transforming the environment and allowing the introduction of exotic crops. Thus agriculture creates new man-made environments or agricultural ecosystems.

Despite the ability of cultivators and herders to modify the natural environment, choices of farming system, crop and livestock enterprises and methods of production are constrained by the climate, soils and biology of the region. Tropical climates are characterized by high levels of solar energy incidence, almost twice as much as is received in temperate zones in the growing season. It should be noted, however, that over 25 per cent of land within the tropics is above 900 m in altitude and is therefore subject to lower temperatures and higher rainfall, than the neighbouring lowlands. Temperate crops such as wheat and barley may be grown, while the keeping of exotic breeds of livestock raises fewer problems than in the hotter tropical lowlands.

In the tropical and sub-tropical lowlands temperatures are adequate to support crop growth throughout the year, so the main constraint on production is the availability of soil moisture. In the absence of irrigation, crop growth is limited by the seasonal pattern of rainfall, which ranges from being perennial in the humid tropics, through bimodal regimes in sub-humid zones, to unimodal distributions in the tropical drylands (Figure 2.1).

The humid tropics occupy a belt roughly 10 degrees north and south of the equator, in Amazonia, Central Africa and South East Asia where, if there is a dry season, it is of less than 5 months duration, so that crop production is possible throughout most of the year. The natural climax vegetation is tropical rainforest. Perennial tree crops are grown, with swamp rice or root crops as the staple food.

The sub-humid tropics, which lie mainly between 10 and 20 degrees of latitude to the north and south of the humid zone, are seasonally well watered, with between $4\frac{1}{2}$ and 7 months of rain. A bimodal rainfall regime, with two peaks separated by a short dry season, exists in parts of this zone. This allows the production of two crops of maize, or pulses within a year or the cultivation of cassava, yams and other roots with a longer growing season. The major cash crops are perennial tree species.

The monsoons of South and South-East Asia result from the seasonal reversal of the winds, from north-east to south-west. They normally bring adequate rain for crop production in each season, but are notoriously subject to fluctuations, from year to year, in time of onset, quantity and distribution. Much of the irrigation in the monsoon region is designed to reduce the risks of seasonal water shortages.

Single peak rainfall distributions are found in the dryer parts of the sub-humid zone, merging into the dryland savannas. The natural climax vegetation in these areas, is open forest, woodland and scrub, where grasses and woody plants compete. Cereals are the staple food crops, traditionally sorghum and millets, but maize production is extending into dryer areas while wheat is grown under irrigation. Cash crops include cotton, groundnuts, soyabean and tobacco.

Semi-arid environments receive sufficient moisture to maintain more-or-less continuous vegetation cover, but they are generally too dry to permit secure, regular rainfed cultivation of cereal or other crops. They have traditionally been used for extensive grazing by ruminant livestock, under pastoral systems, there being few productive alternatives. However, pastoralists are increasingly adopting a more settled agro-pastoral system of land use, while there is increasing encroachment of irrigated and rainfed crop production in the drylands wherever feasible, sometimes only on a temporary basis.

Within these broad climatic regions local variations in topography and

Figure 2.1   Precipitation, evapo-transpiration and soil moisture balance; (a) Semi-arid, single peak rainfall: Samaru, N. Nigeria, (b) Humid, double peak rainfall: Kabanyolo, Uganda

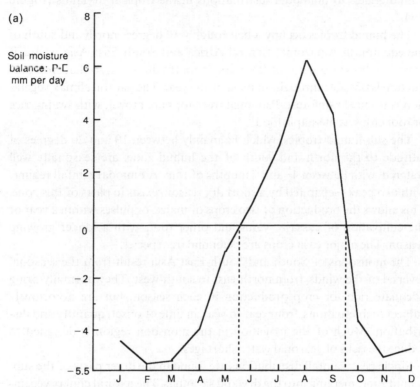

(a)

Soil moisture balance: P-E mm per day

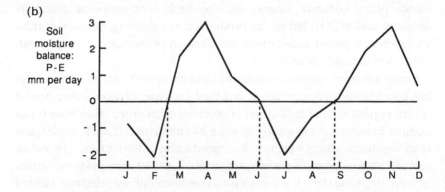

(b)

Soil moisture balance: P-E mm per day

soils also influence the choice of farming system and delimit the main agro-ecological zones. Of particular importance are the lowland flood plains and valley bottoms with relatively fertile and well-watered alluvial soils, which allow greater flexibility in the choice of crops than the less fertile upland soils. In addition, the natural vegetation, for example forest or grassland and prevalent types of weeds, together with the incidence of pests and diseases such as trypanosomiasis, limit the choice of crop and livestock enterprises and the methods of production.

Other elements of the biological environment which affect agriculture are the pests and diseases of crops, livestock, stored products and humans. Unfortunately, where climatic conditions are favourable for plant and animal growth, their pathogens and parasites also flourish. Thus competition from weeds, insects and diseases is generally most severe in the humid zone where crop-growing seasons are longest. Crops such as cotton may be excluded from this zone, because of pests and disease, while cattle are virtually excluded from sub-humid Africa by the existence of *surra* or *nagana* (trypanosomiasis) sickness carried by the ubiquitous *tsetse fly*. Thus the incidence and spread of pests and diseases constrain land-use systems, while traditional practices such as bush burning to destroy weeds, or transhumant livestock movements to avoid the tsetse fly in the wet season are strategies to overcome these constraints.

Intensity of land use

The average area of land, and the amounts of other natural resources, available per household, depend upon the rural population density and intensity of land use. *Intensity* of land use is measured by the amount of effort expended per hectare and the corresponding productivity which, in turn, determines the number of people that can be supported; that is the human carrying capacity. One of the least intensive, or more extensive, forms of land use is pastoralism, which may support only one family or less per square kilometre. Cultivation systems are more intensive, but shifting cultivation with long forest fallows of, say, 20 years following 2 years of cultivation results in only one-eleventh of the available area being used at any one time. Hence productivity per hectare is only one-eleventh of the yield per cropped hectare.

Shorter bush or grass fallows allow more intensive land use and therefore a higher human carrying capacity, but maintenance of soil fertility requires more effort and possibly inputs of plant nutrients from outside the system. Continuous cropping is yet more intensive, but can only be sustained by using more manures and fertilizers and external inputs per hectare. It is further argued that the farmer's choice of technology is associated with the intensity of production, or labour: land ratio. Whereas shifting cultivation requires only a few simple tools, such as a cutlass and a digging stick, continuous cultivation necessitates the use of a plough and other cultivation equipment, together with other 'modern' inputs (Boserup 1965).

Thus human population density is associated with intensity of land use and productivity per hectare; but it is not easy to establish the direction of cause and effect. Some authorities have argued that population growth causes the spread of cultivation at the expense of pastoralism, the shortening of bush-fallows and a general intensification of land use (Boserup 1965, Tiffen, Mortimore & Gichuki 1994). However, as already argued, the choice of land-use and farming systems technology is limited by the natural environment. So too is the human carrying capacity for a given state of technology (Harrison 1983). For instance, irrigated agriculture, which is probably the most intensive form, is impossible without access to substantial water supplies. In fact, people often migrate from areas of low potential to areas of high potential, in search of productive employment and higher incomes, so the population grows faster in the high-potential areas. Thus population density is greater as a result of the higher productive capacity of the natural environment.

There are substantial differences, in the average area of land per person, between the major continents of the tropics, as shown in Table 2.1. Asia, or the Far East, is the most densely populated, with less than a quarter of a hectare of cultivated land per head of rural population. This together with the area of permanent pasture makes up over half of the total land of this region. More than a third of the cultivated land is under irrigation.

The land: labour ratio is more favourable in Africa, with 0.4 hectares of cultivated land per person, and a considerably bigger area of permanent pasture. However, only a very small proportion of the cultivated land is irrigated. In Latin America, there is considerably more land per person, but the inter-personal distribution of natural resources is much wider than in Asia or Africa, so many of the smaller farmers may have no more resources than their Asian or African counterparts.

These broad average statistics, give an indication of the type of farming system common in each of the continents. Asia is commonly associated with small-scale, intensive irrigated agriculture, and Africa with somewhat larger farm areas under rainfed cultivation, together with pastoral livestock-keeping on the rangelands. Latin America has possibly a greater diversity of farm sizes and farming systems than the other two continents.

Table 2.1. *Agricultural land use in developing regions* (hectares per head of rural population)

		Developing countries			
	World	Africa	Far East*a*	Latin America	Developed countries
Land area/head	5.3	6.3	1.1	17.4	59.2
Cropped land/head	0.59	0.41	0.22	1.32	7.23
Permanent pasture/head	1.4	1.9	0.3	5.1	12.9
Percent crops irrigated	16.8	3.6	35.2	10.4	9.6

Source: FAO 1994. Current statistics for 1993; growth rates annual average between 1980 and 1993.
a Far East includes South Asia

Seasonality and risk

In tropical climates, rainfall exceeds evaporation during the growing season, so that plant nutrients, particularly nitrates, mineralized at the start of the season may be rapidly lost by leaching. Given the high temperatures, pests, pathogens and weeds grow and multiply apace. Hence timing of field operations is almost always critical. As a result tropical agriculture is characterized by marked seasonal peaks and troughs of farm work, food availability, market supply and human and animal dietary intakes.

The severity of the seasonal fluctuations depends upon the rainfall regime, being most marked in semi-arid regions with a long dry season and a single short rainy season. With a bimodal sub-humid regime there are generally two work peaks and two harvests each year, as illustrated in Figure 2.2, while in humid regions with year-round rains or where perennial irrigation is possible the peaks and troughs in work and diets are almost eliminated. Where irrigation is used to supplement the rainfall there is likely to be marked seasonal variation in the irrigation water needs.

The seasonality of crop production complicates farm and household decision making in various ways. It is quite difficult to match labour use with labour availability. For the family work force and regular hired workers, the supply of effort is relatively constant throughout the year. It is therefore probable that the farmer will either have less labour than he wants on the farm at work peaks, or more than he wants at slack times, or something of both. Some seasonal unemployment is almost inevitable in agriculture. This is illustrated in Figure 2.2 where in most months, other than

February and March, relatively few hours are worked by family members. Labour availability is an effective constraint on production only during a limited number of critical work peaks.

Food shortages usually occur during the wet season, especially before the first harvest. When food is in short supply then market prices rise, as shown in Figure 1.2. Hence farmers cannot afford to make up the deficit by purchasing food during the so called 'hungry gap'. This means that people are undernourished just at the period when the work load for weeding and tending the crops is high. In contrast, food shortages for ruminant live-stock, mainly cattle, sheep and goats, occur during the dry season when grazing and water supplies are scarce.

Figure 2.2   Distribution of farm activities over one year

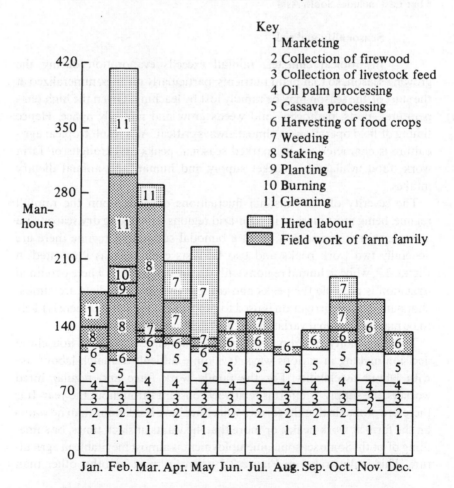

Key
1 Marketing
2 Collection of firewood
3 Collection of livestock feed
4 Oil palm processing
5 Cassava processing
6 Harvesting of food crops
7 Weeding
8 Staking
9 Planting
10 Burning
11 Gleaning

Hired labour
Field work of farm family

Farmers attempt to minimize the effects of seasonal variation in crop production by seeking to spread flows of labour use and harvested production more evenly, for instance by diversification into different on- and off-farm activities which require labour and contribute to household income at different periods of the year. They also respond by storing produce for food, seed and animal fodder, together with inputs such as irrigation water, from one rainy season to the next.

The incidence and timing of tropical rainfall vary a great deal between one year and another, and between adjacent places, especially in the semi-arid zone. In this zone, in particular, rainfall variation is a major cause of uncertainty. Droughts, like those of the 1970s and 1980s in the African Sahel, can prove disastrous for crop and livestock production, and for the dependent farm households. In more humid, lowland areas, disasters may result from occasional excessive rainfall and flooding.

Climatic variation together with the unpredictable incidence of pest and disease outbreaks are major sources of environmental risks for the tropical farm household. Given the limited resources available and the relatively low household income, the outcome of uncertain events can often make the difference between survival and starvation. Crop failure or death of live-stock may indeed prove disastrous (Figure 2.3). The risks faced by tropical farmers are more pervasive and serious than those of farmers in temperate regions.

Tropical farmers are, understandably, risk-averse; they are willing to forego some income, on average, in adopting strategies to avoid or limit the effects of risk. Indeed 'survival', in the face of risk, may be their principal objective. To this end they diversify their productive activities, adopt mixed and sequential cropping, avoid untried or risky products, produce some

Figure 2.3   Income variation and risk

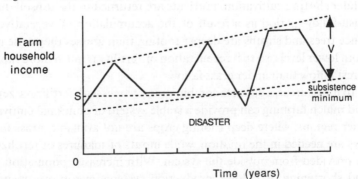

reliable, drought-relief crops and store surplus produce in good years as reserves for use when crops fail. Thus tropical farming systems are adapted to avoid risk and improve the chances of survival of the farm household.

Sustainability

There is much concern, in recent development thinking, with the sustainability of farming systems, although there is some debate regarding the precise meaning of the term. A widely quoted definition of sustainable development is 'Development that meets the needs of the present without compromising the ability of future generations to meet their own needs' (World Commission on Environment and Development, 1987). This a rather broad and general statement, subject to various different interpretations. At the more local farm and village level, the essential concern is that the production system should not collapse in the foreseeable future.

There are two possible ways in which the collapse of the system may occur, illustrated in Figure 2.4. One is as a result of a chance fluctuation or shock, such as a drought or flood, from which the system may be unable to recover (Figure 2.4a). If the system is sufficiently resilient to recover, then it may be sustainable. The other alternative is collapse due to a gradual decline in the stock of resources and household incomes (Figure 2.4b). Sustainability requires that this decline is prevented, by adequate conservation measures.

Most tropical soils are low in organic matter, since they are rapidly broken down by micro-organisms in the warm, moist conditions at the start of the rains. Essential plant nutrients such as phosphates and nitrates are thereby released and leached out of the topsoil quite rapidly. Since all forms of agriculture remove essential nutrients from the system in the harvested biomass, these must be restored by some means to ensure sustainability. Under shifting cultivation, nutrients are returned to the topsoil during the bush-fallow period as a result of the accumulation of vegetative matter. Since trees and shrubs are deeper rooting than grasses they raise nutrients from lower levels, so that regeneration of fertility is much more rapid under forest fallow than under grass fallow.

In forest areas, a suitable combination of trees with fertilizers, zero tillage and mulch farming can provide a stable system of continual cultivation. In drier regions, where deep rooting crops are not available, grass fallows or leys are needed in the rotation, while inputs of manures or fertilizers must be provided from outside the system. With increased population pressure and shortening of fallows, production systems may prove unsustainable without increased use of manures and fertilizers. Irrigated areas may suffer from waterlogging and salination if drainage is inadequate and water-use is not properly controlled.

Another characteristic of low organic-matter soils, is that they are easily eroded under intense tropical rainfall, or by wind in dryer areas, when bare of vegetation. Thus it is important to maintain plant cover to minimize the possibility of erosion and desertification. Traditional practices such as mixed and sequential cropping help to ensure continuous plant cover of the soil. The introduction of monocropping, land clearing for mechanization, collection of vegetation for fuel and overgrazing have all contributed to land degradation and soil erosion. Chemical pollution results from excessive fertilizer and pesticide use.

Figure 2.4 Two views of sustainability; (a) Resilience, (b) Time trend

(a) Resilience

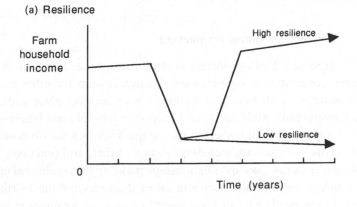

(b) Time trend

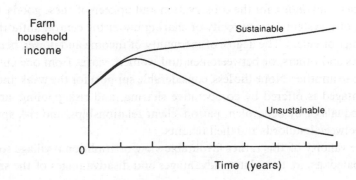

In fact, many cultivation and livestock husbandry practices of the African farmer are rational adaptations to the natural environment. There are serious dangers in abandoning these practices without exploring the environmental impact. At the same time practices for the conservation of soil and water, agro-forestry and integrated pest management should be encouraged as potential means for ensuring sustainable development.

Rangelands, wildlife, fisheries and forests are all renewable, natural resources exploited by rural people. Sustainability requires that the rate of offtake should be less than the rate of new growth. Stocks can only be conserved by careful control of the rate of offtake. The most widely consumed, naturally occurring plant material in the tropics is firewood. It is a renewable resource, but regrowth of timber is slow. Where the rate of consumption exceeds the rate of regrowth, not only are there possible adverse effects on plant cover and soil fertility, but also increasing costs are incurred in travelling further afield to collect firewood. Here, then, is another case for conservation of natural resources.

The socio-economic environment

Traditional village society is often characterized as a small, self-sufficient, community of people linked through kinship and other personal ties. Production, distribution and consumption all take place within the 'closed' community while social and economic relations are based on the status of individuals as members of the village. There is strict observance of social norms and customs, including religious beliefs and practices. These established customs, laws and relationships make up the traditional institutions which govern the allocation and use of resources and the distribution of agricultural products, which are geared to securing a minimum level of subsistence for all community members.

The allocation of *rights*, to the use of natural resources and other village facilities, and *duties*, for the conservation and upkeep of these goods, is the result of a system of reciprocity or sharing under the central authority of the chief or elders. The degree of inequality of income and power, between leaders and others, or between men and women, varies from one cultural group to another. None the less, considerable support for the weak and disadvantaged is offered by co-operative sharing, and risk pooling, among near equals or by benevolent patron–client relationships, and risk spreading, between landlords and their tenants.

The validity of this rather favourable view of traditional village society is debated, as are the relative advantages and disadvantages of the spread of commercial markets (Hayami, 1990). The spread of markets has allowed:

- opportunities for specialization and division of labour, with each type of farming zone concentrating on those products for which it has the greatest comparative advantage,
- a wider range of choice of consumer goods for rural households,
- the use of manufactured chemicals, equipment and other inputs from outside the system,
- easier movement of labour, and other resources between regions,
- greater opportunities for the accumulation of capital.

Overall this should permit increases in productive efficiency, increased incomes for farm households and a general improvement in social welfare.

Disadvantages associated with the spread of markets are the increased social differentiation between capitalist, commercial farmers, traditional farmers and landless labourers, and changes in social attitudes towards individual enterprise and acquisitiveness and less concern for mutual support. There are other causes of 'market failure', which are used to justify government intervention in rural development. They will be discussed in more detail below but first we consider locational, and other, effects on prices and farming systems.

Interregional and intertemporal price variation

Since the major assembly points for export commodities, the largest retail markets for food and for supplies of material inputs to farmers are all located in towns, distance from these centres, or from their main transport routes, has an important influence on farm prices and hence farming systems. As transport costs increase with increasing distance, the prices farmers must pay for their material inputs rise and the price they receive for their marketed commodities falls; in other words their terms of trade deteriorate with increasing remoteness. This means that the profit margin earned per hectare declines and so too does the incentive to produce for the market (Figure 2.5). At distance OX the profit per hectare falls to zero, so it is not worth producing for the market in such remote areas. Thus location influences both the intensity of land use or level of output per hectare and the choice of enterprise, since transport costs per unit of value vary between different commodities, depending on their bulk and perishability.

Most tropical cities are surrounded by a 'close-settled' zone, where continuous, and intensive cultivation is maintained. Vegetables and other high-value crops are produced for the urban markets. Within this peri-urban zone are frequently found specialist large-scale poultry units and dairy holdings, run on a commercial basis. Sophisticated technology, exotic livestock and large amounts of capital are involved.

Beyond the close-settled zone there is a wide belt of, mainly, crop production for the market with land-use intensity and product perishability declining with distance from the market. In many countries such a belt of 'commercial' production is found along the main line of rail and main roads. More remote areas must depend increasingly on production for their own subsistence. Livestock, however, can be moved large distances relatively cheaply on the hoof. Some of the more remote areas in the semi-arid and arid zones are devoted to pastoralism, based on milk production for subsistence and the sale of animals in order to buy cereals and other consumer goods.

Clearly the development of roads, railways and other communications, together with more widely dispersed market-places, storage facilities and processing plants will improve the terms of trade for those farmers that are reached. The problems and costs of extending delivery systems in this way are beyond the means of private individuals. Such elements of the social infrastructure are examples of 'public goods'.

Prices also vary, inversely, with changes in supply as illustrated by the seasonal fall in price of most crops at the time of harvest when the supply is increased. Chance variations in climate or disease incidence are important in this respect, with marked price increases occurring in drought years, when crop yields, and hence supplies, are reduced. Price, or market, uncertainty then adds to the risks faced by tropical smallholder farmers. There are several reasons why market failure may occur. They are summed up

Figure 2.5   The effect of location on price and income

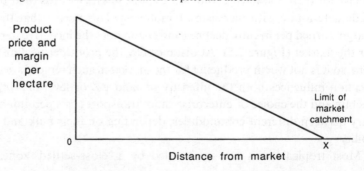

under three headings; transaction costs, imperfect competition and public goods.

Transaction costs

A key requirement for markets to function effectively, is that all potential buyers and sellers should have perfect information regarding the states of supply and demand and prevailing prices. This is manifestly not the case for most agricultural input and product markets since the population of farmers is widely dispersed and communications are difficult. Thus the costs of acquiring information, negotiating contracts and enforcing them, together known as 'transaction costs', are high. Indeed, in some circumstances these transaction costs are so high, in relation to the value of the items to be traded, that no market develops.

Over time, communications and information systems have improved, but in some of the remoter areas the level of transaction costs may preclude the development of competitive markets for farm inputs. Of course, if high delivery costs to remote areas render agricultural production uneconomic, then there is no loss of efficiency due to the absence of a market, as shown at point *X* in Figure 2.5. However this implies that, in such areas, some other means must be found of allocating resources among alternative activities.

An additional cause of high transaction costs is the problem of enforcing contracts. Thus collection of water dues on irrigation schemes, or charges for vaccination or dipping of cattle, or indeed credit repayment, may cause problems. Collection may necessitate repeated visits or even legal action. A point could be reached where the cost of recovery exceeds the original sum owed.

Imperfect competition

As a result of high transaction costs, an individual, a group of people or a commercial company can gain unfair advantage at the expense of others. This situation is particularly likely to arise because of the high costs of establishing a distribution and delivery system to large numbers of widely dispersed farmers. The average cost of distribution, per unit of the good or service, must diminish as deliveries increase. Thus there are economic advantages in operating on a large scale, known as 'economies of scale'. Once one supplier has established such a delivery system, it would be uneconomic for competitors to duplicate the delivery network in order to enter the market. The sole supplier has a 'natural monopoly'. For instance a single fertilizer distributer may be the only supplier in a rural district and is therefore able to restrict the quantity available to farmers and thereby raise the price which they pay.

This is illustrated in Figure 2.6, where the line *KHFC* represents the demand curve for fertilizer within the district. Because the monopolist is the sole supplier, and the demand curve slopes downwards, he knows that to sell more fertilizer he must reduce the price of all the fertilizer he sells. Hence, the extra income, or 'marginal revenue' he will receive by selling an additional bag of fertilizer is less than the price per bag, as shown by the line through *K* and *E* labelled 'MR'.

To illustrate, let the demand function be as follows,

$$p = K - bQ \tag{1}$$

where p=price per bag, Q=number of bags sold, K=a constant and b=slope. Then,

$$\text{total revenue} = R = pQ = KQ - bQ^2 \tag{2}$$

and

$$\text{marginal revenue} = \frac{dR}{dQ} = K - 2bQ \tag{3}$$

Note that this downward slope is twice as steep as that of the demand curve (equation 1).

If the minimum cost at which the fertilizer can be supplied is *OD* per bag then, whereas under competitive conditions quantity *OB* would be supplied and sold at *BF=OD*, the monopolist would only supply quantity *OA*, and

Figure 2.6   Welfare loss due to monopoly

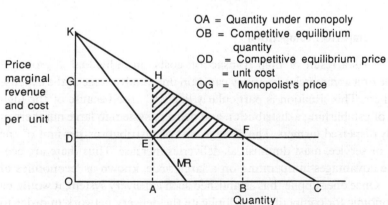

OA = Quantity under monopoly
OB = Competitive equilibrium
       quantity
OD = Competitive equilibrium price
      = unit cost
OG = Monopolist's price

Price
marginal
revenue
and cost
per unit

sell at price $AH=OG$. In both cases the trader adjusts sales to the point where the marginal revenue per bag of fertilizer equals the cost per bag, as this results in maximum profit. However, under competitive conditions the individual trader sells only a small proportion of the total so the marginal revenue is equal to the price. As suggested above, the monopolist sells a smaller quantity at a higher price than would prevail under competitive conditions.

On balance, there is a loss to society as a whole, represented by the shaded triangle. This is based on the assumption that the demand curve represents the consumer's willingness to pay, so that the area below the curve but above the price line represents the 'consumers' surplus'. If a price of OG is paid rather than OD, there is a loss of consumers' surplus represented by the area $DGHF$. Of this, the area $DGHE$ is a transfer to the seller as a monopoly profit. This leaves the triangular area EHF as a dead-weight loss.

Given that the many of the consumers are resource-poor farmers, and the monopoly supplier more likely to be a relatively well endowed commercial firm, or even a transnational, this income transfer may be considered particularly undesirable. Similar arguments can be used to show that a single buyer, or monopsonist, operating in an agricultural product market, can restrict purchases and thereby lower the price paid to farmers. Again there is a dead-weight welfare loss to society.

Public goods

There are two main characteristics which distinguish public goods from private ones. These are, first, whether potential users can be excluded and, second, whether consumption is joint or rival. Potential users can be excluded from using a typical private good, such as a bag of fertilizer; if farmer X uses it, then farmer Y is excluded. The two farmers cannot both benefit from it jointly; they are rivals for its use. This is not true, however, of natural resources which are common property, of extension advice provided through the mass media or of measures to eradicate tsetse fly or to control soil erosion. The benefits are available to all members of the community; no one can be excluded from enjoying them. Furthermore the benefits are enjoyed jointly, since the extra cost of providing the benefit to an additional user is negligible.

Public goods, as the name suggests, are inherently unsuited to private provision. Because they are jointly consumed, the total value to consumers is the sum of all the individual valuations or amounts that individuals would be willing to pay. It would be very difficult, and the transaction costs would be excessive, for a private supplier to collect all these payments. Furthermore, because it is impossible to exclude anyone from enjoying the benefits, some individuals may take advantage of facilities others have made available, whilst not contributing themselves. This is the 'free rider' problem.

These ideas are illustrated in Figure 2.7, which represents a simple situation where the community is made up of just two individuals, A and B, each with a demand curve for public goods in general. The joint market demand for them both is the vertical summation of the individual curves. The (constant) cost per unit of public goods is represented by the line *CC*. Net benefits to society (both individuals) would be maximized where the market demand curve cuts the cost line, at quantity Q^*. Reliance on private enterprise would result in a lower level of provision.

Individual B, acting alone would contribute quantity q_b. Individual A could then free-ride on B's contribution and simply provide the additional quantity $q_a - q_b$. Thus the total provision q_a is less than is socially desirable. Since the demand curves differ for the two individuals, the prices they are willing to pay for the socially desired level of public goods also differ. Individual A would pay price p_a while B would only pay p_b. Thus arrangements for financing public goods are necessarily complex, and private markets cannot be relied upon to make adequate provision.

Figure 2.7   The failure of private markets to supply sufficient public goods

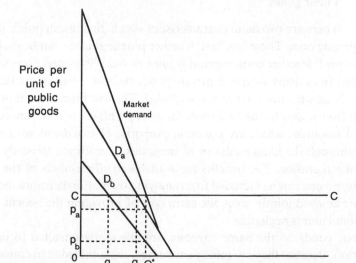

Table 2.2. *Pay-offs for the prisoner's dilemma*

		B's strategy	
		Do not contribute	Contribute
A's strategy	Do not contribute	0,0	3,−1
	Contribute	−1,3	2,2

The free rider problem is also illustrated by the theory of non-co-operative games, such as the so-called 'Prisoner's Dilemma'. In the original formulation it related to the prisoner's willingness to confess to a crime, but in the present context it is best interpreted in terms of the participant's willingness to contribute to the provision of a public good.

Again we consider just two individuals A and B. The 'payoff matrix' is shown in Table 2.2. The first number in each cell represents A's payoff, while the second number represents B's. The top left cell shows the situation where neither contributes, so none of the public good is provided, and both have zero benefit. In the top-right and bottom-left cells only one individual contributes and suffers a net loss as a result. The other, who is a 'free rider', derives the advantage of the public good at zero cost, so benefits substantially. However, if both could be persuaded to contribute, and share the costs, the total payoff, or combined net benefit, would be greater. The best choice for a selfish individual is to free ride, and let the other pay, but, if both think this way, the outcome will be that neither contributes, so none of the public good is provided, with a net social loss overall.

Yet another expression of a similar idea, relating to open access to natural resources, is the 'Tragedy of the Commons' (Hardin 1968). On open-access common grazing land, it was suggested, there is an incentive for individual livestock keepers to increase the numbers of stock carried, irrespective of the potential damage caused by overgrazing and rangeland degradation. This argument was probably overstated, since there are costs associated with the purchase and maintenance of livestock, which will set limits on the number of livestock kept by any individual. None the less, this illustration again serves to emphasize the idea of free riding, in that an individual livestock owner can afford to ignore the need for careful management of livestock numbers and conservation of the rangeland pasture.

The 'tragedy of the commons' argument has been used in favour of the 'enclosure' and private ownership of common property natural resources, of rangelands, forests, fisheries and rivers and streams and aquifers. This would allow market forces to operate effectively in the allocation and conservation of these resources. However, enclosure and privatization may impose constraints on the effective management of natural resources, for instance in preventing transhumant movements of cattle grazing the range-land. Furthermore it may create serious inequalities in the distribution of incomes between owners and users.

Together these theories serve to demonstrate the dangers of relying on individual decisions and private markets for the provision of public goods. The most likely outcome is inadequate provision and maintenance of social goods and services, such as feeder roads and other communication links, water and electricity supplies, and agricultural research and advice; together with inadequate attention to the conservation of common property resources. These arguments have been used to justify government inter-vention, but many instances have been cited of 'Government Failure'; that is distortions and inefficiencies caused by these interventions. Current development thinking generally favours a reduced role for governments.

The role of government

National and local governments are important components of the socio-economic environment, capable of influencing the pace and direction of agricultural and rural development. Development theories prevalent in the early post-independence years in many tropical countries, emphasized the importance of industrial expansion. Agriculture as the largest sector was expected to release the necessary capital and labour resources. The gov-ernment's role in promoting development, was seen as extracting the surplus from agriculture to finance the growth of other sectors.

This 'urban bias' was reflected in pricing and investment policies that dis-criminated against agriculture. Where, as in Africa and Latin America, these policies acted as a brake on agricultural development, they appear to have slowed the pace of general economic growth, as was discussed in Chapter 1. These issues, together with the impact of the international eco-nomic crisis of the early 1980s, and increasing debt and foreign-exchange problems, led to the need for structural adjustment programmes in many tropical countries.

Pre-structural reform trade and exchange-rate policies of many countries involved the maintenance of an overvalued currency, or an artificially low price for foreign exchange, supported by strict import and foreign-currency controls. This served to hold down prices farmers received for export crops, and the price paid for imported cereals and other foodstuffs, for which foreign exchange was released. Thus imports were encouraged and food prices were depressed to the disadvantage of domestic producers. These policies together with taxes on export crops and widespread price controls on staple foods, had a substantial adverse impact on the farmer's terms of trade.

Policy reforms, introduced in many countries over the last decade, have been aimed at reducing price distortions, through currency devaluation, removal of taxes, subsidies and price controls and a return to free-market prices. These changes may provide the necessary price incentives for agricultural growth besides improving rural incomes. However, the improvement of farm price incentives is only one of several necessary conditions for agricultural growth. Investment in public goods, and the promotion of appropriate institutions for rural development are also important, not least in agricultural research and the spread of new technology.

Institutional change

Along with these price reforms, most structural adjustment programmes have involved the privatization of many services previously provided by government agencies. The twin aims are to reduce the drain on government budgetary expenditure, and to increase efficiency. Some economists argue that a state run monopoly is even less efficient than a private monopoly, since it is not subject to the discipline imposed by the need to make a profit. Thus structural adjustment regimes have often included the abolition of agricultural marketing boards, and rural development agencies, and the abandonment of service provision in rural areas.

The belief that private markets can effectively replace agencies like marketing boards, engaged in the sale of tradable commodities, appears to be borne out by the experiences of structural adjustment programmes in several countries. However, as might be expected, private enterprise is less effective in substituting for state provision of public goods. Indeed for some public goods there is no satisfiactory alternative, at least in low-income countries, to provision by the state. This applies to major roads and communications links, basic health and education services and clean drinking water and electricity supplies.

However, there are a range of, so-called, impure public goods or 'club goods' which are partially excludable and partially rival, and which may not require provision by the state. A 'club' in this context, is a voluntary group whose members share certain common characteristics and share in the costs of providing the 'club good'. This definition may apply to a village community, a water user's group or a non-government organization (NGO). This form of co-operative organization may have advantages over both private and public institutions for the allocation of natural resources and the provision of local social infrastructure.

Non-members of the group can be excluded from enjoying the benefits, while continued membership can be made dependent on an individual's willingness to contribute to the costs so that free-riding is eliminated. Risks too are shared among members. Partial rivalry exists, in that 'over-crowding' may occur with excessive use; for example of common grazing land, or a village well. Therefore management and control is needed, provided by a locally accepted leader.

The size of the group is important in determining the likelihood of successful operation. Success is more likely if the number of members is small enough for them all to know each other personally. Mutual respect and trust are then sufficiently strong to minimize transaction costs and avoid free-riding. However, external assistance may be needed to enforce exclusion of non-members. In the case of communal use of natural resources, this may best be provided by the state vesting the group with 'communal user rights'.

Colonial and national governments are accused of attempts to increase their central power by curtailing the autonomy and authority of traditional local community organizations. In particular natural resources, such as communal grazing land and community forests, have been nationalized and made available, under 'open access' to all comers. This, it is suggested, has led to overexploitation and degradation, which would have been avoided had the resources remained under local, community control.

Thus, there are some grounds for hope that local group activity may replace, and possibly improve upon, some of the rural services which governments can no longer afford to deliver. However, care is needed in attempting to foster such communal activity and farmer participation. In the case of the management and conservation of natural resources, restoration of traditional communal user rights may be appropriate. The provision of social services through communal activity may only be feasible with financial and technical assistance from the government or some other outside agency. However, outside assistance must be limited so as to avoid compromising the integrity of the local community.

New technology

The development and spread of new technology is essential for the continuing growth of agricultural production and incomes. In the past some agricultural growth has been achieved by expanding the area of land under cultivation, that is by increasing the amounts of resource inputs used. Today most of the available 'virgin' land has been brought into agricultural use, particularly in Asia. It is now recognized that most of the desired output growth must come from increasing productivity of the land, labour and other resources, even in Africa and Latin America. This requires the widespread and continuous adoption of new technology in the forms of both new methods of production (process innovations) and new products (product innovations).

The 'green revolution', which was based upon the development of new high-yielding varieties of wheat and rice and their spread through Asia and parts of Latin America, provides a dramatic illustration of the beneficial impacts of new technology. As a result, a country such as India has changed from a situation of periodical shortages and famines to a net exporter of these cereals. However, the 'green revolution' is not an isolated success story, rather it is part of the long-term continuing processes of pure and applied research and of gradual improvement in agricultural productivity.

Some 'indigenous' technology is developed and used by the farmers themselves, while research is also conducted by private agri-business firms, such as food and other crop-processing companies and the suppliers of agro-chemicals and farm machinery. However, it is unlikely that the private sector will provide adequate investment in agricultural research and development, so some public sector provision is essential.

New technology, in the form of technical knowledge, is a 'public good'. There is no rivalry between users of knowledge; there is no extra cost incurred when another farmer adopts the innovation. Furthermore, it is difficult to exclude potential adopters. The main exceptions are cases where the innovation is embodied in a new marketable product, such as a machine, a drug or a pesticide. Most innovations are pure public goods, and, as already shown, private markets are unlikely to provide such goods in adequate quantities.

Two further arguments, raised in favour of publicly funded research and development, and agricultural extension, are that these activities are associated with economies of scale and high-risk levels. Economies of scale derive from the advantages of groups of scientists working together as teams, and the often expensive equipment needed. The risks of failure to meet research objectives are particularly high. Farmers, and even relatively small-scale input suppliers, cannot benefit from the economies of scale nor afford to take the associated risks.

Most governments do invest in agricultural research and development and fund agricultural extension services, while major support has been provided from the research institutes of the Consultative Group on International Agricultural Research (CGIAR). Available evidence suggests that the levels of current funding are inadequate, in that the additional benefits of research generally far exceed the extra costs. Furthermore, it is increasingly realized that appropriate and acceptable new technologies will only be developed if they are based on a sound understanding of existing farming systems and local farming practices.

Summary

1 Farming systems are strongly influenced by the natural, social and market environments in which they operate. The natural tropical environment is one in which plant growth is constrained by the seasonal availability of water.

2 Whereas the humid tropics have sufficient moisture, for crop growth, through most of the year, the sub-humid zone varies from bimodal rainfall regimes of about 7 months duration to single peak rainfall seasons of only 4 to 5 months. Semi-arid environments are unsuited to regular rainfed cultivation and are used mainly for pastoralist grazing.

3 Intensity of land use varies from extensive systems such as shifting cultivation or pastoralism, through rotational fallow systems to continuous cultivation, with irrigated multi-cropping the most intensive of all, with high inputs and outputs per hectare. Of the three main tropical continents, Asia is most intensively cultivated and Latin America the least.

4 The marked seasonality in crop growth creates managerial problems due to seasonal variation in work requirements and in the nutritional status of humans and livestock. Environmental risks of crop failure are high and poor farmers are understandably risk averse.

5 The sustainability of tropical farming systems is of increasing concern. Soil and water conservation measures are necessary, together with careful management of natural resources.

6 Traditional village society supported an institutional framework of rights and duties which provided for the allocation and management of resources and the survival of the populace. The spread of markets has widened the range of choice of consumption and production activities of rural people, but may reduce social cohesion.

7 The prices of agricultural commodities vary by location in relation to the main markets. Farmers located near to urban markets benefit from

higher prices than those received in more remote areas. Land in more favourable locations is farmed more intensively and farmers in those areas earn higher incomes. Farmers in remote areas may be limited to subsistence production.

8 Seasonal variations in supply cause variations in prices, which are at a maximum just before the next harvest. Seasonal price variations provide incentives for storage.

9 Market failures are due to the existence of transaction costs; of collecting information, and negotiating and enforcing contracts. High transaction costs are associated with the sparse populations and poor communications often found in tropical countries.

10 Imperfect competition, in the forms of monopolistic supply of inputs and monopsonistic demand for products, is likely in rural areas as a result of the high transaction costs.

11 The provision of extension advice through the mass media and the control of animal and human diseases are public goods; meaning that no one can be excluded from the benefits, and an additional user does not add to the costs of provision. Because of the likelihood of 'free riding', private markets cannot be relied upon to make adequate provision of public goods.

12 Governments intervene to influence farm prices, to provide services and institutions and to fund agricultural research and development (R&D). Price interventions, including macro-economic and trade policies, have generally had an adverse impact on development. However, investment in rural services and institutions and in agricultural R&D is still needed.

13 Given the causes of market failure discussed here, and many instances of government failure due to mismanagement and/or inadequate funding, increased attention is being given to communal or group activity and the so-called 'theory of clubs'. Within relatively small groups or communities, free-riding is much reduced, and the prospects for co-operative, democratic decision-making are high. Such activity should be encouraged by governments whilst avoiding compromising the integrity of the local community.

14 Research and development are essential areas of public investment, since knowledge is clearly a public good, while research is risky and subject to economies of scale. Returns to public investment in research are generally found to be high.

References

Boserup, E. (1965). *The Conditions of Agricultural Growth: The Economics of Agrarian Change under Population Pressure*, London, Allen & Unwin (*Republished 1993, London, Earthscan*)

Bromley, D. W. (1991). *Environment and Economy: Property Rights and Public Policy*. Oxford UK & Cambridge USA, Blackwell

Bunting, A. H. (1975). 'Time, phenology and the yields of crops', *Weather*, **30**, 312–25

Hardin, G. (1968). 'The tragedy of the commons', *Science*, **162**, 1243–8

Harrison, P. (1983). 'Earthwatch: land and people, the growing pressure', *People*, **13**, 1–8

Hayami, Y. (1990). 'Community, market and state' (The Elmhirst Memorial Lecture) in Maunder, A. & A. Valdes. *Agriculture and Governments in an Interdependent World. Proceedings of the 20th International Conference of Agricultural Economists*. Aldershot, Dartmouth

Pearce, D., E. Barbier & A. Markandya (1990). *Sustainable Development: Economics and Environment in the Third World*, London, Earthscan

Richards, P. (1985). *Indigenous Agricultural Revolution: Ecology and Food Production in West Africa*. London, Hutchinson

Tiffen, M., M. Mortimore & F. Gichuki (1994). *More People, Less Erosion: Environmental Recovery in Kenya*, Chichester, John Wiley

World Commission on Environment and Development (1987). *Our Common Future* (The Brundtland Commission Report), Oxford University Press.

3

The farmer's production choices

The farm household as both producer and consumer

Tropical farm houschold systems are relatively complex, involving both production (of crops, livestock and off-farm income) and consumption (of food, other basic needs and some leisure). The allocation of productive resources and the choice of activities are the result of decisions made by members of the farm household. For simplicity we proceed as though these decisions are made by a single individual, the 'farmer', whilst recognizing that the real world situation is more complicated. In this chapter we explore in more detail how these decisions are made.

It is assumed that farmers are rational, in the broad sense, in pursing certain meaningful objectives. Studies of tropical farm households have shown that farmers have a consistent set of objectives which guide their behaviour. For example a survey of 150 farmers in Bendel State, Nigeria, in 1991, showed that they identified six main objectives and ranked them, on average, in the following order of priority;

1 food: provide food for family from own farms,
2 educate: provide for the education of own children,
3 debt: strive to repay debts and avoid more,
4 profit: make the most profit from farming,
5 employ: employ family members on own farm,
6 leisure: arrange work so as to have more hours off farm work (Akatugba 1992).

It seems reasonable to suppose that for most of these items, except debt and perhaps employment, the farmers would prefer more rather than less. Like most humans their wants are not fully satisfied and they seek to improve their well-being or 'utility'.

However, their scope for decision-making is restricted by the range of possible alternative activities that can be undertaken and the constraints imposed by the limited availability of land, labour and capital resources. Hence it appears that economics, which has been defined as 'the science which studies human behaviour as a relationship between ends and scarce means which have alternative uses', should be applicable to the analysis of farmers' decision-making.

Conventional economic theory generally treats firms, which are responsible for production, and households, which consume the products, as separate agencies. Firms are supposed to purchase all their inputs and sell all their products with the aim of maximizing profits, while households supply labour and other resources for hire and use the proceeds to purchase the goods and services they desire. In smallholder agriculture, both roles are combined in the same decision-making household.

Thus in presenting 'the theory of the farm household' an attempt is made to integrate the analysis of production and consumption decisions. Two, relatively new, analytical approaches are applied. The first 'multi-criteria decision-making' (MCDM) is commonly based on the weighting or ranking of multiple goals, which may include a target level of profit besides other consumption goals. The other known as 'new household economics' relies on the assumption of utility maximization, where utility depends upon the levels of consumption of all commodities, including those produced at home and including leisure time.

Given the large number of interactions involved in a farm household system, the analysis is presented here in several separate stages. Of course real-world decisions cannot be separated in this way, but it simplifies the exposition. In this chapter we deal only with the choice of what commodities to produce and consume. The labour–leisure choice is examined in the following chapter.

Constraints and the feasible set

The idea of a limited feasible set of production alternatives, from which the farmer has to choose, may be illustrated by a simple example. Consider a farmer who has the choice of growing two alternative crops, one (maize) grown for food and the other (groundnuts) grown for cash. The constraints on production of these crops are land, which is limited to 2 ha in total, and labour in the two busy periods of planting and weeding in each of which 36 person-days are available. Each hectare of maize requires 6 days for planting and 20 days for weeding. Each hectare of groundnuts requires

Table 3.1. *Activities and constraints determining the feasible set*

	Activities		Constraint level
	Maize	Groundnuts	
Land (hectares)	1	1	2
Planting labour (days)	6	24	36
Weeding labour (days)	20	10	36

Figure 3.1 Constraints and the feasible set

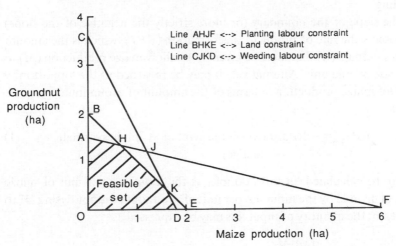

24 days of labour for planting and 10 days for weeding. This information is set out in Table 3.1.

These data can be used to determine the feasible set of combinations of the two crops, subject to the three constraints of land, planting labour and weeding labour. This is illustrated in Figure 3.1, where the number of hectares of maize is measured on the horizontal axis and the number of hectares of groundnuts on the vertical axis.

This diagram is constructed as follows. First consider the land constraint. This would allow the production of 2 ha of groundnuts, point B, or 2 ha of maize, point E, or any combination of the two crops on the straight line joining these two points. For instance point H represents $\frac{4}{3}$ ha of groundnuts and $\frac{2}{3}$ ha of maize, while point K represents $\frac{2}{5}$ ha of groundnuts and $1\frac{3}{5}$ ha of maize. Line *AHJF*, representing the planting labour constraint, and line *CJKD*, representing the weeding labour constraint, are constructed in a similar fashion. The set of feasible combinations of the two crops is represented by the area *OAHKD*, while the segmented line *AHKD* is the 'production possibility boundary'.

Points inside the area, and not on the boundary, represent combinations of the two crops which may be described as 'technically inefficient', since more of either or both crops could be produced with no extra resources. Points outside the boundary, such as *B* or *J*, are infeasible given the fixed land or labour constraints. Between *A* and *H* planting labour is the 'effective-' or 'binding-constraint'; between *H* and *K* it is land; while between *K* and *D* it is weeding labour. Hence at point *H* both planting labour and land are binding constraints, while at point *K* both land and weeding labour are binding.

The slope of the boundary (or more strictly the negative of the slope) represents the rate of product transformation (*RPT*), which is the amount of groundnuts (*G*) that must be given up to allow maize production (*M*) to increase by one unit. Alternatively it may be regarded as the 'opportunity cost' of maize production in terms of the amount of groundnuts foregone. Thus:

$$RPT_{gm} = -dG/dM \text{ (where the symbol 'd' implies a small} \qquad (1)$$
$$\text{change)}$$

It can be calculated, in this example, as the input use per unit of maize output divided by the input use per unit of groundnut output. Using '*X*' to represent the quantity of input this may be expressed as;

$$dG/dM = \frac{dX/dM}{dX/dG} \qquad (2)$$

This equals;

(between points *A* and *H*) $\quad \frac{6}{24} = \frac{1}{4}$

(between points *H* and *K*) $\quad \frac{1}{1} = 1$

(between points *K* and *D*) $\quad \frac{20}{10} = 2$

As more maize is produced the opportunity cost, in terms of groundnut production foregone, increases.

In this simple example, the two crops are assumed to compete for all three resources of land, planting labour and weeding labour, albeit at different rates. However, this is not necessarily the case. For instance, crops grown during the short rains do not compete for resources with crops grown during the long rains, because they require resources at different times of the year. This is true of any kind of sequential cropping when one crop is grown after the other. Such activities are said to be 'supplementary', since they supplement farm household income without requiring any additional resources.

Crop–livestock interactions are important in analyzing any mixed farming system. Livestock which are tethered or housed and fed on crop by-products or purchased feed, do not compete with crops for the use of land, so these are supplementary activities in the use of land. However, the interactions may be of a 'complementary' or a mutually beneficial kind. This applies if an increase in livestock production results in increased availability of manure as a by-product, which then produces increased crop yields. If this in turn leads to increased availability of crop by-products for animal feed, then animal production may be further increased.

The exploitation of supplementary and complementary relationships between activities can lead to valuable increases in household income.

Objectives and goals

The farmer's choices are limited to points within, or on the boundary of, this feasible set. We first consider how these choices would be made on the basis of multiple goals or targets. For this analysis it is assumed that farmers have a set of 'goals', meaning that they have particular target levels for each objective which they try to achieve. These goals might then be treated as constraints, which the farmer strives to satisfy. For example, the farmer faced with the feasible set of crop production activities shown in Figure 3.1, may decide that he needs to grow, at least, one tonne of maize in order to feed his family. This is shown in Figure 3.2 (which is derived from Figure 3.1, by assuming that each crop yields 1 tonne of produce per hectare) by the vertical line LMN. Similarly he may consider that he needs to sell, at least, half a tonne of groundnuts in order to produce enough money to survive; shown by the horizontal line PMQ. The area below and to the left of these two lines is now infeasible, because these new constraints would not be satisfied. The feasible set is reduced to the shaded triangle NMQ.

Such a farmer may be quite satisfied with any combination of the two crops, represented by a point within this triangle. Unlike a profit maximizer or a utility maximizer, he is not seeking an 'optimum' or best choice, which must lie on the production possibility boundary. Decision-making which is

aimed only at achieving an acceptable or satisfactory set of outcomes, is
designated 'satisficing' behaviour to distinguish it from 'optimizing' behaviour.

However, it is possible that the farmer may have difficulty in achieving his
goals. For instance, if he needed to produce 1.6 tonnes of maize and 1 tonne

Figure 3.2   The farmer's goals

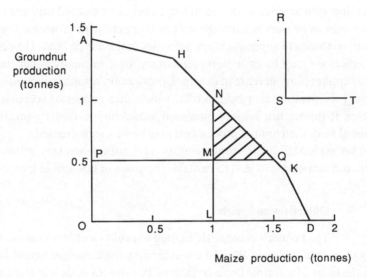

Figure 3.3   The ranking or weighting of goals

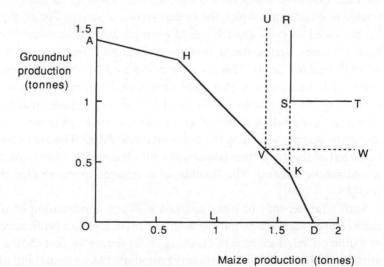

of groundnuts, these targets would be represented by the lines *RS* and *ST*. It would then be impossible to attain both goals simultaneously, so some compromise is required. The farmer might then strive to minimize the extent of underachievement of the goals (the deviations from the target levels), but they may not be equally important to him. Thus the goals must either be ranked in order of priority, to give what is known as a lexicographic ordering, or they must be allocated weights.

These two alternative formulations of decision-making are illustrated in Figure 3.3. The lexicographic ordering is demonstrated by assuming that the goal of producing 1.6 tonnes of maize, to meet household food needs, has a higher priority than the production of groundnuts. Thus the line *RS* is projected down until it meets the production possibilities boundary at point *K*. At this point only 0.4 tonnes of groundnuts are produced so the second goal is not attained. However, given the ranking of the goals, this point represents the optimum choice for this farmer. Alternatively if he weighted the 'maize goal' as twice as important as the 'groundnut goal', the deviation for the latter would be twice that for the former. Thus the optimum would then occur at point *V* representing 1.4 tonnes of maize and 0.6 tonnes of groundnuts, which is 0.2 tonnes short of the maize target and 0.4 tonnes short of the groundnut target.

This approach to the analysis of farmers decisions is useful in many contexts. However, there are problems in determining levels of farmers goals and their relative weights or priorities. Further details are given in Chapter 16 (also see Romero & Rehman 1989).

Prices, profit maximization and supply response

If both groundnuts and maize can be sold, and the prices are known, then it is possible to determine the most profitable combination of the two crops. In practice it may be necessary to subtract the variable cost from the gross revenue, or output, per tonne to arrive at the gross margin. The aim then would be to maximize the total gross margin.

For example let us assume that the gross margins per tonne are £42 for maize and £60 for groundnuts. Since the optimum, or most-profitable combination must lie on the production possibility boundary, and there are only four corners on this boundary, it can easily be found by evaluating each of these corners. The results are shown in Table 3.2, the areas of the two crops represented by each corner being estimated from the Figure or by solving the pairs of constraint equations.

Clearly point *H* represents the most profitable combination of the two

Table 3.2. *Corner solutions and the economic optimum*

Corner	Maize (tonnes)	Groundnuts (tonnes)	Total gross margin £
A	0	1.5	90
H	0.67	1.33	108
K	1.6	0.4	91.20
D	1.8	0	75.60

crops, consisting of $\frac{2}{3}$ tonne of maize and $\frac{4}{3}$ tonne of groundnuts. Land and planting labour are the binding constraints, while $9\frac{1}{3}$ days of weeding labour are left unused, or 'in disposal'. These results can be calculated as follows.

> Let M=quantity of maize produced in tonnes
> let G=quantity of groundnuts produced in tonnes

The equations for the two binding constraints can now be written as:

> $1M+1G=2$ for the land constraint
> $6M+24G=36$ for the planting labour constraint.

The solution to these simultaneous equations is;

$$M=\tfrac{2}{3} \text{ and } G=1\tfrac{1}{3}$$

The total weeding labour required for this cropping plan is;

$$20M+10G=20*\tfrac{2}{3}+10*1\tfrac{1}{3}=26\tfrac{2}{3}$$

which means that $36-26\frac{2}{3}=9\frac{1}{3}$ days of weeding labour are left unused.

The 'shadow prices' or 'opportunity costs' of the binding constraints can be calculated as £36 per ha for land and £2.50 per day for planting labour. Note that, since there is surplus unused weeding labour, its opportunity cost is zero. (Linear programming, which is the method of analysis used here, will be described in more detail in Chapter 16).

An alternative method of finding the optimum, and most profitable combination of the two crops is shown in Figure 3.4, where iso-revenue lines, each representing a different level of total gross margin, have been added to the production possibility boundary. These lines are parallel, with the common slope given by;

$$\frac{T/P_g}{T/P_m} = T/P_g * P_m/T = P_m/P_g \tag{3}$$

Total gross margin increases in the direction of the arrow; hence the maximum is achieved at point *H* where the £108 iso-revenue line just touches the boundary.

We can carry this analysis further to predict how the profit-maximizing farmer would respond to variations in the price of one commodity (e.g. maize) with all other prices and constraints held fixed. In fact we will consider variations in the gross margin per tonne of maize, but, if the variable cost per tonne remains constant, this depends directly on the price per tonne (P_m). From Figure 3.4 it should be apparent that if P_m is zero then no maize will be grown, and the farmer will operate at point *A*.

In fact P_m must rise above £15 before it is worth growing any maize. The optimum then moves to point *H* where $\frac{2}{3}$ tonne of maize is produced. This remains the optimum until the P_m rises to above £60 when point *K* becomes the optimum, representing 1.6 tonnes of maize. Finally if the P_m exceeds £120 it is most profitable to grow 1.8 tonnes of maize alone, represented by point *D*.

These results, which are summarized in Table 3.3 and Figure 3.5, map out the profit-maximizing farmer's production response to changing maize

Figure 3.4   The economic optimum

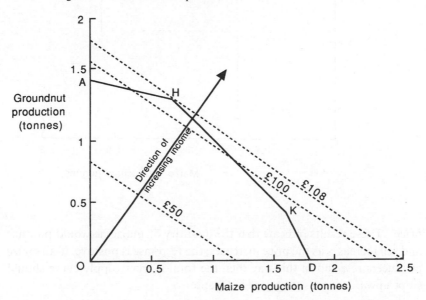

Table 3.3. *Supply response for maize*

From lower GM$_m$ £	To upper GM$_m$ £	Maize produced (tonnes)	Point on boundary
0 (strictly − infinity)	15	0	*A*
15	60	0.67	*H*
60	120	1.6	*K*
120	+infinity	1.8	*D*

Figure 3.5   The farmer's supply response for maize

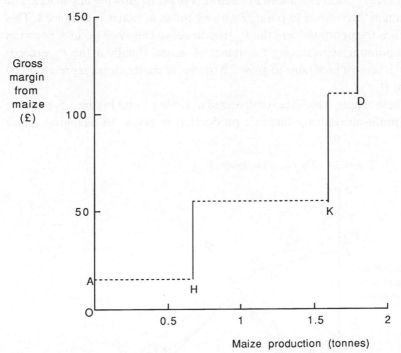

prices. These results indicate that the quantity of maize he would produce and sell increases as the price increases; the response is positive. If all maize producers respond in this way then the total market supply curve should slope upwards as was suggested in Chapter 1.

Smoothing out the production relationships

Before proceeding to discuss choices based on utility maximization, it is convenient to modify the production possibility boundary diagram (Figure 3.1) and the associated analysis by assuming that it is a smooth curve, with continuous first- and second-order derivatives. Such a curved boundary is illustrated in Figure 3.6. It normally slopes downwards as the crops compete for the scarce limiting resources; maize production can only be expanded at the expense of giving up some groundnut production.

As before, the negative of the slope of the boundary gives the rate of product transformation (*RPT*), which reflects the opportunity cost of maize in terms of groundnuts:

$$RPT_{gm} = -dG/dM$$

If both maize and groundnuts can be sold for the prices of £42 and £60 per tonne respectively, the iso-revenue lines can be added to the diagram as before. The maximum obtainable revenue is again found where the corresponding iso-revenue line just touches the production possibility boundary. However, this is now a point of tangency where the two slopes are equal. Thus:

Figure 3.6   A curved production possibilities boundary

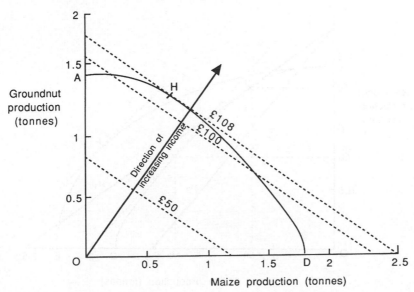

$$-(RPT_{gm})=dG/dM=P_m/P_g \tag{4}$$

the negative of the rate of product transformation is equal to the inverse price ratio. Alternatively multiplying both sides by $dM * P_g$ gives;

$$dG * P_g=dM * P_m \tag{5}$$

The value of groundnuts foregone is equal to the value of the additional maize. Finally, if in equation (4) both sides are multiplied by P_g this gives;

$$dG/dM * P_g=P_m \tag{6}$$

which means that the additional (marginal) opportunity cost per tonne of maize is equal to the price.

The analysis may now be extended to explore the effects of changes in relative prices. Let us assume that the price of groundnuts remains constant, but that the price of maize rises (e.g. to £72). This means that the same total revenue as was earned at the old price, can now be obtained by selling a smaller quantity of the maize (in Figure 3.7, the equal-revenue line shifts from P_1 to P_2). However the farmer, if he is an optimizer, will continue to operate on the production possibility boundary, so will move to a higher level of total revenue or profit (represented by the broken line through J). This rise in profit is the first effect of a rise in product price. A second effect

Figure 3.7   The effect of increasing the price of maize

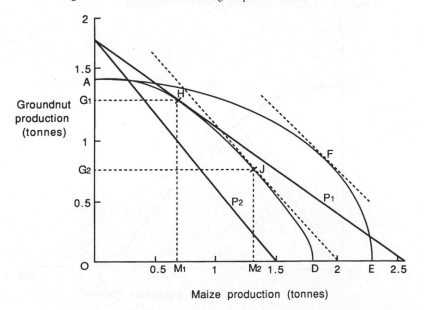

Maize production (tonnes)

is that maize production and sales are substituted for those of groundnuts. The economic optimum combination of the two crops moves around the boundary, in a clockwise direction, from *H* to *J*.

A third effect of the rise in maize price is a possible increase in the quantities of inputs used. In practice the price rise may encourage the farmer to use more fertilizer and other inputs on his maize crop, and thereby to increase production and move the production possibility boundary outwards, as shown in Figure 3.7 by the line *AFE*. The farmer might even be induced to acquire more land and other 'fixed' resources, given the increased returns that can be produced. However, such changes may take time to implement, so there is a difference between the short-run response, within say one year, and the long-run response over a period long enough for fixed inputs to be changed (see Askari & Cummings 1976).

The short-run relationship between maize price and quantity supplied is illustrated in Figure 3.8. As the price of maize rises, the (negative) slopes of the iso-revenue lines in Figure 3.8a, become steeper. Hence the economic optimum choice of products moves around the boundary from point *A*, through *G*, *H* and *J* to *D* representing increased production of maize and reduced production of groundnuts.

The elasticity of supply (*E*) is defined as the percentage change in quantity supplied divided by the percentage change in price, or:

$$E = \mathrm{d}Q/\mathrm{d}p \cdot p/Q$$

Supply is said to be inelastic if *E*<1, and the supply curve has a relatively steep slope. It is elastic if *E*>1, and the supply curve is flatter. As shown the supply response is more elastic in the long-run, since time is needed to adjust inputs of land, labour and capital. These arguments apply equally when the focus is changed from an individual farm to aggregate production response for a country or region.

Available evidence from empirical supply response studies suggests that, although the elasticity of supply for a single commodity is generally positive, aggregate supply of all farm products does not vary much in response to prices, at least in the short-run (see Binswanger 1990). In other words aggregate supply is inelastic, which suggests that resource inputs are not changed much when prices rise or fall. The observed elasticity of supply for an individual crop reflects the transfer of resources from other alternative enterprises.

The elasticity of supply, and the speed of response, differs as between different commodities. Generally speaking the supply of permanent crops such as cocoa, coffee, oilpalm and rubber is less elastic than that of annual

Figure 3.8   Price change and supply response; (a) Changing optima from *A* to *D*, (b) Supply response

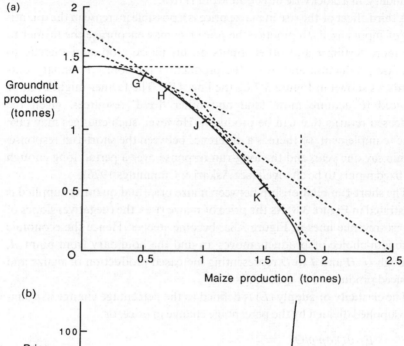

(a)

Groundnut production (tonnes)

Maize production (tonnes)

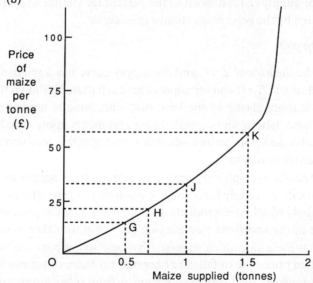

(b)

Price of maize per tonne (£)

Maize supplied (tonnes)

crops. Investment in establishing tree-crops is a long slow process. For similar reasons the short-run elasticity of supply for slow-breeding live-stock such as cattle or camels is very low. Indeed supply response in the first year may be negative, as cattle keepers respond to a rise in price by first building up their herds.

The supply of food crops is generally less elastic than that of cash crops, and may even be negative, because of the tendency for farm households to increase home consumption as income rises. To illustrate this possibility we now turn to the analysis of the utility maximizing household.

Utility maximization

Let us now revert to the result given in Figure 3.4, with maize priced at £42 per tonne and groundnuts at £60, and assume that farmers (and their families) can ascribe subjective values to commodities such as maize and groundnuts, and indeed to other sources of satisfaction, or 'goods', such as leisure. An increase in the availability of any one 'good' results in an increase in total utility, but at a diminishing rate. In short, we assume diminishing marginal utility.

An indifference curve represents all the combinations of a pair of 'goods' which yield the same level of utility. It is implied that the decision-maker, in this case the farmer, is indifferent between the various combinations shown on the curve.

Indifference curves for maize and groundnuts are illustrated in Figure 3.9, by $I_0 I_0$ and $I_1 I_1$. Note that the latter represents a higher level of utility than the former, and that they slope downwards as utility from increased maize consumption substitutes for utility from groundnuts foregone. The negative of the slope is known as the 'marginal rate of substitution', and is equal to the inverse ratio of the marginal utilities of groundnuts and maize.

$$-dG/dM \text{ (for the indifference curves)} = MRS_{mg} = MU_m/MU_g \quad (7)$$

These curves are convex to the origin and the marginal rate of substitution diminishes as more of one good is substituted for the other, reflecting the diminishing marginal utility as consumption is increased.

It is assumed that the household aims to achieve the maximum possible level of utility and attain the highest possible indifference curve. For the subsistence household, unable to buy or sell the food-crop, maize, this point is found at L, where the indifference curve, $I_0 I_0$, just touches the production possibility boundary and the two slopes are equal. At this point, then,

$MRS_{mg} = RPT_{mg}$ which implies that $MU_m/MU_g = -dG/dM$

where the latter reflects the opportunity cost. Rearrangement gives:

$$dM * MU_m = -dG * MU_g \tag{8}$$

which means that the utility of the extra maize produced equals the disutility of consuming fewer groundnuts. Thus utility would be maximized by producing 1.1 tonnes of maize, for household consumption, and 1 tonne of groundnuts. Note that, in practice, the direct measurement of marginal utilities or the *MRS* is extremely difficult. None the less if the *RPT* can be estimated from a knowledge of the production relationships, and the farmer is assumed to maximize utility, then the *RPT* provides a measure of the *MRS* at the chosen levels of production. In this example, at point *L* it is approximately equal to 1.

However, if there were a market for maize, as well as for groundnuts, consumption and production decisions could be dealt with separately. At the prices of £72 and £60 respectively, the profit maximizing household would choose to produce 1.55 tonnes of maize, and only 0.5 tonnes of groundnuts (point *K*). However, utility is maximized by consuming 1.15 tonnes of maize, and 1.1 tonnes of groundnuts, or its monetary equivalent (point *M*). This household would then sell 1.55 − 1.15 = 0.4 tonnes of maize

Figure 3.9   Utility maximization

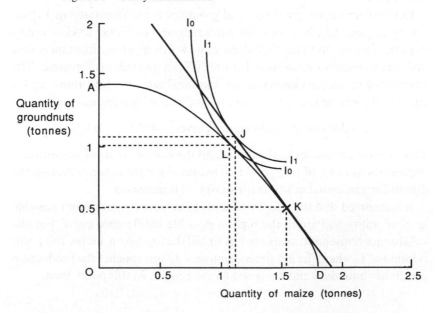

which would earn the equivalent of the reduction in income from ground-nuts. The MRS_{mg} must equal the inverse price ratio $72/60=1.2$ at point J.

The opportunities offered by the access to a market for the food crop allows this household to increase total utility with an increase in consumption of both maize and groundnuts. Incidentally it should be noted that, since groundnuts are sold rather than consumed, the vertical axis effectively measures money income. The convexity of the indifference curve reflects the diminishing marginal utility of increasing money income as well as the diminishing marginal utility of increasing food consumption. Thus market access allows the farm household to increase income by selling maize, whilst at the same time increasing consumption above the original sub-sistence level.

We now consider the effect of an increase in the relative price of maize, represented by the shift from iso-revenue or price line P_1 to P_2, in Figure 3.10. The economic optimum level of maize production increases from OM_3 to OM_4, so there should be more maize available for sale. However, household income has increased as a result of the rise in maize price, and the family may decide to take advantage of this to consume more maize. This increase in income is, in fact, due to the extra farm profit produced. Hence the effect on consumption is called the 'profit effect'. In Figure 3.10, the increase in food consumption is from OM_1 to OM_2. This increase in

Figure 3.10 Consumption and market supply

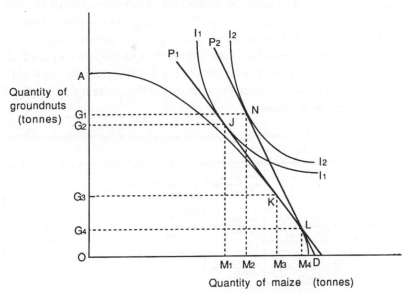

consumption M_1M_2, must be subtracted from the increase in production M_3M_4 to determine the effect on marketed surplus. As shown, the increase in consumption is less than the increase in production, so the market supply response, measured by the elasticity of supply, is still positive. However, it is considerably lower than it would be if none was consumed at home.

The whole set of effects of the price change on production and consumption, and hence on the marketed surplus, of a food crop is shown in Figure 3.11. The possibility exists that the increase in consumption could exceed the extra production, in which case market supply would fall and the elasticity would be negative. Since supply elasticities are usually positive, this is known as a perverse supply response (see Bond 1983). Thus household economics analysis, which takes account of both production and consumption choices may lead to quite different estimates of supply and demand elasticities from those obtained by separate analyses of supply and demand.

Summary

1 Farm households have multiple objectives concerning both production and consumption. Choices are limited by the available resources and production technology.

2 A simple example is developed with two activities, maize and groundnut production, and three constraints, land, planting labour and weeding labour. These constraints limit the feasible set of combinations of the two crops which may be grown, and define the 'production possibility boundary' (PPB). The (negative) slope is the 'rate of product transformation'.

3 Goals may be expressed as 'target' quantities of the two crops, which limit the range of choice within which the farmer may be 'satisfied'. Alternatively goals may be ranked in a 'lexicographic ordering' or weighted to achieve an optimal choice.

Figure 3.11   Household-firm response to increase in output price (adapted from Adelman and Taylor, 1989)

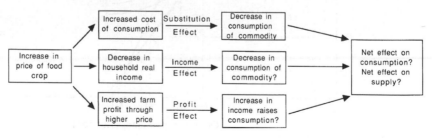

4 If prices, or gross margins, are known then the combination of activities which maximizes total revenue can be found. It must lie on a corner of the PPB where some, but not necessarily all, the resource constraints are binding.

5 The 'shadow prices' or 'opportunity costs' of the binding constraints can be calculated and reflect resource scarcity. For a non-binding constraint the shadow price is zero.

6 Similarly the opportunity cost of maize production, can be calculated as the value of groundnuts foregone. The extra (marginal) cost per tonne of maize increases with increased maize production. On the assumption that the farmer will expand maize production so long as the price is greater than the marginal cost, the step-wise shifts in marginal cost represent the farmer's maize supply response.

7 If the PPB is assumed to be a smooth, differentiable curve, the revenue maximizing choice is found at the point of tangency of a line of equal revenue, rather than at a corner. The (negative) slope of the boundary, known as the rate of product transformation (*RPT*) then equals the inverse price ratio.

8 The individual (revenue maximizing) farmer's short-run supply response may now be represented as a smooth curve derived from the production possibility boundary and given prices for competing products. Elasticity of supply, defined as the percentage change in quantity over the percentage change in price, depends upon the slope of the curve. Supply response is more elastic in the long-run, since time is needed to adjust inputs of land, labour and capital. These arguments apply equally when the focus is changed from an individual farm to aggregate production response for a country or region.

9 Where crops are grown for home consumption, choices may be based on the maximization of household utility. It is maximized where the indifference curve just touches the PPB, and its slope (the marginal rate of substitution) equals the *RPT*.

10 However, if markets exist for subsistence crops, consumption and production decisions can be separated. Production activities are chosen to maximize revenue, or gross margin, while produce is sold or purchased to maximize utility. The optimal or best choice is found where the marginal rate of substitution is equal to the inverse price ratio.

11 An increase in the relative price of a food crop will induce (i) an increase in its production (ii) increased farm income (profit) leading to increased home consumption (iii) substitution by other food items because of its higher price and (iv) an effective decrease in income and consumption

because of the rise in food cost. The sum of all these may affect home consumption in either direction. The market supply response is likely to differ from that of a pure commercial producer, and may even be negative.

References

Adelman, I. and D. Taylor (1989). *Econometric approaches to utilising farm household data in agricultural policy analysis*, Farm Management and Production Economics Service, Agricultural Services Division, FAO, Rome

Akatugba-Ogisi, O. D. (1994). 'Multiple objectives and small farmer behaviour in Delta and Edo States of Nigeria: an application of Goal Programming', Ph.D. thesis, Department of Agricultural Economics and Management, The University of Reading, UK

Askari, H. & J. T. Cummings (1976). *Agricultural Supply Response*, New York, Praeger

Binswanger, H. P. (1990). The policy response of agriculture: a survey of the econometric evidence. Washington, DC. *Proceedings of the World Bank Annual Conference on Development Economics 1989*, Supplement to the World Bank Economic Review

Bond, M. E. (1983). *Agricultural Responses to Prices in sub-Saharan Africa*. International Monetary Fund Staff Papers 30, No 4

Colman, D. & T. Young (1989). *Principles of Agricultural Economics*, Cambridge University Press

Ellis, F. (1988). *Peasant Economics: Farm Households and Agrarian Development*, Cambridge University Press

Romero, C. & T. Rehman (1989). *Multiple Criteria Analysis for Agricultural Decisions*, Developments in Agricultural Economics 5, Amsterdam, Elsevier

4

Labour and leisure

The input–output relationship

In our discussion so far we have assumed that the farmer controls a fixed set of resources, of land and labour, to be allocated between alternative productive activities in pursuit of given objectives. The labour inputs per hectare of sorgham or groundnuts, given in Table 3.1, are assumed to be fixed regardless of the number of hectares grown. In practice some inputs may be varied, for instance labour use for a key operation, seed rate, irrigation or fertilizer application on a particular crop; feed inputs to a livestock enterprise. The relationship between the quantities of inputs used and the product obtained is known as a 'Production Function'. Product output (Y) is a function of, or is determined by, the quantities of inputs used (X_i), thus;

$$Y = f(X_1, X_2, \ldots, X_n)$$

There are many practical and theoretical problems involved in estimating a production function, and these will be discussed in some detail in Chapter 13. None the less it seems reasonable to assume that the farmer knows the amount of yield he can expect, on average, when he decides to allocate inputs to, say, growing a plot of maize. In short, he has a mental picture of his production function.

In the simplest case, with a single variable input, for example weeding labour (X), the relationship may be expressed as

$$Y = f(X).$$

which simply means that the maize crop output, or yield (Y), depends upon the amount of labour used in weeding. The farmer's knowledge of this relationship is based on past experience on his own, and other, farms. The figures given in the first two columns of Table 4.1 serve to illustrate the

Table 4.1. *The effect of varying weeding effort on maize yield*

Days of weeding labour	Maize yield (Total product)	Average product	Marginal product[a]
		Bags of maize	
0	0	—	
1	2.5	2.5	2.5
2	6.0	3.0	3.5
3	8.0	2.67	2.0
4	9.2	2.3	1.2
5	9.9	1.98	0.7
6	10.2	1.70	0.3
7	10.2	1.46	0

[a] The marginal product is calculated as the difference between successive values in the total product column.

relationship which might exist between the number of days spent weeding a maize plot and the yield obtained. The important point to note about these figures is that the yield, or total product, increases with increased labour inputs, but at a diminishing rate.

The effect is seen rather more clearly, when we calculate the average product (*AP* equals total product divided by the number of man-days worked) and the marginal product (*MP* equals the *increase* in total product for each additional day of weeding labour) as shown in columns 3 and 4 of Table 4.1. Clearly, both average and marginal products diminish as weeding labour is increased. The effects are also shown in Figure 4.1 which is based on the information given in the Table. The shaded blocks in the diagram represent the marginal products of each additional man-day of weeding labour. It may be noted that for any particular level of weeding labour use the total product is equal to the cumulative sum of the marginal products. For instance, when three days are spent on weeding, the total product is

2.5+3.5+2.0=8.0 bags.

If we assume that labour can be hired by the hour, or even by the minute, rather than by the day so that inputs can be varied continuously, the input–output relationship may be represented by a smooth curve as in Figure 4.2. Such a curve is called a 'response curve' since it shows how the crop yield *responds* to variations in inputs. The marginal product, over any small interval of the curve, is measured by the slope. If we use X to represent the quantity of weeding labour and Y to represent maize yield, while d means a small change then the slope may be written as dY/dX=marginal product (MP).

Thus the marginal product curve can be estimated as shown in the lower diagram. Now the total product for any particular level of weeding labour use is equal to the area under the marginal product curve, up to that level of input. For example, the area under the curve when 6.5 days of labour are used represents 10.2 bags of maize, which equals the total product.

The assumption that all inputs other than weeding labour, for instance, the area of land and the amount of seed, are fixed is important. It means there are limits on the amount of maize that can be produced from this particular plot, and that is why extra weeding labour becomes less and less effective in raising the yield. This case of diminishing returns to weeding labour in maize production is an example of a general rule, the so-called 'law of diminishing

Figure 4.1   Diminishing marginal returns to weeding labour; (a) Total labour produce, (b) Marginal produce

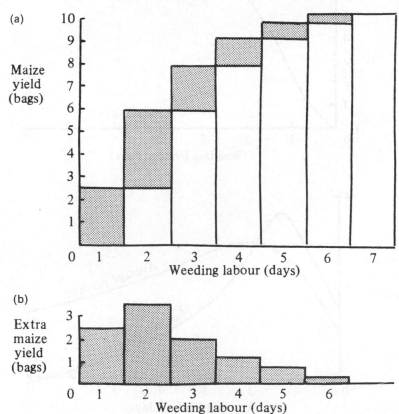

returns', which we can now state precisely. *If one input is varied, the amounts of all other inputs being held constant, the marginal product per unit of the variable input eventually diminishes.* This 'Law' applies very widely and explains why we cannot produce all the food we need from a single plot. It is likely to apply as farming population pressure increases on a fixed area of land. As the labour input rises, the marginal product per person is likely to fall, unless new, more-productive systems of farming can be found.

Figure 4.2   Response curve for weeding labour; (a) Total product, (b) Marginal and average product

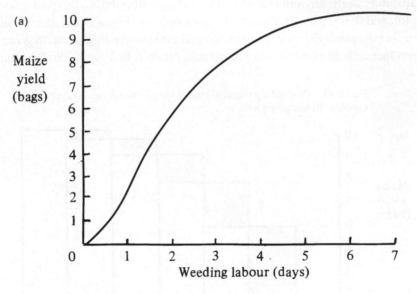

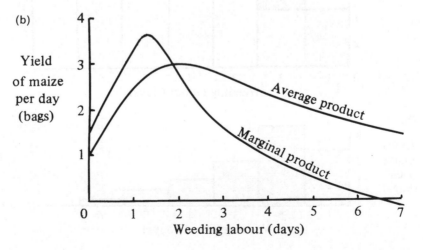

Generally speaking the average product, often referred to as the 'productivity', of a variable input diminishes along with the marginal product when inputs are increased, as shown in Table 4.1 and Figure 4.2. However this only occurs where the marginal product is less than the average product of labour. Initially the marginal product is greater than the average product and pulls the average up so productivity rises.

The point where total product is at a maximum and marginal product is zero, at about 6.5 days of weeding labour in this case, is sometimes known as the technical optimum or technically the best choice. In this case it represents the highest attainable yield per hectare of land. However, this is to ignore the cost of weeding labour. If, in fact, labour for weeding is scarce and costly while land is freely available it might be better to maximize the productivity of labour, which from these figures implies less than two days of weeding effort.

The economic optimum

For simplicity in this first example we assume that labour can be hired at a wage rate of £3 per day, while maize can be sold for £4 per bag. This means that each day of labour costs the equivalent of $\frac{3}{4} = 0.75$ bags of grain to hire, or one day of weeding labour exchanges for three-quarters of a bag of grain. It is now relatively straightforward to calculate the economic optimum, where the surplus over the variable cost is maximized. Since all inputs except weeding labour are supposed to be fixed, their cost is constant regardless of the amount of weeding labour used. As a result, when the surplus over variable cost is maximized so too is the farmer's profit, which is simply the surplus over the variable cost minus the fixed cost.

The economic optimum, or profit maximizing level of weeding labour, for the assumed prices, is shown in Table 4.2 to be four days. At this level the surplus over the cost of weeding labour is maximized (see column 4) although total yield is below the maximum.

An alternative approach to finding the economic optimum, is to compare the cost per unit of labour input with the marginal product earned. The economic optimum is then found where the marginal (value) product equals the unit factor cost. In this example the unit factor is 0.75 bags of grain, and the marginal product is closest to this value for the fourth day of weeding labour. However, if inputs can be varied continuously, the precise economic optimum can be found using the response curve as shown in Figure 4.3. This is identical with Figure 4.2 except that the line *BD* has been added to represent the cost of hiring weeding labour. In the upper (total

Table 4.2. *Costs and the economic optimum*

Days of weeding labour	Cost of weeding labour	Total product	Surplus over weeding cost[a]	Marginal product
		Bags of maize		
0	0	0	0	
1	0.75	2.5	1.75	2.5
2	1.5	6.0	4.50	3.5
3	2.25	8.0	5.75	2.0
4	3.0	9.2	6.20	1.2
5	3.75	9.9	6.15	0.7
6	4.5	10.2	5.70	0.3
7	5.25	10.2	4.95	0

[a] This is the difference between total product (third column) and cost of weeding labour (second column).

product) diagram, *BD* represents the total cost of weeding labour so it has a slope of 0.75 (the cost, in bags of maize per day of labour). The maximum surplus over labour cost is obtained when, as shown, the cost line just touches, or is tangent to, the response curve at *C*. At this point the slope of the curve is equal to that of the tangent, so marginal product equals unit factor cost of 0.75 bags ($MP = dY/dX = P/R$ where P=wage and R=price of maize). Surplus *OB* is maximized at 6.25 bags, when 4.4 days of weeding labour are employed.

In the lower (marginal product) diagram, *BD* actually represents the unit factor cost, at 0.75 bags of maize per day. Total weeding labour cost is given by the area under this line (e.g. *OBCA* when *OA* days of labour are used). The marginal product is equal to the unit factor cost where the two lines cross at *C*, so this is the economic optimum. Since the area under the marginal product curve represents the total product, the shaded area *BCE* represents the surplus over weeding labour cost. This surplus would be smaller if less than *OA* (equals 4.4) days were spent weeding. For instance, if only three days were used, the surplus would be reduced to the area *BGFE* on the lower diagram, or *OF* (5.75 bags) in the upper diagram. If, on the other hand, more weeding labour was employed, say six days, the surplus would again be reduced. Referring back to the lower diagram, the area *CHJ* would be lost from the total surplus. Thus, for the given response curve and prices, the maximum surplus of 6.25 bags of maize cannot be improved upon.

Alternatively, total product may be measured as average product times total variable input. In Figure 4.3(b) this is represented by the area *OAKL* at the economic optimum. Thus the surplus over labour cost is represented by the area *BCKL*.

If the price of labour rises, or the price of maize falls, the economic optimum level of weeding falls. For example, at a labour cost of 1.5 bags of maize per day, the economic optimum weeding rate is only three days, as the

Figure 4.3 The economic optimum input; (a) Maximum surplus, (b) Marginal product equals unit factor cost

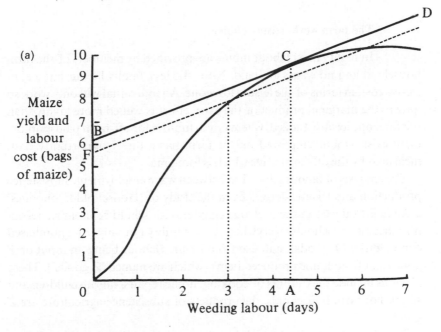

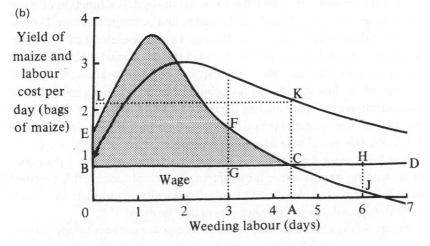

reader may check from Table 4.2 or Figure 4.3. At the price of more than three bags per day it is not worth employing weeding labour at all, since this cost exceeds the maximum average product. Conversely, if the relative cost of labour falls, the economic optimum use of labour rises. Hence, if the farmer's objective is to maximize the surplus over weeding costs, he will employ more weeding labour if the wage falls and less if it rises. His 'demand curve' for weeding labour slopes downwards to the right.

The farm work–leisure choice

In reality most labour inputs are provided by members of the farm household and no wages are paid. None the less, family labour has a subjective cost, in terms of the leisure foregone. An individual will only work so long as the marginal product of the extra effort is valued more highly than the foregone leisure. Indeed, where opportunities for off-farm paid employment exist, labour employed on the farm has a direct opportunity cost, measured by the off-farm wage which is foregone.

The analysis of labour allocation between wage employment, subsistence production and leisure, derives from the study of 'Household Economics' already introduced in the previous chapter. Household economists recognize that all households, everywhere, derive utility not only from purchased commodities (Y goods), but also from leisure (labour being an input or X good) and from home produced items (which are named 'Z goods'). These Z goods include the outputs of cooking, home repairs, raising children and so on. For farm households, the products of subsistence agriculture are Z goods.

Thus household utility, which is to be maximized, is a function of these three components: purchased goods, leisure and home production. If these can be evaluated in money terms, the first by the household cash income, assumed spent and not saved, the second at the going market wage rate and the third at the market value, they can be summed to arrive at the 'full income' of the household. The household objective is then assumed to be maximization of this full income. The set of possible effects, of a change in the wage or opportunity cost of labour and leisure, is illustrated in Figure 4.4. These effects will now be analysed separately in more detail.

The farm work–leisure choice is first analysed for a pure subsistence farm, with no opportunities for off-farm wage employment. It is assumed that the farm household can evaluate both agricultural products and leisure subjectively, and that indifference curves may be drawn.

Figure 4.5(a) illustrates the production response curve (OB) for varying labour inputs, at a peak work period, in maize production. Thus it is similar to Figure 4.2. The corresponding marginal product curve is shown in Figure 4.5(b). Even though constant returns to scale may apply, it is appropriate to assume diminishing marginal returns to labour for a specific operation. The maximum number of hours that can be worked is set by the basic minimum leisure essential for eating and sleeping represented by the constraint line *AB*. Within the range *OA* increased work means less leisure. An additional constraint is set by the need to produce sufficient food for subsistence. This is represented by the line *CDE* in the upper diagram, and by the shaded area in the lower diagram. Thus, the feasible range of choice between work and leisure is limited to the range *FA*.

Utility is maximized at point *G* (in the upper diagram) where the indifference curve between maize output and leisure just touches the production response curve. (Note that the indifference curve slopes upward from left to right since a reduction in leisure is only acceptable if production is increased. However, it may also be noted that the horizontal axis could be reversed to measure leisure rather than work, in which case the diagram would resemble the production possibility boundary of Figure 3.9.)

In the lower diagram, the line *JGK* represents the subjective marginal value of leisure, which increases as the hours of leisure diminish. The optimum utility maximizing choice occurs where the marginal value per hour of leisure is equal to the marginal value product of work, at *G*, when *OH* hours are worked.

Income and substitution effects

A rise in labour productivity as a result of new technology would have both a substitution effect and an income effect on the hours worked. The rise in the return per hour of work and the consequent rise in opportunity cost per hour of leisure provides an incentive to substitute work for

Figure 4.4 Household-firm response to an increase in off-farm wage rate (adapted from Adelman and Taylor, 1989)

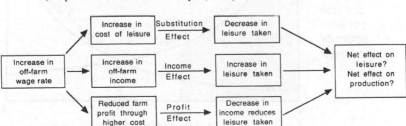

leisure, by working longer hours. However, the income effect works in the opposite direction. With an increased income resulting from his increased productivity, a person is better off and can afford to 'buy' more leisure.

These effects are illustrated in Figure 4.6 in which the rise in productivity is respresented by the upward shift of the response curve and the marginal product curve.

In the upper diagram, the new utility maximizing point *M* lies on a higher indifference curve, reflecting the rise in total income and utility. The effect on labour input in this example is a *fall* in the hours worked. This

Figure 4.5   The income–leisure choice; (a) Total product, (b) Marginal product

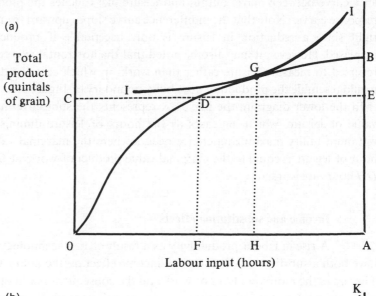

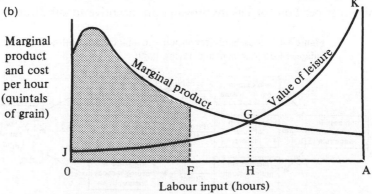

means that the income effect (*PM*) outweighs the substitution effect (*GP*), so the farmer decides to take more leisure.

From the lower diagram we see that if the subjective marginal value per hour of leisure remained unchanged, increased agricultural productivity would result in more hours worked (the substitution effect). However, the rise in income represented by the increased productivity causes a rise in the subjective valuation of leisure (the income effect), and this is sufficient to bring about a fall in hours worked. When a rise in productivity, or product

Figure 4.6   Income and substitution effects; (a) Total product, (b) Marginal product

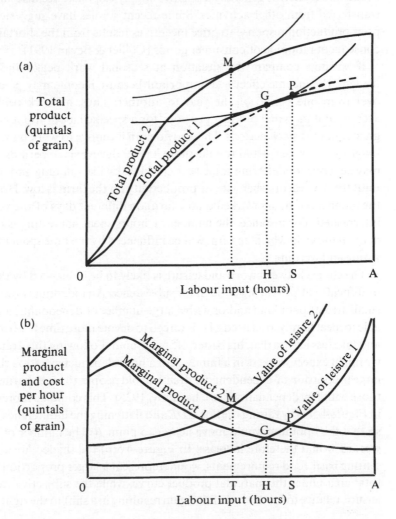

prices, causes a reduction in hours worked, we have what is called a backward-bending labour supply curve. In the case of a product price increase, this may mean a decline in the product output, or negative price response.

This analysis does not allow us to predict whether the income effect will be stronger and labour supply backward-bending, or not. There is no clear empirical evidence either, in relation to *total* labour supply. This is because, in practice, there is not just a simple choice between labour and leisure, but many different alternative activities. If the returns from one such activity increase, there will be a clear incentive to substitute this for other activities, while the income effect may be relatively small. Thus, if the price of one product rises there is generally a positive supply response, because labour is transferred from other activities. Some recent studies have suggested that poor production response to price incentives results from the shortage and consequent rationing of consumer goods (Collier & Bevan 1991).

If we now compare the situation at seasonal work peaks and work troughs, the income effect is unimportant because income may be carried over from one period of the year to another. Thus, at work peaks the average and marginal product per hour for a specific labour input is much greater than at slack periods. This provides an incentive to work harder and longer at work peaks and to take more leisure during slack periods. There may be scope for deferring some household tasks, like building and repairs, until the dry season when labour productivity on the farm is low. However, the numbers of hours worked on the farm on different days of the year are interrelated. For instance, the number of hours spent harvesting is dependent on the yield which, in turn, will be influenced by the time spent in cultivating and weeding.

The choice between work and leisure is likely to be influenced by the ease or difficulty of producing enough for subsistence. An individual cropping a small area of poor land and/or with a large number of dependants, is barely able to meet family food needs. He is forced to devote more time to farm work and take less leisure than his better-off neighbour. Following this argument, we might expect workers in a family with a high 'dependency ratio', that is a large proportion of dependent children and old people, to work harder than those with few dependants (see Chayanov, 1925). This could be represented in Figure 4.5(a) by raising the line *CDE* and flattening the indifference curve, so that the optimum would move nearer to point *B*. The number of hours worked would therefore increase. In Figure 4.5(b) the shaded area, representing basic food requirements, would represent a larger proportion of the total area under the marginal product curve, while the subjective value of leisure, relative to food, would fall, again resulting in a shift to the right of the optimum point. Evidence from many tropical areas generally supports the theory that work input per person is directly related to the dependency ratio (see Norman 1969, Levi & Havinden 1982; and Hunt 1978).

Hired labour

Hired labour is of increasing importance with the spread of production for the market and increased individualism. The wages of hired labour make up the largest single item of expenditure on most farms, despite the fact that hired labour generally provides less than 20 per cent of the total farm work input.

Hired workers are often other farmers, either from the locality or migrants from further afield. Migrant workers may live with the employer's family and share his meals, or they may be allowed to establish food-crop farms of their own.

Share contracts may be viewed as a mechanism whereby those who control the means of production, land, tree crops or livestock, acquire access to the labour of others. Their prevalence may reflect a shortage of cash and a lack of short-term credit facilities which would allow hire of labour for a money wage. However, labour hire for wages often coexists with various sharing agreements in the same village or area. There is no obvious tendency to change from one form of contract to the other. Share-cropping has certain advantages in spreading risks. From the farmer's point of view it is most convenient to hire labour by the hour as and when needed. However, the temporary piece-worker hired by the hour has very little security and no continuity of employment. Possibly for these reasons, wages are generally highest for labourers hired by the hour. This provides the simplest case for analysis.

As explained in detail earlier, the profit maximizing level of labour hire is found where the marginal product is equal to the wage, measured in terms of the product. However, when unpaid family labour is also available, a choice must be made between family and hired labour. The solution is obtained by combining the analysis of labour hire (Figure 4.3) with that of the farm work versus leisure choice (Figure 4.5). The result is shown in Figure 4.7. In Figure 4.7(a) the total labour cost line (*BCD*) is a tangent to the production response curve at point *C*. This then gives the optimum level of labour input (*OA* hours) where the marginal product is equal to the wage as already described. The same labour cost line (*BCD*) is a tangent to the farmer's indifference curve (*II*) at point *Y*. This means that the farmer chooses to work only *OX* hours, and hires the remaining *XA* hours.

Figure 4.7(b) shows the marginal product curve, the horizontal line *BD* representing the constant hourly wage rate, and the rising marginal value of leisure curve. Labour use is extended to point *C* since the marginal product exceeds the wage up to this point. Family labour is used up to point *G*, since each hour of leisure is valued at less than the wage over this range. The economic optimum of family and hired labour is found when (a) the marginal value per hour of leisure is equal to the wage rate, and (b) they are both equal to the marginal product of labour on the farm.

In fact, agricultural wage rates are themselves influenced by the productivity of labour on farms as well as the availability of labour. Where the

Figure 4.7   Labour hiring; (a) Total product, (b) Marginal product

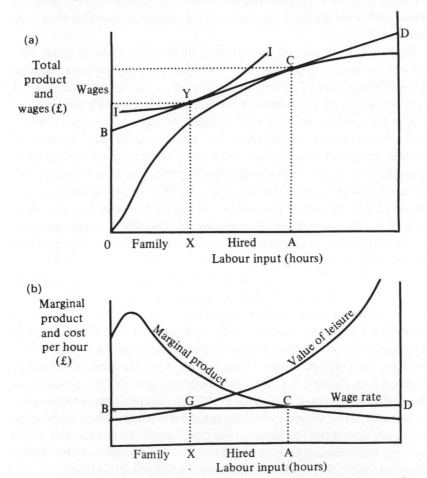

marginal product of labour is high, as in areas of high potential, so too is the demand for labour. As a result wages are likely to be higher than average in such areas. Immigration of workers may increase the supply of labour, and thus reduce the average wage, but this process is unlikely to proceed so far as to eliminate the wage differential. By a similar argument we might expect wages of casual labour to rise at peak work periods; as indeed often happens. It may also help to explain why women and children are paid lower wages than adult males for certain tasks, where their productivity may be lower.

Another consideration is that some tasks, such as bush clearing, are more arduous than others and a higher wage, which includes a 'compensating differential', is necessary to attract sufficient labour. Thus quite large wage differences may exist between regions, sexes and seasons of the year (see Byerlee *et al*. 1976). Other things being equal, a rise in wages would induce a reduction in the desire to hire labour, although the effect on family labour input is uncertain. However, if wages are high enough, farm family members may be persuaded to seek off-farm work.

Off-farm work

Figure 4.7 is readily modified to show the allocation of family labour to off-farm work as in Figure 4.8. The only difference is that the wage rate is higher, so that the optimum level of family work is greater than the profit maximizing level of labour input on the farm (point *Y* is now to the right of point *C*). Now *OA* hours are worked on the farm and *AX* hours off the farm. The same effect would result if the production response curve for farm labour was lower than in Figure 4.7 or the utility curve was flatter, reflecting a higher preference for income rather than leisure. If the off-farm wage were higher than the marginal product of labour in farming at all levels of employment, the best policy would be to leave farming altogether.

Most farm families in the tropics are involved in off-farm work or at least some household members are. Off-farm activities represent an alternative form of employment and source of income, which must also be taken into account in considering the opportunity costs of different farm enterprises.

Since the marginal product or opportunity cost of farm labour varies over the year, so do the relative attractions of off-farm work. Ideally, off-farm work would be fitted in during slack periods, while labour would be hired-in for work peaks. Thus hiring-in *and* hiring-out of labour may occur on the same farm at different periods of the year. In fact, the wage rate for off-farm work may differ from that for hiring agricultural labourers, in which case it may pay a family to hire farm labour at the same time as some family members work elsewhere. Three main categories of off-farm work may be identified:

(i) local employment on other farms in local crafts such as black-smithing or other occupations such as trading;
(ii) urban employment in a neighbouring town which is of particular importance to those dwelling on the urban fringes and people like

Figure 4.8   Off-farm work; (a) Total product, (b) Marginal product

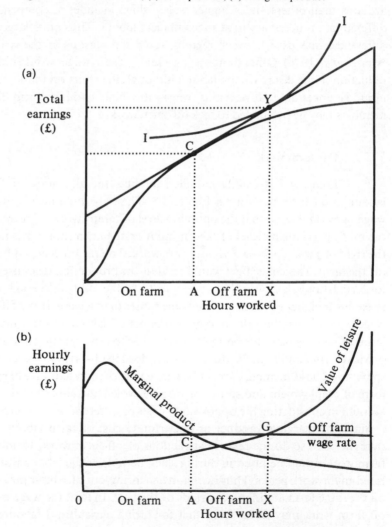

the *Yoruba* of Nigeria who have traditionally lived in towns and
farmed the surrounding hinterland;

(iii) long-range migration of some family members to work in cash-
cropped areas, on plantations or in the mines.

In the third case the migrant faces the risk of not finding employment when
he has made the move. Thus he really needs to estimate his 'expected wage'
(the going wage rate in the region to which he is migrating multiplied by the
probability of finding employment) to compare with the marginal product
in agriculture (which is also an expected value) in assessing whether migration is justified. Due allowance must also be made for travel costs, of course.

Most part-time farmers are loth to give up farming altogether. Their land
holdings represent links with their families and communities and provide
security as a basis for subsistence if the off-farm employment should cease.
However, they may devote less time and effort to the land, than their full-
time neighbours. Because of differences between the sexes and age groups
in off-farm work opportunities, those most likely to move out of agriculture, if only temporarily, are the young adult males. As a result, women face
increased responsibility for farm work, and increased work loads, while the
dependency ratio on the farm may rise. Remittances of off-farm earnings
may resolve the latter problem, but the absence of adult males creates shortages of labour for crucial tasks such as land clearing. As a result land
already cleared, is cropped for more years than normal with resultant
declining yields and loss of soil fertility (see Hunt 1984; Swindell 1985).

Seasonal labour allocation

Although there are seasonal peaks of activity associated with all
crops, they do not necessarily coincide. The labour profile for yams, which is
the pattern of monthly labour requirements per hectare over the year, is
different from that for maize. How then does the farmer decide to allocate
his labour between them? Yams may yield a higher return per man-hour in
one month, while maize yields a higher return per man-hour of labour in a
different month. Yet the areas planted to yams and maize cannot be varied
from month to month according to their returns per hour of labour. Thus,
it is not possible to allocate labour so as to earn equal marginal returns
from all crops in each and every month.

In practice there are complicated management-decisions regarding the
allocation of labour between crops at peak periods of the cropping season.
The fixed-coefficients approach used at the beginning of the previous

chapter (Table 3.1) can be of help in analyzing such decision problems. More details of this method, known as linear programming, are given in Chapter 16. However, the full complexity of such decisions, which also involve risk considerations, may be best explored by farming systems and farmer participatory research (Chapter 10).

If labour can be used productively more evenly throughout the year, the total product of the family labour force will be increased. The well-being of the family is thereby improved. By the same token, the production per unit of peak-period labour is increased. However, it should be noted that the *total* work load over the year may also be increased so much that the average product per unit of annual labour input is reduced. This is likely to be a less important consideration than the gain in household output, but it depends upon the choice between income and leisure to be discussed in the next section.

Given that labour profiles differ for different crops, the work load for a combination of different crops is more level through the year than that for a sole crop. Thus another argument put forward in favour of mixed cropping is that it spreads the labour input more evenly over the year. In Northern Nigeria mixed cropping has been shown to yield a higher return per unit of peak labour input than sole cropping (Norman 1969). However, the crops do not need to be grown in a mixture to achieve this benefit. Clearly, in bimodal rainfall areas with two distinct cropping seasons, the late maize crop does not compete with the early maize crop for either labour or land. The two crops are supplementary enterprises. Similarly, dry-season irrigation may be supplementary to rainfed cropping in the wet seasons, and may help to even out the work load, as shown in Figure 4.9.

Increasing labour productivity

Labour productivity, in terms of the average product per person employed in agriculture, may be increased either by producing more with the existing work force or by saving labour. This distinction is somewhat artificial since labour which is saved might be used to increase output without increasing the work force. However, this is only likely to occur if labour is saved at peak work periods, when seasonal availability is an effective constraint. Labour saved at slack periods simply adds to leisure time. The real distinction to be drawn is that between neutral innovations, such as some new high-yielding crop varieties, which make a net contribution by raising the productivity of all inputs equally, and labour-saving innovations such as mechanization which generally involve the substitution of capital for labour (see Chapter 5 for analysis of technological change).

Labour-saving innovations may include herbicides, zero-tillage techniques, animal draught and various levels of mechanization. The introduction of any of these necessitates capital investments; special equipment is needed for applying herbicides or for seeding through the herbage cover under zero tillage, while oxen, ploughs and machines are also items of capital. The introduction of ox ploughs and tractor mechanization also involves the initial costs of training oxen and operators and clearing and destumping the land. This last cost item may be prohibitive in humid rainforest areas.

There is no assurance that the benefits of such labour-saving innovations will outweigh the costs. First, the elimination of one work peak may simply result in another becoming critical. Thus the introduction of zero tillage, animal draft power or tractors may reduce or eliminate the work peak for cultivation and planting, only to leave weeding labour as a critical constraint. The use of herbicides reduces labour needs for weeding, but then

Figure 4.9   Levelling labour needs with supplementary irrigation

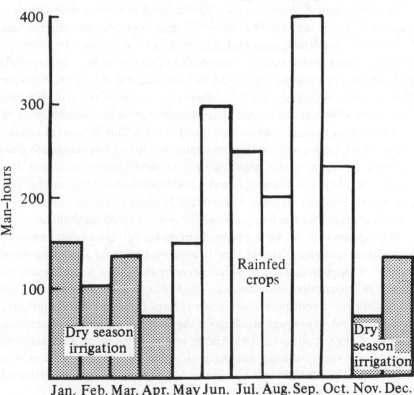

harvest labour may become critical. As a result there may be very little saving in the labour-force required. Second, even when a real reduction in labour needs is achieved there is no benefit, other than the reduction in drudgery, unless the labour saved can be used productively. There are three possible ways of absorbing labour which is saved: (i) intensifying and increasing yields per hectare, (ii) extending the cultivated area, and (iii) finding alternative off-farm work.

In principle, the use of labour-saving technology, especially machinery, should allow greater cropping intensity and increased yields as a result of more timely and effective crop operations. There is relatively little evidence of such benefits being obtained in practice. It is suggested that the introduction of tractors on the Mwea Irrigation Scheme in Kenya was accompanied by increased rice yields. None the less in such cases it is not easy to separate the effect of the labour-saving technology from other changes such as improved management and increased use of fertilizers. It must be concluded that, even if there is scope for increasing yields by the use of machinery, it is limited.

The alternative of extending the cultivated area may be feasible if there is an abundance of unused land, although since ox-teams and tractors are lumpy, indivisible items, a substantial increase in farm area may be needed to cover the costs (see discussion of farm scale in Chapter 5). Where this entails a lengthening of the cropping period and a shortening of fallows, yields are likely to diminish unless alternative means are found of restoring fertility. Indeed, as shown in the second chapter, this represents intensification of land use rather than an extension of the area used. This in turn, of course, implies that land is now a limiting constraint, but it does not necessarily conflict with the argument that peak labour is the *most* limiting constraint. It is usually the case that, if the most limiting constraint is overcome, another secondary one becomes effective. Land is highly likely to become an effective constraint given the large increase in scale associated with mechanization.

The expansion of off-farm employment makes no direct contribution to agricultural output of course, but it may be beneficial in raising rural incomes. Opportunities for part-time farming may allow some families to remain in agriculture, who otherwise could not survive. Thus the promotion of improved transport to urban areas or of rural and cottage industry may help to raise rural welfare. Finally, the provision of improved services, notably water supplies, rural electricity and health centres may improve farm labour supply throughout the year. Apart from the general gain in welfare, farm production may be increased as a result of the labour released for farm work at peak periods.

In summary it is clear that labour productivity may be increased through the introduction of new technology, but additional costs are always incurred. Careful economic evaluation is needed before any innovation is recommended for general adoption. Farming Systems Research and the planning methods discussed later in this book may be used to evaluate specific proposals.

Summary

1 This chapter deals with the optimal use of a single variable input; labour. It concerns the factor:product relationship.

2 The response curve to a single variable input illustrates the 'law of diminishing returns' predicting that beyond some level of input (relative to fixed levels of other factors) both the marginal and average products, per unit of input, decline.

3 For a marketed product and a purchased input, such as hired labour, the economic optimum (most profitable level of use) occurs where the value of the marginal product is equal to the unit factor cost; in this case the wage rate.

4 Typically labour is provided by members of the farm household. Farm household economics is concerned with the allocation of family time between labour and leisure; the latter viewed as a form of consumption, along with produce used for subsistence.

5 For the purely subsistence producer the optimal level of labour use and farm production occurs where the subjective marginal utility of leisure foregone is equal to the utility value of the marginal product of farm work.

6 A rise in labour productivity (e.g. resulting from technological innovation) increases the opportunity cost of leisure, and encourages its substitution by increased work. However it also raises household income which may induce increased consumption of leisure. If the latter 'income effect' exceeds the former 'substitution effect', a negative or backward-bending labour supply response may occur.

7 If a labour market exists, the household may choose to work on the farm only to the point where the marginal rate of substitution of leisure for farm income is equal to the wage rate. If this point is below the economic optimum level of farm labour use, additional labour should be hired in. Alternatively, if the point is above the economic optimum level of farm labour use, family members should seek additional off-farm work.

8 Labour allocation decisions are complicated by the seasonality of farm work and its marginal productivity. Management policies which result

in a more even spread of labour requirements over the year can improve average productivity.

References

Adelman, I. & D. Taylor (1989). *Econometric approaches to utilising farm household data in agricultural policy analysis*,' Farm Management and Production Economics Service, Agricultural Services Division, FAO, Rome

Byerlee, D., C. K. Eicher, C. Liedholm & D. S. C. Spencer (1976). *Rural Employment in Tropical Africa: Summary of Findings*, Michigan State University, Department of Agricularal Economics, African Rural Economy Working Paper 20

Chambers, R., R. Longhurst, D. Bradley & R. Feachem (1979). *Seasonal Dimensions to Rural Poverty: Analysis and Practical Implications*, Sussex, England: Institute of Development Studies. Discussion Paper 142

Chayanov, A. V. (1925). 'Peasant farm organization', in Thorner, D., B. Kerblay & R. E. F. Smith (eds.), *The Theory of Peasant Economy*. (1966), Homewood, Illinois, Irwin

Cleave, J. H. (1974). *African Farmers: Labour Use in the Development of Smallholder Agriculture*, New York, Praeger

Collier, P & D.L. Bevan (1991). 'Income and substitution effects in models of peasant supply response under rationing', *Oxford Economic Papers*, **43**, 340–3

Farrington, J. (1975). *Farm Surveys in Malawi: The Collection and Analysis of Labour Data*, University of Reading, Department of Agricultural Economics: Development Study 16

Hunt, D. (1978). 'Chayanov's model of peasant household resource allocation and its relevance to Mbere Division, Eastern Kenya', *Journal of Development Studies*, **15**(1)

Hunt, D. (1984). *The Labour Aspects of Shifting Cultivation in African Agriculture*, FAO, Rome

Hymer, S. & Resnick, S. (1969). 'A model of an agrarian economy with non-agricultural activities', *American Economic Review*, **59**(4) 493–506

Lagemann, J., J. C. Flinn, B. N. Okigbo, & F. R. Moormann (1975). *Root Crop/Oil Palm Farming Systems: A Case Study from Eastern Nigeria*, IITA, Ibadan

Levi, J. & M. Havinden (1982). *Economics of African Agriculture*, London, Longmans

Low, A. R. C. (1986). *Agricultural Development in Southern Africa: Farm-Household Economics and the Food Crisis*, London, James Currey

Nakajima, C. (1986). *Subjective Equilibrium Theory of the Farm Household*, translated by R. Kada, Amsterdam, Elsevier

Norman, D. W. (1969). 'Labour inputs of farmers: a case study of the Zaria Province of the North Central State of Nigeria', *Nigerian Journal of Economic and Social Studies*, **2**, 3–14

Swindell, K. (1985). *African Society Today: Farm Labour*, Cambridge University Press

5

Costs, scale and size

Two variable inputs

Generally speaking, labour is not the only input which can be varied. Where there are two or more variable inputs then substitution of one for the other may be possible, and decisions must be taken on the appropriate combination of inputs, and method of production. This may be illustrated using the example from the previous chapter, of maize yield response to variations in weeding labour. It is now assumed that the amount of seed sown, per one hectare plot, is a second variable input. An increase in seed use which raises maize yield, thereby raises the average product per day of weeding labour but may reduce the amount of weeding necessary. More specifically there may be scope for substituting seed for weeding labour in producing a particular yield of maize. A possible response surface for these two variable inputs is represented by the data given in Table 5.1 and plotted in Figure 5.1.

The original response curve for weeding labour is now seen to relate to a fixed seed rate of 10 000 plants per hectare, as shown in the first row of Table 5.1 and by the line *AB* in Figure 5.1. Although some yield is obtained, even when no weeding labour is used (at least for seed rates above 15 000), the situation is different for seed. There can be no yield when no seed is used, so the response curves for seed pass through the origin. It is clear from Figure 5.1 that there are diminishing returns when either input is increased on its own or even when both are raised together. This is likely to occur, since other inputs, such as the area of cropped land, are limited.

Each contour line around the surface of the diagram, shows different combinations of seed and weeding labour, which will produce the same particular yield level. Contours are shown for yields of five bags and ten bags. In order to study the scope for substitution between inputs, we will now

Table 5.1. *Maize yield response to weeding labour and seed rate*

Weeding labour (days)	0	1	2	3	4	5	6	7
Seed rate (thousand stands)			Yield in bags of maize					
10	0	2.5	6.0	8.0	9.2	9.9	10.2	10.2
20	2.2	6.0	8.5	10.0	10.8	10.8	11.0	11.0
30	4.6	8.0	10.0	11.0	11.5	11.5	11.5	11.5
40	5.6	8.4	10.3	11.2	11.5	11.5	11.5	11.5

Figure 5.1   The response surface for weeding labour and seed

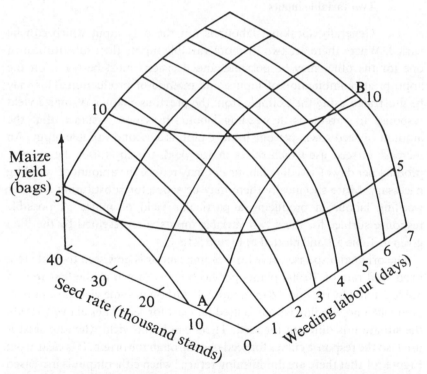

concentrate on these contours which are known as 'isoquants', meaning lines of equal output. A two-dimensional plan-view is given in Figure 5.2, while data for the isoquants are presented in Table 5.2.

In the diagram (Figure 5.2), the isoquants slope downwards from left to right. As *more* weeding labour is used, *less* seed is needed to produce a given yield, since the two inputs are assumed to be substitutes. The negative of the slope is known as the 'rate of technical substitution' (*RTS*) which is the reduction in seed use for each additional unit of labour input. Calculated values of the *RTS*, for the five-bag isoquant, are listed in the third column of Table 5.2(a) while those for the ten-bag isoquant are listed in Table 5.2(b).

It is clear from the figures in these columns, that the *RTS* diminishes, as weeding labour use increases. The diminishing *RTS* is reflected in the fact that the isoquant curve bulges towards the origin in Figure 5.2. This effect can be explained by the law of diminishing returns. It can be proved mathematically, that the *RTS* is equal to the ratio of the marginal products ($RTS = -dX_2/dX_1 = MP_1/MP_2$, where d means a small change, X_1 and X_2 are quantities of weeding labour and seed respectively and MP_1 and MP_2 are their marginal products). In this case the rate at which seed use declines per unit increase in weeding labour is equal to the marginal product of weeding labour divided by that of seed. If the marginal product of labour is relatively high, one unit substitutes for a lot of seed. Conversely, if the marginal product of labour is relatively low, one unit substitutes for a small amount of seed. Hence, as weeding labour use increases, with other inputs fixed and seed inputs falling, the marginal product of labour diminishes and so too does the *RTS*.

Figure 5.2   The isoquant diagram

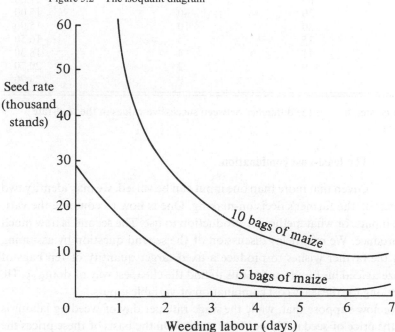

Table 5.2(a). *The five-bag isoquant (for five bags of maize output)*

Weeding labour (days)	Seed rate (thousand stands)	Rate of technical substitution[a]	Cost (£)
0	30		9.00
1	18	12	8.40
2	10	8	9.00
3	5	5	10.50
4	2	3	12.60
5	1	1	15.30
6	1	0	18.30
7	2	−1	21.60

[a] Calculated here as the difference between successive values in the seed-rate column.

Table 5.2(b). *The ten-bag isoquant (for ten bags of maize output)*

Weeding labour (days)	Seed rate (thousand stands)	Rate of technical substitution[a]	Cost (£)
0	∞		∞
1	60	∞	21.00
2	30	30	15.00
3	20	10	15.00
4	15	5	16.50
5	11	4	18.30
6	9	2	20.70
7	9	0	23.70

[a] Calculated here as the difference between successive values in the seed-rate column.

The least-cost combination

Given that more than one input can be varied, we may identify two aspects of the farmer's decision-making. One is how to combine the variable inputs, or what method of production to use. The second is how much to produce. We may delay discussion of the second question by assuming that the farmer wishes to produce a fixed target quantity of ten bags of maize to feed his family and wants to find the cheapest way of doing so. He is seeking for the least-cost combination of variable inputs.

We now suppose that, while the wage rate per day of weeding labour is £3, the price of seed is 30p per 1000 stands. On the basis of these prices the total cost of each combination of weeding labour and seed are given in the last column of Table 5.2(b). It is clear that the least-cost combination for producing ten bags of maize is between two and three days of seeding labour and a seed rate of between 20 and 30 000 stands. For this combination the rate of technical substitution, 10, is equal to the inverse price ratio 3/0.30. In fact this is the usual method of defining the least-cost combination.

The argument may be reinforced by reference to the isoquant diagram. In Figure 5.3 equal-cost, or isocost, lines have been added. Each of these straight lines represents all combinations of weeding labour and seed which can be purchased for a given total cost. For instance, the line *CD* represents a total cost of £12 which would allow the hire of four days of labour at £3 per day, or the purchase of 40 000 seeds or various intermediate combinations of the two inputs. Its slope is again negative, because *more* labour can be hired from a fixed total sum, only if *less* seed is purchased. The negative of the slope is 40 000/4=10(000) which is also equal to the inverse price ratio, as we have already seen. The isocost line for a smaller total cost (*AB*) is parallel to *CD* but nearer to the origin, while that for a larger total cost (*EF*) is also parallel but further from the origin.

Figure 5.3 The least-cost combination

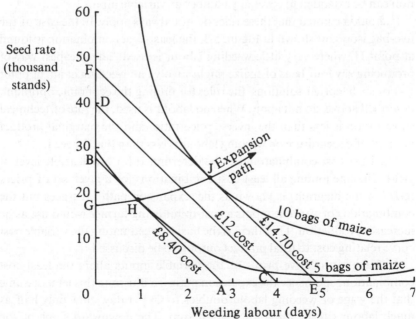

It should now be clear that normally the least-cost method of producing a particular level of yield is found where an isocost line is tangent to the isoquant. For a yield of ten bags of grain this occurs at point *J* representing 2.4 days of weeding labour and 25 000 plants with a total cost of £14.70. At a point of tangency the slope of the curve is equal to that of the tangent so the rate of technical substitution equals the inverse price ratio, which confirms our earlier conclusion.

An alternative method of defining the least-cost combination may be derived mathematically. We may recall that the rate of technical substitution of seed by weeding labour is equal to the ratio of the marginal product of weeding labour to that of seed. Therefore, since at the least-cost combination the rate of technical substitution is equal to the inverse price ratio we may write

$$RTS = MP_1/MP_2 = P_1/P_2$$

where the subscripts 1 and 2 refer to weeding labour and seed respectively. Rearranging the equation gives

$$MP_1/P_1 = MP_2/P_2$$

In words, this means that the marginal produce per unit of expenditure is the same for all variable inputs. This rule for finding the least-cost combination can be extended to cover any number of variable inputs.

It should be noted that these rules do not always apply. In the case of the five-bag isoquant shown in Figure 5.3, the least-cost combination is found at point H, where very little weeding labour is used. The cheapest way of producing say four bags of maize might involve no weeding at all, at point G. For such 'corner solutions' the rules for finding the economic optimum, described above, do not apply. When no labour is used, the rate of technical substitution is less than the inverse price ratio, and the marginal product per unit of expenditure on weeding labour is less than that for seed.

The least-cost combination can be determined for any feasible level of yield. The line joining all least-cost combinations for a given set of prices (*GHJ* in the diagram) is known as the 'expansion path'. It traces out the combinations of variable inputs a cost-minimizing farmer would use as he increases production. This, then, is the basis for estimating the variable cost curve relating cost to total product output, to be discussed.

A change in relative prices of the variable inputs alters the least-cost combination, and hence the expansion path. To illustrate this let us assume that the wage of weeding labour doubles to £6 per day. Now only half as much labour can be hired for a given sum. The downward slope of the isocost lines is therefore twice as steep, as shown by *FK* in Figure 5.4. It is apparent that for the ten-bag isoquant a new point of tangency occurs at point *M* representing a combination of one-and-a-half days of weeding labour and a seed rate of 37 000 stands. The least-cost combination for five bags of maize is now a corner solution at point *L*. Clearly a rise in the wage provides an incentive to use less labour and more seed; to substitute the cheaper input for the dearer one.

In addition to this 'substitution effect' of the wage rise, the total variable cost of producing ten bags of maize has now risen from £14.70 to £15.60. This rise in the cost of labour will cause a reduction in the economic optimum level of labour input and maize output. This is known as the 'output effect'. Thus when the relative price of labour rises both the substitution and the income effects will lead to a reduction in labour use, but, whereas the substitution effect implies more seed use, the output effect implies less seed use. Whether the two effects in combination will lead to a rise or a fall in seed use is an open question.

Figure 5.4 Price change and factor substitution

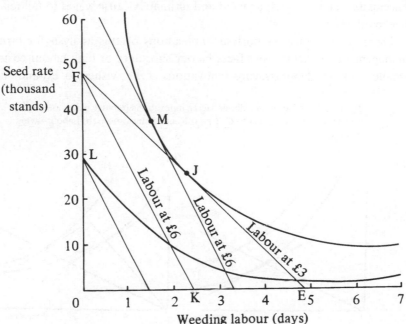

New technology

New technology generally means new methods of production, although it may include product innovations such as new improved crop varieties. Generally speaking, new technology is only worth adopting if it will increase output from a given set of inputs, or reduce costs for a given level of output. If the innovation reduces all costs by the same proportion, its effect is said to be 'neutral'. Thus a new method which increased maize yield per hectare without any change in the quantity of inputs used per hectare would be a neutral innovation. More commonly innovations are 'biased' in that they save some costs more than others. The use of herbicides is biased in the direction of saving labour rather than land. It is a labour-saving innovation.

The distinction between 'neutral' and 'biased' technology may also be illustrated for smoothly curved isoquants as in Figure 5.5. In both diagrams T_1T_1 represents the original isoquant while T_2T_2 represents the new technology. Diagram (a) shows the effect of a neutral innovation which simply causes a parallel shift towards the origin with no change in factor proportions. Diagram (b) shows a labour-saving innovation, which, if prices do not change, results in a bigger reduction in labour use than in the use of land and other inputs. A labour-saving innovation, adopted by many producers, may create unemployment and ultimately cause wages to fall relative to other prices.

There are obviously important implications of this analysis for farm management. A farmer who faces labour shortages or high labour costs, should seek for labour-saving innovations if he wishes to expand his

Figure 5.5   Neutral and labour-saving innovations (relative prices assumed constant: C_2C_2 is parallel to C_1C_1); (a) Neutral innovation, (b) Labour-saving innovation

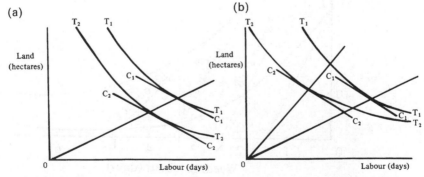

output. If land is the effective constraint, he needs land-saving innovations which increase yields and intensity of land use.

Fixed and variable costs

We have now estimated the economic optimum for a single variable input and the least-cost combination for two variable inputs. This still leaves the problem of finding the economic optimum level of output when there are two or more variable inputs. This problem is best considered in terms of the costs of production, some of which are fixed and some of which are variable. For the example used in Tables 5.1. and Figure 5.1 only the costs of seed and weeding labour are assumed to vary as the yield of maize changes. Costs of bush clearing, land preparation and harvesting are all assumed to be fixed in the sense that they do not vary with the yield of maize and must be met anyway. In other words they are unavoidable.

The estimation of these fixed costs would be very difficult in practice since many fixed inputs are neither bought nor sold. However, we shall see that the level of fixed costs has no effect on the economic optimum, except when they are so high that production is not worthwhile. This possibility will be explained later. For the present let us assume that the total fixed cost of cultivating the maize plot is £10.

The total variable cost of producing ten bags of maize (using the least-cost combination of weeding labour and seed) was found to be £11.70 (see Table 5.2(b) and Figure 5.3). It was also noted that the least-cost combination for five bags of maize is £4.30. Similarly, the total variable cost can be found for any level of maize output up to about twelve bags, always assuming that the least-cost combination of inputs is used. Total variable costs, estimated in this way for each whole number of bags produced, are given in column 2 of Table 5.3. As might be expected the variable cost increases with rising output, but the size of the increase gets bigger and bigger. To be more precise, the extra cost of producing one more unit of output, an extra bag of maize in this case, is called *marginal cost*. Thus the marginal cost increases with rising output, as shown in column 3 of the Table. Note that since fixed costs do not vary with output they do not affect the marginal costs at all. Note also, however, that the reason why marginal costs rise is that some inputs are fixed. These fixed-factor limitations cause diminishing marginal returns as variable inputs are increased, and this is reflected in rising marginal costs. The total cost curves, both fixed and variable are shown in Figure 5.6(a).

Let us now consider the average cost per bag of maize produced. Again

Table 5.3. *Costs of maize production per plot (£) (fixed cost=£10; price of maize £4 per bag)*

Output bags of maize	Variable cost	Total cost[a]	Marginal cost[b]	Average fixed cost[c]	Average total cost[d]	Gross[e] margin
0	0	10.00				0
1	0.80	10.80	0.80	10.00	10.80	3.20
2	1.60	11.60	0.80	5.00	5.80	6.40
3	2.40	12.40	0.80	3.33	4.13	9.60
4	3.30	13.30	0.90	2.50	3.33	12.70
5	4.30	14.30	1.00	2.00	2.86	15.70
6	5.40	15.40	1.10	1.67	2.56	18.60
7	6.60	16.60	1.20	1.43	2.37	21.40
8	8.00	18.00	1.40	1.25	2.25	24.00
9	9.70	19.70	1.70	1.11	2.19	26.30
10	11.70	21.70	2.00	1.00	<u>2.17</u>	29.30
11	14.40	24.40	2.70	0.91	2.22	<u>29.60</u>
12	20.00	30.00	5.60	0.83	2.50	28.00

[a] Total cost=variable cost+£10 fixed cost.
[b] Marginal costs=difference between successive values of variable cost.
[c] Average fixed cost=£10/number of bags of maize (column 1).
[d] Average total cost=Total cost (column 3)/number of bags of maize (column 1).
[e] Gross margin=Bags of maize×£4 − variable cost.

we may distinguish the average *fixed cost* from the average *variable* cost. As output is increased, the fixed cost is spread over more bags of maize so the average fixed cost per bag diminishes. However, the rate at which average fixed cost diminishes is rapid to start with but falls as output grows. This effect is shown in column 5 of Table 5.3 and in Figure 5.6. The average variable cost, on the other hand, rises as total variable cost rises with increasing output. The overall effect on average cost as output rises is that there is an initial fall, caused by falling average fixed cost, then an increase caused by increasing average variable cost. Thus a typical average cost curve, for both fixed and variable costs together, is U-shaped, as shown in Figure 5.6(b).

The marginal cost curve is also shown in Figure 5.6(b). Note that where marginal cost is less than average, the latter is falling; the low marginal cost pulls down the average cost. Conversely, where marginal cost is greater than average cost, then average cost must rise. If follows that marginal and average costs are equal when average cost is at a minimum. Although not shown in the diagram, average cost may remain constant over a range of outputs. Over this range marginal cost must equal average cost.

Maximizing the gross margin

Profit is the difference between total cost and total revenue, which in our example is the cash earned from sales of maize at £4 per bag. At this stage of the analysis we assume that the farmer's aim is to maximise profit. As in the previous chapter, the point where profit is maximized is known as the economic optimum. But, since fixed cost does not vary with the amount of maize produced, the economic optimum can be found by maximizing

Figure 5.6   Cost curves; (a) Total cost, (b) Average and marginal cost

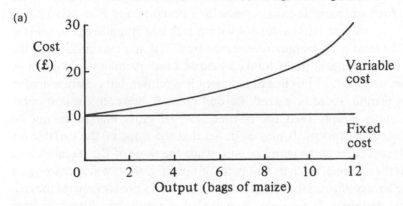

(a)

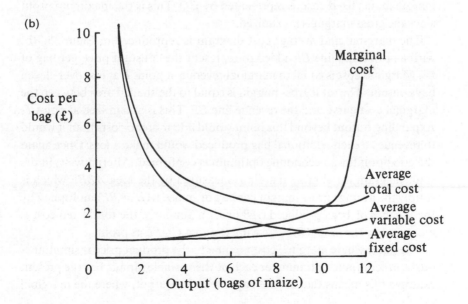

(b)

the difference between total revenue and total variable cost per hectare. This is known as the gross margin. Gross margins, calculated for each level of maize output, are given in the last column of Table 5.3. The maximum gross margin of £29.60 is obtained when eleven bags of maize are produced. By subtracting the fixed cost of £10 we can calculate the maximum profit as £19.60. This then is the economic optimum. It is commonly identified as the point where marginal cost is equal to marginal revenue, which is simply the product price. The reader may confirm from the marginal cost column (column 4) of the Table that the nearest values to £4, the price per bag of maize, lie either side of eleven bags output.

This result may be confirmed from the diagrams. Figure 5.7(a) shows the total fixed and variable costs curves with a straight line *CB* added to represent total revenue. It has a slope of 4 since each bag of maize can be sold for £4. The total gross margin, represented by *CA*, is at a maximum since the line *CB* is a tangent to the total cost curve. Lines parallel to *CB* could be drawn to the left of this line to represent less output, but clearly a smaller gross margin would be earned. Beyond point *B*, however, the cost curve rises more steeply than the revenue line, so gross margin cannot be increased any further. It may be noted that the slope of the variable (or total) cost curve is the marginal cost, while the slope of the revenue curve *CB* is the marginal revenue. At a point of tangency the two slopes are equal so we have confirmed that marginal cost equals marginal revenue at the economic optimum. It may also be noted that profit, which equals gross margin minus fixed cost, is represented by *CO*. This is the maximum profit since the gross margin is maximized.

The marginal and average cost diagram is reproduced in Figure 5.7(b) with a horizontal line *EF* added to represent the constant price per bag of £4. Marginal cost is equal to marginal revenue at point *F* at just over eleven bags output. The total gross margin is equal to the shaded area between the marginal cost curve and the revenue line *EF*. This is maximized at point *F*. Expanding output beyond this point would add more to costs than it would to revenue so each additional bag produced would make a loss. Once again the condition for an economic optimum is confirmed. Alternatively, in the same diagram, total gross margin is measured by the area *ABFE* which is simply the average gross margin per bag of maize (*AE* or *BF*) multiplied by the number of bags produced (*AB* or *EF*). Similarly, the total fixed cost is measured by the area *ABDC*, leaving the area *CDFE* as profit.

The point where marginal cost is equal to the product price is simultaneously an economic optimum for each of the variable inputs. For the present example this means that at 11.3 bags of maize output, where the marginal cost is equal to the price of £4 per bag, the marginal product of weeding labour must equal 0.75 bags of maize as shown in the previous chapter. At the same time the amount of seed used must also be the economic optimum. Figure 5.7(b) may also be used to assess the effect of varying maize price on the quantity a profit maximizing farmer would produce. By comparing points on the marginal cost curve we find that, at a price of £6 per bag, 11.6 bags would be produced whereas, at a price of £2.50, only 10.5 bags would be produced. Thus the marginal cost curve traces out the indi-

Figure 5.7   Economic optimum output; (a) Maximum gross margin and profit, (b) Marginal cost equals marginal revenue

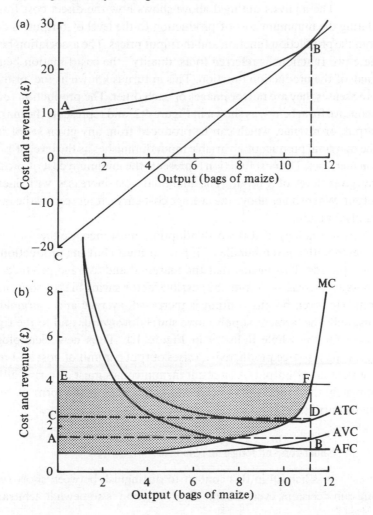

vidual farmer's supply curve relating maize output to price. In this case the curve rises rather steeply implying that price has relatively little impact on quantity supplied; or in other words supply is inelastic. However, this argument only applies so long as average revenue exceeds average total cost; or in other words total revenue exceeds total cost. If, on the contrary, total cost should exceed total revenue, losses would be made. The best or optimum policy might be to abandon production altogether, although this must depend upon what alternative sources of income are available.

Duality and change in technology

The analysis outlined above shows how the direct cost function, relating the minimum cost of production to the level of output, is derived from the production function and the input prices. The association between these two functions is referred to as 'duality', the cost function being the 'dual' of the production function. This in turn is known as the 'primal'. In some senses they are mirror images of each other. The production function is concave from below, as shown in Figure 4.2, and represents the maximum output, or revenue, which can be produced from any given set of inputs. The marginal product of a variable input diminishes as the level of production increases. The cost function represents the minimum cost of producing any given level of output. The marginal cost increases with increased output. Where it lies above the average cost curve, it represents the farmer's supply function.

New technology, if it is worth adopting, must increase the total output achieved with a given bundle of inputs. It must shift the production function upwards. This means that the marginal and average products of all inputs are increased, despite the possible factor-saving bias of some innovations. However, because output is increased, average and marginal costs must fall. The farmer's supply curve shifts downwards and to the right, as shown for the whole industry in Figure 1.1. Thus new technology, by increasing resource productivity, raises output per unit of cost and reduces cost per unit of output. As a result farm incomes must also rise, although ultimately the benefits may accrue to consumers in the form of reduced product prices.

Short-run and long-run response

It is helpful in this context to distinguish between short-run and long-run decisions even though the distinction is somewhat arbitrary. We have been considering a short-run decision of how much seed and weeding labour to use and hence what yield to produce on a fixed area of land. Given that the land has already been cleared and many of the fixed costs are already incurred, there is no way of avoiding them this year. It may be worth continuing to grow and harvest the crop even though it will make a loss. So long as the revenue is sufficient to cover the variable cost and a small gross margin is earned it is better than nothing.

In the longer run, however, even by the next season, it should be possible to vary the area of maize grown and, if necessary, substitute some other crop. Thus, other inputs such as the area of land devoted to maize growing, may be varied. With fewer fixed inputs there is less cause for marginal returns to diminish or for marginal costs to rise. If long-run marginal costs do rise, they rise more slowly so the slope is likely to be flatter. In short, it is argued that farmers are likely to be more price responsive the more time they have to adjust. This means that their long-run supply response is more elastic than their short-run response.

Before leaving this subject we should note that the term gross margin has a precise meaning as the difference between revenue and variable costs per hectare of crops or per head of livestock. The term is not applicable if general farm costs, such as the cost of family subsistence, are assumed to vary. Gross margins are used, however, in farm accounting and planning (see Parts II and III).

Returns to scale

It is arguable that, in some situations, *all* inputs may be varied in the long-run. For instance, where there is a surplus of uncultivated land, the area under cultivation may be expanded to keep pace with population growth. Thus as family size grows so too does the farm size. If all other inputs of seed, manures, tools, livestock and the rest, are increased in proportion, then an 'increase in scale' is said to occur. The effect on output depends upon the 'returns to scale'. Where there are increasing returns, the proportionate growth in output is greater than the proportionate growth of inputs; where there are constant returns the proportionate growth in output is the same as that of inputs; while, where there are decreasing returns to scale, the proportionate growth in output is less than that of inputs.

It might well be asked whether an increase in *scale*, that is in strict proportion, ever occurs in practice. After all a growth in family size is likely to result in a change in the land:labour ratio, that is a change in factor proportions. However, if an increase in scale is possible, for instance, if all inputs can be doubled, then we might reasonably expect output to double also; that is for constant returns to apply. In these circumstances marginal and average costs are constant, represented by a horizontal straight line.

It is often assumed that smallholder agriculture, dependent on hand labour, is subject to constant returns to scale. However, there may be advantages in having a large family, which would be reflected in increasing returns to scale and decreasing average costs. For example, where team work is needed in digging a well or clearing dense bush, a large family can provide the necessary team. Also there may be advantages in division of labour, since one family member may be away at market while another tends small-stock, another is at work in the fields and yet another is fetching firewood or water. Furthermore, a family with several labour-force members, is less likely to be prevented by hazards such as ill health from undertaking the timely planting of seasonal crops (see Hunt 1984). Yet these advantages, if they exist, are limited especially since small families often share work loads, and provide mutual assistance in times of trouble.

Studies of traditional agriculture in Asia and Latin America have shown an inverse relationship between output per hectare and size of the farm in hectares, after making due allowance for variations in the quality of land (see Berry & Cline 1979). This evidence might be interpreted as demonstrating decreasing returns to scale. Indeed, the authors found that average cost per unit of output was generally lower on the smaller farms, *especially when the price of labour was assumed to be zero.* However, the situation analysed is one of changing factor proportions, rather than differences of scale. Smaller holdings are cultivated more intensively, with higher labour inputs per hectare responsible for the larger output. The average cost per unit of output must depend on the relative values of land and labour. Average costs are only lower on smaller holdings when labour is cheap relative to the value of land. In much of Africa land is less scarce, and therefore less valuable relative to labour than in the Asian and Latin American countries studied. This is related to the fact that, under African communal land tenure, the amount of land cultivated can be adjusted to match up with the family labour supply and food needs. This may result in a shortening of the fallow with consequent lowering of fertility; a case of diminishing marginal returns to increased labour inputs. However, it may be possible to increase farm scale rather than varying the intensity of land use. On balance it seems reasonable to assume constant returns to scale for hand cultivation resulting in constant long-run average costs as shown in Figure 5.8.

However, most observers would refer to all family farming by hand as 'small-scale'. 'Large-scale' production is then taken to mean some form of commercial mechanized system. Here again the difference is not really one of scale, since factor proportions differ between the two systems, large farms using more capital per person employed. Thus capital, mainly in the form of machinery, is substituted for labour. In fact, there is a difference in the technology used, between hand-tools on the one hand and machinery on the other. Despite the possible confusion over the precise meaning of 'differences in scale', the terms 'small-scale' and 'large-scale' are so commonly used to describe these different technologies that we will continue to do so.

The technical advantages of 'large-scale' production are generally due to the indivisibility of certain inputs, such as tractors and field machinery, crop and livestock processing plants and irrigation reservoirs. The same applies to expensively trained and skilled manpower. Each item represents a large fixed cost which is spread, or averaged, over the total product output. On a small farm, with a small output, the average fixed cost of such an item must be high, whereas on a larger holding the average fixed cost is lower. This effect of spreading fixed costs on average total cost was illustrated in Table 5.3 and Figures 5.6 and 5.7. Similar average cost curves for tractor cultivation are shown in Figure 5.8.

These curves are only loosely based on field studies (e.g. see Joy 1960).

Figure 5.8   Comparative costs of hand labour and tractor cultivation

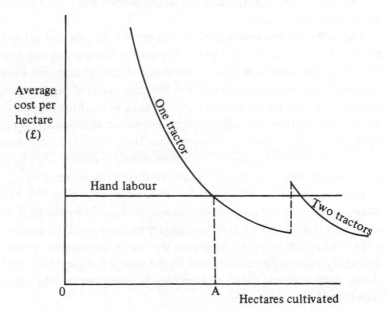

The situation must differ from one part of Africa to another depending upon the relative availability and costs of labour, credit, machinery, servicing and spare parts and the natural environment. Thus the cost of introducing the plough must be higher in forest areas, where destumping would be involved, than in grassland savannah. None the less, two broad implications of this diagram are generally valid. These are, first, that on very small holdings hand cultivation has the lowest cost, and therefore the highest profit per unit of output and, second, that if the average cost of tractor cultivation falls below that of hand labour it will only do so beyond a certain 'minimum efficient size' of mechanized holding, represented by output OA.

An alternative view

Some researchers suggest that input–output relationships are not curved, as we have assumed so far, but are made up of straight lines as shown in Figure 5.9. This is known as 'bent-stick' response for obvious reasons. Because of the practical difficulties of estimating production functions, no one can be sure which theory gives a better description of the real world. In fact Figure 5.9 is similar to Figure 4.2 in that both show diminishing marginal returns. The only significant difference is that now the marginal product is constant, reflected in the constant slope, until the maximum feasible yield is reached at which point the marginal product suddenly diminishes to zero.

The difference has significant implications for the effect of price changes on the level of input use and yield. Whereas with a smooth response curve the economic–optimum level of weeding labour changes for even small changes in relative prices, this is not the case for bent-stick response. By considering alternative weeding labour cost lines through point B, the reader will see that this represents the economic optimum for wage costs from zero up to two bags of maize per day. However, if the wage should rise above this level, the economic optimum would suddenly shift to point A representing only three bags of maize produced with *no* weeding.

The maximum feasible yield is determined partly by the biological characteristics of the crop variety grown, and partly by the level at which other inputs are fixed. Thus if the seed rate was increased the maximum feasible yield might be raised. However, the law of diminishing returns must still apply; there is an absolute limit to the amount of yield that can be produced from a given plot in a given season, regardless of the amounts of inputs used.

The theory of straight-line, or bent-stick, production response is closely akin to linear activity analysis, or linear programming which will be discussed in more detail in Chapter 16.

There is a minor difference, however, in that a linear activity ray is supposed to pass through the origin; since the input–output ratios and factor proportions are assumed to be constant for all levels of output. This implies that the activity is subject to constant returns to scale, so that marginal and average costs are also constant.

Such a fixed-factor proportions activity may be represented in a two-dimensional diagram like Figure 5.10. This is based on data given in row 1 of Table 5.4. Although this diagram, in common with Figure 5.2, shows the relationship between two inputs, it is quite different in form. First, it may be

Figure 5.9   Bent-stick response; (a) Total product, (b) Marginal product

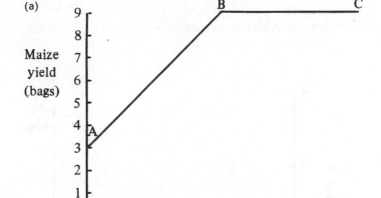

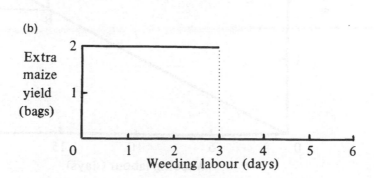

Table 5.4. *Alternative activities for maize production*

	Weeding labour per hectare (days)	Yield per hectare (bags)	Weeding labour productivity (bags per day)	Maximum product from twenty days weeding labour (bags)
Activity 1 Hand weeding	10	25	2.5	50
Activity 2 Using herbicides	5	20	4.0	80

Figure 5.10   A fixed factor proportions activity

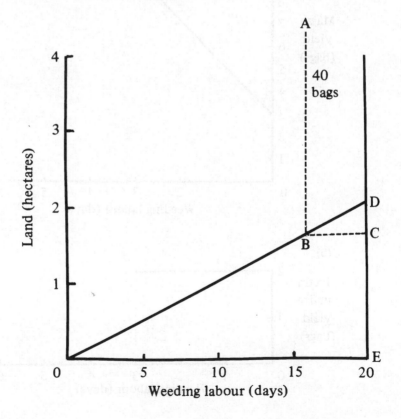

noted that we are now treating land as one of the variable inputs. This is because, when an activity is expanded, *all* inputs including the land area used must be increased together. Seed use also must be increased but we have omitted this input from the diagram. Second, the ray from the origin *OD* shows the fixed ratio of labour to land inputs for all levels of production. The line *ABC* may be viewed as an isoquant but, being right-angled, it simply shows that, since substitution is impossible, an increase in either input *on its own* has no effect on the level of product output.

A productive activity may be expanded until the limited availability of one of the inputs becomes an 'effective constraint'. In Figure 5.10 we assume that the availability of weeding labour is limited to twenty days, represented by the line *ED*, while land is relatively abundant. Thus labour is the effective constraint and maize production cannot be expanded beyond fifty bags (point *D*).

However, there is another possibility for expanding production, namely switching to an alternative method. For instance, the use of herbicides

Figure 5.11   New technology and activity substitution

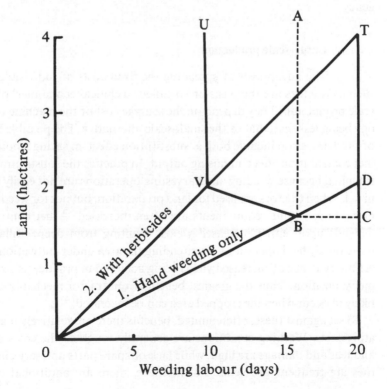

might bring about a substantial reduction in weeding labour. Thus a new activity, 'maize production with herbicides', might be compared with the original as in row 2 of Table 5.4 and in Figure 5.11. Since this new activity requires less weeding labour per hectare of land than the original activity, factor proportions are different and so too is the slope of its ray in the diagram. As a result the area of maize grown can be increased from fifty bags (point *D*) to eighty bags (point *T*). Although the yield is assumed to be lower when herbicides are used, the increase in area allows an increase in total maize production.

Now we are admitting that factor substitution is possible after all. By switching from activity 1, hand weeding, to activity 2 with herbicides, land and herbicides are substituted for labour. Slightly more land and a lot less labour are used to produce a bag of maize, when herbicides are used. Indeed, if it is assumed that part of the maize crop can be hand weeded while another part is treated with herbicides, combinations of the two activities are possible and an isoquant such as *UVBC* can be drawn. This is similar to the isoquants of Figure 5.2, although a least-cost combination would occur at a corner representing a single activity, not at a point of tangency.

Large-scale production

The advantages of spreading the fixed costs of indivisible inputs such as tractors are the basis of so-called 'technical economies' of large-scale production. They depend on the average cost of the machine technology being less than that of the small-scale alternative. The possible benefits of mechanization include both a 'substitution effect' in saving labour and a 'net contribution effect' in raising output. In practice the substitution effect is limited because weeding and harvesting operations are not easily mechanized. When tractors are used for land preparation, but not for weeding and harvesting, labour requirements are often increased. A net contribution depends upon either increased yields, resulting from deeper tillage and more timely field operations, or extending the area under cultivation. There is little evidence of increased yields being achieved in practice as a result of mechanization. Thus the greatest benefits from tractor mechanization are likely to occur when the cropped area can be increased.

To set against these, often limited, benefits there are relatively high operating costs. Working conditions are generally tough so the costs of wear and tear and damage are high, while lack of spare parts and servicing facilities are frequent problems. Furthermore, there are additional costs of maintaining soil fertility under continual cultivation and possible dangers of increased soil erosion. But large-scale production also suffers from '*diseconomies*' associated with the problems and costs of management and control. Partly for these reasons many large-scale mechanized schemes in tropical Africa have proved to be costly failures, including the East African Groundnut Scheme, State Farms in Ghana and Sierra Leone, and Nigerian Farm Settlements.

In contrast, large-scale commercial farms exist in many parts of Africa and appear to provide their operators with an acceptable margin over costs. However, their apparent success may be associated with 'financial economies' rather than the technical advantages discussed above. First, the large producer often has easier access to markets for his produce. He may well have contractual arrangements to supply a particular buyer at a guaranteed price. Transport costs per unit are generally lower for large shipments of produce. Thus, for one reason or another, the large-scale producer often receives a higher net price for his produce. Similarly, he is able to buy inputs such as seed and fertilizer in large quantities. Bulk buying may enable him to obtain price discounts and assured deliveries. Probably most important of all, the large-scale producer is much more creditworthy than his smaller neighbour. The ownership of capital assets provides security for loans, while the per unit costs of servicing large loans are less than those for small amounts. In short, the large-scale borrower finds it easier to obtain credit, and on more favourable terms, because there are economies of large-scale lending. These financial advantages alone may explain the relative profitability of large-scale farming.

In so far as the costs of marketing and the provision of credit are lower for large-scale producers, society as a whole may benefit from their activities in terms of lower cost production and more efficient use of national resources. But, where large producers simply use their political power to change the terms of trade in their favour, then society will lose out as resources are diverted away from more efficient users. Other possible social costs of large-scale mechanized agriculture are the gradual degradation and erosion of certain tropical soils under continual monoculture and the displacement of labour when there is no alternative employment. It is argued, on the other hand, that there are important social benefits in transforming agriculture through mechanization; commercial attitudes are engendered, farmers are absorbed into the 'modern' sector and rural–urban migration of school leavers may be discouraged (see Hart 1982).

It is difficult to generalize regarding the overall impact of large-scale mechanized technology. As remarked already, this must vary from one ecological and economic environment to another. Very careful analysis and assessment is needed before policy decisions are made either to promote or discourage this form of production. There are two alternative policy approaches to the promotion of mechanized farming among smallholders whilst possibly deriving some of the financial economies of large-scale trading. These are, on the one hand, the encouragement of producer co-operatives and, on the other, the provision of tractor hire and marketing services by government. The organizational and administrative problems of these institutions will not be discussed here. However, it may be noted that there are major difficulties in imposing a co-operative system on farmers. Indeed some of the large-scale failures mentioned earlier, such as the Nigerian Farm Settlements, were intended to be operated as co-operatives. Most government tractor-hire schemes have operated at a loss, whilst agricultural marketing boards have not always benefited the farmers.

Summary

1 Where more than one input can be varied the factor:factor relationship may be explored for a given fixed level of output. The resulting production contour is known as an isoquant, and its negative slope as the rate of technical substitution (*RTS*).

2 The least-cost combination of inputs occurs where the *RTS* equals the inverse input price ratio. This is where the marginal product per £ spent is equal in all uses. The line joining these points for varying output levels is known as 'the expansion path', since it specifies the combinations of inputs that would be used by a cost-minimizing farmer as output is expanded. If the relative price of an input rises, less of it will be used; (i) the substitution effect means that other inputs will be used as substitutes, (ii) the output effect means that the rise in costs causes a reduction in input use and a fall in output.

3 New technology shifts the production function upwards to increase average productivity of all inputs. It is defined as neutral if the *RTS* is unchanged for a given input ratio, or biased if the *RTS* changes; e.g. with a labour-saving bias the *RTS* of land or capital for labour is reduced so that either relatively less labour is used for a given set of prices or the relative wage rate falls.

4 For most decisions some costs are fixed, or unavoidable, while others are variable. The minimum variable cost for each feasible level of output is derived from the expansion path. The average fixed cost per unit of output must decline as the total is spread over increasing quantities, whereas the

marginal and average variable cost is likely to rise eventually as a result of fixed-factor constraints. Overall the average cost curve is generally U-shaped.

5 A gross margin is the difference between total revenue and total variable cost. This is maximized, and so too is profit, where the product price (which, if constant, represents the marginal and the average revenue) equals the marginal cost. Since the economic optimum output level moves along the marginal cost curve as product price varies, this curve represents the individual profit-maximizing farmer's short-run supply curve. This applies only where marginal cost exceeds average (variable) cost, since if product price fell below the average cost, the most profitable choice would be to cease production altogether.

6 Some inputs which are fixed in the short-run may be variable in the longer run. Thus the long-run supply response is likely to be more elastic than the short-run response.

7 If, in the long-run, **all** inputs can be varied in proportion, a change in scale may occur. Constant returns to scale apply if output increases by the same proportion as the inputs. However, there may be economies of increasing size as indivisible cost items are spread over more output.

8 An alternative analysis assumes linear activities with constant returns to scale and fixed-factor proportions. Given fixed resource constraints and activity substitution, diminishing marginal returns and *RTS* may be demonstrated. The optimum is now found as a corner solution.

9 Technical 'economies of scale' are associated particularly with mechanization. Financial economies in marketing and provision of credit may also apply. However, many large-scale schemes have foundered on managerial diseconomies.

References

Adegeye, A. J. & J. S. Dittoh (1982). *Essentials of Agricultural Economics*, Ibadan, Nigeria, Centre for Agricultural and rural Development (CARD)
Berry, D. A. & W. R. Cline (1979). *Agrarian Structure and Productivity in Developing Countries*, Baltimore, Johns Hopkins University Press
Dillon, J. L. (1977). *The Analysis of Response in Crop and Livestock Production*, 2nd edn, Oxford, Pergamon Press
Doll, J. P. & F. Orazem (1984). *Production Economics: Theory with Application*, 2nd edn, Chichester, John Wiley & Son
Hart, K. (1982). *The Political Economy of West African Agriculture*, Cambridge University Press
Hunt, D. (1984). *The Labour Aspects of Shifting Cultivation in Africa*, Rome, FAO

Joy, J. L. (ed.) (1960). *Symposium on Mechanical Cultivation in Uganda*, Kampala, Argus

Olayide, S. O. & E. O. Heady (1982). *Introduction to Agricultural Production Economics*, Nigeria, Ibadan University Press

Upton, M. (1976). *Agricultural Production Economics and Resource Use*, Oxford University Press

6

Risk avoidance

Uncertainty in agriculture

A farmer, when he embarks on any productive activity, is uncertain what the actual outcome will be. Uncertainty has three main causes: (i) environmental variations causing production and yield uncertainty, (ii) price variation causing market uncertainty and (iii) lack of information. All of these are significant in African agriculture, where unreliable rains and pest and disease outbreaks cause wide variation in resource availability and in crop and livestock yields. Human diseases are frequent, unpredictable and costly to treat. Ill health or injury of a family member at a critical period may cause serious loss of production and income. Generally there are wide seasonal and unpredictable fluctuations in market prices, while information on alternative technologies or the market situation outside the immediate locality is often lacking. Hence the farmer cannot plan with certainty; his decisions are subject to risk.

Risk is a measure of the effect of uncertainty on the decision-maker. There are differences of opinion as to how risk should be measured. Some argue that it is variation or instability of income, while others claim that it is the possibility of disaster or ruin. Both these alternatives will be explored. In any case there is fairly general agreement that most people, including farmers, are risk-averse. This means that they are willing to forego some income or face extra costs in order to avoid risk. They are cautious in their decision-making.

These ideas are best illustrated by a simple example comparing the hypothetical returns from two alternative crops, maize and sorghum, with variable yields. The so-called 'pay-off matrix' is given in Table 6.1. Since we are only concerned with yield uncertainty here, the pay-offs are in quintals of grain rather than in cash terms, a quintal of sorghum being valued equally

117

Table 6.1. *A pay-off matrix (yields in quintals of grain per ha)*

	States of nature		
	Wet years	Normal years	Dry years
Maize	70	60	30
Sorghum	40	50	50

with a quintal of maize. The pay-off from a particular activity is supposed to depend upon the 'state of nature' which obtains during the subsequent cropping season. We have further simplified the analysis by assuming only three possible states of nature; wet years, normal years and dry years. In practice, there is an enormous range of possible states of nature. The farmer does not know which of these will occur. To start with, we assume he does not know the likelihood of their occurring.

The figures have been chosen to show that sorghum yields are less variable than maize yields. Also, whereas maize yields are higher in wet years, sorghum yields are higher in dry years. If a choice had to be made between the two crops, a cautious farmer would clearly choose to grow sorghum as the less risky. He is then assured of a yield of at least 40 quintals of grain even under the worst conditions. This is known as the MAXIMIN choice since it maximizes the minimum or worst possible outcome.

This is really a *very* cautious policy, since it assumes that 'nature' will always do her worst. By growing sorghum the farmer foregoes 30 quintals of grain in wet years and 10 quintals in normal years, while he only gains 20 quintals in dry years. There is, in effect, some trade-off between net gains and risk avoidance. The choice would be clear cut, however, if one crop, say maize, yielded more than the other under *all* states of nature, in which case maize production would 'dominate' sorghum. In this example neither activity dominates.

Probability and expectations

In practice, the farmer's choice is likely to be influenced by the probabilities of occurrence of the different states of nature. Clearly, if dry years occur only one year in ten, that is their probability of occurrence is only 0.1, sorghum is less likely to be chosen than if dry years occur more frequently. It is reasonable to assume that farmers can judge the probabilities of wet and dry years or different states of nature on the basis of their past experience and that these judgements influence their choices. Incidentally, the distinction which used to be made between 'risk', where probabilities are known, and 'uncertainty' where probabilities are not known, is no longer accepted since it is argued that decision-makers have to make judgements of the relevant probabilities in every risky situation.

Returning to the example, let us assume that dry years are judged to occur three years in ten on average, while wet years occur two years in ten. Since there are only three states of nature and their probabilities must sum to one, the probabilities of wet, dry and normal years are 0.2, 0.3 and 0.5 respectively. The expected yields for the two crops can now be calculated using the formula

$$E(Y) = \sum Y_i P_i = Y_1 P_1 + Y_2 P_2 + \cdots + Y_n P_n \tag{1}$$

where the amounts Y_1, Y_2 ... or Y_n are the yields under the various states of nature, $P_1, P_2 \ldots$ and P_n are the respective probabilities, and the $\sum$ sign means the sum of n similar terms as shown. The expected yield for maize is therefore

$$70 \times 0.2 + 60 \times 0.5 + 30 \times 0.3 = 53 \text{ quintals}$$

and for sorghum

$$40 \times 0.2 + 50 \times 0.5 + 50 \times 0.3 = 48 \text{ quintals.}$$

If the farmer were risk indifferent, rather than risk averse, he would choose maize production, since it yields the highest expected return. Indeed, this is arguably the only rational choice, since the expected value is simply an average. In the long run, better than average years will cancel the effect of worse than average years so, provided the family survives, on average returns will be maximized in this way. However, if worse than average years could prove disastrous, it is perfectly rational to avoid risk.

Given estimates of the probabilities of different outcomes, variation can be quantified by either the variance, which is the square of the 'standard deviation'

$$V(Y) = \sum (Y_i - E(Y))^2 P_i = E(Y^2) - (E(Y))^2 \tag{2}$$

(note the two alternative methods of calculation) or the mean *absolute* deviation

$$MAD(Y) = \sum |Y_i - E(Y)| \cdot P_i \tag{3}$$

The variance and mean absolute deviation of yield per hectare of maize (Y_1) are therefore

$$V(Y_1)=241$$
$$MAD(Y_1)=13.8$$

while for sorghum yields (Y_2) they are;

$$V(Y_2)=16$$
$$MAD(Y_2)=3.2$$

as the reader may care to check.

Both measures lead to the same conclusion, namely that sorghum has less variable yields than maize. Of course, this is obvious from inspection of Table 6.1 without making these calculations. However, when analyzing more complicated, real-world situations it is useful to have some measures of variation. Generally, both measures described here give the same ranking of alternatives.

Minimizing variation of returns cannot be the farmer's sole objective. After all he could reduce variation to zero by producing nothing at all. We must therefore assume he has a second objective of maximizing expected or average return. Clearly, he has a difficult choice. Expected return is maximized by growing maize, while the yields of sorghum are less variable.

Diversification and risk

An obvious possibility, not yet considered, is to grow both crops in a mixture. For simplicity we now assume a constant rate of product transformation between the two crops. This means that for a given state of nature, the total grain yield $Y(T)$ from a combination of K_1 hectares of maize and K_2 hectares of sorghum is given by

$$Y(T)=K_1Y_1+K_2Y_2 \tag{4}$$

This equation is readily extended to cover cases where there are more than two alternative activities. In our example we assume only one hectare of land is available so $K_1+K_2=1$.

Using equation (4) and the data given in Table 6.1, yields can be calculated for various combinations of the two crops under the alternative states of nature. Results are presented in Table 6.2. It is apparent that the yields from mixtures of the two crops are less variable than yields of either crop on its own. Further analysis of the effect of diversification on risk may be pursued (i) in terms of worst possible outcomes or alternatively (ii) in terms of variation of outcomes.

Perusal of Table 6.2 will make it clear that for sorghum-based mixtures

Table 6.2. *The effects of diversification (yields in quintals of grain per hectare)*

Percentage of maize in mixture	States of nature			
	Wet years	Normal years	Dry years	Expected value[a]
0	<u>40</u>	50	50	48
20	<u>46</u>	52	<u>46</u>	49
40	52	54	<u>42</u>	50
60	58	56	<u>38</u>	51
80	64	58	<u>34</u>	52
100	70	60	<u>30</u>	53

[a] Based on p(wet)=0.2; p(normal)=0.5; p(dry)=0.3.

Figure 6.1   The maximin mixed strategy

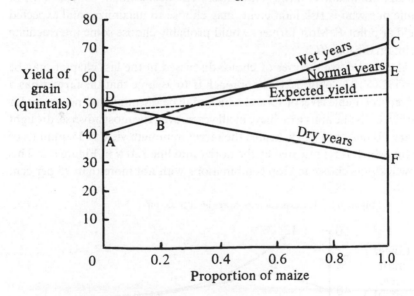

with less than 20 per cent maize, the worst outcomes occur in wet years. For mixtures with more than 20 per cent maize the worst outcomes occur in dry years. For a mixture of exactly 20 per cent maize and 80 per cent sorghum the lower yield of 46 quintals is obtained in wet or dry years. Furthermore, this is the maximum or best of the worst outcomes. It therefore represents the 'MAXIMIN' mixed strategy.

This result is illustrated in Figure 6.1 where the horizontal axis represents the proportion of maize in the combination, while yields are measured on the vertical axis. The lines *AC*, *DE* and *DF* show how total yields vary with an increasing proportion of maize in wet, normal and dry years respectively. The minimum outcomes for all combinations of the two crops are given by the line *ABF*. Clearly point *B* represents the maximum level of these worst yields, that is the maximin point.

As already noted, a maximin strategy has an opportunity cost in terms of reduced expected, or average, returns. The total expected return $E(T)$ from a mixture of activities can be calculated from the expected yields of the component activities using equation (4). In the present two-activity example, maize has the higher expected yield, so total expected return increases directly with the proportion of maize in the mixture. The trade-off with risk may be expressed by plotting minimum return against total expected return, as in Figure 6.2 which is derived directly from Figure 6.1. Between points *B* and *F*, expected return can only be increased by accepting a lower minimum. A farmer who is very risk averse might choose point *B*, while one who is risk indifferent, may choose to maximize total expected yield at point *F*. Most farmers would probably choose some intermediate point on the line *BF*.

The alternative theories of choice discussed in the last chapter may be applied to risky choices. One approach is to assume that the farmer has a target acceptable level of return, which may be the minimum necessary for survival, that he aims to achieve in all years, even the most adverse, drought years. To illustrate let us assume the target minimum yield is 35 quintals of grain, which is represented by the horizontal line *LMN* in Figure 6.2. This now restricts choice to crop combinations with not more than 75 per cent

Figure 6.2   The expectations–lower limit trade-off

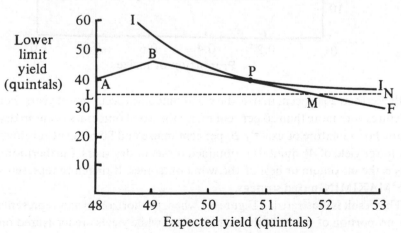

maize. A 'satisficer' might be content with any combination which will achieve this target.

A closely related alternative is to assume that the farmer is a lexicographic optimizer, who aims at meeting the target minimum survival level as first priority and maximizes expected returns as second priority. This is known as a 'safety-first strategy' for obvious reasons. In our example this would lead to a choice of point *M* representing 25 per cent sorghum and 75 per cent maize, as the optimum. The total expected yield for this combination is $0.75 \times 58 + 0.25 \times 43 = 54.25$ quintals.

Alternatively, we could assume that the minimum income is a variable in the farmer's utility function. His indifference curves, such as *II* in the diagram then determine his optimum, in this case at the point of tangency *P*. The farmer's attitude to risk is reflected in the slope of the indifference curves; the more risk averse he is, the flatter are his indifference curves and the nearer to the maximum combination is his optimum.

It should be noted that, in more realistic analyses with many more possible states of nature, such concern with the worst possible outcome may be inappropriate, since the probability of this outcome may be very small indeed. A more appropriate criterion for the 'lower limit' might be that there is a relatively small probability of falling below it. Indeed, the objective could be formulated as minimizing the probability of falling below the disaster level or maximizing the probability of survival. Yet another alternative is to assume the farmer can identify a 'focus-loss' which is the most unfavourable outcome he will consider. This is not necessarily the worst possible outcome, since results which are very unlikely may be ignored.

Variance minimization

We can broaden our understanding of the effect of diversification and risk avoidance, if we now assume that the farmer's aim is to minimize variance, rather than to avoid disasters.

Diversification does not always reduce variance. It all depends upon the relationship between the yields of the different activities, which is measured by the covariance or the correlation coefficient. The covariance between variables Y_1 and Y_2, $COV(Y_1 Y_2)$ is given by:

$$COV(Y_1 Y_2) = \sum (Y_{1i} - E(Y_1))(Y_{2i} - E(Y_2))P_i = E(Y_1 Y_2) - E(Y_1)E(Y_2) \qquad (5)$$

The correlation coefficient, normally denoted by *r*, is then

$$r = COV(Y_1 Y_2) / V(Y_1)V(Y_2) \qquad (6)$$

which has a maximum of one and a minimum of minus one. For the data given in Table 6.1 the covariance is -34 and the correlation coefficient is -0.55.

The negative correlation between crop yields, obtained in this case, means that they move in opposite directions: when the yield of one is high the yield of the other is low. In these circumstances variance of total yield must be reduced by diversification. The effect on variance of total yield $V(T)$ may be calculated as follows

$$V(T) - K_1^2 V(Y_1) + K_2^2 V(Y_2) + 2K_1 K_2 COV(Y_1 Y_2) \tag{7}$$

where K_1 and K_2 are the areas of each of the two crops as before. This form of equation is known as a 'quadratic' function and is readily extended to allow for more different crops, in the mixture.

We can now see from this equation that where the covariance is negative so too is the last term, so that the combined variance $V(T)$ is less than the sum of the individual variances $K_1^2 V(Y_1) + K_2^2 V(Y_2)$. But, even where the yields are independent, so the covariance is zero, the combined variance will be reduced by diversifying as may be shown if we assume $V(Y_1) = V(Y_2) = V$ and $K_1 = K_2 = \frac{1}{2}$. Then substituting in equation (7) gives:

$$V(T) = (\tfrac{1}{2})^2 V + (\tfrac{1}{2})^2 V = V/4 + V/4 = V/2,$$

so that the variance of the combination is only half that of each individual crop.

Variance *may* also be reduced in this way even when the correlation is positive. However, it is likely to be *increased* by combining crops with strongly positive correlation between yields, as often occurs in practice; all crops fail together in a drought, while all yields are high in favourable years. Whether diversification will reduce variance of total yield, actually depends upon whether the covariance is smaller than the yield variance for each of the crops on its own.

Maximizing expected utility

Let us now return to our original example of Table 6.1 and consider the trade-off between variance and expected values. These have been calculated for various combinations of maize and sorghum and are presented in Table 6.3. Since we assume that resource contraints limit the farmer to growing only one hectare of the two crops (so that $K_1 + K_2 = 1$) the data recorded in the Table, other than for sorghum alone, represent points on the expectations–variance (E–V) boundary, which is plotted in Figure 6.3. This curve is a boundary or frontier since points inside and to the left of

Table 6.3. *Diversification, variance and mean absolute deviation*

Percentage of maize in mixture	Expected value	Variance	Mean absolute deviation
0	48	16	3.2
20	49	9	3.0
40	50	28	4.8
60	51	73	7.8
80	52	144	10.8
100	53	241	13.8

Figure 6.3   The expectations–variance (*E–V*) boundary and the expectations–mean absolute deviation (*E–M*) boundary

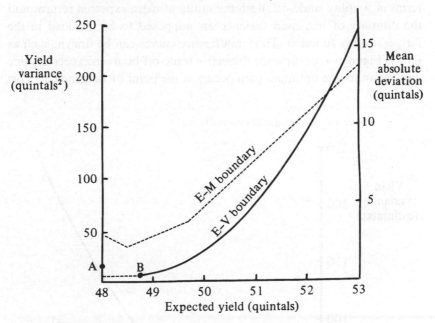

it, such as point *A* representing a pure stand of sorghum, are feasible but inefficient. A larger expected return with a smaller variance may be obtained by choosing a combination on the frontier. From the Figure we see that variance is minimized by combining 0.154 of a hectare of maize with 0.846 of a hectare of sorghum (Point *B*). This point does *not* coincide with the maximin combination, although it still represents a low expected return and a very cautious choice. Mean absolute deviation measures are also given in Table 6.3 and plotted in Figure 6.3. The minimum mean absolute deviation combination is very close to that of minimum variance, and, as already mentioned, the two measures usually lead to similar results. However, there is one important difference. Whereas the variance of any combination of activities can be calculated directly from a knowledge of the variances and covariances using equation (7), calculation of the mean absolute deviation, or indeed the worst possible outcome, involves estimation of the return under each state of nature using equation (4) before combining them in a single measure of risk. Thus the variance of returns from a combination of activities is easier to estimate than other measures of variation. However, 'linear programming' can be used to find the *minimum* mean absolute deviation, while finding the *minimum* variance requires more complicated 'quadratic programming' (see Chapter 16).

Choices between expected return and variance are usually viewed in terms of a utility trade-off. Both the utility of extra expected returns and the disutility of increased variance are supposed to be included in the farmer's utility function. Thus indifference curves can be drawn, such as *QPI* in Figure 6.4, to show the subjective trade-off between expected value and variance. The optimum then occurs at the point of tangency, *P*. This

Figure 6.4   Expected utility maximization

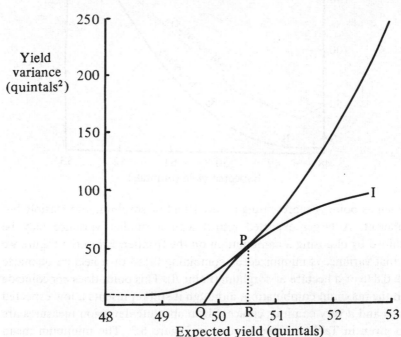

point represents an expected yield of 50.5 quintals of grain, which is below the maximum feasible expected yield of 53 quintals. The difference of 2.5 quintals is the amount of yield the farmer is willing to forego, on average, to reduce risk. Indeed, he would give up even more in order to avoid risk entirely. Point Q is on the same indifference curve as point P, so it represents the same level of utility, but at point Q the variance is zero, so the outcome is certain. Thus point Q may be described as the 'certainty equivalent' of point P for this farmer. The amount QR (70 kg of grain) is what the farmer would be willing to pay, say for crop insurance, in order to eliminate risk entirely. This is the cost of risk for him, or his risk premium if expressed as a fraction of his expected return.

Some researchers have treated the indifference curve as though linear, and used the slope of the tangent at P as a measure of the rate of trade-off between expected money value and standard deviation (which is the square root of the variance). If the slope is λ then the farmer's objective is assumed to be maximization of the certainty equivalent (CE) where,

$$CE = E(Y) - \lambda \sqrt{V(Y)}$$

Much research has been done in recent years, involving the estimation of utility functions of this type for individual farmers, in order to measure their attitudes to risk. The estimation procedure is based on farmer interviews in which the respondent is asked to choose between alternative hypothetical gambles, with different sets of prizes and/or different probabilities. (Further details are given in Anderson, Dillon & Hardaker 1977.)

Choices under risk

From this discussion, it appears that there are several alternative theories, or models, of decision-making under risk. Some are based on the concept of a lower limit or disaster-level income, while others are concerned with income variation. There is no general agreement over which model is the most useful.

Some have argued that none of the models are very convincing as descriptions of the way decisions are made in practice. Given the complexity of the real world, decision-makers may not be aware of all the possible states of nature and or possible strategies. It is even less likely that they can estimate probabilities of all states of nature and rank alternatives so as to find an optimum. Thus it might be concluded that most people are cautious sub-optimizers or satisficers, guided by fairly crude 'rules of thumb'. The counter-argument is that, although decisions are not consciously made according to these theoretical models, the rules of thumb used in practice lead to similar results. Decisions are made *as if* an optimum is sought.

Whatever the case, these theories have confirmed, first, that risk aversion has a cost in terms of income foregone on average, second, that some activities are more risky than others and may therefore be avoided, and, third, that diversification reduces risk provided that the component activities are not strongly positively correlated. Thus risk aversion may explain why farmers are reluctant to adopt new crop varieties with high but variable yields, why they prefer to grow subsistence crops even when food may be purchased more cheaply, why they practise mixed cropping and why they pursue many on- and off-farm activities. However, there may be other good reasons for adopting these policies. Expected returns may be increased as was shown for the case of mixed cropping in the last chapter. We should be cautious in imputing farmers' motives from their observed behaviour.

A study of 1500 smallholder farmers in Kenya (Wolgin, 1975) provided rather stronger evidence of risk averse behaviour. First, it was found that the marginal value products for most inputs were higher than their unit costs. This implies that farmers used less than the economic optimum level of input (see Chapter 4) and may be explained by farmers' willingness to forego income in exchange for a reduction in risk. Stronger evidence that this was the main reason is provided by the fact that the ranking of crops by marginal value product correlated closely with their marginal contributions to risk. In other words, the riskier the crop, the higher was the marginal value product, which implies that inputs were further below the 'economic optimum'.

In so far as farmers do take precautions against risk, they will differ in the extent of their risk aversion. This may cause or exacerbate income and wealth disparities between households. The cautious risk avoider will pay more, or forego more income on average, than will the expected value maximizer. Given that the wealthy farmer, with plentiful resources, can afford to take risks and innovate while his poorer neighbour cannot, there is a natural tendency for the rich to get richer while the poor may stagnate. Financial assistance to the poor may enable them to become less risk averse and more innovative.

Sequential risks

In practice, the final outcome of a risky decision generally depends upon a sequence of events. Thus the crop yield obtained depends upon the soil moisture status at several stages of the growth season, for instance (i) at planting and germination and (ii) at grain fill. Furthermore, the moisture availability at grain fill may depend upon the moisture available at planting. The probability of a given moisture level at grain fill is then conditional upon the moisture level at planting. In such circumstances, a tree diagram, such as Figure 6.5, is useful for estimating the probability distribution of final outcomes.

In this diagram, the probabilities of different moisture levels are written alongside the relevant branches, those for the later period being conditional probabilities (the conditional probability of event B given that event A has occurred is written as $P(B/A)$ while the probability of both A and B occur-

Figure 6.5   Tree diagrams; (a) Joint probabilities, (b) Expected values

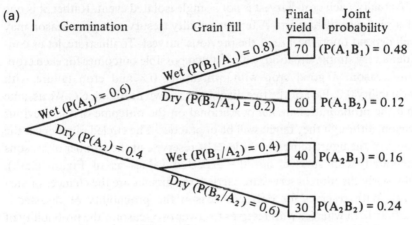

(a)

| Germination | Grain fill | Final yield | Joint probability |

Wet $(P(A_1) = 0.6)$

Wet $(P(B_1/A_1) = 0.8)$ — 70 — $(P(A_1B_1) = 0.48$

Dry $(P(B_2/A_1) = 0.2)$ — 60 — $P(A_1B_2) = 0.12$

Dry $(P(A_2) = 0.4$

Wet $(P(B_1/A_2) = 0.4)$ — 40 — $P(A_2B_1) = 0.16$

Dry $(P(B_2/A_2) = 0.6)$ — 30 — $P(A_2B_2) = 0.24$

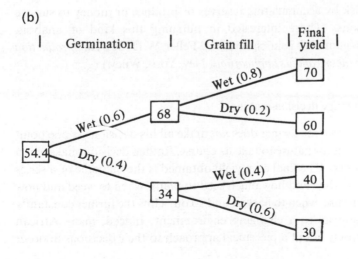

(b)

| Germination | Grain fill | Final yield |

54.4

Wet (0.6) — 68

Wet (0.8) — 70

Dry (0.2) — 60

Dry (0.4) — 34

Wet (0.4) — 40

Dry (0.6) — 30

ring is written as $P(AB)$). The probabilities of the final outcomes are calculated by multiplying the probabilities together along each branch as shown in Figure 6.5(a) (that is $P(AB) = P(A) \cdot P(B/A)$). Alternatively an expected value can be calculated for each node, or junction, as shown in Figure 6.5(b).

This extension of the theory makes little difference to the analysis, except that each state of nature is now seen to represent a series of events or outcomes. However, care must be taken in using simple averages to estimate expected values, where events are not independent. For instance, it would be wrong to calculate expected revenue per hectare as the product of average yield and average price, if the price received is dependent on the yield obtained (see Upton & Casey 1974).

Actually, each crop harvest is not a single isolated event. Rather, it is one of a sequence of harvests. A farmer's ability to survive a poor season may well depend upon the size of the previous harvest. To illustrate, let us consider a very simple situation, with just two possible outcomes for each cropping season; a good crop with probability 0.8 and crop failure with probability 0.2. Part of the tree diagram is shown in Figure 6.6. We assume that the probabilities are *not* conditional on the outcome of the previous season, although they might well be in practice. The circled numbers at the nodes of the figure represent the level of reserves, or the number of seasons the family can survive, not the expected values as in Figure 6.5(b). Obviously the more reserves are carried, the greater are the chances of survival. With reserves for only one season the probability of disaster is $0.2/0.8 = 0.25$ whereas with reserves to cover two seasons, the probability of disaster is reduced to $0.25 \times 0.25 = 0.065$. Most cultivators and pastoralists try to limit risk by accumulating reserves of produce or money to survive adverse seasons. (Those interested in pursuing this kind of analysis, referred to as 'gambler's ruin' should read Feller, W. (1950). *An introduction to probability theory and its applications*, New York, Wiley.)

Multistage decision-making

In practice the farmer does *not* make all his decisions at one point in time, then wait for nature to take its course. Rather, decision-making is a sequential process. The final crop yield obtained is the outcome of a series of decisions of when and how much seed to plant, when to weed and how much labour to use, when to harvest and so on. Thus the farmer constantly adapts and adjusts to a changing environment. Indeed, many African farmers purposely adopt a piecemeal approach to their decisions in order to maintain flexibility. Typically, only a part of the cropped area is plantcd at the first rains, decisions about cropping of the remainder being delayed until more is known about the pattern of the weather.

Such multistage decision problems may be represented by decision trees, a simple example of which is given in Figure 6.7. It shows an alternating sequence of actions and outcomes, starting from the left and moving across to the right. Actions stem from decision modes represented by black squares, while outcomes stem from chance modes which are unmarked. As before, probabilities are shown (in brackets) alongside outcome branches. In this example, the initial decision is whether to plant at the outset of the rains. The second decision whethcr to interplant, extend the cropped area, or plant for the first time is taken a month later, in the light of whether the rains have continued. For simplicity, the decision tree finishes at this point, although in practice further decisions would arise before the final yields are obtained. A three-stage decision tree of this type was used in a World Bank study in Northern Nigeria to show how a multiplicity of different crop scquences and mixtures can result (Balcet, 1982). In our example hypothet-ical expected money values (*EMV*s) for each branch are shown (boxed in) on the right-hand side of the diagram.

The optimal sequence of decisions is determined by working backwards from the right-hand side using a process of 'averaging out and folding back'. This means that at each decision mode, the branch with the highest *EMV* is chosen, while at each chance node the *EMV* is averaged out. Figure 6.8 which is derived from Figure 6.7 illustrates the process. From the upper branches on the right, it is clear that the *EMV* from extending the planted area is greater than that from interplanting or stopping. Hence the latter

Figure 6.6 Sequential risks of disaster

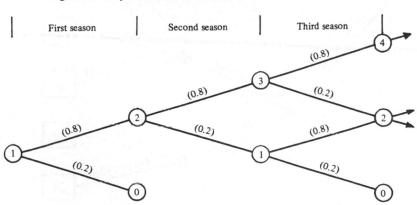

options are rejected and the *EMV* at the decision node is the same as that for extending the area. Now the *EMV*s for the two possible outcomes can be averaged out at each chance mode. Since the *EMV* at the planting mode is the greater, this is the option chosen. The optimal sequence of decisions in this case is to plant at the first rains and then to interplant, this sequence giving an *EMV* of £88.

Figure 6.7   A multistage decision problem

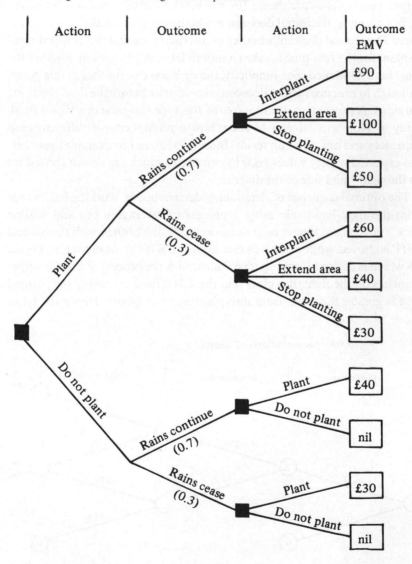

benefit when everyone faces the same risks so their incomes are positively correlated. Thus, in a rural community, if everyone's crops fail and livestock die in a drought, all suffer together.

An alternative, known as 'risk-spreading' occurs when a single risky project is shared by more than one individual. Returns are then shared, but so too is the risk for each individual. This situation arises in the various forms of crop sharing and livestock caretaking widely practised in Africa. Crop sharing is common in the case of tree-crops, which are tended and harvested by labourers who do not own the trees. Produce is then shared in some agreed proportion between owner and labourer. Caretaking of breeding animals, is based on sharing the progeny between owner and herdsman. In either case the risk is less if shared between the partners in the transaction.

Any method of reducing risk to the individual producer, who is risk-averse, is beneficial, first, because his utility is increased by the reduction in risk, and second, because it may enable him to concentrate on maximizing expected returns, thereby increasing productivity. For these reasons policy-makers and planners may seek to reduce income variation and risk for farmers. Almost any change in the rural environment may affect the riskiness of rural life, but four types of innovation deserve special mention. First, new technologies are likely to influence production and yield uncertainty. Some high-yielding crop varieties have proved more variable than traditional ones, use of nitrogenous fertilizers on drought prone crops may increase risk, while the use of pesticides and irrigation tends to reduce risk. The need to assess the riskiness of new technology is increasingly recognized.

Second, price stabilization policies and minimum price guarantees reduce market uncertainty, as do improved input supply services. However, where yields and prices are negatively correlated, so that low prices result from bumper harvests and high prices result when crops fail, product price stabilization may destabilize incomes. Provided this is not the case, market stabilization should reduce risks. Third, the provision of information to farmers regarding new technologies, market prices and new policies will also reduce uncertainty and risk.

Finally, mention should be made of crop insurance schemes as a direct method of reducing risk. Under such schemes each farmer pays an annual premium or levy on his crop, but in the event of crop failure receives compensation. The financial viability of crop insurance depends upon pooling the risks of the many farmers insured. By pooling risks, the average variance and cost of risk per farmer might be substantially reduced. But, as we have seen, this result requires that individual incomes are not positively correlated. When everyone's crop fails at the same time, the cost to the insurance agency might be very high indeed. Risks might still be spread, over a number of years, but the agency would require huge reserves to cover the occasional bad year.

An additional problem with crop insurance is 'moral hazard' which means that farmers who know their crops are insured against failure may not bother to tend them properly. This problem may be overcome by only providing insurance on an area basis; that is only to pay compensation when the district average yield falls below the critical level. The best policy for the individual producer is then to maximize his returns as he would if no insurance was offered.

For a voluntary insurance scheme, 'adverse selection' is another problem. This means that only those farmers who are most at risk would bother to join the scheme. Compensation payments per farmer would be higher than if some less risk prone farmers were insured. High premiums are required to cover high costs which further discourages farmers from joining the scheme. Many crop insurance schemes are therefore made compulsory for all growers. However, for reasons given above, most crop insurance schemes have run into financial difficulties. They may be justified none the less on welfare grounds as a means of subsidizing victims of natural disasters.

Summary

1 This chapter deals with the risks farmers face, resulting from (i) environmental uncertainties, (ii) market uncertainties and (iii) lack of information.

2 Decision-making under uncertainty is illustrated using a pay-off matrix, which shows the outcomes under all the alternative possible states of nature, for different strategies; in this case the two crop production activities, maize and sorghum. The 'maximin' decision criterion indicates choosing the strategy which yields the best of the worst pay-offs; in this case sorghum production. Reliance on this criterion reflects cautious, risk-averse behaviour.

3 Further analysis uses the probability distribution of the set of possible outcomes. For this purpose it is assumed that the farmer (decision-maker) can form subjective, judgemental probability estimates based on past experience. The mean of the probability distribution of financial outcomes, known as the expected money value (*EMV*), is maximized by choosing maize production. This then is the optimal choice for a risk-indifferent farmer.

4 Probability estimates, together with the corresponding outcomes, also provide measures of the spread or variation; such as the variance or the mean absolute deviation (*MAD*). A risk averse decision-maker would seek to minimize this variation. In practice there is generally a trade-off between *EMV* and variation, so risk avoidance has a cost in terms of reduced *EMV*. In this example maize has a higher *EMV* than sorghum, but also a higher variance and *MAD*.

5 It is demonstrated that a mixed strategy, or diversification into more than one activity, yields a higher maximin return than does a pure strategy, or sole cropping. Different combinations of the two crops (strategies) may be compared to show the trade-off between *EMV* and the minimum possible return. A 'safety-first strategy' is aimed at achieving a target minimum level of income as first priority before maximizing *EMV* as second priority.

6 Diversification only reduces risk, however, when the returns from alternative activities are not positively correlated. The example data show returns which are negatively correlated.

7 An alternative analysis of risky decisions is based on the trade-off between *EMV* and variance (*V*) or mean absolute deviation (*MAD*). This trade-off is represented by the slope of the $E-V$ (or $E-MAD$) frontier between feasible and infeasible plans. The farmer's preferred choice depends upon his expected utility function, or marginal rate of substitution between *EMV* and variance. This determines a 'certainty equivalent' for any risky choice, which provides a criterion for comparing alternatives.

8 Both theories of risk, the one based on disaster avoidance, the other on variance minimization, may appear unrealistic. However, it is clear that most farmers are risk-averse despite the fact that this has a cost in terms of *EMV* foregone, that some activities are riskier than others and that diversification often reduces risk.

9 In practice, the final outcome of any productive activity depends upon a series of risky events. Tree diagrams may be used to display all possible sequences of events and outcomes. The probability of a particular final outcome is the product of the conditional probabilities of the intermediate steps leading to that outcome.

10 Decision trees are used to analyse multistage sequences of risky decisions. By averaging out (at outcome modes) and folding back (by deleting dominated alternatives at choice nodes) the best sequence of decisions can be identified. This approach is known as 'dynamic programming'.

11 Risks can be shared between households. Risks are pooled when households share in co-operative activities. Risks are spread under crop sharing and livestock caretaking arrangements.

12 Governments may reduce the risks faced by farmers, by promoting drought-resistant crops and other risk-reducing technologies, by establishing price stabilization policies, by improving information flows and by introducing crop insurance. This last option suffers from problems of moral hazard and adverse selection.

References

Anderson, J. R., J. L. Dillon & J. B. Hardaker (1977). *Decisions Analysis in Agricultural Development*, Ames, Iowa State University Press

Balcet, J. C. (1982). Adoption of Farm Technology on the Northern Nigerian Agricultural Development Project. Paper presented at the First National Seminar on the Agricultural Development Projects, Ibadan, 14–15 July 1982

Moore, P. G. (1972). *Risk in Business Decisions*, London, Longman

Roummasset, J. A. (1976). *Rice and Risk: Decision Making among Low Income Farmers*, Amsterdam, North Holland

Roummasset, J. A., J. M. Boussard & I. Singh (1974). *Risk, Uncertainty and Agricultural Development*, Agricultural Development Council

Upton, M. & H. Casey (1974). 'Risk and some pitfalls in the use of averages in farm planning', *Journal of Agricultural Economies*, **25**(2) 147–52

Wolgin, J. M. (1975). 'Resource allocation and risk: a case-study of small-holder agriculture in Kenya', *American Journal of Agricultural Economics*, **57** 622–30

Part II

Rural resource economics

Part II

Rural resource economics

7

Capital and credit

Types of capital

Everything used in production, which is not a gift of nature but has been produced in the past, is called capital. It includes not only machines and tools but also buildings, roads, footpaths, drainage ditches, terraces, irrigation equipment, growing crops, livestock and stocks of food, seed, fertilizers and other materials. Clearly, many very different items are included. All they have in common is that they were produced in the past and will contribute to production in the future.

It should be clear that some capital is needed for any kind of productive activity. For instance, the spears and food and water containers of pre-agricultural, food-gathering societies are items of capital. A typical arable farmer may own three cutlasses or machetes, two hoes, an axe and a grain store which may together be valued at about £20. Capital valuations are often much higher where permanent crops are grown, livestock are kept and machinery used. Each item of capital controlled is known as an asset.

We are concerned here with the assets used in the process of agricultural production, but two other forms of capital should be noted in passing. One is social overhead capital, which includes communications, market-places, public utilities, research stations and agricultural extension services, and is best considered as a feature of the farmer's environment. The other is consumer capital, made up of durable consumer goods such as houses and furniture. It may be difficult to decide whether a particular asset is productive or consumer capital. For example, a bicycle may be used for pleasure or for transporting farm produce to market. A house, furniture and cooking utensils are necessities which must be available before man is capable of productive work. The problems of definition are acute in family farming where there are close links between farm and household.

141

A farmer's capital assets may be classified according to the length of their productive lives into long-, medium- or short-term capital. Long-term capital has a life of many years and may be virtually permanent. It includes items like buildings, wells, dams and land improvements. Certain tree crops may come into this category. Capital with a medium lifespan of just a few years includes workstock such as bullocks, breeding and milking stock and many items of tools and equipment. Short-term capital is generally consumed within one year and includes stocks of food, seed, agricultural chemicals and cash. The harvesting of annual crops usually occurs in one or two discrete periods of the year, so not only do stocks of seed have to be provided some months before benefits are obtained, but also family consumption must be met during the period between one harvest and the next. For these purposes capital in the form of stored seed and food (or the cash to buy them) is needed for at least part of the year. This short-term capital is also known as circulating or working capital, to distinguish it from other assets which are not consumed within a single year and are therefore known as fixed or durable capital.

Capital is made up of so many different items that it can be misleading to treat it as a single resource. Land and labour vary in quality, as we have seen, but it is generally reasonable to assume that these resources can be transferred from one enterprise to another, say from cattle grazing to cotton production, without too much difficulty. With capital it is less straightforward. Since capital is embodied in durable physical assets, transfer from one use to another is difficult. They are fixed items of cost.

Investment and saving

Investment means adding to the stock of capital. It can take place in several apparently different ways, although in effect they all amount to the same thing, namely, saving, which means foregoing current consumption. The first way in which a farmer invests is by actually saving some of his produce. For instance, cereals, legumes or yams which are stored either for seed or future consumption represent an addition to the stock of capital, and are therefore investments. Goats and cattle which are kept for milk or breeding or just to fatten into bigger animals also represent savings and investment. Secondly, assets are created by the farmer's own physical efforts. If he clears land, plants trees, builds a dam or a cattle kraal he is investing. Again he foregoes current consumption because he might have spent his time either in producing more food or in leisure, which in itself is a form of consumption. Investment by foregoing leisure is particularly suited to the small farmer. Especially if his total output is little above the subsistence minimum he cannot afford to forego consumption of produce, but even the poorest producer will almost certainly have some leisure time, particularly during the seasonal troughs in the pattern of labour requirements. The opportunity cost of this labour may be very small indeed.

The third method of investment is by purchase. This can, of course, only occur in an exchange economy where produce is sold or bartered, but this is true of most of Africa today. Again, current consumption is foregone if the money or bartered goods would otherwise have been used for consumption purposes. Certain assets cannot be manufactured on the farm and must be purchased. This is particularly true of tools, machinery, stocks of improved seed and agricultural chemicals. It may occur to the reader at this point that capital assets are sometimes hired or purchased with the aid of a loan. We will return to these possibilities later, but it is worth noting that hired or borrowed capital is still the outcome of saving by someone other than the user. Furthermore, although investment is ultimately dependent upon saving, it does not follow that all savings are necessarily invested. They may be used for consumption, for festivities or hoarded as a reserve against risk.

Saving, no matter for what purpose, represents a cost to the user, namely, the cost of waiting. Why then do individuals save? The answer is that the benefits that are obtained by waiting are greater than the value of the consumption foregone. In the case of productive investment, greater returns are obtained in the long run by using indirect or roundabout methods of production. Thus the farmer who spends time making a plough, training bullocks to draw it and destumping his land must work harder than his neighbours who use hoe cultivation, and he may produce less food than they while he is making this investment. In future years, however, he hopes that plough cultivation will add to his output more than enough to make up for his original efforts. This surplus, over and above the cost of the investment, is known as the 'return on capital'.

Return on capital from goats

Most rural families and some urban dwellers in much of Africa keep a few sheep and goats. These small ruminants are often left to forage for themselves in free-roaming village flocks with minimal management. Labour and other costs are very low, but mortality may be quite high. Sheep and goats kept for breeding are clearly capital assets. They have been produced in the past, and will contribute to future output by producing young.

Table 7.1. *Goat flock structure over two years with no offtake*

	Initial flock	End of one year	End of two years
Adult female	4	4	6
Adult male	1	1	3
Immature female	—	2	2
Immature male	—	2	2
Total	5	9	13

Thus we may illustrate the concept of return on capital by considering production from a small goat flock (see Upton 1985).

West African dwarf goats, of the rainforest region, are highly prolific. They reproduce every eight or nine months on average, frequently bearing twins. As a result each doe bears two or more kids each year. However, mortalities are such that only half the kids survive to maturity at about 12 months of age. Thus a typical household flock of 4 does would produce 4 surviving animals each year. Predicted flock structures at yearly intervals over 2 years if there were no off-take, are presented in Table 7.1. In practice it is not necessary for every family to keep a buck since each one may serve about 20 does. An adult male is included in this simplified example to avoid dealing with fractions of an animal. Note that we are arbitrarily dividing continuous time into yearly intervals. More accurate results could be obtained by dividing time up into shorter intervals and correspondingly increasing the number of age cohorts. However, this would necessarily lead to increased occurrence of fractional numbers in the calculations.

The number after 1 and 2 years are predicted by assuming each doe bears one surviving kid annually and that half of all kids born are female. By the end of the second year the kids born in the first year have matured and joined the stock of adult goats, while more immatures have been born. The mortality of adult goats is ignored for the present.

Clearly, with this set of assumptions the flock would grow steadily over time. Alternatively, from the end of year one, the family could consume four animals, two males and two females, each year and maintain a constant flock size of nine animals. On this basis a capital stock of five breeding animals appears to yield a return of four animals per year.

However, this could not continue indefinitely, since eventually the breeding stock will need replacing. Given that, on average, adults spend 5 years in the breeding flock, this is the maximum period that an offtake of four animals per year could be maintained. Allowances for replacement are necessary if a steady-state, constant-sized flock is to be maintained. Of course, the productive lives of individual animals vary considerably around the average of 5 years. Thus it is more convenient to think of the replacement cost as an annual rate of 20 per cent. There is then an annual cost of replacing one-fifth of the adult animals, which in our example means one replacement every year. This annual replacement cost is generally known as 'depreciation'.

We now adjust the results for depreciation of breeding stock, to give an annual offtake of three animals (four minus one) from a steady-state breeding flock of six animals (five plus one replacement). The annual rate of return on capital is therefore

$$\tfrac{3}{6} = 50 \text{ per cent}$$

This is a rather crude estimate based on rounding-off the productivity estimates and assuming all animals are equally valued. In fact, the value of a one-year old animal is less than that of a breeding adult. Thus the rate of return in money value terms is lower; estimated at 34 per cent by Upton (1985). However, for present purposes the cruder estimate based on animal numbers may be used.

Note that we now have two alternative ways of viewing a capital asset, either as a stock of past production, in our example six goats already produced, or as a stream of future incomes, in this case three kids per year continuing indefinitely into the future. This case represents a very simple example of a 'flock growth model'. To build such a model, the flock structure is described by the numbers (proportions) in each of the various age and sex cohorts. The new flock structure after a given time period has elapsed is predicted on the basis of productivity and mortality parameters. Thus the number of kids is determined as the number of breeding does multiplied by the kidding rate and multiplied by the survival rate for kids. The number in an older age group is given by the number in the next younger group in the previous period multiplied by the survival rate, and adjusted for offtake if any, (see Figure 7.1). In this way the development of the flock structure over time may be predicted for different off-take policies or different production parameters (Upton, 1985).

Intertemporal choice

In this example the steady-state policy was emphasized. A depreciation allowance was made to allow for the maintenance of a constant

breeding stock. Net investment (i.e. net of depreciation) or capital forma-
tion, was assumed to be zero. This is a convenient approach for estimating
the rate of return, but maintenance of a constant breeding flock is not the
only feasible policy. Other feasible alternatives are shown in Figure 7.2. The
farm family could, for instance, have a grand feast and consume all nine
goats in the first year. They would then have no goats left in year two (point
A). The steady-state alternative of consuming only three animals and
retaining the rest for breeding purposes is represented by point *B*. Another
alternative would be to consume none and retain all the offspring to maximize flock growth (point *C*). If we assume that numbers of animals can be
varied continually (which may be justified if treated as expected values
rather than actual numbers) intermediate policies may be represented by
other points on the line *ABC*. This may be viewed as a production possibilities boundary for the two commodities, goats this year and goats next year.

Along the horizontal scale, the distance *OA* represents the flock or stock of
capital in year one. The amount consumed is measured along this scale from
the origin (*OX*), the remainder (*XA*) being retained or invested for future
production. When *XA* units are retained, the stock next year will be *OY*

Figure 7.1   Goat flock growth model

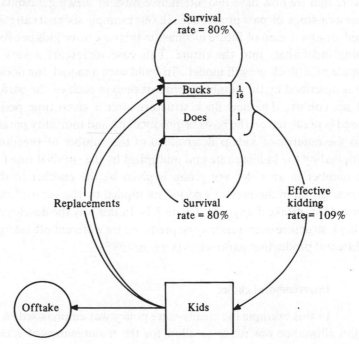

goats. Clearly, there is a trade-off between offtake of goats this year and the number of goats available next year, so the boundary has a negative slope. The (negative) slope, or *RPT*, for this boundary is equal to $(1+r)$ where r is the rate of return. Thus between points A and B the (negative) slope is

$\frac{9}{6} = 1.5$. Hence $r = 0.5$ or 50 per cent

The rate of return between B and C is lower since three more goats invested produce only four additions to next year's stock. The slope is $\frac{4}{3}$ $= 1.33$ so $r = 33$ per cent. This decline in the rate of return reflects diminishing marginal returns to increased investment. (The perceptive reader may question how thirteen goats can be produced if one is needed for replacement. The answer is that the additions to the flock are assumed to start breeding from twelve months of age.)

Figure 7.2   The choice between present and future consumption

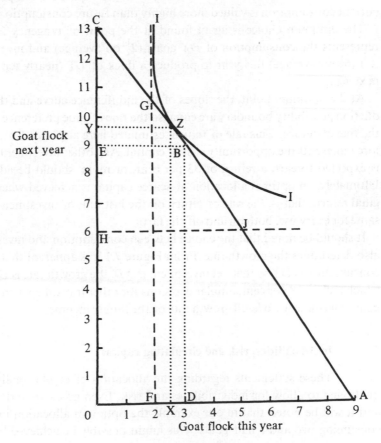

Intertemporal choice may be illustrated on this diagram along similar lines to our earlier analyses (particularly Chapter 3). First, the family may have a target consumption need of say two goats per year represented by the vertical line *FG*. This restricts the amount of investment and hence the size of next year's flock to about ten animals. Note that, if more than three goats are consumed, disinvestment occurs and the breeding flock is reduced.

The family may also aim to retain the flock of at least six animals, represented by the constraint line *HJ*. Given the other constraint *FG*, the choice is limited to the segment of the boundary *GJ*. If we assume that the farmer's utility depends upon his expected future consumption as well as his current consumption, indifference curves may be drawn, showing the subjective trade-off between goats this year and goats next year as shown. The (negative) slope is equal to $(1+p)$ where p is the rate of subjective time preference also known as the 'personal discount rate'. When p is positive it implies that current consumption is valued more highly than future consumption.

The optimum choice is again found at the point of tangency Z. This represents the consumption of *OX* goats ($2\frac{1}{2}$ on average) and investment *XA* ($6\frac{1}{2}$ on average) this year to produce a flock of *OY* (nearly ten goats) next year.

At the optimum point, the slopes of the indifference curve and the production possibility boundary are equal so the rate of time preference equals the rate of return. This rate of return, estimated here at 33 per cent, therefore represents the opportunity cost of capital. Any other investment which is expected to earn a return of 33 per cent, or more, should be adopted. Ultimately, an optimal allocation of scarce capital is achieved when marginal return, that is, the rate of return on the last unit of investment is the same for every use, both on and off the farm.

It should be noted that the choice between consumption and investment also determines the growth rate. From Figure 7.1 it is apparent that, when consumption is *OX* so that net investment is *XD*, the growth rate is *EY/OA*, which is about 8 per cent. Similar decisions for other investments, in aggregate, determine the overall growth rate of the family income.

Indivisibilities, risk and circulating capital

These statements regarding the allocation of capital really need qualifying to allow for indivisibilities and risk. Even goats are indivisible, and it will be noted that in our example the optimum allocation involves consuming two and a half goats! This might possibly be achieved by consuming two animals in one year and three the next, or vice versa. However, it is clearly not possible to attain exact equality of marginal returns for all uses in every year. The opportunity cost principle may still be applied; namely, to maximize utility, each unit of capital should be used where it will earn the highest return.

There is a further problem in that capital already invested in goats cannot readily be transformed into another form of capital which might earn a higher rate of return. Once capital has been invested in durable assets it is committed; flexibility is lost. Only when new investments are planned is there scope for adjusting the allocation to maximize utility.

However, when new investments are planned, the outcome is uncertain; all such decisions are necessarily subject to risk. Although a farmer may allocate his investments so as to equalize *expected* marginal returns in all uses, he cannot be certain that the *actual* marginal returns will be equal. Indeed, if he is risk averse he will not base his decisions on the expected returns only. Generally, the riskier a project, or the greater the potential variation in outcomes, the higher must be the rate of return to justify the investment (see Chapter 6). A crude but simple method of allowing for risk in this context is to arrive at a 'certainty equivalent' by means of a 'risk-discount'. For example, suppose the expected rate of return is 50 per cent, then it may be reduced by a risk discount of 10 points to a figure of 40 per cent for a mildly risky investment, or by a risk discount of 20 points to give a 'risk-discounted return' of 30 per cent for a more speculative project. The risk-discounted value of the prospective return is then the basis for allocating new investment. A low expected-return, low-risk investment might be preferred over a potentially more profitable but riskier choice.

Returns to working capital cannot be calculated in the same way as outlined above, because it is used to provide other inputs such as labour. Thus it is impossible to distinguish the marginal return on working capital from the marginal product of the labour. None the less, working capital is essential for continued production, so in that sense it is productive.

Requirements of working capital vary within each year according to a fairly regular cycle. Over the cropping season the costs of seed and of supporting the labour force must be met some weeks or months before the returns are obtained at harvest time. Thus the working capital requirement usually rises to a peak just before harvest. If the produce is stored after harvest, the capital requirements continue to rise until the produce is finally sold or consumed. However, the peak capital requirements of different enterprises may occur at different times of the year. Where this is the case, the working capital requirement for a combination of enterprises will be more level through the year than the requirement for a single crop. Enterprises may be supplementary in the use of working capital in much the same way as they may be supplementary in the use of labour.

Stored produce may earn a return in the sense that it gains in value as the dry season progresses and food becomes more scarce. Against this benefit must be set the costs of storage, which are the capital costs of the storage barn or granary and the storage losses due to insect, fungal and rodent damage. Grain storage losses in the drier Savannah regions may be as low as 3–4 per cent, but they are higher in more humid zones and for cowpeas and root crops. None the less, storage can generally be justified economically since the gain in value is sufficient to cover costs and earn an acceptable return on the capital invested in the store and the produce itself, (see Upton 1962). Note that in this case the return is earned over a part of a year and needs adjustment to give the equivalent annual rate.

Discounting for longer-term investments

For longer-term investments an alternative method of evaluation is needed. To illustrate let us consider a rather artificial example of a calf bought purely for fattening and sale three years later. This animal is supposed to forage for itself so there are no feed or labour costs as was assumed for the goat flock. However, the value of the animal is now measured in money terms.

The use of money values was avoided in the goat example in order to emphasize the physical productivity of capital and the idea that even pure subsistence farmers face capital-investment decisions. However, in the new example the benefit is simply a gain in value. Energy value of the carcass might have been used, where the animal was kept for home consumption, but we assume the calf is purchased for cash and later sold. The purchase price of the calf is £20 and the expected sale price three years later is £60. Clearly there is a gain of £40 over the three years but it is not yet clear whether this is sufficient to justify the investment. The opportunity cost of investment funds is 30 per cent or 0.3.

The results in Table 7.2 show how the cumulative cost of the initial investment and its opportunity costs increase over the life of the animal. After the animal has been kept for one year the cumulative cost C, of purchase (V=£20) and the opportunity cost (pV=0.3×£20) is £26 given by

$$C_1 = V(1+p)$$

Table 7.2. *Compounding investment costs*

	Cumulative cost	Interest	Total
Outset	20	6	26
End year 1	26	7.80	33.80
End year 2	33.80	10.14	43.94
End year 3	43.94		

In the following year the opportunity cost applies to this total sum so that total cost after two years C_2 is

$$C_2 = C_1(1+p) = V(1+p)^2$$

Similarly after three years

$$C_3 = C_2(1+p) = V(1+p)^3$$

This process of predicting accumulated future costs over time is known as 'compounding' and is the method used for adding 'compound interest' on bank loans. The general formula for an initial sum V, and an opportunity cost rate p calculated over n years is $V(1+p)^n$. Thus £20 compounded over three years at 30 per cent amounts to

$$£20(1+03)^3 = £43.94.$$

On this basis this project is clearly worth undertaking. The cumulative cost at the end of three years is £43.94, although it sells for £60. Thus there is a terminal net gain of £16.06 (£60–43.94). However, this gain will not be obtained for three years. For the farmer deciding whether to make the investment, it would be more useful to know what the gain is worth now; what is its 'net present value'. This is easily arrived at by 'discounting' which is simply the converse of compounding (see Figure 7.3). Thus if £1 now is worth £1.30 next year (if compounded at 30 per cent) then £1.30 received next year is only worth £1 now (if discounted at the same rate). In short, since investment has an opportunity cost, £1 in the hand now is worth more than £1 expected in the future. Similarly, given that the future value F of a sum V compounded at a rate p over n years is

$$F = V(1+p)^n$$

by rearranging, we find the present value of F is V thus

$$V = \frac{F}{(1+p)^n}$$

Using this formula or the discount factors from Appendix Table I we find the present value of £16.06 in three years' time at a discount rate of 30 per cent to be

$$\frac{£16.06}{(1.3)^3} = £16.06 \times 0.4552 = £7.31$$

In fact, this could have been estimated more simply by discounting the £60 expected revenue, to give a present value of £27.31 (60×0.4552) and subtracting the initial investment of £20.

An investment which yields a positive terminal net gain must also yield a positive net present value (*NPV*). Thus on either criterion it is worth undertaking, provided that the associated risk is acceptable.

We now have a method of defining the value of any capital asset. It is the discounted, present value of expected net benefits. Thus the present value of this beef animal after keeping it for one year is $60/(1.3)^2 = £35.5$. The discounted present value of a plot of land expected to produce an annual net return of £90 per year is obtained simply by dividing by the discount rate thus

$$£90/0.3 = £300$$

In short £300 invested at 30 per cent would earn £90 per year.

Figure 7.3   Discounting – the converse of compounding

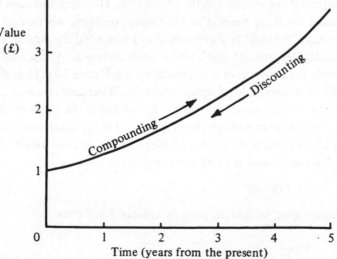

The internal rate of return and replacement

In this calf-fattening example there is clearly a 200 per cent return over the three years; £40 gain in value for a £20 investment. The annual rate of return *r* is easily calculated by discounting so that

$$\frac{60}{(1+r)^3}=20 \text{ or compounding } 20(1+r)^3=60$$

which gives $r=0.44$ or 44 per cent. This is known as the internal rate of return (*IRR*) and is that discount rate which results in a net present value of zero.

The internal rate of return can only be calculated in this way when there is a single input cost followed, after some years, by a single lump sum receipt as in our example. Generally it is necessary to use a trial and error procedure, calculating the *NPV* for different discount rates and interpolating as shown in Figure 7.4.

Figure 7.4   Finding the internal rate of return

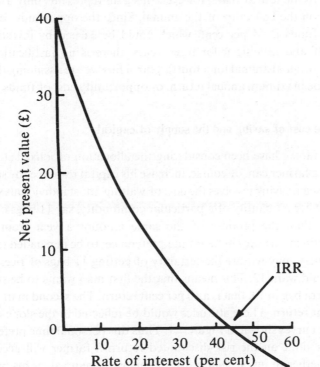

Real-world investments generally involve a series of costs, (e.g. annual food costs for the fattening calf) and may yield a series of benefits (e.g. milk from a cow or draft power from an ox). All these costs and benefits need to be evaluated in the same terms, usually money, and the resultant cost and benefit streams must be discounted to find the *NPV* or the *IRR*. Details of this planning procedure are given in Chapter 15. For present purposes, it must be recognized that a farmer faces difficult judgements in making long-term investment decisions. In so far as he can 'judge' the *IRR*, he can use it as described earlier to arrive at the optimum allocation of new investment.

A further capital investment decision problem may be illustrated using our simple example; that is to find the optimum age for replacement. How long should the investment last? At first sight it might appear that the investment should continue so long as further gains can be made. However, this is not the case since investment funds have an opportunity cost. The general rule is to adjust the life of the investment so as to maximize the annual gain.

Let us suppose our beef animal could be kept for a fourth year at the end of which it could be sold for £85. Thus it continues to gain in value by £25 (£85 – £60) in the fourth year. However, this gain represents only a 42 per cent return on the £60 value of the animal. Since the opportunity cost of investment funds is 44 per cent, which could be earned by investing in another calf and keeping it for three years, there is no justification for keeping the original animal for a fourth year. Thus we are assuming that 44 per cent is the maximum annual return, or opportunity cost of funds.

The cost of saving and the supply of capital

So far we have been considering the allocation of a fixed stock of capital, but a farmer can, of course, increase his capital resources by saving. As we have seen, saving involves the cost of waiting; most individuals would prefer to receive a quantity of a particular commodity, say 11 bags of rice, now rather than the promise of the same amount a year from now. However, individuals vary in their time-preference; to be persuaded to wait a year one man may require the certainty of getting 11 bags of rice, while another would want 12. This means that the first man wants to be sure of getting 1 extra bag in 10, that is a 10 per cent return. The second man wants a 20 per cent return. These attitudes would be reflected in the slope of the indifference curves shown in Figure 7.1. Thus this personal time preference sets a lower limit on the risk-discounted return a farmer will accept in deciding whether to invest. Naturally, the higher a man values his present consumption in relation to future consumption, the higher this minimum acceptable rate of risk-discounted return will be.

It should not necessarily be inferred from this that if, because of improved technology or improved product prices, the risk-discounted return on capital rises, farmers will save more. The supply curve for savings may be backward sloping as is possible for labour. A rise in risk-discounted return increases the income of the investor and he may consequently prefer to increase his level of consumption and therefore save less. Indeed, the level of risk-discounted return probably has relatively little influence on the amount saved from any given level of income, but much influence on the use of savings. The amount saved is likely to be affected much more by the level of farm incomes and the saving habits of the farming population. The saving habits of a person or a community are measured by the 'marginal propensity to save' which is the proportion that is saved from each additional £1 (or other unit) of income.

It is usually found that rich people save more than poor people, not only in absolute amounts, but also as a proportion of their total income. The very poor are unable to save at all. Instead, they 'dis-save' or spend more than they earn, the difference being covered by going into debt or using up previously accumulated savings. As incomes rise, so too does the marginal propensity to save. Thus, if we compare African farmers with wealthier societies elsewhere, we find that savings and capital investment per person is low because incomes are low, but it may be argued that incomes are low in turn because the amount of capital per person is low. This is known as 'the vicious circle of poverty' because it implies that poor people must remain poor unless capital is introduced from outside to break the circle. It also implies that poor farmers will have a greater preference for present consumption than will wealthier people. The poor farmers are more concerned with survival from day to day until the next harvest rather than with investment for the future. This means that they will only invest in activities which are expected to yield a relatively high rate of risk-discounted return. All we are saying really is that, where capital is scarce in relation to labour and land, it will be costly in relation to these other resources.

Other reasons for saving and investing are (i) to create a reserve against risk and (ii) to help children to become established on their own and to provide for old age. Some fruit orchards and poultry units are established to provide a low labour-input source of income after the owner is too old for full-time work.

So long as there is some net investment every year the total stock of capital will increase continually. This means that if there are diminishing returns to extra units of capital used with a fixed area of land and a fixed labour force, the rate of risk-discounted returns on the additional investments will fall over time. Eventually, the rate of return may fall to a minimum acceptable level where no further investment is justified. Thus a point of stagnation might be reached where farmers are capable of acquiring more capital by saving, but where there are no further opportunities for productive investment.

In practice, the situation is complicated by the process of change. As shown in Chapter 4 some net investment is necessary to keep pace with family growth even if there are no innovations; but where agricultural change is taking place, new investment opportunities are constantly being introduced. Such technical innovations generally yield higher risk-discounted returns per unit of capital than do extra investments in traditional productive activities. Thus technical innovations provide new opportunities for productive investment, to which some farmers may respond without outside assistance.

A good example is the rapid expansion of cocoa production in West Africa during the last half-century. The massive investment in establishing the trees was provided by the farmers themselves as they became aware of the possibility of growing this new crop for export. Similarly in Kenya more recently the establishment of tea and coffee was largely financed by the farmers themselves. In fact, among cash-cropping farmers the rate of saving and investment is often high by any standards. Studies in Nigeria, Zambia and elsewhere have suggested that they may save as much as one-third of their incomes.

Borrowing and lending

Opportunities for borrowing and lending may increase farm incomes and welfare as shown in Figure 7.5. This is based on Figure 7.1, but now the line *CK* has been added to represent the possibility of borrowing or 'caretaking' of breeding goats. This practice is very common in West Africa, where the payment for the loan consists of half the offspring which are returned to the owner. Since we have estimated a return of 50 per cent from goat breeding, the hire charge is estimated at half this, namely 25 per cent. The hire charge represented in this way is similar to 'interest' charges on a financial loan.

Given this alternative prospect, the optimal policy is to maximize investment, and keep nine goats for breeding (point *C*) but to maintain consumption levels by borrowing two or three animals each year. In this way the household utility is raised from point *Z* to *Z**. Next year the flock will have increased to 13 animals but three of these are owed to the lender. Note that in this case, point *C* is a corner solution, where the rate of return exceeds the interest rate. If the farmer could increase his herd to more than nine animals, by borrowing more, it would pay him to do so.

The question may be asked why the owner is happy to lend animals on terms which are rather unfavourable to him. There may be an element of social duty to poorer kinsmen, but there may also be physical constraints limiting the size of flock an individual can conveniently keep. He is then happy to make *some* return by lending.

However, in some circumstances utility may be increased by lending as shown in Figure 7.6. Now the production possibility curve represents

Figure 7.5   Gains from borrowing

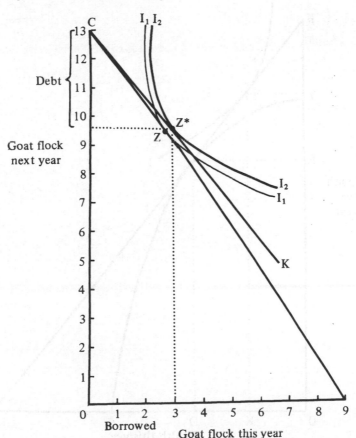

money values of wealth this year and wealth next year, and is drawn as a
curve to illustrate diminishing marginal returns to investment. In this case
the line *FK* represents the lending activity. Its (negative) slope is $(1+i)$ where
i is the rate of interest.

The optimal solution now is for the farm family to consume quantity *OX*,
to lend quantity *XD* and invest quantity *DA*. Next year total assets will
amount to *OE* produced on the farm plus *EY*, the loan with interest. This
choice of activities ensures that the slopes of the production possibility
boundary, the lending activity line and the indifference curve are all equal.
Thus the marginal rate of return on investment, the rate of interest and personal time-preference rate are all equal. The present value of the entire

Figure 7.6   Gains from lending

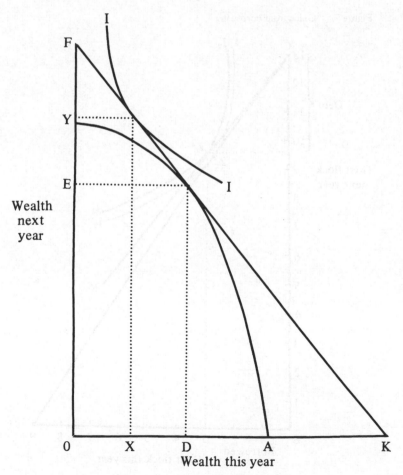

system, discounted at this rate, is given by OK. Similar analysis would apply to off-farm investments offering a constant rate of return.

Unfortunately, rural credit markets do not function as smoothly as implied here. Farmers may have difficulty in borrowing as and when they wish or in lending their savings out at interest. In any case, risk has an important influence on the costs and volume of credit.

First, let us consider the borrower's situation. Generally, he must undertake to repay instalments and interest on the loan annually regardless of the state of the harvest. In good years he should produce a surplus over and above the cost of servicing the loan, but in bad years, even if he makes a loss, he still has the loan service charges to meet. His residual net income will therefore fluctuate more widely than if he had not incurred the debt. Indeed, the more that he borrows the greater will be the variation in his residual net income. This is known as the 'principle of increasing risk' and may be restated as follows. The greater is the ratio of borrowed to owned or 'equity' capital (the ratio being referred to as leverage or gearing), the larger is the risk. Clearly, for any risk-averse individual, this sets a limit on the amount he would wish to borrow.

However, the lender also faces a risk, that the borrower will default and the loan will not be repaid. Before making a loan he may require some reassurance that the borrower is creditworthy. This can be provided in two main ways:

(i) personal knowledge of the borrower or even control and supervision of his operations; or
(ii) collateral security, meaning some possession of the borrower which the lender can keep if the loan is not repaid. Under a mortgage, land or buildings provide the collateral security. The same is true when land and tree crops are pledged. Machinery or equipment bought under hire-purchase is itself collateral security in case the payments are not made. Many small farmers have nothing to offer as collateral security.

Interest rates charged on loans should cover

(i) the opportunity cost of the funds, that is the base rate of interest,
(ii) administrative costs, which are proportionately higher the smaller is the loan, the more remote is the borrower's location and the greater is the need for personal contact and supervision,
(iii) losses due to default; for which a 'risk premium' is included,
(iv) inflation, which effectively means a fall in the value of money.

These costs in combination may result in relatively high interest rates on unsubsidized rural credit.

Credit needs and sources

Despite the possible high rates of saving achieved by some farmers, there is little doubt that credit can improve the productivity, incomes and welfare of rural people. Short-term credit may alleviate seasonal needs for working capital, or the problems arising from crop failure, sickness within the family or unexpected social commitments. Note that credit may be used for production or consumption and some argue that it should be restricted to the former use. However, the distinction is really very hard to draw since funds are 'fungible', which means they can be moved around between uses. Credit provided for productive purposes may simply allow the family to spend more of their own savings or equity on consumption.

However, savings which are already invested in the farm or in non-agricultural activities are no longer fungible. A household with savings tied up in goats cannot immediately release these funds to buy sheep if the latter prove more profitable. Since practically all technological innovations are embodied in new forms of capital, liquid funds are needed to finance their introduction. The provision of credit will facilitate and accelerate the necessary investment and hence the adoption of the technology. However, in the absence of any new technology, provision of credit alone may have little impact on agricultural production.

Credit agencies are frequently classified into two groups; formal and informal. Formal institutions include banks and co-operative credit unions, while informal agencies may be further sub-divided into two groups. On the one hand, family members, kinsmen and farmers' credit associations (such as *esusu* clubs in Nigeria) lend money or assets at little or no interest. On the other hand, village traders and moneylenders sometimes charge very high interest rates. None the less, informal sources, even of the latter kind have certain advantages over formal institutions.

(i) They are convenient, available locally, require no documentation and can provide credit quickly.
(ii) The informal moneylender has local knowledge to help in appraising household credit needs and credit worthiness.
(iii) There is little risk of default because the lender is generally well placed to apply pressure on the borrower to ensure payment.
(iv) Administrative costs are low.
(v) With some types of informal credit such as the caretaking of live-

stock and the pledging of tree crops, the risks of borrowing are shared between the two parties involved.

The disadvantages of informal credit are that

(i) the borrower feels he has an obligation to the lender and loses his independence,
(ii) there are few alternative sources to choose from, and
(iii) only short-term and relatively small loans are available.

Formal credit institutions have standardized lending procedures and make loans on a contractual basis. Such agencies may make longer-term and large loans available but they face special problems in lending to farmers.

(i) Since farms are widely scattered and many are remote from urban centres and main roads, the costs of travel and administration are high. When rural branches are established they may do much less business than comparable town branches.
(ii) Compared with urban industry, farmers' loans are relatively small. The cost of administration and supervision of a small loan is the same as for a large one.
(iii) Many farmers lack knowledge and experience of formal application procedures. They are discouraged by the need to complete application forms and other documents, which naturally introduce delays.
(iv) Agricultural production is particularly risky. As a result risks of default are high.
(v) Farmers lack suitable collateral security. Formal mortgaging of property is often not feasible because farmers do not have legal title to their land. In any case it may be difficult, socially and politically, to foreclose on a smallholder's main productive assets (see Chapter 6).

As a result of these difficulties, formal credit agencies rarely operate in rural areas without government support and promotion. Farmers are often forced to rely on informal sources.

Promotion of rural credit

Four main topics deserve brief mention. These are (i) subsidized credit, (ii) lending through marketing agencies, (iii) co-operation and group loans and (iv) lending as an element of integrated rural development.

Subsidized credit is provided to farmers in many African countries, through their Agricultural Development Banks. At first sight this appears a straightforward method of assisting small farmers and promoting agricultural production at the same time. However, there are several possible disadvantages. First, the low interest rate may discourage farmers from saving themselves. Second, it cannot be self-supporting, a continued subsidy is needed, which means that the total amount of subsidized credit must be limited. Third, since it cannot be rationed by price, that is by allowing the interest rate to vary, it must be rationed in some other way, usually on the basis of estimated credit worthiness. Fourth, as a result the bulk of loans go to the larger farmers, who since they have more equity to offer, inevitably appear more creditworthy. Finally, the large farmers, who are able to get the loans, have less incentive to use the credit productively when it is cheap. Farmer surveys suggest that other factors such as ease of securing credit, timeliness of loans, transaction costs and collateral requirements are more important in influencing use of formal credit, than the rate of interest charged.

Lending through marketing boards and similar marketing agencies is particularly suited to short-term loans offered at the start of the cropping season. Repayment is then deducted from the price of the crop after harvest. The system is somewhat inflexible and involves strict control of the marketing operation.

Group loans have some advantages over individual loans. Generally, since a larger sum is lent to the group, the per unit administrative costs are reduced. In addition, since the group takes joint responsibility for repayment, there is less risk of default. Thus considerable cost savings may be made. At the same time, co-operation in production and marketing may be encouraged through the joint action in raising the loan. Indeed, once a national structure of primary village co-operatives and credit unions has been established, this may serve as a banking system providing funds to farmers from the central co-operative bank. Farmers may also be encouraged to save and deposit their savings with the co-operative.

The main advantages of linking credit with Intergrated Rural Development is that opportunities for profitable investment are presented along with the credit needed to implement them. Indeed, some of the credit may be provided in kind. At the same time agricultural extension agents may assist in drawing up plans and making credit applications. They may also be involved in supervision of its use and repayment. The provision of tractor and other hire services is another means of making more capital available to farmers. However, Integrated Rural Development Projects and tractor-hiring services have often proved costly and of limited success in increasing agricultural productivity.

Summary

1 Capital consists of assets produced in the past and not yet used up. Short-term, circulating or working capital (seed, food, chemicals, fuel) is used up and replaced within one production cycle (a year). Durable, medium- and long-term capital assets (animals, trees, land improvements, buildings, machinery and equipment) have longer lives.

2 Investment, an addition to the stock of capital, either produced by the household or purchased, necessitates saving. This cost is justified by the resultant increased future household productivity.

3 Return on capital is the additional annual income earned from the investment. Allowance should be made for depreciation, needed to cover the costs of replacement. The return is usually expressed as a percentage of the value of the capital invested.

4 Saving and investment decisions involve intertemporal choice. Increased investment implies current consumption foregone in exchange for increased future consumption. Two-period analysis of the trade-off between consumption this year and investment to raise consumption next year, of the same good, is similar to the theory of choice between two different products discussed in Chapter 3. The optimum is found where the (subjective) marginal rate of substitution or time preference is equal to the marginal rate of return.

5 In practice, capital investments are 'lumpy' and risky, so the rate of return should be greater than the rate of time-preference for an investment to be justified.

6 Requirements for working capital vary over the year, as illustrated by stored produce, which gains in value despite possible storage losses.

7 Benefits and costs of longer-term investments may be discounted (for time) to arrive at their 'present values'. Thus the value of a capital asset is the net present value (*NPV*) of the expected future income stream.

8 The internal rate of return (*IRR*) is that discount (interest) rate which yields an *NPV* of zero. It is a more reliable measure of the rate of return than that outlined in paragraph 3 above.

9 Capital investments should be replaced when the average income per year is maximized; that is where the marginal income from a further year's delay is equal to the average income.

10 If the rate of return on investment rises (due to improved technology or prices) saving and investment may be substituted for current consumption. However, the income effect may cause a rise in current consumption and a fall in investment, although it is generally found that the proportion

of income saved rises as income is increased. The availability of new technology provides an incentive for new investment.

11 Borrowing and lending activities may raise household income. If the (marginal) rate of return on investment exceeds the interest rate, borrowing will raise expected income. Lending may be profitable if the interest rate exceeds the rate of return on home investments.

12 Risks of default are associated with lending, so personal knowledge of the borrower, control and supervision of the use of the loan or collateral security are desirable precautions.

13 Informal sources of credit (e.g. moneylenders) may have advantages over formal institutions (e.g. banks) in terms of personal contact and lack of formal procedures, despite high interest rates. Formal sources may make larger loans but do not easily reach the poor without subsidisation. However, low interest rates may benefit the rich rather than the poor.

14 Credit may be effectively organized through marketing agencies, co-operative group lending or as an element of integrated rural development.

References

Ahmed, I. & B. H. Kinsey (1984). *Farm Equipment Innovations in Eastern and Central Southern Africa*, Aldershot, UK, Gower

Hill, P. (1970). *Studies in Rural Capitalism in West Africa*, African Studies Series No. 2, Cambridge University Press

Howell, J. (ed.) (1980). *Borrowers and Lenders: Rural Financial Markets and Institutions in Developing Countries*, London, Overseas Development Institute

Hunt, D. (1975). *Credit for Agricultural Development*, East African Publishing House

Miller, L. F. (1977). *Agricultural Credit and Finance in Africa*, New York, The Rockefeller Foundation

Upton, M. (1962). Costs of maize storage 1959–60: the cost of guinea-corn storage in silos 1959–60. *West African Stored Products Research Unit: Annual Report 1962*, Ibadan, Nigeria

Upton, M. (1966). 'Tree crops: a long term investment'. *Journal of Agricultural Economics*, **17**(1), 82

Upton, M. (1976). *Agricultural Production Economics and Resource Use*, Oxford University Press, Chapter 7

Upton, M. (1985). 'Returns from small ruminants production in South West Nigeria', *Agricultural Systems*, **17**, 65

8

Natural resources

Land, wildlife and water

Agriculture and pastoralism may be viewed as ways of exploiting the natural environment. Human labour and man-made capital are employed in harvesting some of nature's bounty. As was mentioned earlier, man actually modifies his natural environment and its flora and fauna. The application of science and technology allows him to do so to an increasing extent. None the less the availability of natural resources still limits what can be harvested from a given area using a given technology.

In so far as natural resources may be destroyed by over-exploitation or misuse, choices arise between current and future consumption. Resources which are conserved for the future might otherwise have been used to increase consumption now. The analysis of such choices really comes into the realm of capital theory discussed in Chapter 7.

For present purposes it is convenient to assume that users aim to sustain productive capacity over time; or in other words to maintain a steady state. This means that the stock of natural resources is not allowed to deteriorate over time. Naturally, yield may vary from season to season as a result of chance climatic and other variation, but a steady state implies no long-term downward (or upward) trend in the resource stock. There are three main categories of natural resources of importance to the farmer, which are:

(i) biological, renewable resources such as forests, wildlife and natural rangeland grazing;
(ii) non-renewable resources of land, meaning the 'original and inde-structible properties of the soil'; although we know that soil fertil-ity may be destroyed by overcropping or overgrazing and soil may be lost by erosion; and
(iii) water.

165

This last resource is difficult to categorize. In one sense it is renewable; both surface-water ponds, drains and rivers *and* groundwater aquifers are replenished by the precipitation phase of the water cycle. On the other hand, the total amount of rainfall in a given season is fixed. In this sense water is a non-renewable resource.

Water resources may be further divided into three main classes:

(i) *Drinking water* is essential for human and animal life; and may be treated as a fixed requirement or constraint. Thus the availability of drinking water influences the location of human settlements and the areas of rangeland which can be grazed. In fact some pastoralists only water their cattle every three days during dry seasons, which, despite some loss of condition of the animals, does allow a larger area to be grazed. Drinking water is a variable input in this case subject to the pastoralists' choice of optimum frequency (see Nicholson 1986).

(ii) *Soil moisture* is essential for crop growth, and its availability is an important influence on the productivity of the soil. For many purposes it may simply be treated as a characteristic of the land.

(iii) *Irrigation* generally yields substantial increases in productivity per hectare, which may justify considerable expenditure on pumping, storage and transport. In this way it becomes possible to control the allocation of water between crops and between time periods. In principle, the optimal allocation of water requires that the value of the marginal product per cubic metre is the same in all uses and equal to the supply cost, after having made due allowance for risk (see Chapters 4 and 6). Reduction of the risk of losses due to drought may be a major benefit of irrigation. In practice there are many special problems associated with the control and distribution of irrigation water.

The exploitation of biological resources

The following analysis may be applied to any biological, renewable resource, be it a fishery, a herd of wild game, a forest harvested for firewood and building materials or natural rangeland.

Provided that the rate of harvest offtake does not exceed the natural growth rate, the stock will not be depleted. A steady-state ecological equilibrium may be maintained. If, on the other hand, over-exploitation occurs, the natural resource stock will be depleted or even destroyed.

To illustrate let us first consider the growth of a biological population or stock of plant biomass, which is not harvested. The growth curve is usually S-shaped, as shown in Figure 8.1, since growth is slow when the stock is sparsely distributed, increases exponentially as the stock grows, but gradually slows down as the stock increases further, due to 'environmental resistance'. Environmental resistance may be due to overcrowding, pressure on food supplies for animals or shading effects for plants. Growth ceases once the environmental 'carrying capacity' is reached. This is a somewhat simplistic approach in not distinguishing between reproductive and other phases in the population and ignoring interactions between different species, but it will serve our purpose.

Figure 8.2 which shows the relationship between the total biomass and its rate of growth is easily derived from Figure 8.1. In reality the curve could not originate at zero, because some minimum initial stock is necessary to

Figure 8.1   A biological growth curve

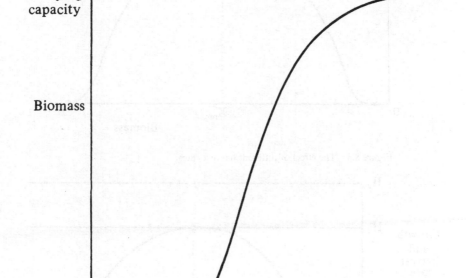

reproduce and grow. However, the important features to note are *M*, the point of maximum growth, at stock OX_m and *OK*, the natural equilibrium stock. Without human exploitation the stock would stabilize at this maximum level.

Now let us assume that humans harvest some of the resources by fishing, hunting, felling trees or putting cattle to graze on the rangeland. The effects of three different harvest rates are shown in Figure 8.3. First consider an annual harvest offtake of OH_1 on rangeland where it would represent a rel-

Figure 8.2   The effect of biomass on growth rate

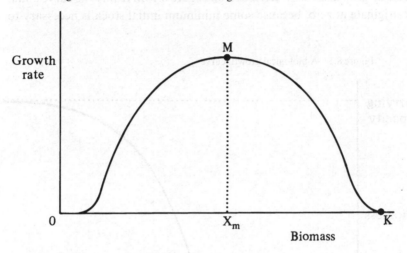

Figure 8.3   The effect of different harvest rates

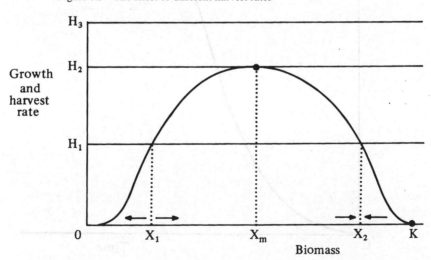

atively low stocking rate. A steady-state equilibrium would result with a biomass of OX_2. This rate of exploitation could be sustained indefinitely, barring disaster, because the natural growth rate is just sufficient to replace the harvested offtake. Furthermore, this is a stable equilibrium, which means that if the balance is disturbed it is automatically restored. Thus, if as a result of a poor growing season, the biomass is reduced below OX_2, the natural growth rate will increase. Since the offtake rate remains constant, the total biomass must increase, thus restoring the stock to level OX_2. Similarly a chance increase in the biomass above this level would be self-eliminating.

A steady-state equilibrium also exists at a much lower biomass, a smaller population of wild animals or a more denuded landscape, at OX_1. However, this is an unstable equilibrium. In a bad year, if natural growth fell below the harvest rate, further depletion would occur. A reduction in harvested offtake would be needed to arrest disaster. In a good year, on the other hand, the stock would increase and with it the natural growth and regeneration rate. This self-sustaining growth would continue until the stable equilibrium is reached at OX_2.

A harvest offtake of OH_2 represents the 'maximum sustainable yield' (*MSY*). It is the maximum possible offtake which is a steady-state equilibrium. By contrast a harvest rate of OH_3 cannot be sustained. It may be possible to harvest this yield for a short period, but only at the expense of depleting the resource stock. This process of overexploitation or resource mining, if continued, must ultimately result in total destruction of the resource.

Now it might appear that the maximum sustainable yield is the optimal rate of exploitation, since biological resources are free gifts of nature. However, there are two main reasons why this might not be the case. First, there are risks in trying to operate at this level, since even a slight fall in natural growth during a poor season must result in a reduction of the total biomass below OX_m. This in turn means that growth will fall below *MSY* in future seasons. If the level of offtake is not reduced accordingly continual depletion is inevitable. Risk averse users of the natural resource are likely to aim for a larger steady-state biomass than OX_m.

Second, costs are incurred in harvesting natural resources; in hunting, fishing, collecting firewood or keeping livestock. Furthermore, the marginal and average returns per unit of cost or effort are likely to diminish as the activity is increased. To see why we may refer again to Figure 8.3. With no exploitation the total biomass is given by OK, but as the harvesting effort is increased first to OH_1 and then to OH_2 the biomass is reduced through OX_2 to OX_m. Thus harvesting takes longer. Returns to hunting or fishing fall as the population of game is diminished. The same is true of wood-gathering as the forest is thinned out, or of keeping more livestock on rangelands as the grass cover is reduced. Similar arguments might even be applied to ground water, since the yields of wells and boreholes may diminish as the water table is drawn down. In all these instances the situation of diminishing returns to effort is similar to that for weeding labour analysed in Chapter 4 (see Figures 4.1 to 4.3). Now it is quite feasible that the economic optimum rate of harvest lies below the MSY, provided that the product value is not too high in relation to the effort required. Increased human population pressure may raise the scarcity value of natural resources and cause a higher rate of exploitation.

To summarize this section we may conclude that

(i) provided the rate of offtake does not exceed MSY and the biomass does not fall below OX_m, a steady-state equilibrium harvest can be maintained, and

(ii) diminishing returns are likely to result from increased harvesting effort and the optimum rate may lie below the MSY.

Intensity of land use

In those parts of Africa where there is still some unexploited virgin bush, land use per household can be varied. The economic optimum policy is to operate an 'extensive' system with a large land:labour ratio and hence low labour inputs and yields per hectare, for instance under long-fallow shifting cultivation. This is illustrated using the marginal and average product curves for labour shown in Figure 8.4. The average product of labour is maximized at point B so this is the optimum. Labour input per hectare is limited to OA and total product per hectare is limited to $OABC$. Population growth can be accommodated simply by increasing the area of land use to scale (see Chapter 5). In these circumstances land is truly a free resource.

Once all available land is in use, as a part of a crop rotation, increased labour inputs must mean intensifying the system of land use to produce more per hectare. The effects may be illustrated in Figure 8.4. When labour input per hectare is increased from OA to OD, marginal and average products per hour of work fall to OG and OH respectively. However, the total product per hectare is increased from area $OABC$ to area $ODJH$. Alternatively, measuring total product by the area under the marginal product curve, the increase is given by area *ABED*. Thus returns per hour of labour fall with increased labour use per hectare, while returns per hectare of land rise.

Although there is some scope for varying the intensity of land use within a given system, pastoralists can vary the stocking density of the rangeland for instance, bigger changes can be accommodated by changing the system. A change from pastoralism to arable cultivation, generally allows increased intensity of land use. Instead of relying on natural regrowth, the cultivator actually harvests the entire crop biomass (*OK* in Figure 8.3) each season and re-establishes the crop in the following season. This requires more labour, but produces more yield per hectare.

One way of describing the intensity of cultivation is in terms of the frequency with which the land is cropped. This is measured by the 'cropping index', which is the number of crop seasons as a percentage of the total rotational cycle including fallow. On this basis arable cropping systems may be classified, according to the intensity of land use, along the following lines:

   1. Natural fallow systems
   1.1 Shifting cultivation usually with forest fallows and a cropping index of below thirty-three
   1.2 Fallow systems, usually involving bush or savannah grass fallows, with a cropping index of between thirty-three and sixty-six
   2. Permanent cultivation systems
   2.1 Annual cropping under which land is only fallow between seasons

Figure 8.4 Returns to labour under different intensities of land use

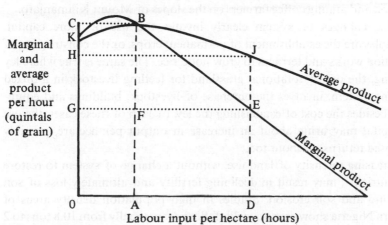

Labour input per hectare (hours)

Table 8.1. *Labour input in shifting and fallow systems, Kiberege Strip, Kilombero Valley, Tanzania*

	Shifting cultivation on the escarpment	Fallow farming in the valley
Cultivated area as a percentage of total cultivated and fallow (cropping index)	15.0	55.0
Total area cultivated and fallow (ha/ME)[a]	4.0	1.7
Land productivity (kg rice/ha)	252.5	654.0
Labour input (man-days/ha)	41.0	136.0
Labour productivity (kg rice/man-day)	6.2	4.8

[a] ME=man-equivalent. After Baum (1967)

or at most one year in three. The cropping index lies between sixty-six and one hundred

2.2 Multi-cropping with each plot bearing two or more crops per year, giving an index of over one hundred.

From the analysis of Figure 8.4 we might expect increases in returns per hectare and decreases in returns per man-day of labour with increases in the cropping index. Many field studies support these conclusions; such as the example given in Table 8.1 (Baum 1967). Widely quoted examples of intensive, high labour input systems are found in the close settled zones around major cities in Northern Nigeria, on the island of Ukara in Lake Victoria and among coffee farmers on the slopes of Mount Kilimanjaro.

Some changes of system clearly involve the use of more capital. Examples are the establishment of permanent crops, or the construction of irrigation works and terraces to grow flood rice. The same is true where ley farming, the use of rotational grassland for feeding livestock in a mixed farming system, involves the purchase of livestock, buildings and equipment besides the cost of establishing the ley. In each of these cases, the use of capital may bring about an increase in output per hectare, possibly increased returns to labour too.

Increasing intensity of land use, without a change of system to restore soil nutrients, may result in declining fertility and ultimately loss of soil structure and soil erosion. Studies in high population density areas of Eastern Nigeria show cassava yields falling dramatically from 10.8 tons to 2 tons per hectare as the length of fallow is reduced from 5.3 years to 1.4 years (see Lagemann 1977). The situation is rather like that of exceeding the *MSY* for a biological resource. If continued long enough the resource may be destroyed. These problems will be taken up again in discussing property rights and tenure.

Variations in returns to land

In theory, the returns to land and labour can be separated according to their marginal productivities. For simplicity we ignore returns to capital and assume that land and labour are the only inputs. Referring again to Figure 8.4, it may be argued that the return to labour, which is the marginal product times the labour input, changes from area *OABC* to area *ODEG* with increased intensity. But, for the extensive system, the return to labour *OABC* is the same as the total product. There is no separate return to land; it is zero. However, with increased intensity, the surplus over the labour cost, area *GEBC*, (which equals *GEJH*) may be viewed as a return to land, or 'rent'.

Alternatively, if labour could be hired at a wage of *OG*, then the economic optimum level of employment per hectare would be *OD*, so the amount *ODEG* would be paid out as wages. The area above this, which we have identified as rent, is the surplus remaining for the land holder. In practice, where both land and labour are provided by the farm family, factor shares cannot be distinguished in this way.

However, in order to make efficient allocation decisions it is important to identify opportunity costs as we have seen in Chapter 3. An alternative view of the allocation problem is given in Figure 8.5. This shows the marginal product curves for labour applied to two different 1 hectare plots of land. Note that the marginal product curve for Plot B is drawn back to front, since labour applied to this plot is measured from right to left, starting from point *T*. The total labour hours available for cultivating the two plots are measured by *OT*. Given that no labour is wasted, an increase in employment on one plot must mean less labour employed on the other. Plot A is more fertile than Plot B so the marginal product of labour is higher on A for a given intensity of labour use.

Several useful conclusions may now be drawn.

  (i) The optimum, most productive, allocation of labour is found when the marginal product is the same for both plots, at point *D*, where *OX* hours are allocated to Plot A and *XT* hours to Plot B. This is simply an application of the equi-marginal returns principle; that scarce resources should be allocated so that marginal returns are the same in all uses. It is readily seen in Figure 8.5 that an increase in labour used on plot A beyond *OX* would result in a smaller gain in yield than would be lost from the reduced labour input on Plot B. A similar net loss would occur if labour was transferred to Plot B, away from the optimum allocation.

  (ii) At the optimum allocation, more labour is used on the more fertile plot (A). In short the more fertile plot is cultivated more intensively.

 (iii) This marginal product of labour, which is the same on the two plots, represents the opportunity cost of labour. If this hourly cost is applied to the total labour input *OT*, the area *OTFC* represents the return to labour. The areas *CDE* and *DFG*, above this, represent returns to land.

 (iv) The return or rent per hectare of the more fertile plot (area *CDE*) is greater than that of the less fertile plot (area *DFG*).

Major differences in land quality are often found within the area of a single farm and cropping systems are organized accordingly. The crops chosen for fertile valley bottoms, such as rice, sugar cane and vegetables, probably yield a larger surplus per hectare, which means that they are more intensive crops than upland sorghum or millet for instance. Similarly yam is

Figure 8.5   Efficient labour allocation between two plots of land

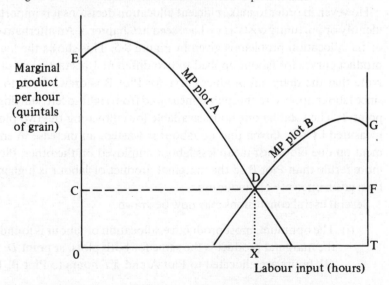

a more intensive crop than cassava. Such comparisons require that money, or some other common unit of value, is used to compare the returns from different products. However, for present purposes it is useful to remind ourselves, by using a physical measure of output, that land allocation decisions are made even by pure subsistence farmers.

In reality there are added complications in that there may be more than two classes of land and it is not neatly divided up into one hectare plots. However, there must be a limit on the amount of each class of land available. Thus once all the top-quality land is in use, as the intensity is increased, a stage will be reached when labour can be used more productively on poorer quality land. This is illustrated in Figure 8.6, which shows the marginal product curves for labour on three different classes of land. Once *OA* hours of labour are used on the most productive land, further labour would be used more productively by extending on to second-quality land.

As yet more labour is used, the marginal product falls on second-quality land until eventually (when *AC* hours are worked on this land) it becomes worthwhile to start cultivating even poorer, third-class land. There are two important effects. One is that as the marginal product of labour falls on second quality land, that is the opportunity cost falls, the intensity of using top-quality land increases from *OA* hours of work to *OB* hours. This is known as the effect on the 'intensive margin', when costs fall or returns rise.

The second effect is that the area of cultivation is extended on to poorer quality land. Note, however, that poorest quality land is freely available and sufficient is used, with low labour inputs per hectare, for the labour cost to account for the total product. There is no surplus over labour cost on the

Figure 8.6   The intensive and extensive margins of cultivation

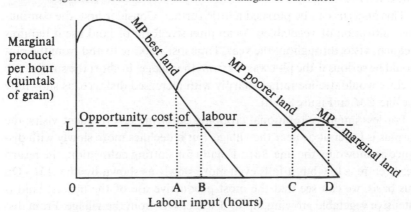

poorest land, which is therefore known as 'marginal land'. It is only just worth cultivating. The return to labour on this marginal land determines the opportunity cost. A surplus is produced over and above this on better-quality land. These ideas may become clearer when we consider the effect of location which also influences the surplus produced per hectare.

Location

Most farm families maintain a compound or kitchen garden close to the house, which is fertilized with ashes and household refuse and continuously cropped. Land further from the home is used less intensively under a rotational bush fallow system for instance. This may reflect a conscious choice to build the settlement on the most fertile soil in the area. However, even if all the land was of equal fertility, that near the home would be cultivated more intensively because of its location. Time is lost walking to and from more remote plots, so the surplus over labour costs must be lower. As we have seen from Figure 8.4, this means the remote plots will be cultivated less intensively.

Figure 8.7(a) shows a continuous decline in the surplus produced per hectare with increasing distance. At distance OM, there is no surplus, so land is marginal in this vicinity because of its remoteness from the village. Beyond this, there may be unused land, which is sub-marginal or not worth using. Assuming there are no obstacles, so that access is equally easy in all directions, the margin of cultivation may be represented by a circle around the village. Note that a general increase in productivity represented by the broken line in Figure 8.7(a) would cause both an increase in intensity on land already cultivated (the intensive margin) *and* an extension of the area (the extensive margin).

This analysis can be pursued a little further. Consider first, the continuous cultivation of vegetables. As an intensive form of land use it requires frequent visits throughout the year. Time lost walking to and from the plot would be serious if the plot was far from the village. In short the surplus per hectare would decline rather sharply with increased distance, as shown by the line CM_1 in Figure 8.7(b).

For less intensive rotational cropping requiring less frequent visits, the surplus is lower at or near the village, but it declines more slowly with distance as shown by the line BM_2. Finally for shifting cultivation, the return per hectare is low but it falls even more slowly as shown by line AM_3. On this basis, we can see that the most productive use of the nearest land is intensive vegetable growing, up to distance OD from the village. From distance *OD* to *OE*, rotational bush fallowing is more profitable. Beyond this, and even on land which is sub-marginal for continuous cropping, shifting cultivation may be justified. The shaded areas represent the differential rent or surplus earned over the next best alternative form of land use.

Thus location has an important influence on farm systems. A pattern of concentric rings of different forms of land-use has often been observed around villages as shown in Figure 8.8 (after Pelissier 1966).

Figure 8.7   The influence of location on land use; (a) The distance-decay function, (b) Alternative forms of land use

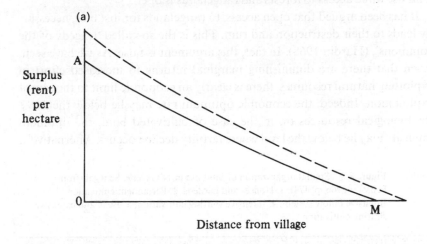

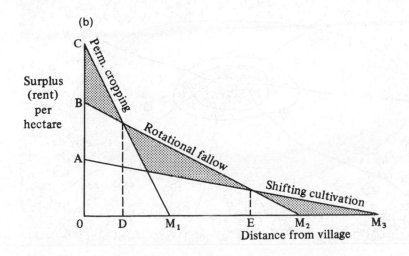

Common rights and conservation

Natural resources are generally treated as the common property of the whole of society. In the well-known words of a Nigerian chief 'land belongs to a vast family of which many are dead, a few are living, and countless numbers are still unborn' (Elias 1962). Of course, access is not open to anyone; it is generally limited to members of the nation, lineage or village society. Furthermore, user rights to cultivated land are allocated to individual households. However, in much of Africa no rents are paid for land use while access to forests and rangelands is open.

It has been argued that open access, to rangelands for instance, necessarily leads to their destruction and ruin. This is the so-called 'tragedy of the commons', (Hardin 1968). In fact, this argument is false. As we have seen, given that there are diminishing marginal returns to increased effort in exploiting natural resources, there is clearly an economic limit to the rate of exploitation. Indeed, the economic optimum rate may lie below the *MSY* for biological resources or, in the case of cultivated land, the optimum intensity may lie below the level where fertility decline occurs. Alternatively,

Figure 8.8   Spatial organization of land use in N'Gayene, Senegal (from Pelissier 1966, p. 474). 1. Houses and gardens. 2. Permanent cultivation. 3. Intensive fallow system. 4. Intensive shifting cultivation. 5. Bush and extensive shifting cultivation

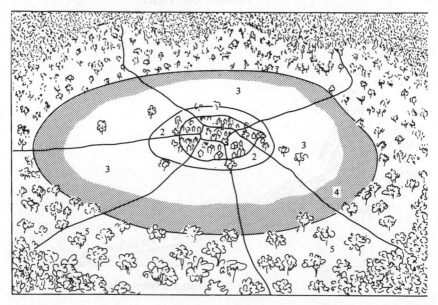

measures for fertility maintenance and conservation may be incorported in
the optimal policy. In these cases a steady-state equilibrium may be maintained.

The only germ of truth in the 'tragedy of the commons' is that open
access may result in a higher rate of exploitation than would occur under
private ownership. This is illustrated in Figure 8.9, which shows the marginal and average product curves to labour or effort applied to natural
resources. As already emphasized, the economic optimum (under private
ownership) occurs where the marginal product is equal to the unit cost of
effort (level *OA*). However, at this point, there is a surplus or 'rent' since the
average product exceeds the average cost. Under open access, where no rent
is paid, there is an incentive to exploit the resource further and increase the
effort to the point where average product equals the unit cost (level *OB*).
There are differences of opinion as to how this effect should be interpreted.
To the environmentalist it represents over-exploitation, but to the developer
it may be seen as fuller and more productive use of available resources. The
interpretation should depend upon whether the resource is being depleted.

Natural resources may be depleted either as a result of chance, droughts,
floods or disease outbreaks or because of a conscious decision to do so. In
the latter case the users place a higher value on their current consumption
than on the welfare of future generations; they discount the future. This
might arise as a result of (i) opportunity, such as high prices for wild game,
or (ii) need, because of rapid human population growth. In these circumstances, open access might hasten the rate of resource depletion. Social

Figure 8.9   Exploitation of natural resources under open access

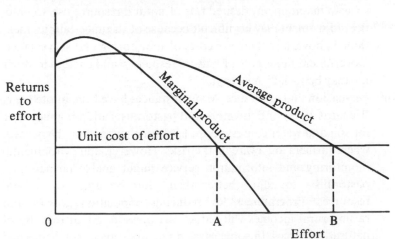

costs are incurred, in terms of loss of future production, which are not necessarily felt by current users.

Chance effects are important since much uncertainty surrounds the use of natural resources. It is difficult for farmers, and scientists, to monitor and evaluate when over-exploitation and resource depletion is occurring. Random variations around a steady-state equilibrium may be either self-correcting *or* self-perpetrating. This implies that a safety margin is desirable; the planned intensity of exploitation should be below the expected *MSY*.

Where there are risks of depletion the Government may wish to impose some control on the exploitation of natural resources. One or other of the following alternative approaches may be appropriate depending on the circumstances:

(i) Privatization; for instance, by enclosing, fencing and issuing titles to grazing land, or allocating and registering private water rights, should in theory, provide the necessary incentive to operate at the point where marginal product equals cost of effort. Furthermore, given security of tenure, it should also provide an incentive to conserve the resource. However, overexploitation may still occur for the reasons given above, social inequalities may develop under private ownership and the concept may be socially unacceptable.

(ii) Compulsion, of which there are two main forms (a) imposition of quotas, on the number of livestock grazed or the amount of game, firewood or water taken annually and (b) taxes per unit harvested or per head of livestock. In theory, quotas or taxes can be adjusted so as to maintain any desired rate of natural resource use. In practice, adjustment may be difficult because of the uncertainties mentioned above, and there are costs of monitoring and surveillance. Government monopoly of natural resources, and charges for their use may be socially unacceptable.

(iii) Persuasion and assistance. Many instances have been quoted (e.g. Richards 1985) of cultivators and pastoralists adopting measures for soil and water conservation. Little persuasion may be needed, where farmers are aware of the risks. However, an environmental monitoring and information service might enable farmers and pastoralists to adjust better their rates of usage of natural resources. Programmes for reducing population growth and raising rural incomes will reduce the pressure on current use of natural resources. In some cases direct assistance may be needed for terracing, reforestation, land reclamation and other conservation measures. As with all spending on rural development the costs must be weighed against the future benefits.

Land tenure

The system of land tenure is the set of laws and customs which establish rights and duties relating to land use. From the national point of view, the two main requirements of a system of land tenure are, firstly, that it should lead to the most productive distribution of land among potential users and potential uses; and, secondly, that it should provide sufficient security of tenure to justify measures to maintain or improve the productivity of farms. To some extent these two requirements are in conflict, since the greater the security of tenure, the more difficult it becomes for efficient farmers to obtain control of land occupied by the less efficient. Most of the customary tenures in Africa also emphasize a third feature: the right of each family to some share in the natural resources belonging to the community, the lineage or village. Sale or lease to strangers may be prohibited but, subject to these overriding controls, individuals belonging to the community have the right either to use particular pieces of land which may have been inherited, or to occupy plots under shifting cultivation.

African patterns of land tenure have proved to be flexible in allowing for differences in the needs of families and for changing circumstances. It has generally been possible for the more energetic or capable farmers to obtain extra land, either from that controlled by the community and still unused, or by way of pledge or loan from other families, who have more land than they can use. Again, the introduction of tree crops in both East and West Africa led to extension of individual rights in land to cover the prolonged period of occupation and to allow the pledging and even sale of cocoa or coffee plots which a man has built up by his own work. In such cases systems of land tenure may evolve naturally through increasing individualization to the stage of a commercial market in land, where plots can be bought and sold like other commodities.

However, the existing pattern of land tenure may not evolve quickly enough to avoid acting as a constraint upon agricultural changes which are urgently required in view of the rising populations and the expansion of export crop production. In the first place the loan or pledging of land, based on close personal relationships, provides neither the security of tenure nor the incentive for efficient farming by the occupiers. Secondly, the sale of land becomes associated with lengthy and costly legal disputes regarding the true ownership, particularly if it is sold to strangers from outside the community. Hence, with the development of a market in land, it becomes important to establish individual rights on a legal basis by survey and registration of ownership. Thirdly, the system of inheritance may lead to excessive fragmentation, which causes time loss in walking to and from isolated plots and creates problems for any kind of mechanization. Land consolidation and legal control of subdivision may contribute to increased agricultural productivity.

Where the individual owner has the sole right to use a piece of land or to dispose of it as, and to whom, he wishes it is known as freehold tenure. It is widely believed, particularly in East Africa, that individual freehold tenure is a highly desirable, even an essential, component of any agricultural development programme. The pride of ownership and the security offered to the farm family by this form of tenure are thought to encourage long-term improvement and conservation of the land and associated water resources. Furthermore, privately owned land can be offered as security for loans, to be given up to the lender in the event of failure to repay the loan; that is it can be mortgaged, thus enabling small farmers to raise money for farm improvement. However, this argument is of doubtful validity since few banks and commercial moneylenders are prepared to accept land as security for loans because of the practical and political difficulties of removing farmers from their land if they fail to repay their loans. It is also argued that the market in freehold land encourages the able and industrious farmers to expand production by buying the land of the less successful thus encouraging the development of a commercial attitude to farming.

This last feature of private-land ownership has its disadvantages in the potential for increasing inequality of land holdings and the development of a rural landless labouring class, as is occurring in Kenya (Hunt 1984). Where, in addition, the leasing of land is prevalent, class distinctions may be established between landlords and tenants. This was the case in Ethiopa before the 1974 revolution and subsequent land reform. However, the alternative to private-land ownership, of communal farming of land held in common has had limited success there and in Tanzania. Cultivation of individual family holdings still continues in both countries.

In those countries of Eastern and Southern Africa where large-scale commercial farms were established under colonial governments, some of these have survived alongside much smaller semi-subsistence holdings. Redistribution of land was one of the objectives of the independence movement, and, as we have seen, production per hectare may well be higher on small farms. Both equity and efficiency objectives may be served by the subdivision and resettlement of the large-scale farms. However, substantial costs may be involved in compensating the occupiers and resettling smallholders, while problems may arise in maintaining urban food supplies since most of the marketed surplus comes from commercial farms.

Leasehold

Forms of leasehold tenure, met with in African countries, include formal fixed-rent tenancies, crop-sharing agreements and pledging in which case the payment is in the form of a loan. Where there is competition between potential tenants, with the lease being awarded to the highest bidder, the rent paid will equal the total surplus over operating costs. More precisely, the rent is the same as the marginal product per hectare. Arguably the payment of rent promotes efficiency. The tenant must operate at the economic optimum intensity in order to afford the rent. Any increase in crop prices or productivity will cause the demand for rented land to rise and so will the rent. This effect does not apply, of course, where rents are fixed below the free market rate and eviction of tenants is forbidden as was the case under the *Mailo* system introduced in Buganda. There, tenants were able to retain some of the surplus and accumulate enough to buy the land. This reminds us that, even when no rents are paid, the producer still has an incentive to use land productively. The supposed advantage of charging rents must be set against the lack of security of leasehold tenure and the income distributional impact of a landlord–tenant system. Note, however, that on many irrigation and settlement schemes the state is the landlord.

It used to be argued that crop-sharing agreements are inefficient. The tenant, since he only keeps a share of the produce, has less incentive to maximize the surplus over production costs. He would only apply labour up to the point where his share of the marginal product equals the wage rate. It is now recognized that costs per hour of labour are not fixed, and the tenant might well aim to maximize total production rather than the surplus over some notional labour cost. In any case, if this system really were less efficient, it would presumably be replaced by a fixed-rent system. Share-cropping is really, as the name suggests, a system for sharing productive resources, the associated risks and the benefits.

Increasing output per hectare

Although there are high land/man ratios in Africa, we must not assume land is unlimited. Much is under fallow in rotational systems, and effectively in use. Furthermore, as we have seen, better quality and better located land is likely to be fully used before production is extended onto poorer and more remote land. Thus the area of more productive land is a constraint on output. New technology which increases output per hectare will bring about growth at both the intensive and the extensive margins. Examples of such technology are new high-yielding crop varieties, fertilizers and pesticides. For instance, introduction of short-season maize may allow two crops to be taken in place of one each year, and production to be extended to drier areas. Systems of agro-forestry, with soil mulching, may help maintain fertility and increase intensity of land use, thereby also increasing output per hectare. Although less obvious, increases in livestock productivity through improved health, nutrition and breeding also raise output per hectare.

Such innovations are sometimes described as 'land-saving', in the sense that less land is needed in total to produce a given output. However, strictly speaking, this description which implies that capital and labour are substituted for land, may be misleading. In general, new technology which raises crop and animal yields is neutral, at least between land and labour so that yields per hectare *and* per man-day are raised together. Admittedly more harvest labour may be needed for a larger crop yield, and mulching requires extra labour. To set against this, any extension of the feasible number of years of continuous cultivation reduces the need for bush-clearing labour. Overall, labour productivity is likely to be raised.

Furthermore, although costs may be involved, there are no large items of capital (except perhaps for pesticide sprayers). Thus most of these innovations are scale neutral. They can be introduced equally easily on small or large farms. In practice, large farmers may have easier access to the new inputs and credit to buy them, so they may adopt new technology more quickly. Where there are effective input supply systems such innovations can spread rapidly even among small farmers. One well-documented example is the introduction of hybrid maize to Western Kenya, where the innovation spread to most farms within two or three years (Gerhart 1975).

To derive the full potential benefit of introducing modern varieties, may require application of fertilizers and use of pesticides, so a package of these innovations is likely to be more productive than one on its own. Furthermore the impact may be felt throughout the farm household system. The introduction of hybrid maize for instance may cause a shift away from mixed cropping, more land devoted to maize for cash sale, or less land and labour devoted to maize if a target quantity is needed for subsistence, and the purchase of seed rather than retaining it from year to year. Thus careful testing and evaluation of the over-all impact is needed before innovations are launched. This must include an assessment of the risks involved. Generally speaking, yield increasing innovations also increase the total interseasonal yield variation. The *proportionate* variation (coefficient of variation) may well decline. Some new varieties have been unacceptable to farmers because of the appearance, processing characteristics, cooking qualities or taste. Clearly, such factors are as important as the economic impact on the farming system in determining the acceptability of the innovation.

Summary

1 Natural resources may be classified into (i) biological renewable resources (ii) non-renewable resources, mainly land and (iii) water.

2 Biological resources, such as forests, wildlife and rangelands, in the natural state reach an equilibrium level, where growth is just matched by decay, so the stock remains constant. The maximum sustainable yield (*MSY*) is produced at a lower stock level. To avoid depletion of the stock, and ensure sustainability, the rate of offtake must be no greater than the *MSY*. Furthermore stability is only ensured if the stock level exceeds that corresponding with maximum sustainable yield. The economic optimum rate of offtake may lie below the *MSY*.

3 Increasing intensity of land use is associated with increasing population density and labour inputs per hectare. The results are increased output, and marginal product (rent), per hectare of land, but reduced marginal and average productivity per man-day of labour.

4 Where land varies in fertility (productivity) labour should be allocated between different plots so that the marginal product of the last hour worked is the same for all plots. This will normally ensure that more labour is used per hectare and that the return (rent) per hectare is higher on the more fertile land.

5 Because the costs of transporting inputs to, and products from, the field, increase with distance from the homestead, intensity of cultivation tends to decline also. While compound gardens are continuously cultivated, more distant fields may be subject to rotational fallowing or indeed just used for grazing.

6 Communal tenure is not the same as common, or open-access, ownership. None the less, even under communal tenure there may be a tendency to over exploitation, to the point where unit cost equals average product per unit of effort, and the marginal return to land is zero. However, the alarmist 'tragedy of the commons' view is unfounded.

7 Traditional forms of land tenure generally provide, for each household in the community, the right to cultivate land or harvest other natural resources. Ownership rights generally apply to tree crops. Systems of freehold ownership of land have evolved in some countries and have been introduced through land reform measures in others. In some cases this has resulted in greater inequality of farm sizes.

8 Under leasehold tenure, an annual rental payment is made to the landlord. This may provide an incentive for the tenant to use inputs efficiently, to the point where the marginal value product equals the unit factor cost (see Chapter 4). The supposed inefficiency of share-rents (since the tenant only receives a share of the marginal value product of other inputs) is not valid. They are more correctly viewed as a method of risk sharing (see Chapter 6).

9 Land-saving innovations, such as high-yielding crop varieties, fertilizers, pesticides and irrigation are most appropriate where population density is high and land is scarce. None the less, provided that the innovation does not greatly increase labour inputs per hectare, a general increase in productivity should be beneficial even in land surplus areas.

. **References**

Adegboye, R. O. (1977). 'Land tenure', in Leakey, C. L. A. & J. B. Wills (eds.), *Food Crops of the Lowland Tropics*, Oxford University Press
Baum, E. (1967). 'Land use in the Kilombero Valley', in Ruthenberg, H. (ed.) *Smallholder Farming and Smallholder Development in Tanzania*, Afrika-Studien, No 24, IFO Institute, Munich
Boserup, E. (1965). *The Conditions of Agricultural Growth*, London, George Allen & Unwin
Carruthers, I. & C. Clark (1981). *The Economics of Irrigation*, Liverpool University Press
Cohen, J. M. (1980). 'Land tenure and rural development in Africa' in Bates, R. H. & M. F. Lofchie (eds.), *Agricultural Development in Africa: Issues of Public Policy*, New York, Praeger
Dasgupta, P. (1982). *The Control of Resources*, Oxford, Blackwell
Elias, T. O. (1962). *Nigerian Land Law and Custom*, London, Routledge & Kegan Paul
Gerhart, J. (1975). *The Diffusion of Hybrid Maize in Western Kenya*, CIMMYT, Mexico
Guillard, J. (1965). *Golonpoui, Analyse des Conditions de Modernisation d'un Village du Nord-Cameroun*, Mouton, Paris
Hardin, G. (1968). 'The tragedy of the commons', *Science*, **162**, 1243
Hartwick, J. M. & N. D. Olewiler (1986). *The Economics of Natural Resource Use*, New York, Harper & Row

Hunt, D. (1984). *The Impending Crisis in Kenya: The Case for Land Reform*, Aldershot, Gower

Lagemann, J. (1977). *Traditional African Farming Systems in Eastern Nigeria: An Analysis of Reaction to Increasing Population Density*, Munich, Weltforum

Nicholson, M. (1986). 'How water shortage can benefit pastoral society', *ILCA Newsletter* 5(2)A

Pelissier, P. (1966). *Les Paysans du Senegal*, Imprimerie Fabregue Saint-Yrieux

Richards, P. (1985). *Indigenous Agricultural Revolution: Ecology and Food Production in West Africa*, London, Hutchinson

9

The economics of irrigated farming systems

The benefits of irrigation

As we have seen in Table 2.1, about 17 per cent of the world's cropped land is under irrigation. Yet irrigated agriculture produces over 36 per cent of the total world output of crop products. It is forecast that by the year 2000 the share of total agricultural output produced under irrigation will increase further (Alexandratos 1988). These facts alone serve to emphasize the importance of irrigation as a means of increasing agricultural productivity. Table 2.1 also shows the wide intercontinental differences in the extent of irrigated agriculture. Whereas in Africa and Latin America irrigated farming systems are relatively unimportant, other than in a few countries, in Asia more than a third of all cropped land is irrigated. It can be inferred that most of Asia's food and other crop output is produced from irrigated farms.

Wet-rice cultivation is particularly important in humid areas of the Far East, such as China, Vietnam, Thailand, Indonesia, Malaysia and the Philippines, together with parts of Burma, Sri Lanka, and Eastern and Southern India. Other tropical irrigated crops, such as cotton, sugar cane, groundnuts, and vegetables are also grown in these and other more arid and semi-arid areas, where water supplies can be augmented. This is the case for major river-basin development schemes such as those of the Indus, the Nile and the Laguna area of Mexico.

Irrigation, which can be broadly defined as the supplementation of precipitation by storage and/or transportation of water, increases agricultural productivity and human carrying capacity, per hectare of land, in several ways (adapted from Ruthenberg 1980).

- First, it allows the introduction of high-yielding crops (e.g. rice), or high-value crops (e.g. cotton, wheat or vegetables) which could not otherwise be grown in that locality.

- Second, higher yields are obtained from crops which may be grown without irrigation, especially when complementary inputs such as seed for high-yielding crop varieties and fertilizer are used; as reflected in the so-called 'green revolution'.
- Third, it allows extension of the cropping season, before and after the rains, so that cropping intensity can be increased.
- Fourth, it reduces the year-to-year fluctuations in yield and the risks of crop failure due to drought. This greater stability of production and associated reduction of risk is of direct benefit to risk-averse producers and consumers alike. The justification for risk-avoiding behaviour is reduced, and farmers have an incentive to expand their use of purchased inputs for increased production and to invest for the future.
- Fifth, it allows the adoption of continuous cultivation, provided that waterlogging and salination can be avoided. Whereas some form of rotational fallowing is still practised in many rainfed farming systems, continuous rice-cropping has been practised for centuries in some areas, without any apparent impairment of fertility. The control of water reduces erosion.

As a result, irrigated areas support very high rural population densities. Parts of the Ganges and Tonkin Deltas and Java carry more than 1500 persons per km². Irrigated crop production is the most intensive form of agricultural land use.

However, there are substantial costs associated with irrigated agriculture, for both the initial capital investment involved in establishing a permanent water supply, together with an effective drainage system, and for the recurrent annual operation and maintenance (O&M). The precise form of these costs depends upon the type of irrigation system. For large-scale river diversion schemes capital costs are those of dam building, which should include the present value of the production foregone from the land inundated and of resettling the people displaced, and constructing the distribution system. O&M costs are incurred in desilting and maintaining water channels and control structures. *External costs* of irrigation development, which are imposed on people outside the scheme, as well as within, include the spread of water-borne diseases such as *schistosomiasis*, malaria and river blindness. For *groundwater systems*, investment is incurred in sinking wells and purchasing pumps, while recurrent costs involve those of operating the pumps.

The establishment of irrigation facilities therefore represents a capital investment which enhances the productivity of natural resources of land

and water. Decisions regarding the design and implementation of major large-scale irrigation projects fall under the heading of agricultural policy which is not the main subject-matter of this text (but see Ellis 1992, Chapter 11). Suffice it to say that ideally the incremental benefits of a new irrigation project should be sufficient to cover not only the O&M costs, but also the recovery of the original capital investment cost together with an acceptable rate of return. For an already established scheme it can be argued that the initial capital investment is a 'sunk cost', which is now unavoidable. This cost is therefore irrelevant to current decisions on whether to maintain the system in operation. This is justified so long as the incremental benefits exceed the incremental costs of operation and maintenance.

When irrigation systems are introduced, appropriate institutional structures must be established for the allocation of water, distribution of complementary inputs such as seed and fertilizer, maintenance of the system and conflict management. Special knowledge and skills are required of the cultivators to make effective use of the available water, and to ensure sustainability of the system. As human population and the demand per head for agricultural products both grow, so pressures on the limited water potentially available for irrigation will rise. This in turn will raise the opportunity costs of irrigation water and necessitate improvements in the efficiency of water-use.

The classification of irrigated farming systems

There is a wide diversity of different irrigated farming systems, some based on long-established traditional practice, others depending upon modern engineering technology. They may conveniently be classified in terms of;

(i)   water supply (engineering criteria),
(ii) water use (agronomic criteria) and
(iii) forms of organization (social criteria).

Water supply is derived either from natural flows of *surface water* above ground or from so-called *groundwater*, which is retained in underground aquifers. The surface water may be acquired by the capture and retention of floodwater or surface water runoff in small field-sized basins where the crops will be produced. This is the basis for much of the wet rice (paddy) production. Alternatively rivers and other surface water sources may be diverted, and/or stored in tanks or dams for distribution to cropped fields. Water is normally distributed by gravity through a system of canals and watercourses. The transport of water through underground pipes avoids evaporation and seepage losses, but the high capital costs are only justified in high-value production of horticultural products for urban high-income consumers. Surface-water systems can range in scale from a single farmer's catchment tank to massive schemes with huge storage dams and diversion canals commanding thousands of hectares of irrigated land.

Surface water may be raised from rivers or streams using traditional methods, such as *shadoufs* for hand-lifting or persian wheels operated by bullocks, or using mechanical diesel or electric-powered pumps. However, these lifting devices are more closely associated with the use of groundwater from shallow hand-dug wells or tubewells sunk to greater depths by drilling. Over the past 50 years there has been a massive increase in tubewell irrigation. For India it is estimated that the area under groundwater irrigation increased by 9.5 per cent per year between 1950 and 1985 (Sangal 1987). In some areas, such as the Indus Basin, *conjunctive use* of pumped groundwater, with gravity-fed canal irrigation, increases the water supply per hectare and allows a greater cropping intensity to be achieved. There may also be complementary relationships between the two methods of water acquisition in that groundwater is recharged from canal seepage, while the tubewell pumping reduces the risks of waterlogging.

The feasibility of the introduction of alternative systems of water supply is strongly influenced by environmental factors, such as the suitability of soils and topography for irrigation, the existence of surface flows, and of a suitable dam site or an accessible aquifer. Once established, the physical infrastructure of the irrigation system determines the pattern of water supply, its spatial and seasonal distribution. These variables may be influenced by the design of the scheme, for instance in terms of decisions regarding how widely and thinly the water is spread, per hectare of land and per irrigator household.

In some wet-rice areas of Asia, at least in the rainy monsoon season, water supply is such that it is virtually unlimited, with zero opportunity cost. In that case irrigable land is the main binding constraint, so efficiency depends upon production per hectare of land and equity depends upon the allocation of land between households. In most less-humid areas, water is a binding constraint on production. It therefore has a positive opportunity cost so productive efficiency and equity depend upon its allocation and use. With inadequate drainage, waterlogging and salination problems may arise, in which case additional water may create a disutility and have a negative value.

In wet-rice systems, the paddies are flooded and the crop is grown in standing water from sowing or transplanting until shortly before harvest. This represents a fairly extravagant use of irrigation water, and various alternative cropping strategies are adopted to optimize its use. Other crops, except perhaps sugar-cane, are less demanding of water, and these may be grown in place of, or in rotation with, rice. Additionally only a part of each holding may be irrigated, income being supplemented from other rainfed crops grown in rotation on the irrigable land or on separate upland areas.

Irrigation systems also differ in the seasonal distribution of water supplies and the extent to which rainfall is supplemented. Whereas groundwater and water stored in large dams may be delivered to growing crops continuously throughout the year, catchment of floodwater or discharges from rivers may be highly seasonal in nature, meaning that the period of irrigation is similarly restricted. Water storage in surface reservoirs or underground aquifers allows rainfall supplementation in dry years or for pre-wetting or extending the season for a particular crop. Although many schemes are designed to allow watering for maximum yield, this cannot be justified where water supplies are limited.

Forms of organization of land, water and people are closely linked with the sources of water and the scale of the operation. It is convenient to distinguish three forms, or scales of operation: (i) the individual household lifting water from a well or riverbank, (ii) small groups or *minor*, community irrigation systems and (iii) bureaucratically operated *major*, large-scale schemes. The first two forms are sometimes grouped together under the heading of 'small-scale' or 'farmer-managed irrigation', which some authorities believe to be more effective than large-scale schemes in furthering efficient, equitable and sustainable development (Underhill 1990). Different issues arise regarding the allocation of water, under these different forms of organization, but as a basis for further discussion we first review the analysis of crop–water relations.

Crop–water relations

The relationship between the total quantity of water applied and the yield of a specific crop is a complicated one, since the applications are spaced out in a series of irrigations, which may vary in frequency and intensity. For at least part of the year, natural precipitation (i.e. rainfall) contributes to the soil moisture content, and is supplemented by irrigation. In addition there are often considerable water losses in the conveyance and application of water, so the amount reaching the crop is less than the amount delivered.

Problems associated with the sequential nature of irrigation-water inputs stem from the fact that crop-yield response depends upon the timing and adequacy of individual water applications, those applied at certain critical growth stages having a greater impact than those at other times. Thus the marginal product per m^3 of water varies over the life of the crop. Yet, because the final yield is the result of the cumulative growth over the crop life, it is difficult to measure the effect on yield of varying water inputs at a particular growth stage.

Crop scientists generally think in terms of crop–water requirements for maximum potential yield. These in turn depend upon the potential evapotranspiration, meaning the water potentially evaporated from the leaves of a crop and the ground surface. Any moisture deficit, which causes the actual evapotranspiration to fall below the potential rate causes a reduction in yield (see Doorenbos & Kassam 1979).

This approach provides a basis for the accurate matching of irrigation applications to water requirements day by day, under sophisticated systems with piped supplies and sprinkler or trickle application, possibly under computer control. Given the high capital cost of such methods, they are unlikely to be of direct relevance to the majority of tropical smallholders. However, the approach also provides a basis for further research on the effects of water stress on different crops at different stages of growth. Recent research has shown that limited stress at some stages can actually enhance yields of many irrigated crops (Turner 1990).

Potential evapotranspiration can be calculated from local meteorological data in most parts of the world. This provides a measure of the total crop-water requirement for maximum yield, in m^3, over the crop life. Alternatively the measure may be averaged over the appropriate number of water applications. Average, expected rainfall is subtracted to arrive at 'net consumptive use'. In practice, the amount of water delivered to a farmer at the 'turnout' or supply point must exceed the net consumptive use because of water losses due to runoff, seepage and deep percolation, and to allow a safety margin given the inevitable irregularities in delivery.

The ratio of the volume of water actually utilized by the crop to the volume of water applied in the field is the 'field irrigation efficiency' and this may range widely from 25 per cent to over 90 per cent, averaging about 60 per cent. In arid zones the application of surplus water is recommended to leach out accumulated salts from the soil profile. Thus the total crop-water requirement, including allowance for application losses, a safety margin and special needs, can be calculated for each crop. This may then be used as a fixed input–output coefficient for the design of irrigation systems, both for the area that can be irrigated and for appropriate crop rotations.

In order to design the irrigable 'command' area of a scheme, the quantity of water available must be compared with the water requirement per hectare. Where there is a continuous flow, from a river or well, the daily discharge is divided by the daily water requirement per hectare to determine the irrigable area. For a storage dam or tank, the command area is determined by the total annual storage capacity. When planning a crop rotation it is convenient to assume that each crop has a specific fixed seasonal pattern of water requirements. A crop rotation can then be designed to make most profitable use of the limited seasonal water supplies. Indeed, if the land–water ratio is assumed to be fixed and the same for all crops, the rotation can be planned to make best use of the irrigated land.

However, the theory that a moisture deficit generally causes a reduction in crop yield accords with the idea of crop-water response to variable water inputs. The economic optimum level of water-use may well differ from that required for maximum yield. This can be illustrated using a hypothetical production function relating wheat yield to the quantity of water reaching the crop, at a critical growth stage, shown in Figure 9.1(a). The response curve, like those shown in Chapter 4, is ultimately subject to diminishing marginal returns, as shown by its decreasing slope, the value of which is plotted in Figure 9.1(b), together with the average product curve.

It is assumed that a certain minimum level of moisture availability (OA) is necessary to allow the crop to survive and produce a yield. Point A, represents the 'permanent wilting point', below which the crop cannot survive. From point A up to point P where OB m^3 of water are available, the yield increases steeply initially but then flattens. The slope ($dY/dX = MPP$) first increases but then diminishes through P and M. At point 'P' the average product per m^3 of water is maximized. From this point on it declines through point M (OC m^3 of water) and beyond. The maximum yield point M represents 'field capacity' which is the moisture status of a free-draining soil when it is holding all the water it can against the force of gravity. Further increases in water availability have an adverse effect on yield, and, at point F where OD m^3 are available, in the absence of adequate drainage, additional water can cause crop damage through flooding and waterlogging. The marginal product is negative for levels above OC m^3.

This hypothetical model serves to illustrate the argument that if irrigation is economically justified then sufficient water should be applied to raise the soil–moisture balance above the permanent wilting-point. Thus, if there is not enough water to irrigate the whole farm area up to this level, it is better to reduce the area irrigated, rather than the water applied per hectare of land. This practice of concentrating scarce water on part of the farm may be observed in the North Indian and Pakistan Punjab where canal water supplies are inadequate to irrigate the whole command area fully. The basis for this argument is the fact that at low levels of water application the average product per m^3 is rising. Productivity of both land (per ha) and water (per m^3) is increased by raising the level of water application to point *P* in Figure 9.1. Only if the opportunity cost of water was extremely high in relation to the price of wheat would it be worth operating to the left of point *P*, in which case it would probably be uneconomic to irrigate anyway.

Figure 9.1 also illustrates the argument that irrigating for maximum yield is unlikely to be optimal. Because the marginal product of water is low between *P* and *M*, a reduction in water use from *OC* to *OB* m^3, reduces yield by a much smaller proportion from *OZ* to *OY*. Wherever water is scarce,

Figure 9.1   The crop–water response relationship

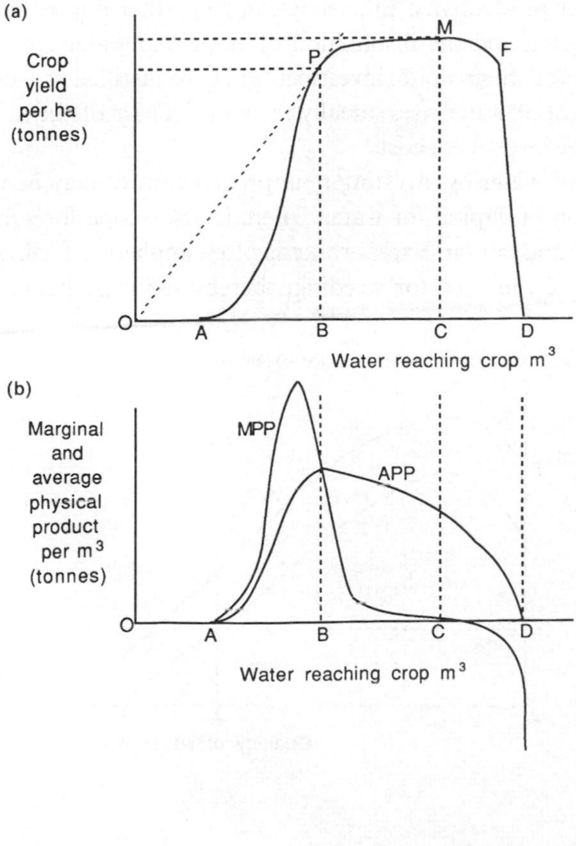

and has a positive opportunity cost, the economic optimum level of water use is likely to be nearer *P* than *M*.

Finally this Figure serves to emphasize the dangers of excessive water-use and the need for effective drainage as a complement to irrigation. Improved drainage can also help to reduce salinity which is a serious problem in many irrigated areas.

The farmer's demand curve for water is derived from the value of the marginal product obtained from irrigation. However, it differs from the marginal product curve of Figure 9.1b which applies to a single water application on a particular crop. When we consider the demand for water for the whole farm other influences come into play, generally supporting the assumption of diminishing marginal returns and a downward sloping demand curve, as shown in Figure 9.2.

First there may be scope for increasing field irrigation efficiency. Given that runoff and seepage are likely to increase more than proportionately with increased water usage per hectare, water-use efficiency, and with it the overall marginal product per unit of water, is likely to decline. Tighter management and control can lead to reduced water inputs per hectare and increased water productivity. Efficiency can be further improved by levelling and terracing and the installation of improved water-control structures. The costs of these capital investments may be justified in order to save water, if the cost of water rises. Ideally the beneficiaries of the saved water should meet the investment cost.

The saving of water by investing in improved control may be viewed as the substitution of capital for water. There is also scope for substitution between water and labour. Excess water is often applied to facilitate planting or to reduce the need for weeding, thereby reducing labour require-

Figure 9.2   The farmer's demand for irrigation water

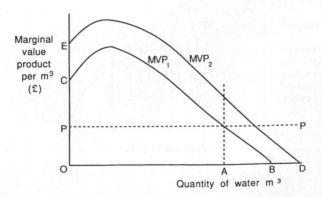

Quantity of water m³

ments. If water becomes scarce and expensive, such practices may be abandoned, possibly causing an increase in labour inputs but improving water-use efficiency.

The choice of crops may also affect the demand for water. Crops with a shorter than average growing season, use less water than other crops and should therefore yield a higher margin product per unit of water, even though the yield per hectare may be lower than average. However, the introduction of a new, high-yielding crop variety represents a change to new technology with a shift in the associated demand curve for water; from MVP_1 to MVP_2 in Figure 9.2. This raises the value of the marginal product for any given level of water-use and is therefore likely to have an impact on the demand for irrigation water. In addition, there will certainly be a positive impact on the demand for other complementary inputs such as fertilizer.

Water allocation

Given that irrigation water is productive and scarce, its availability is often an effective constraint on production. Hence individual farmers and communities of farmers compete for the available supplies. The allocation of available supplies between individuals and communities is an important issue affecting both efficiency of production and equity of social justice. Unfortunately, free market forces cannot be relied upon to perform the function of allocating available supplies in an efficient and equitable manner. Although water (e.g. tubewell water) is bought and sold in some situations, it is usually only a small proportion of the total quantity used in the region, while the problems of delivery restrict the market for an individual supplier to a limited number of neighbouring farms. Thus even where a market exists it is likely to be restricted and highly imperfect. More generally it is argued that *transaction costs* are high and water allocation is subject to *market failure*.

Reasons for the absence of markets include the physical characteristics of water, particularly in that as a liquid it is transported and delivered as a flow rather than as a fixed quantity or stock. The flow must be controlled in channels or pipes and allowance must be made for conveyance losses. Measuring and monitoring the flow is not easy or cheap and this is an obstacle to the establishment of water rights (as private property or on a usufructuary basis). Furthermore, water falling as rain or drawn from rivers, streams and aquifers appears as a free gift of nature. Thus there may be strong social and cultural, even religious, objections to the idea of paying for water.

Where markets fail some alternative institutional means must be found for allocating or rationing the limited supplies efficiently and equitably. The alternative institutional arrangements can be classified as follows (adapted from Chambers 1980):

Individual acquisition either directly from a natural source such as a private dam or well, or through contractual agreement with a supplier in exchange for goods or services. The acquisition of water is often linked with tenure of the land on which it is used. Thus 'riparian rights' allow a land holder to draw water from a source adjoining the land or an aquifer beneath that land. Frequently contracts for acquiring water are embodied in agreements for the tenancy of irrigated land.

Community allocation, whereby water from a communal source, such as a village tank, is shared among a community of users.

Bureaucratic allocation, often found on large-scale canal irrigation schemes, in which the administrators or managers responsible for the allocation of water are separate and distinct from the users. Each user is allocated an agreed quantity of water according to either a fixed or a flexible schedule. In the majority of cases the administrators are paid from a central government budget. In other cases their salaries are recovered from the fees paid by water users.

These alternative approaches are not mutually exclusive. For instance under bureaucratic management water may be supplied on contract to individual farmers or allocated to individual farmers by communal water-users' groups. However, the list illustrates the range of possible alternative situations from one where the supply of water is variable and the rate of use is determined by price, to one where the supply is fixed and there is an implicit opportunity cost. The same allocation of water may be obtained using either of these institutional arrangements.

The principles involved may be illustrated by considering the allocation of a fixed quantity (or flow) of water between two users, as illustrated in Figure 9.3. The horizontal axis OT measures the total quantity of water available. User A's demand curve reflects the value of the marginal product (MVP_a) of irrigation water, like that shown in Figure 9.2. User B's access to water is measured from right to left, with zero use at point T. Thus his demand curve, assumed identical with A's, is reversed (MVP_b). The optimal allocation is found where the two curves intersect at H, with equal shares to both users.

If user A takes more than his fair share of water (e.g. he takes $OF\,\mathrm{m}^3$) as might be possible for a farmer near the head end of a watercourse, then user

B will receive less. The extra output produced by user A (*EFGH*) is considerably less than the loss of output of user B (*EFJH*). Overall there is a loss of production equal to the shaded triangle (*GHJ*). Thus inefficiency results from unequal allocation. However, this follows from the assumption that the two users are equally efficient in their use of water; they both operate on the same response curve. If, on the other hand, the marginal product of water was higher for user A, at any given level of water-use, as shown in Figure 9.4, for instance because user A controls more land, or grows higher-yielding crops, then total production would be maximized by allocating more water to user A as shown. Land and water are complementary inputs, so there may be a conflict between the efficiency and equity of water allocation, when inequalities of access to other resources and technologies exist.

The main purpose of this analysis is to show that the same efficient

Figure 9.3   The allocation of water between two equal users

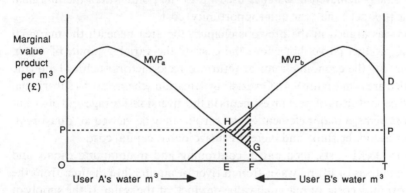

Figure 9.4   The allocation of water between two unequal users

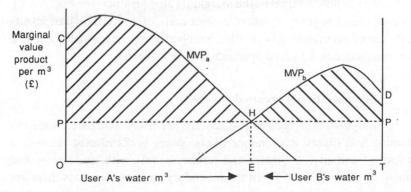

allocation of available water could be achieved by either,

- bureaucratic regulation of the quantities delivered to each user,
- communal agreement as to how water should be shared, by members of a water users group, or
- sale of water at a price equal to the opportunity cost (OP in Figures 9.3 and 9.4).

The last alternative is not easily achieved given the problems of monitoring and control mentioned earlier. Where water charges are imposed they are generally set at a rate per irrigated hectare, rather than in relation to the volume of water used. The charges are well below the opportunity cost. These alternatives are discussed in more detail below.

Similar considerations apply to the allocation of water between plots on a single holding. The optimal allocation of water is obtained when the marginal return per unit of water is the same for all activities. The same outcome is achieved if water is used up to the point where the marginal value product equals the unit (opportunity) cost.

As was argued in the previous chapter, the area beneath the marginal value product curve, but above the cost of the variable input, of water, represents the economic rent, or return to fixed factors such as land (the shaded areas in Figure 9.4). On existing irrigation schemes, with substantial sunk capital costs of past investments in the diversion, storage and distribution systems, a major element of the surplus may be viewed as 'quasi-rent' or return on the sunk, and therefore unavoidable, capital cost.

The O&M costs, incurred in controlling and maintaining canals and watercourses or lifting water from a river or aquifer, are distinct from the opportunity costs, or marginal value product, of the water. If the supply of water could be varied and O&M or pumping were the only costs incurred in supplying the water, then optimum water use would occur where the marginal cost of supply is equal to the marginal value product (see Figure 9.6). However, there are generally other implicit costs, of a return on past investments and of external effects on other members of society, which should be taken into account if a social optimum is to be achieved.

Bureaucratically operated systems

Large-scale irrigation systems are generally associated with the damming and diversion of major rivers. Water is distributed through a network of primary, secondary and tertiary canals, with sluice gates and weirs to control the flow. From the secondary or tertiary canals there are controlled outlets into field distribution channels or watercourses. Operation and administration of the system, at least down to tertiary canal level, is in the hands of a department of government or a parastatal agency.

In such cases there is a separation of responsibilities between the water users and the water authorities. The user's role is usually restricted to activities 'below the outlet', while in general the officials of the irrigation agency are not farmers and may have little understanding of irrigated agriculture and its economic imperatives. Thus agency–farmer interactions are important for the efficient operation of an irrigation scheme. There are persuasive arguments in support of greater farmer participation in scheme management (Uphoff 1986). The main managerial tasks relate to:

(i) the allocation and distribution of water to the users,
(ii) the maintenance and upkeep of the physical structure; canals, control structures and drainage systems,
(iii) conflict management and resolving disputes between users.

A set of interrelated operational problems occur on many large-scale schemes and result in a failure of irrigation investments to produce their intended benefits. Some of these are the result of faulty design and construction of distribution and control structures, but others are caused by weaknesses in management, including the following:

- insufficient resource provision for recurrent operational and maintenance activities,
- deterioration of physical structures, silting of canals and obstruction by weeds, damage to control structures, waterlogging and soil salination,
- unreliable water supplies, which lead farmers to adopt unorthodox coping mechanisms, or even to steal extra supplies,
- unequal and inefficient water allocation as farmers at the head end of a canal or water-course have readier access to scarce water, and can acquire more, than those at the tail end (see Figure 9.3),
- opportunities arise for irrigation officials to impose unofficial charges for water, on the basis of their control of water deliveries. This is known as 'rent seeking', since such charges are extracted from the 'rent' or surplus over any official charges (see Figure 9.4).

Three broad approaches are recommended for overcoming these problems and improving scheme management, namely:

- technical improvements such as refurbishing control structures and lining canals with concrete or bricks,
- introduction of economic incentives, through a system of water charges,
- organizational modifications and in particular greater farmer participation.

The lining of canals has been widely adopted in recent years, but its value is still under debate. Arguments in favour of lining are:

(i) a substantial reduction in seepage, thus saving water for distribution elsewhere and reducing waterlogging along the canal,
(ii) faster transport of water, which both reduces evaporation in transit and brings forward the timing of its application with consequent improvements in efficiency and equity between users,
(iii) better control of water supplies, which may facilitate rotational watering of rice, saving of water and reduction of waterlogging,
(iv) possible reduction of the need for weeding and desilting, although where maintenance *is* needed it is generally more costly for lined canals.

Arguments against lining are:

(i) it is an expensive operation and the costs are increased substantially if it is necessary to close down the system,
(ii) unless carefully maintained, lining can quickly deteriorate, so that, within as few as five years, seepage rates may return to the levels which obtained before lining, while the costs of repair exceed those of earth-lined canals.

The rate of return on investment in lining a canal further depends upon the number of days per year over which the canal is used, as this determines the volume of water transported, the porosity of the subsoil, the value of the crops grown on the saved water and whether there is conjunctive use of tubewell water. If there is, then seepage water is not lost since it is recovered by pumping from the aquifer (Upton & Chancellor-Weale 1988).

The institution, or increase, of water-user fees is widely recommended as a means of recovering the costs of operation and maintenance and maybe the initial capital investment, whilst also giving incentives to the farmers to economize in their use of water (Small & Carruthers 1991). Furthermore farmers who do not pay user fees are effectively subsidized from public funds. Given that the incomes from irrigated agriculture generally exceed those from rainfed cultivation, a case can be made on equity grounds for recovering costs from the irrigators through some form of taxation. To ensure that the fees are used to improve the operation and management of the scheme they should be collected by a financially autonomous irrigation agency. Dues that are collected by central government may well be diverted to other sectors of the economy. Costs of collection and risks of default are likely to be reduced if farmers are allowed to participate more in the management of the scheme.

Instances are often quoted where farmers cannot afford to pay water-user fees, either because the project was the subject of grant aid and set up only to ensure subsistence, or because deterioration of the distribution system has caused a reduction in water supplies to tail enders below the level needed to produce an adequate income. However, if the farmers cannot afford to pay for the variable costs of operation and management, the sustainability of the system must be in doubt. Rehabilitation is needed to ensure survival of the scheme and the farmers.

The argument that the charging of fees provides an incentive for more efficient water-use is weak. As was shown in the previous section, provided that scarce water supplies are effectively rationed between users, and discipline is adequate to ensure that no one exceeds his or her ration, then there is no need to impose charges in order to make the user aware of the opportunity cost. None the less this may be the most appropriate way to meet essential maintenance costs. Other issues of farmer participation and the establishment of water-user groups are conveniently dealt with in the next section.

Communally operated systems

Communally operated systems are found where the water source exceeds the needs of one household and where community co-operation is well established. Such systems are operated and maintained by the community of users, which generally differs from the residential community or village. Many irrigation societies are traditional indigenous institutions like the Balinese *subak*, the village tank committees of India and Sri Lanka, the Philippine *zangjeras*, and water-user groups of West Africa and Madagascar. Other schemes have been established with outside assistance from NGOs or other agencies. In some cases (e.g. SAED, Senegal), they may be encouraged by government help through extension services. In other cases government involvement is more comprehensive; a number of small groups become part of an administered policy with a large capital commitment (e.g. Zimbabwe, Kenya). However, this may result in excessive overhead costs, which render the scheme uneconomic (see Tiffen 1990). In India and Bangladesh, group ownership of wells is part of official policy to reduce rural poverty.

A communally operated system does not operate in isolation. It may be part of a larger irrigation system, and receive water from an outside agency. State intervention may be needed on occasion for repairing canals or other structures or settling disputes regarding water rights. None the less the main managerial activities of water allocation, maintenance of physical structures and resolving conflicts between members are the responsibility of the community.

The advantages of this kind of communal activity were discussed in Chapter 2. Many communal irrigation systems have operated effectively for decades and longer. It is therefore argued that they offer important insights into the solution of organizational problems, and may indeed be the most appropriate form of management for the terminal units of large-scale schemes. It is a direct means of ensuring farmer participation in scheme management.

Two factors, which influence the performance of communal systems are, first, the size of the operational units and, second, accountable leadership (Coward, 1980). As suggested in Chapter 2, communal activity is more likely to succeed in small groups, since transaction costs are lower, it is easier to negotiate agreements, and altruistic concern for other group members is more likely. Many communal irrigation schemes are sub-divided into smaller sub-units of from 10–70 ha, and a similar number of members. Accountable leadership is achieved, in such small units, where the leader is selected by the members, and is recompensed from their farm incomes.

Groundwater management

The rapid increase in the exploitation of groundwater for irrigation has already been emphasized. It is estimated that, in countries such as India, there is a huge potential for further expansion (Chambers, Saxena & Shah 1989). Groundwater, especially at shallow depths, is generally the most easily controlled, readily established and economical source of irrigation water.

Investment in a single well (or tubewell) is within the means of a single farmer or small group of farmers, so most wells are under private ownership. Water storage and conveyance costs are at a minimum as are water losses through evaporation and runoff. Whereas surface water supplies vary from season to season and from year to year, water stored in an aquifer is continuously available, provided that the rate of withdrawal does not exceed the rate of recharge. The sinking of a well generally takes less time than the building of a dam, and does not require the flooding of land areas that might have been used for other purposes.

Given the continuous availability and easier control of groundwater, irrigation from this source is considerably (2 to 3 times) more productive than surface-water irrigation (Dhawan 1982; Lowdermilk *et al.* 1978). In fact the greatest benefits are obtained under conjunctive use of surface and groundwater, as in both southern and northern India and Pakistan. Drainage is improved and waterlogging avoided by the pumping of groundwater, while the risks of increasing soil salinity from the use of groundwater are reduced by flushing the soil with surface water. In addition there is some interseasonal complementarity with greater reliance on surface water in the rainy seasons and on groundwater in the dry seasons (see Figure 9.5).

Alternative technologies for tapping groundwater aquifers range from traditional hand-dug wells, and *quanats* (horizontal wells) through drilled or jetted tubewells of different depths and degrees of sophistication. Some shallow tubewells have locally produced bamboo linings and screens, which allow the ingress of water. Deep tubewells generally have metal or fibreglass

Figure 9.5   Integration of surface and groundwater supplies

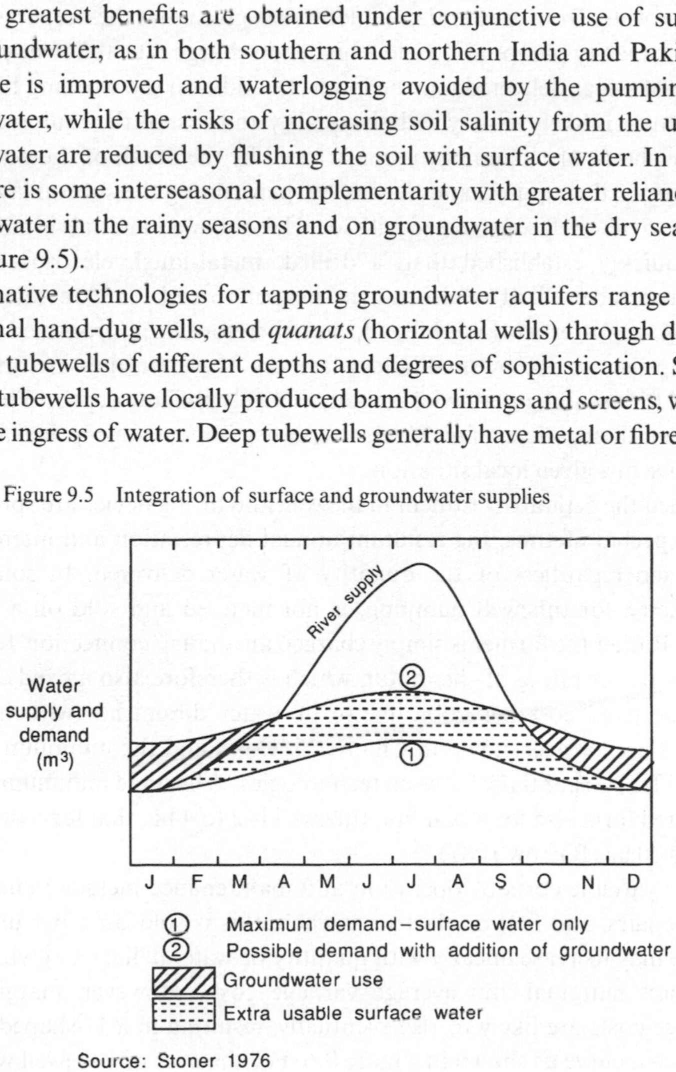

Source: Stoner 1976

screens and linings. Similarly lifting devices range from traditional hand- or animal-driven equipment used with open hand-dug wells, through improved manual, wind, solar or water-driven pumps used with some shallow tubewells, to the now widespread use of electric motors or diesel engines. Submersible electric motors are used to drive deep-well turbine pumps.

In general the capital costs of sinking the well and installing the lifting device increase across the range from hand-dug wells to deep tubewells. Operating costs also increase with the size and capacity of the pump needed to raise water from greater depths. However, given that the deeper wells and larger capacity pumps also yield a higher discharge rate, the costs per cubic metre of water delivered may be lower. In addition the working life of the equipment is likely to vary with the quality and cost of the equipment.

The choice of technology is constrained by the depth of the water-table (surface of the aquifer) and the ease of penetrating the subsoil layers. The bamboo tubewell constructed with local labour and materials is more easily and quickly established than a drilled, metal-lined, electric or diesel-powered tubewell. It is also much cheaper to sink and operate, despite having a shorter working life, and has therefore been promoted as more appropriate for use by smallholder farmers. However, they are only really suited for use in light alluvial soils at relatively shallow depths. Thus many different factors determine which alternative is most appropriate and cost-effective in a given local situation.

When the capital investment in the well and lifting device are spread over the expected lifetime, the resultant annual depreciation and interest costs are fixed regardless of the quantity of water delivered. In some areas electricity, for tubewell pumping, is not metered and sold on a per unit basis. Rather the farmer is simply charged an annual 'connection' fee, based on the power rating of the motor, which is therefore also a fixed cost. The average fixed cost per cubic metre of water diminishes with increased annual use, as was shown in Chapter 5. Costs and the minimum efficient size differ substantially between technologies. Whilst the minimum efficient irrigated farm size for a bamboo tubewell is 2 to 4 ha, that for a deep tube-well is 20 ha (Barrow 1987).

The variable costs of operation and maintenance include maintenance and repairs, and fuel or electricity where this is sold on a per unit basis. These may increase linearly with quantity of water delivered, giving rise to constant marginal and average variable costs. However, marginal and average costs are likely to rise eventually, resulting in a U-shaped average total cost curve as shown in Figure 9.6. For the user of tubewell water, the economic optimum rate of water supply is found where the marginal cost is equal to the marginal value product of irrigation water as shown, at quantity *OA*.

The demand (marginal value product) curve for water on a single smallholding may lie below the minimum efficient size of a deep tubewell, and possibly even of a shallow bamboo tubewell. Such a limited demand curve is illustrated by the line MVP_2 in Figure 9.6. Investment in the tubewell cannot be justified if there is insufficient demand for water; there being economies of scale in the exploitation of groundwater. To overcome these limitations state governments have established and operated public tubewells, non-government organizations have promoted lift irrigation groups while other groups have formed spontaneously. However, public tubewells generally have a record of poor performance, while group activity is difficult to start and sustain. In India such groups only account for between 2 and 4 per cent of the total area under groundwater (lift) irrigation (Chambers, Saxena & Shah 1989, Chapter 4).

It is suggested that far greater scope exists for spreading the benefits of lift irrigation through the development of water markets. Small and marginal farmers may then rely on selling water to make their tubewell systems viable, while others who cannot afford to invest in a well of their own can irrigate their land using purchased water. Despite the difficulties of metering water for sale, mentioned earlier, the marketing of groundwater is widespread in India and Bangladesh (Chambers, Saxena & Shah 1989, Chapter 5). Methods of payment include flat charges per hectare, a charge per hour of pumping or a share of the crop being irrigated. In some cases the crop is shared three ways between the landlord, the water supplier and the cultivator.

Figure 9.6 The economic optimum use of groundwater

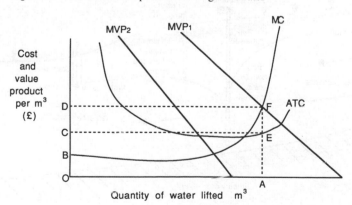

Where an owner of a deep tubewell is the sole water supplier in a particular locality, the resulting monopoly power may be used to restrict supplies and force up the price of water. Policies to promote the sinking of more wells in the area should result in increased competition between sellers and a lowering of prices. For this reason it has been argued that, at least in water surplus areas, all restrictions on the sinking of wells should be removed. The aquifer is then effectively under 'open access'.

However, the natural recharge rate of an aquifer is limited. If the rate of water consumption exceeds the natural recharge rate, reserves are depleted and the water-table falls. Ultimately this may cause permanent damage to the aquifer, soil subsidence or, in coastal regions, saline water intrusion. In any case the lowering of the water-table may cause shallow wells to run dry, requiring the sinking of deeper wells, which may only be afforded by the wealthier so increasing income disparities, and generally increasing the costs of pumping for current and future generations (see Figure 9.7).

Once the recharge rate is exceeded, each cubic metre of water raised from the aquifer carries an associated external cost of depletion of the water reserves. Its effect on the economic optimum rate of water use is illustrated in Figure 9.8. The 'private' marginal cost to the tubewell owner is depicted by the curve labelled MPC. However the 'social' marginal cost, shown by MSC includes the external costs of aquifer depletion. If the tubewell owner faces no controls on the rate of water extraction the 'private' optimum is found when quantity OA is used. However, this results in excessive use, or mining, of the groundwater. The 'social' optimum is at OB, and there is an overall loss of welfare to society represented by the shaded triangle.

Figure 9.7   Groundwater lifting

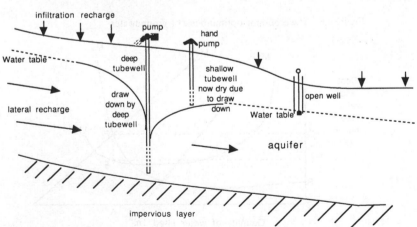

Depletion of the aquifer and a falling water-table are more likely to be caused by sinking too many tubewells, rather than by pumping too much water from each. Thus it is frequently argued that government controls on the spacing of new tubewells are needed in order to avoid this problem. Unfortunately such controls limit competition in the supply of water, may give an unfair economic advantage (monopoly power) to those who sink the first tubewells and provide government agencies with opportunities for 'rent seeking'. Furthermore the monitoring of water-table levels, assessment of the rate of depletion, and calculation of the maximum sustainable density of wells is very difficult. None the less, in water-scarce areas some form of control is desirable.

Irrigator household decision-making

Three basic types of decisions, affecting the efficiency of water-use, are made by the irrigator household. These are:

- *cropping decisions* regarding the number, type and timing of crops grown,
- *water conservation decisions*, which affect the field irrigation efficiency,
- *water acquisition decisions* regarding the amounts and timing of deliveries.

The degree of autonomy exercised by water users varies between schemes, from very little in the Sudan Gezira where water deliveries and cropping patterns are centrally decided, to a great deal under the

Figure 9.8 The social cost of using groundwater

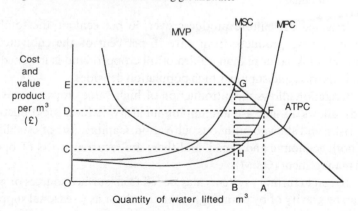

Warabandi systems of Northern India where the farmer can choose where to concentrate the water supplied, whether (if he can afford it) to supplement canal water with wells and what sort of crops to grow. Tubewell owner irrigators have the greatest freedom to make independent decisions, and the greater productivity of tubewell irrigation is attributed to this cause.

Where the farmer is free to decide on the acquisition of water, the choice should be based on equating the marginal value product of water in all uses to the price of water or its opportunity cost, as already discussed. Cropping decisions may be based on the analysis of Chapters 3, 4 and 5, with water treated as an additional constraint or set of seasonal constraints, or alternatively treated as an additional set of variable inputs in the production function. Given the time-dependency of all these decisions, they are complicated and difficult. Where water supplies are unreliable, risk considerations are also involved. Careful analysis and experience are important for effective decision-making in this area.

Water conservation and increased field irrigation efficiency may be achieved by:

- improving the field channels (in S. India there is an On Farm Development Programme in which farmers are assisted to line their channels);
- improving water distribution within the fields from, say, border to ridge-and-furrow irrigation.

Clearly where water is a scarce resource, outside the very humid tropics, any measure which conserves water at a cost below the value of the water saved is worth adopting.

Summary

1 Irrigated agriculture produces over 36 per cent of the total world output of crop products, from only 16 per cent of the cultivated land. However, in Asia more than a third of all cropped land is irrigated, much under wet-rice, and supports high population densities.

2 Irrigation allows the introduction of high-value crops, increases crop yields, allows an increase in cropping intensity, reduces yield fluctuations and risks, and allows continuous cultivation. Capital costs of establishment are both economic and social, and there are recurrent costs of operation and management (O&M).

3 Irrigated farming systems may be fed from surface sources or groundwater, by gravity or by pumping, continuously or as a seasonal supplement

to rainfall, with or without water storage, on a large or small scale, and individually, communally or under bureaucratic organization.

4 Although several water applications are spaced out over the growing season, there is a functional relationship between the total quantity of water applied and the crop yield, reflecting both increasing and diminishing marginal returns. The optimal rate of water use is beyond the point of maximum yield per m^3 of water but below the point of maximum yield per hectare. Field efficiency is also improved by reduction of distribution losses.

5 Water should be allocated between competing users and competing crops so that the marginal product per m^3 is the same in all cases. This will ensure that the overall productivity of this scarce resource is maximized. Given that effective water markets rarely exist, allocation is usually by direct acquisition, or communal or bureaucratic decisions.

6 Large-scale schemes are usually subject to bureaucratic management for the allocation and distribution of water to the users, the maintenance and upkeep of the physical structures and resolving disputes between users. Problems often result from inadequacy of resources for O&M.

7 Canal lining may improve distributional efficiency but has a high capital cost and may deteriorate rapidly.

8 The charging of water-user fees is justified economically but may be difficult to implement.

9 Communally operated systems may be traditional institutions, or established by governments or NGOs. Success depends upon limited scale and effective leadership. Terminal units of large-scale schemes may be best managed communally.

10 Tubewell water, especially at shallow depths is generally the most easily controlled, readily established and economical source of irrigation water. The minimum efficient irrigated farm size for a bamboo tubewell is 2 to 4 ha, that for a deep tubewell is 20 ha. The area watered may be expanded by state or group ownership of wells and development of water markets. Controls are needed to avoid depletion of the aquifer.

11 Where the farmer is free to decide on the acquisition of water, the choice should be based on equating the marginal value product of water, in all uses, to the price of water or its opportunity cost. Increased field irrigation efficiency may be achieved by improving the field channels and improving water distribution within the fields from, say, border to ridge-and-furrow irrigation.

References

Alexandratos, N. (1988). *World Agriculture Toward 2000*, Rome, FAO and London, Belhaven Press, pp. 132–3

Barrow, C. (1987). *Water Resources and Agricultural Development in the Tropics*, Harlow, Essex, Longman

Carruthers, I. & C. Clark (1981). *The Economics of Irrigation*, Liverpool University Press

Chambers, R. (1980). 'Basic concepts in the organization of irrigation', in E. W. Coward (ed.), *Irrigation and Agricultural Development in Asia: Perspectives from the Social Sciences*, Ithaca and London, Cornell University Press

Chambers, R., N. C. Saxena & T. Shah (1989). *To the Hands of the Poor*, London, Intermediate Technology Publications

Coward, E. W. (ed.) (1980). *Irrigation and Agricultural Development in Asia: Perspective from the Social Sciences*, Ithaca and London, Cornell University Press

Dhawan, B. D. (1982). *Development of Tubewell Irrigation in India*, New Delhi, Agricole Publishing Academy

Doorenbos, J. & A. H. Kassam (1979). Yield response to water, *F.A.O. Irrigation and Drainage Paper* No. 33, Rome, FAO

Ellis, F. (1992). *Agricultural Policies in Developing Countries*. Cambridge University Press, Chapter 11

Levine, G. and E. W. Coward, Jr. (1989). *Equity considerations in the modernisation of irrigation systems*, ODI/IIMI Irrigation Management Network Paper 89/2b

Lowdermilk, M. K., A. C. Early & D. M. Freeman (1978). *Farm Irrigation Constraints and Farmer's Responses: Comprehensive Field Survey in Pakistan*, Water Management Research Project Technical Report 48, Fort Collins, Colorado State University

Malhotra, S. P. (1982). *Warabandi System and its Infrastructure*, Central Board of Irrigation and Power, Publication No. 157

Ruthenberg, H. (1980). *Farming Systems in the Tropics*, 3rd edn, Oxford, Clarendon Press, Chapter 7

Sangal, S. P. (1987). Minor irrigation and groundwater resource, paper for *Proceedings of the First National Water Convention*, Vol II. Sponsored by Ministry of Water Resources, Government of India, New Delhi, October 1987

Small, L. E. & Carruthers, I. (1991). *Farmer-financed Irrigation: the Economics of Reform*, Cambridge University Press

Stoner, R. F. (1976). Conjunctive use of surface and groundwater supplies. Paper to ODI Workshop on *Choices in Irrigation Management*, University of Kent, September 1976

Tiffen, M. (1990). Socio-economic parameters in designing small irrigation schemes for small-scale farmers. *Nyanyadzi Case Study; Report IV. Summary and conclusions on water distribution and farm incomes on the Nyanyadzi Irrigation Scheme, Zimbabwe*. Report OD 117. Wallingford, Hydraulics Research

Turner, N. C. (1990). 'The benefits of water deficits', in Sinha, S. K., P. V. Sane, S. C.

Bhargava & P. K. Agrawal (eds.), *Proceedings of the International Congress of Plant Physiology, New Delhi, India. 15–20 February, 1988*, vol. 2

Underhill, H. (1990). *Small Scale Irrigation in Africa in the Context of Rural Development*, Bedford, Cranfield Press

Uphoff, N. (1986). *Improving International Irrigation Management with Farmer Participation: getting the Process Right*, Studies in Water Policy and Management, No. 11, Boulder and London, Westview Press

Upton, M. (1994). 'Spreading the benefits of irrigation', *ICID Bulletin*, **43**(1), 1–12

Upton, M. & F. Chancellor-Weale (1988). *A Method for Evaluating the Economics of Canal and Watercourse Lining: the Case of the Indian Punjab*. Report OD104, Wallingford, Hydraulics Research and Amritsar, Irrigation and Power Research Institute

Wade, R. (1984). 'Managing a drought with canal irrigation: a South Indian case, *Journal of Agricultural Administration*, **17**(4)

Part III

Field investigations

10

Farming systems research

The approach

Farming systems research (FSR) is aimed at identifying options for improving the well-being of rural households in specific local environments. Much of this research has been conducted by staff of the International Agricultural Research Institutes, mentioned in Chapter 2, with the prime objective of developing new, improved farm-level technology. However, the introduction of new technology is not the only way of improving the well-being of rural households. Other possibilities include the provision of rural social infrastructure such as roads, market-places, health and education facilities, water and electricity supplies and opportunities for off-farm employment. Assured supplies of farm inputs and markets for farm produce and improved price incentives also benefit farm families. In principle, farming systems research may be used to identify options for improvement in all these areas.

There are four main characteristics of farming systems research. First and foremost it is focussed on the farm household. Thus it is based on a recognition that rural change and development ultimately depend on rural people whose existing practices are well adapted to environmental constraints and household objectives. Attempts to develop and impose innovations or policies from the top down, without previous reference to those who will be affected, rarely succeed. Those of us, research scientists or development planners, who are concerned to promote rural development must work with farmers and try to understand their aims, their methods and their problems if our outside assistance is to be acceptable and useful to them. Furthermore, proposed innovations should be subjected to on-farm testing to identify practical management problems or constraints on their adoption before introducing them more widely.

The second characteristic follows from the first: namely that FSR is locale specific. Since its central concern is with farm households and since there are large differences between localities in the resource base and the farming systems practised, each FSR programme relates to a limited number of similar farms in a given locality.

The third main characteristic is that FSR is holistic, which means that it is concerned with the whole system and its interdependencies rather than with individual elements. In this respect it may be contrasted with commodity programmes which are aimed at increasing output of a single crop or livestock product. This single commodity approach fails to consider the repercussions a new product or process will have on the rest of the farm household system. To the commodity specialist, 'every isolated improvement is another brick in the building of a more efficient agriculture. In reality, however, every improved technique affects the whole structure of the farm. Its introduction does not represent the laying of a brick on top of a building, but the removal of one part way down and replacing it by a better one. This replacement can be as disturbing to a farm as to a building' (Jolly 1957). Although commodity programmes may be more effective in generating new technology they should always be complemented by FSR.

However, this argument begs the question of where the boundaries of the whole system lie. Much FSR has concentrated exclusively on the farm or even on a sub-system as in the case of Cropping Systems Research. Given that the central concern is with the well-being of the rural household, off-farm activities should be included in the system being studied. Links with rural services such as credit, input delivery, product markets and agricultural extension are also important and should form part of the study. Pastoral Systems Research, which is also included under the broad heading of this chapter, incorporates (i) rangeland ecology, (ii) livestock husbandry and (iii) the study of pastoral society and the household economy. Here again external trade is likely to have an impact on family welfare and should be included in any study of pastoral systems (see Upton 1986).

The fourth main characteristic is that FSR is multidisciplinary. In particular it integrates the perceptions of both the technical and the social sciences to analyse existing systems and to identify options for improvement. Technical sciences are needed to explain the physical relationships between inputs and outputs and to develop new products and new methods. The social sciences can contribute to understanding how the society is organized, how resource allocation decisions are made, how the disparate parts of the system are integrated and which new products and new methods are likely to be accepted. Within these two broad areas there are many scientific disciplines that could contribute as suggested in the opening chapter. One essential discipline, however, is agricultural production economics or farm management.

Thus FSR usually involves multidisciplinary teams of researchers. The team size, and hence the number of separate disciplines represented, is limited by cost considerations, frequently to one crop scientist and one production economist or farm management specialist. No matter how large or small the team, FSR requires a flexible open-minded outlook by team members. Each one must be able and willing to think in disciplines outside his own and to learn from his colleagues as well as from farmers and their families. The, perhaps unattainable, ideal farming systems researcher would be competent in more than one discipline encompassing both technical and socio-economic knowledge.

Research procedures: description and diagnosis

There are four main stages involved in an FSR programme. These are:

(i) description and diagnosis,
(ii) design of improved systems,
(iii) testing and evaluation of improved systems, and
(iv) implementation and extension of promising alternatives.

Although most farming systems researchers agree with the general philosophy outlined above and that these are the four main stages, their views differ considerably with regard to detailed procedure and indeed the general scale and timing of these stages. While Collinson, working in East Africa, suggests that an FSR study can be completed within three months, 'including a two-week input from the relevant technical scientists', others such as Norman who worked in Northern Nigeria operated on a time span of several years (see Collinson 1979, Norman 1980). In fact, the general philosophy and the four main stages may be executed at different levels. On the one hand, the entire research programme of an institute may be planned for several years ahead along these lines. On the other hand, the procedures may be used for a series of relatively short studies in different localities within a broad agro-ecological zone. Figure 10.1 illustrates how such a series of studies might be linked together and with the experimental station activity. The four main stages will now be discussed in more detail.

The first step in description and diagnosis is to identify the target population of farmers the research is aimed at. This involves grouping farmers with similar, though obviously not identical, farming systems into zones or 'recommendation domains'. The target population for a particular FSR study consists of all farm families within the selected recommendation domain. A considerable amount of local information is needed and some preliminary investigational work may be involved before recommendation domains can be identified. There is therefore an overlap with the next step which is the assembly of background information. This includes agro-ecological data such as monthly rainfall, topography and soil types which determine the crops that can be grown and may be critical constraints on the system. It also includes measures of population density and, where available, production and yields of major crops and livestock. Information on local social structures and institutions, markets and prices for inputs and outputs and government policies is also relevant as all these factors may influence or constrain what is produced. Most of this background information can be obtained from secondary sources, such as published reports, unpublished records and experienced local government officers or development agents.

More detailed description of farming systems and diagnosis of limiting constraints requires field investigations of the target population. There are

Figure 10.1   The farming systems research cycle

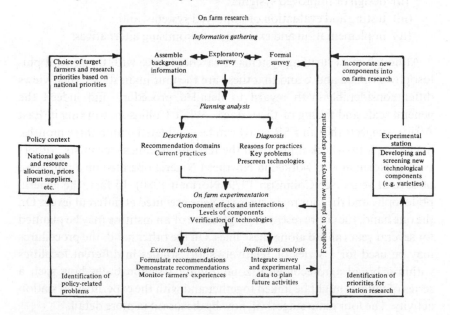

wide differences of opinion as to the appropriate investigational methods to use. Some authorities recommend 'rapid rural appraisal' based on a tour of the zone, purposely visiting areas remote from the main roads, and in-depth interviews of a few representative farmers. Others argue that such details as the seasonal pattern of labour inputs, needed for the identification of seasonal labour constraints, can only be obtained by regular farm visiting over at least one cropping season. Opinions also differ as to whether reliable data can be collected from a few case studies or whether a random sample survey of a large number of farms is needed. Clearly, the so-called 'quick and dirty methods' save time and costs in comparison with full-scale socio-economic surveys and may allow direct contact between researcher and farmer rather than through enumerators. Yet there are dangers of error and bias in relying on non-random samples and on farmer recall. These issues are discussed in more detail in the next Chapter.

Having collected information from farm families, the next step is its analysis in order to identify their objectives and preferences and the diagnosis of their problems arising from resource constraints, and environmental risks. This diagnosis should indicate points in the system where the introduction of new technology or the modification of government policies will have the greatest impact. It should identify where change is needed or where there is a potential demand for change. The methods used will generally include accounting procedures to summarize results for individual households and statistical procedures for aggregating and comparing these results to draw conclusions about the whole population. Some methods of analysis will be discussed in Chapters 12 and 13. Planning methods such as linear programming (Chapter 16) may also be used to model the existing system and diagnose constraints.

Research procedures: design, testing and extension

The scale and duration of the design stage depends upon whether appropriate technologies have already been developed and are available, on the shelf, to be taken down and used when needed. If this is not the case, then substantial scientific and technical research programmes may be required to produce new technology. In fact, there is no guarantee that the desired technology will be developed within a given budgetary and time allocation. The outcome of any research programme cannot be predicted with any degree of certainty so the supply of new technology will not necessarily match up with the demand. There are no grounds for assuming that FSR is a panacea which will *ensure* the generation of appropriate new technology. However, it should help to establish whether the technology that is generated is appropriate.

To this end the development of new agricultural technology may be set in an FSR framework even though it may be based on an experimental station. Such programmes are described as 'upstream FSR,' to distinguish them from farm-based or 'downstream' programmes, although a more apt description might be 'resource management research'. The research on minimum tillage systems at IITA has hitherto been of this type.

The design of new improved systems may be assisted by the use of planning tools such as partial budgeting, or investment appraisal. In some circumstances more sophisticated models such as linear programming may be appropriate. Although time, effort and skill are involved in building models, they are potentially very useful in allowing the assessment of the impact of new technology and other changes before they are implemented. In short, models may be used in place of real farms to explore the effects of proposed changes on an experimental basis. It is generally much cheaper to experiment with models than with real-world farming systems. The main planning tools are described in Part IV of this book.

On-farm testing and evaluation is an important stage in FSR. This involves the introduction of the new improved system on a sample of farms with a view to measuring its feasibility, performance and impact in practice. Farmers may introduce modifications and improvements to the system during the testing phase. Careful monitoring is needed over at least one season in order to make an evaluation. Here again rigorous measurement of the advantages of the new system requires monitoring a representative sample of adopters as well as an otherwise similar sample of non-adopters. Statistical methods may then be used to test whether differences between adopters and non-adopters are significantly greater than zero. However, in practice, time and resource constraints may limit testing to a small number of case-study farms.

Once a new system has been tested and shown to be an improvement on existing methods, the production stage may be launched. This involves promoting the spread of the new system throughout the target population. As local agricultural extension agents are generally responsible for this stage, it is highly desirable that they should be involved throughout the FSR programme. There should be a constant flow of information and knowledge between farmers, researchers and extension staff. The feedback of information regarding farmers' attitudes to the innovation and the managerial adjustments they make may be useful in designing future programmes. Reliable delivery systems for the necessary inputs and markets for new products are essential preconditions for the success of the production stage and the widespread adoption of innovations.

Issues of farmer involvement

There are several unresolved issues relating to FSR, not least of which is the question of farmer involvement. Despite widespread agreement that new technology should be appropriate to rural household needs and compatible with existing farming systems, there are different schools of thought regarding the extent to which farmers should be involved in the research and development process. One school favours commodity programmes and upstream FSR. It claims that this is the most promising approach to making radical new discoveries and achieving large and significant improvements. In its view, the downstream farming systems researcher, by concentrating on what farmers are currently doing, takes too narrow a view of what is possible and will probably only identify minor or marginal improvements. (Eicher & Baker 1982).

Following this approach, social scientists based at the research station are engaged in evaluating ongoing research and conducting field investigations. These are often based on a full-scale random sample survey of farm families, with formal questionnaires, regular visiting and possibly even direct measurement of plot areas, yields and dietary intake for instance. If the aims can be achieved, such a survey should provide accurate and reliable estimates of the main variables measured. However, it is costly, time consuming and necessitates the use of enumerators. Thus direct contact between researcher and farmer is limited. Although the survey is focussed on the farm household system, farmers are not active participants in the research and development process. Similarly, where the agricultural extension service takes sole responsibility for communication with farmers, there is little scope for direct interaction between researcher and farmer.

The informal, 'quick and dirty' survey, on the other hand, may be carried out by the researcher himself with the aid of an interpreter where necessary. Thus there is direct contact between research scientist and farmer. Although a checklist of important issues may be used, there is no formal questionnaire so interesting and relevant issues can be pursued in great depth and detail. The farmer is then a more active participant in the study. Indeed, he may frequently lead the discussion. Supporters of this approach suggest that a much deeper understanding of the farmers' attitudes, objectives, constraints and indigenous technology may be acquired than is possible using more formal methods. However, it may require a change in attitude by the research scientist towards a greater willingness to accept and learn from farmers' opinions. Special skills, derived from field experience or training, are needed to arrive at a full understanding of a farming system on the basis of a single interview. Some critics of this approach doubt whether it is possible to identity farmers' objectives simply by asking questions. On-farm testing of new technology is another element of this approach to farmer involvement.

Another school of thought presses the case for farmer participation even further. According to this view, a great deal of 'informal sector R&D' (research and development) already occurs on farms and in villages. Many successful innovations have been developed in this way without outside intervention. Thus there is a case for 'participatory research' much of it undertaken by farmers themselves. 'The role of the scientist is that of consultant: to collaborate rather than direct' (Richards 1985). This, it is argued, is an efficient way of meeting localized research needs and of mobilizing local skills and initiative. Problems that might be associated with the widespread adoption of this approach are first, that of organizing and administrating effective farmer panels, second, the dangers of creating an élite class of 'panel farmers' and, third, the training of scientists to adapt to this kind of work.

Clearly, there is a wide range of opinion regarding the appropriate level of farmer involvement. However, the different approaches are not all mutually exclusive. Thus Collinson recommends that informal diagnostic pre-survey by research scientists should be followed by a formal survey of farmer circumstances (Collinson 1979). On the other hand, scientists working in teams on a research station cannot easily operate as consultants to local farmer panels. Unfortunately, it is very difficult to evaluate and compare these approaches objectively. Apart from the problems of identifying and measuring all the costs and benefits of any FSR programme, comparisons may not be valid because the success of a particular approach is likely to be influenced by the type of farming system, the natural and the socio-economic environments, the type of innovation developed and the personalities of the individuals involved. All these key factors differ from one case to another. Thus, in practice, the choice must depend on personal judgement of what is appropriate to the particular circumstances.

Other unresolved issues

One of the main justifications for FSR is that it provides a focus or aim for agricultural research, the aim being to overcome constraints and

However, farm accounts are only likely to be kept on large-scale commercial or state farms and estates. This approach has little relevance to the vast majority of small farms. Early studies in Kenya relied on literate children to keep farm records and accounts for survey purposes (MacArthur 1968) while 'emergent farmers' in Zambia were able to provide bank statements of their financial position (Bessell *et al.* 1968) but such cases are atypical of the majority of farmers.

Interviewing respondents

This is the usual method of investigating attitudes and objectives, and may be used for collecting factual information on farming systems, resource use, crop and livestock yields and research constraints. It is likely to require less frequent visiting and to be less costly than direct observation and measurement, but may produce some inaccuracies or biases.

Attitudes and objectives are described as 'latent variables' existing in the individual's mind but not necessarily easily expressed. Very few of us could specify precisely what is our aim in life in response to a simple question. There is a temptation to give answers which will satisfy or please the interviewer, rather than carefully exploring one's own motives. With regard to factual information, there is the problem of recall. Clearly, this is a possible source of inaccuracy or error. We return later to the question of frequency of visiting and errors of recall. However, there are possible advantages in relying on farmer recall when there is substantial year-to-year variation in the weather, resource use and yields. The study period may well be atypical in some sense, so that data collected by direct observation will also be atypical. The farmer's estimates of resource use and yields may be influenced by his judgement of what is, rather than by what has occurred in the current season.

We may remind ourselves at this point of the possible difficulties in defining the basic unit of analysis: the household and the farm. There are difficulties in deciding exactly who should be included in the household in terms of both their contribution to household resources and their dependence upon household income. There are difficulties in identifying who makes the decisions and therefore who should be interviewed regarding his attitudes and objectives. In some cases decisions are made jointly by household members, and group interviewing is more appropriate than individual questioning. There may also be difficulties in recording all the resources under the family control. Distant plots of land, areas under bush-fallow and herds of livestock grazing far afield may easily be overlooked. Some authors have argued that the household is too small a unit to capture the multidimensional relationships affecting decision-making on African farms (Ancey 1975 or Gastellu 1980). Arguably the whole village or lineage should be the basic unit of investigation.

Direct observation

This clearly involves regular visiting by the investigator or his enumerator and is therefore very time-consuming and costly. However, if it is done properly the results should be accurate and reliable. Clearly, it is impracticable to follow every member of the farm household all the time and record their every movement, besides observing crop and livestock growth and development. Hence direct measurement is always used in conjunction with interviews, to collect missing data. Direct estimations can be made of land areas and the resource stock with periodical measurement of labour use, crop yields and other input and output flows.

The three main types of field investigation are: (1) case studies; (2) farm surveys of the rapid rural appraisal kind and (3) the cost-route method (Spencer 1972). These are distinguishable in terms of (a) the number of farms involved in (b) the frequency of visiting. All three methods have been used in Africa.

Farm case studies relate to a few farms which are studied in great depth with regular visits, observations and possibly record-keeping. Clearly whole village studies must be limited to very few cases, but some farm household studies have been of this nature (e.g. see Clayton 1961). Unit farms, which are case studies established by the researcher, often on a research station, have been used to provide data and for on-farm testing in various parts of Africa; at the International Institute for Tropical Agriculture, Ibadan, for example.

Rapid rural appraisal is based mainly on interviews and informal observation. It involves few visits to each household, possibly only one, so the cost per household is relatively small and a larger sample can be covered for a given total expenditure than using the cost-route method. This approach is increasingly favoured because of its low cost and the advantages of completing a study within a short period of a few months (see Collinson 1982; Byerlee *et al.* 1980). By contrast, case studies or the cost-route method usually involve record-collecting over a period of at least twelve months often with a similar additional period devoted to analysis and presentation of results. The greater timeliness achieved with rapid rural appraisal is a major advantage in providing data which are still relevant in a rapidly changing situation.

The cost-route method refers to repeated visiting of the same sample of farms over an extended period to collect data on inputs and outputs, costs and returns, some by questioning and some by direct observation. It is generally claimed that this method provides the most accurate and reliable data, particularly for items such as labour use and crop yields. However the cost per household of regular visiting is substantial. There is therefore an important trade-off between sample size and visiting frequency for a given total expenditure.

Summary statistics

The information collected from a farm household survey may be quantitative: areas of land, hours worked, or kilogrammes of grain for instance, or qualitative, as in response to questions regarding attitudes. It may be further categorized in terms of the number of possible response classes. Thus we may identify:

(1) binary data with only two response classes, such as whether the household head is male or whether any permanent crops are grown;
(2) multiple category data where there are a number of discrete categories:
    (a) non-numerical and unranked, as in a set of alternative farmer objectives;
    (b) numerical or ordered data; such as the number of ox teams owned, the number of the month of planting or soil quality;
(3) continuous data on plot areas, crop yields or length of time worked.

For most practical applications we need to summarize the data, and different summary measures are suggested for each of the above categories. In the first case the appropriate summary measure is the *proportion* of positive responses. For category (2), the *mode* or most frequently occurring response may be used. Indeed if continuous data are grouped into classes, a *modal class* may be identified as the most frequently occurring class. However, for numerical or ranked data, whether discrete or continuous, the most common measure of central location is the *arithmetic mean*, or simply the mean. This is defined in the same way as the 'expected value' given that each observation is assumed to have a probability of $1/n$ where n is the total number of observations or sample size. For some purposes (e.g. risk analysis) it may also be useful to have a measure of the variation, such as *the variance* (see Chapter 6). In the case of a simple random sample, as described below, the variance (now written as S^2 to emphasize that it is the square of the standard deviations) is estimated by:

$$S^2 = \sum (X_i - \bar{X})^2 / (n-1)$$

where X_i is an individual observation and $\bar{X}$ is the mean.

Each of the statistics discussed above relates to a single characteristic or measurement for each household. However, the objective in farm household surveys is to arrive at a description of the whole system, which requires estimates of many inter-related characteristics. A problem then arises in deciding which statistics to use to describe the typical farm. This is often referred to as the 'modal farm', but clearly it is most unlikely that any individual farmer will fall into the modal class for every variable that is measured.

The alternative is to create a theoretical model of an imaginary farm that is typical of the sample. In taking this approach it would be inappropriate to use the sample mode for each variable, since this measure is unsuited to accounting and other arithmetical manipulations. For instance, we cannot assume that the modal quantity of maize produced times the modal price equals the modal value of maize produced. Mean values, on the other hand, can be manipulated in this way. Hence there is a stronger case for using the mean of each variable in describing and analyzing the typical farm. The only possible disadvantage in using the mean is that, for indivisible items such as cows or machines, unrealistic fractions may result. However, it is questionable whether this need invalidate the analysis.

Another advantage in using the mean, rather than the mode, is that we can measure its 'precision' as an estimate of the true population mean. For a simple random sample the error of the mean is calculated by

$$\text{Standard error} = \sqrt{(S^2(1-f)/n)}$$

$$= \text{approx } \sqrt{S^2/n} \text{ when } f \text{ is small where } S^2 \text{ and } n \text{ are as already defined and } f = \text{sampling fraction}$$

$$= n/N \text{ where } N \text{ is the population size.}$$

The standard error may be used either (i) to estimate the confidence interval for the population mean, such that we can assert with a given probability (e.g. 95 per cent) that the interval actually contains the population mean; or (ii) to test hypotheses regarding the population mean (see any basic statistics text, e.g. Freund 1979). It is argued that presentation of a confidence interval is more meaningful and useful than a single point estimate of the population mean in descriptive studies, since it gives some guidance as to the precision of the estimate. Hypothesis tests may be used in on-farm testing of innovations to investigate whether there is a significant difference (one unlikely to have occurred by chance) in performance between adopters and non-adopters.

Several points should be noted, however, First, estimation of confidence intervals and hypothesis tests are only valid if appropriate random sampling techniques are used. Second, in these circumstances precision can be increased by increasing the sample size (note that the standard error is proportional to $1/\sqrt{n}$). More sophisticated sampling techniques may further increase precision for a given sample size or survey cost. Third, in practice, non-random sampling methods and measurement errors may introduce *bias* in the estimation of the population mean. The overall precision or size of the error depends upon both sampling error and bias:

$$(expected\ error)^2 = (standard\ error)^2 + (bias)^2$$

the latter often being much larger in practice.

There is probably a trade-off between these two influences. Sampling error can be reduced by increasing the sample size but, given a limited budget, this will necessitate less careful measurement on the individual farm with a possible increase in measurement bias.

Sampling

(i)   *Why random sampling is desirable*

The sampling problem is to decide how to select the sample from the population. This sounds, and indeed is, a simple thing to do, but, unless we ensure that there is no bias involved in our sampling method, there is no hope whatever of our being able to make scientific statements about the population from the knowledge we obtain from the sample. It is by no means easy to ensure that there is no bias.

Suppose, for instance, the agricultural extension service is asked to recommend names of farmers likely to be willing to co-operate in providing farm management data. These farmers are likely to be more progressive than their neighbours and may have introduced new techniques not commonly employed on the majority of farms in the population. If this error is avoided by eliminating these farmers from consideration when selecting the sample, this would be little better, for the bias would be in the opposite direction.

We do not usually know what biases there are in our sampling procedure if we choose it for reasons of mere convenience, speed, or cheapness, or because it has no obvious disadvantages. In sampling it is never enough not to have detected a bias; the sample should be drawn in such a way that no possibility of bias can arise. We are only really safe in this respect if the sample is selected in some way which is completely unrelated to any conceivable variable. To ensure this, we employ a chance mechanism to select the sample, that is we take a random sample. With a simple random sample every farm in the population has an equal chance of being selected.

(ii)   *The simple random sample*

The random sample is therefore the ideal to be aimed at to avoid bias. However, a random sample is not always possible for farm management surveys. Thus a great deal of information, some of it of a highly personal nature, must be collected over at least one cropping season and preferably longer. This may require many visits by the enumerators and may take up a great deal of the farmer's time. It is therefore essential to find farmers who are able and willing to co-operate. Not all members of a random sample will be agreeable. Furthermore, in many parts of Africa there is no complete list of all the farmers in the population. Without such a list or 'sampling frame' it is impossible to ensure that every farmer has an equal chance of being selected.

For some purposes, such as land-use surveys, it is possible to use areas of land (or their equivalent on maps) as the sampling frame, but where, as with a farm management survey, contact with the individual farm families is necessary, the best frame to use is one based on a list of the human population. Such a list may be prepared from the returns of the most recent population census, or, in their absence, from the records of local administrators, tax collectors or a centralized marketing agency. Most of these lists are likely to be either out of date, or incomplete, or both. If no comprehensive and up-to-date information for a sample frame exists, it may be desirable to make a reconnaissance survey of all farms covering only a few items, such as farm area, type of land and family size, in order to compile a complete list of farms in the area. Thus every effort should be made to obtain a complete sample frame and to select a random sample. Where this is not possible, the danger of bias must be borne in mind.

(iii)   *Systematic sampling*

Systematic sampling involves choosing every jth member of the population systematically, where $1/j$ is the desired sampling fraction. Thus a

5 per cent or 1 in 20 sample of households in a village might be obtained by selecting every 20th dwelling passed in a tour of the village. It is generally easier to draw a systematic sample than a simple random one, but there is a danger of introducing bias if the sample units are not arranged in a random order.

(iv) *Stratification*

There are possible modifications to the simple random sample in which every farm has an equal chance of selection, although these modifications involve random selection at some point. For the 'stratified random sample', the population is divided into a number of groups or strata. These strata may consist of: (1) administrative units, (2) ecological/agricultural zones, (3) village or farm size groups, or any other means of classifying farms. Within each stratum a random sample of farms is selected, which means that every farm has an equal chance of being selected. This chance, however, might not be equal to that in a different stratum of the population. A stratified random sample is thus, in effect, a collection of simple random samples from a collection of populations.

It is generally the case that a stratified random sample gives more precise results than a simple random sample, especially if the strata are selected so that the variation between strata is as large as possible and hence the variation between farms within each stratum is minimized. The results are more precise, simply because the variation within each stratum is less than the variation in the whole population. However, in order to define the strata, it is necessary to have some additional information on the population, besides the sampling frame. This additional information will obviously be available if the sample is to be stratified by administrative units, but this method of defining strata is likely to be less effective in improving precision than stratifying by ecological zone and farm size.

Obviously, since many items are being recorded on each farm, one basis of stratification may not be equally effective in improving precision for each item. For example, the types of crops grown and the area of each crop per farm are likely to differ considerably between climatic zones, *but* family sizes or the amount of capital used might vary more between farms within zones than between zones. Unless we are very fortunate, therefore, we must expect the gains from stratification to be relatively modest, *but* it will practically always bring about some improvement for every item, no matter what the basis of stratification.

(v)   *Cluster sampling*

The random cluster sample involves dividing the population into a number of groups. A random selection is made from these groups. All the individuals in the chosen groups then constitute a cluster sample. Whereas, with the stratified random sample, all groups or strata are included but only a sample of farms within each group are surveyed; with the random cluster sample only a sample of groups are included but all farms within the sample groups are surveyed. Unless the clusters are very carefully defined so that each one includes as much variation as possible, or reflects the full range of variation in the whole population, this method is likely to be less precise than simple random sampling for a given sample size. However, its big advantage is that it is likely to be cheaper than other forms of sampling, because the cost of enumerator's travel from one farm to another is much reduced. Hence the level of precision per unit expenditure may be increased.

Random cluster sampling is particularly useful (1) where there is no population list to serve as a sampling frame, and (2) where there is a large dispersed population or where communications are bad. Cluster sampling was used in a farm survey in Zambia.

Generally speaking, some of the advantages of both techniques can be obtained by means of a multi-stage random sample. For a two-stage sample, the population is divided into a number of groups, villages, for example: a simple random selection is made from the groups; then a simple random selection is made from the farms in each selected group. All the individuals selected in this way, taken together, constitute the two-stage sample. Thus the two-stage sample may be viewed as a cluster sample, in which only a sample of the farms within each cluster are studied, or a stratified random sample in which only a sample of the strata are included. Most of the field inquiries in the agricultural sector in developing countries have been based on multi-stage samples. Thus the first-stage groupings may be ecological/agricultural zones; the second-stage groupings villages; the third-stage groupings farms or families; and for some purposes the fourth-stage groupings are individual plots.

Where there are no population data available to serve as a sampling frame, ecological zones and villages may be distinguished and sampled from aerial photographs or maps if available. Each village in the sample may then be subjected to a population census in order to provide data for sampling farms at random within the villages.

This very brief review of sampling methods should show that selection is by no means the simple and obvious matter that it at first appears. Before embarking on any survey it is advisable to get the help of a statistician or to study the theory of sampling methods before drawing the sample.

One general point regarding sampling is worth noting, namely that it is *sample size* and *not* the fraction of the population sampled which almost entirely determines the precision of estimation for a given population. For most purposes a sample size of thirty farms in each stratum for which an independent estimate is required is probably adequate. There is little point in surveying a sample of a thousand or more farms. Resources would be better used in improving the accuracy of the data collected or in collecting additional data. Even where the number of farms studied is an insignificant fraction of the total population, a random sample of sufficient size can be used to draw reliable, unbiased results and to test the accuracy of these results. If, however, it is impossible to draw a random sample then it is important to check as thoroughly as possible whether the results are biased in any way.

Where a survey is made in just a single year or only a few years, the years are in fact a sample from the whole population of an infinite series of years. Random sampling is not possible in this respect, so it is important for the investigator to determine to what extent the information gathered each particular year represents normal or average conditions, particularly for crop yields, animal production and price levels. This, of course, does not apply where farm management surveys are made continuously year after year. Indeed, there is much to be said for establishing surveys on a permanent basis. Farm conditions and factors which influence farm business are constantly changing. Thus data rapidly become outdated. After a farm management survey has been repeated in the same area for a number of years, the data become more and more accurate, and the time involved and money spent diminish because farmers become more familiar with the nature of the survey and the type of information required. Enumerators become more experienced and do not need to repeat the initial training. Furthermore, data from repeated surveys make it possible to identify trends in yields, prices and factor inputs.

Questionnaires and schedules

There are two types of form that may be used:

(i) the schedule for collecting factual information, in tables or lists;
(ii) the questionnaire for collecting opinions, attitudes and aptitudes by asking the respondent questions framed in a precise way.

The schedule is often designed for ease and convenience of coding and summary of the data, although it is also necessary to set it out in such a way that the enumerator is unlikely to miss any items. Sometimes sets of schedules are bound together to form record books. One possible set of schedules for farm management data collection and analysis have been designed by FAO (Friedrich 1977).

With a questionnaire it is important that every respondent should be asked the same question in the same way. It is therefore necessary to translate the questions into the local language on the questionnaire to avoid any slight misinterpretations by the enumerator.

All the terms used in schedules and questionnaires must be clearly understood by enumerators and agreed before the survey starts. Difficulties may arise over the definition of 'a farm' for instance. It may be defined as 'all the land and other resources under the control of one farm family', but then problems may arise in defining the 'farm family' and deciding how to treat resources under family control but not used in farming. The correct translation of local crop names must also be agreed.

Pre-testing of schedules and questionnaires is highly desirable, either as part of a pilot survey or as part of the training programme for enumerators. This allows the opportunity to correct omissions, or ambiguous questions and to discover terms, the meaning of which may not be clear to farmers or enumerators.

Organizing the survey

Preparation

The organization of a survey is a major administrative task which involves:

(i) formulating objectives,
(ii) delineating the study area,
(iii) choosing samples,
(iv) designing and testing questionnaires,
(v) selecting and training enumerators,
(vi) preparing for their needs in the field and back-up services in the office,
(vii) carrying out a pilot survey,

all before the main survey can begin. Thus it is important that adequate time is allowed for all these preparatory tasks before the main survey period, and that plans and phasing of the whole operation are worked out in advance.

It is also desirable in most cases, to hold meetings with chiefs, village councils and farmers before the main study in order to explain the aims and objectives and to enlist farmers' support and co-operation.

Some investigators have thought it necessary to provide incentives in the form of free issues of fertilizer or other inputs or in the form of cash. However, apart from the cost, the promise of a gift may alter the farmer's behaviour so that it becomes atypical. It is likely that observing local customary procedures of communication and keeping farmers informed at all times about the purpose and progress of the study is more important than the provision of financial or physical incentives.

Arrangements must also be made for housing, transport and equipment for enumerators, as well as communications for returning questionnaires, supervision and payment of wages. Generally, the enumerators can be left to make their own accommodation arrangements, but it is important that they should live in the survey area to minimize travel time and cost.

Generally enumerators need some form of transport to visit farms and this can prove a costly item. If cluster sampling or multi-stage sampling is used, it may be convenient and not too costly to take a small group of enumerators by motor vehicle to a sample village, dropping them one by one at sample farms or allowing them to walk between farms. Where the sample farms are too widely scattered for this approach, it may be necessary to provide each enumerator with a bicycle or, where distances are greater still, a motorcycle. Careful planning and budgeting is needed to find the most suitable form of transport in terms of convenience and cost.

Enumerators require, besides a stock of schedules and questionnaires, clipboards and writing materials. They may require other equipment, depending upon the records to be collected, such as surveying equipment for measuring areas of plots of land, harvesting tools and weighing balances for crop-cutting and weighing of yields or stop watches for timing labour use. All such equipment should be acquired in advance, before the main study begins.

Communication between the enumerator and the survey office is probably best maintained by regular supervisory visits, when the enumerator can be paid, completed survey forms can be checked and collected while progress and problems can be discussed. Unless enumerators are very experienced and trustworthy employees, regular supervision is essential.

The enumerators

The personality and behaviour of the enumerators has an important effect on the willingness of farmers to co-operate. A good working relationship must be established. Thus choice of enumerators, their training, motivation and supervision are all important considerations.

Enumerators must be fluent in the language used by the farmers and it is desirable that they should know something of local farm conditions and practices so that they ask questions intelligently and check on the accuracy of the farmer's replies.

There are, therefore, advantages in recruiting local inhabitants of the survey area. However there are also possible disadvantages if the enumerator is a member of a particular faction, religious group or political party whose opponents may refuse to co-operate. Also it may be difficult to sack an enumerator who is unsatisfactory in the work, if he is a member of the local community, since this may turn farmers against the study and create problems for his replacement.

Another consideration in choosing enumerators is the educational standard required. This must depend upon local circumstances. In some places there may be unemployed university graduates who could be recruited for such work, whereas in other places, primary school leavers are the most highly educated people one could hope to recruit. Generally speaking, a high educational standard is not needed provided that the applicants are reasonably literate and numerate and adequate training is provided. Selection may be based on an interview and a simple test of ability to write clearly and make simple calculations.

The possibility of employing part-time enumerators should be borne in mind. People such as extension agents or school teachers may be used. However, there is always a problem of dual allegiance which makes supervision and control difficult. There is a danger that they will withdraw from the project when an opportunity for promotion occurs or when annual leave is due. University students may be used if the main survey work can be restricted to the vacations. Such experience can be very valuable to students of agricultural subjects.

Motivation of enumerators is important and they should be paid adequate wages comparable with those they could earn in similar employment elsewhere. Ideally, where there is regular and fairly continuous survey work in progress, a permanent cadre of professional enumerators should be established with opportunities for promotion resulting from good service. However, this may not be possible if there is inadequate work to keep them fully employed.

Whatever the background of the enumerators, some training is needed before they start work in the field. Generally a period of two to three weeks, made up of say one week of office training and the rest in field training, will be adequate. During the office training the purpose and importance of the study can be explained. The survey questionnaires and schedules should be studied in detail with some discussion of the ways in which the results will be summarized in order to give trainees a thorough understanding of their interview procedures. They should also be instructed in the techniques of assessing areas, weights and measures. Field training is devoted, in the main, to giving enumerators practice in completing questionnaires and schedules with farmers.

The number of farmers each enumerator can be expected to visit each week must depend upon

  (i) The time it takes to travel from one farm to another, which in turn depends upon distances and means of transport,

 (ii) the time it takes to complete each interview which depends upon the amount of information collected and the method of measurement used,

(iii) whether farmers are only available at certain hours for interview or at any time.

A decision may, perhaps, be delayed until after a pilot survey which will give a clearer picture of what is possible, but, as a crude guide, four or five visits per day or twenty to twenty-five visits per week should be possible if sample farms are relatively close together. When most of the time is spent in travelling, the number that can be visited is, of course, reduced.

Frequency of visiting farmers

A critical decision which affects both the cost per farm surveyed and the accuracy of the data collected, is the number of times each of the chosen farms is visited. It may range from once only to daily visiting over a whole year or longer. There is apparently a trade-off between savings in cost and gains in accuracy per farm. However, certain gains in reliability are obtained by increasing the sample size, so if the reduction in cost per farm allows an increase in the number of farms studied there may be an overall *gain* in reliability of the results.

In part the decision may be whether to rely on recall (i.e. the farmer's ability to remember inputs used and yields obtained in the past) or direct observation. Clearly direct observation of amount of seed used as well as amount of crop harvested is impossible when the farm is only visited once.

However, even with quite frequent visiting, it is necessary to rely on the farmer's recall, though only over the short period since the last visit. Accuracy is likely to be greater, the shorter is the period of recall.

The scope for saving by infrequent visiting depends upon the complexity of the farming system. In the case of a simple system with a single, short cropping season, no perennial crops or livestock, a single visit just after harvest might be sufficient to provide acceptable data. More frequent visiting would probably be essential to study systems with two or more cropping seasons, some perennial crops and livestock.

A distinction may be made between (i) 'single-point data' such as area of land, numbers of livestock, or productive trees and stocks of machines, equipment and materials and (ii) continuous data such as daily labour use and quantities of other inputs and outputs. Whereas 'single-point data' may be collected in a single visit, reliable records of continuous data may require regular and frequent visiting.

Within each of these categories of 'single-point data' and continuous data, a further distinction may be made between 'registered' and 'non-registered items'. The former consist of items such as rented land areas, hired labour use or cash crop sales which are associated with market transactions and therefore are 'registered' in the farmer's mind if not on paper. Non-registered items include family labour use and household consumption of food stuffs which are far less likely to be recorded. Registered items can be recalled more easily and hence can be collected satisfactorily with infrequent visiting. Overall then, reliable information on single-point, registered items may be collected in a single visit, but to get accurate information on continuous, non-registered items may require regular and fairly frequent visiting; say every two or three days (See Collinson 1979.)

Where farmers have more than one dwelling, for instance, where, as in parts of central and southern Africa, the cattle post is located at quite a long distance from the cultivated plots, it may be necessary to visit each of the holdings to make observations and collect records. The risk that the farmer may not be 'at home' on a single visit is perhaps greater than in a more settled system of farming.

Measurement

Measurement of land areas

The area of land farmed is clearly a single-point item, but it may not be registered: that is the farmer may not have a very precise idea of the exact area. Direct measurement may be necessary.

The first requirement is to locate and identify which plots or fields are cultivated by the sample farm household, since many family farms are made up of several scattered plots. Omissions and errors may occur at this stage for several reasons.

(i) The farmer may not wish to disclose how much land he controls because he fears he will be taxed upon it or for other reasons.
(ii) Wives or other household members may have their own plots which the family head may fail to mention although strictly speaking these plots form a part of the family farm.
(iii) The farmer may only mention those to which he has long-term usufructory rights and may fail to mention land which is rented or pledged.
(iv) He may fail to mention very distant plots.

Having identified the plots on the ground it may be useful to make a sketch map of the whole farm for inclusion with the other records as a visual check that information is collected on all the plots. It is also desirable to paint some identifying mark or number for each plot, on a convenient tree or rock.

Difficulties may arise in defining crop boundaries, especially where crop plants tend to spread or ramble. Furthermore boundaries may change over the season as more land is cleared or some reverts to bush. More than one visit will be necessary to discover this.

Generally, if the farmer does not know the area of his plots, direct measurement is required. Methods which might be used include

(i) triangulation (i.e. dividing the area up into triangles) and measuring the sides by pacing, surveyors chains, tapes or a measuring wheel (see Figure 11.1).
(ii) measuring offsets, perpendicular to a straight, base-line using survey chains and tapes.
(iii) compass survey, again using any of the devices mentioned above to measure distance.
(iv) plane table.
(v) aerial survey, though costs may be prohibitive for this last method.

Some of these alternative methods are discussed in Upton & Anthonio (1965) Appendix II, and Hoyoux (1979).

Areas are either calculated using the formula for the area of a triangle for instance, or estimated from a scale drawing over which a squared grid, of the same scale, is placed. The area is then found by counting the squares.

Intercropping raises special measurement problems. The simplest approach, and perhaps the most realistic, is to treat a mixture of, say, maize intercropped with beans as a single crop different from sole crop maize and from sole crop beans, with its own pattern of labour requirements, cost and returns. Unfortunately, mixtures frequently include many more than two crops and since the proportions in the mixture can vary, the range of possible alternative combinations is practically infinite. Hence, in order to distinguish between different crop mixtures (and possibly to assess their relative merits), some information on plant densities is needed. It may possibly be based on visual assessment of the plot by the enumerator, or on quantities of seed used or on plant counts of sample areas within the plot. None of these methods is wholly satisfactory.

Special problems arise in assessing the areas of fallow land and communal grazing land per family. However, in both these cases, the collection of accurate data may not be considered very important. The area of fallow land might be estimated by asking the farmer how many years of fallow and how many years of cropping occur in a rotation, then multiplying the area cropped by the ratio years of fallow/years of cropping.

This is not very reliable, especially where different rotations are practised on different plots or where the length of fallows is changing over time.

Figure 11.1   Area measurement by triangulation. The sum of the areas of triangles *ABC*, *ACE* and *CDE* may be compared with the sum of the areas of the triangles *ABE*, *BDE* and *BCD* for checking purposes.

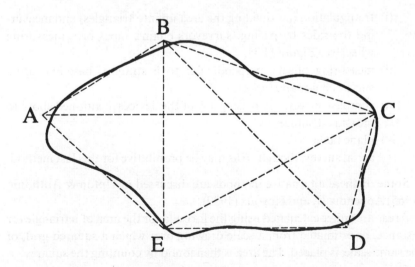

For communal grazing land the only solution may be to estimate the total area and divide it by the number of families using the land.

Measurement of labour inputs

A very crude assessment of the total labour input can be based on the numbers of men, women and children in the labour-force multiplied by the number of hours each is expected to work. However, since the number of hours worked can vary widely from one individual to another, the margins of error may be very large and this method gives no detail of the allocation of labour between different activities.

For most farming-systems analysis and farm planning, information is needed on the seasonal pattern of labour requirements for individual crops (or crop mixtures) and livestock enterprises. As already mentioned, labour use is continuous and (except perhaps for hired labour) unregistered, so the collection of reliable data requires regular and frequent visiting. At each visit the enumerator records, the date, and (day by day since the previous visit) the operations carried out on each crop plot and the time spent on each. Similar details are collected for work connected with livestock.

For completeness, as a means of checking records and for other uses, it is desirable to record hours of sickness, hours spent in entertainment and relaxation and hours of non-farm work. Difficulties may arise in defining whether a particular task is farm or non-farm work, for instance processing and marketing of produce. Decisions on categories of work must be made and agreed by all enumerators before the survey begins. Time spent travelling to and from the fields may take up a significant portion of the working day. It is normal practice to include travelling time as a part of the work time.

In collecting labour records it is necessary to separate different categories of worker, say (i) family head (ii) other adult male family members (iii) adult female family members (iv) children (under 14 years old) of the family (v) hired men (vi) hired women (vii) hired children. This is necessary because there is generally some division of labour between sexes and classes of labour so they are not perfect substitutes. Even when one category can substitute for another, hourly work performance may vary with physical strength and motivation. Thus, whilst on light work there may be little difference in performance between men and women, on heavy bush clearing and cultivations men may achieve much more per hour. For hired labour, wage and other payments must be recorded together with information on associated bullock or equipment hire.

Assessment of hours worked may be unreliable without clocks and watches. It may be necessary to relate periods of work to the movement of the sun, or to prayer or meal-times in questioning the farmer.

All this assumes that labour records are based on recall by the farmer of the hours worked. However, direct measurement of rates of working, using work-study techniques may be an alternative, (see Farrington 1975). The time spent carrying out a specific task on a measured area of land or quantity of produce, is timed accurately by stopwatch. The advantages of this approach are:

(i) work-study requires a far smaller volume of labour data than do frequent visit surveys to produce mean values with comparable errors;

(ii) the costs involved in the separate surveys of areas and yields required for estimates of per hectare labour requirements by frequent-visit surveys are avoided by work-study where measurement of the work achievement is performed directly at the end of each observation;

(iii) the directness of the technique excludes the possibility of respondent confusion or omission inherent in memory-based techniques.

The disadvantages are:

(i) there are certain operations for which it is practically impossible to measure the work achieved during observations of only a few hours length, e.g. tobacco-curing or bird-scaring.

(ii) work-study only provides information on work rates, survey data are still needed to provide information on the seasonal pattern of operations and the number of times they are carried out.

Nevertheless, some saving might be made by using a combination of survey and work-study.

Most farm-survey data collectors in the past have been concerned to find a means of aggregating different categories of labour into a total labour input in 'standard man-hours' or 'man-equivalents'. Weighting factors are used for converting the work of women and children into man-equivalents; for instance, weights of 1.00 for adult males, 0.67 for adult females and 0.33 for children under 14 have been proposed for this purpose. However, for reasons given above, any such weighting system must be arbitrary and there may be advantages in keeping labour records subdivided into separate categories.

Measurement of crop yields

Very often harvesting is fairly continuous, rather than a single-point operation, and unless the crop is sold immediately quantities are not registered. Thus estimates based on long periods of recall are likely to be vague and inaccurate. Regular visiting is desirable over the harvest period so that amounts harvested can be recalled more easily.

To avoid total reliance on recall, direct measurement by crop-cutting on sample plots may be used. These sample plots should be marked out within the standing crop sometime between planting and harvest, generally the earlier the better as this limits crop damage. Each sample plot is of a standard area (e.g. 3 metres square or 9 sq metres) marked out with pegs and wire or string, but is located randomly within the whole cropped area. The number of samples taken in any one parcel of land ranges from one up to ten or more, but it must depend, in part, on (i) the size of the parcel, (ii) the variability of the crop stand, (iii) the level of accuracy desired and (iv) the costs that can be afforded (see Spencer 1972).

The sample plots are cultivated along with the rest of the field but are harvested separately, the yield from each plot being weighed accurately. Since the weight of most crops can vary significantly according to their moisture content, it is advisable to measure the moisture content when weighing the plot yield so that the yield can be adjusted to a standard moisture level. The yield estimates obtained are then multiplied by the total area of the crop to arrive at an estimate of total output. The main disadvantages of crop-cutting are

(i) it is somewhat inconvenient for the farmer so he may not be ready to co-operate;

(ii) it is costly and time-consuming for the enumerator, especially where many sample plots are involved;

(iii) yields are usually overestimated because the useful yield (actually available to the farmer) is often less than the total biological yield which is measured from the sample plots (see Zarcovich 1965);

(iv) it may be difficult to arrange the crop-cutting at the most appropriate time, when the rest of the crop is being harvested, especially where mixed cropping is practised and the component crops are harvested at different times.

It has been suggested that experienced enumerators may be able to make reasonably accurate estimates of crop yields simply by looking at the mature crop and judging the yield. Clearly, this must give rather crude estimates, less satisfactory than actual measurement.

For some tree crops, where the fruit grows in bunches, yield estimates can be based on a count of the total number of bunches and sample weighings of a few of them.

It is a good idea to ask farmers at some stage whether they consider the yields obtained this year to be about average, better or worse than average to give some idea as to whether the results are typical.

Other yields

For livestock such as dairy cows or laying hens, yield recording, if it is not already done by the farmer requires regular visiting by the enumerator. Births, deaths and slaughterings of most classes of livestock are more easily recalled and can be collected at relatively infrequent intervals.

If records are kept of produce disposals, both sales and home consumption, these may provide a cross check on the estimated yields and total production. Discrepancies may arise as a result of wastage, losses in store, gifts and so on.

Another reason for recording sales is to collect data on the market prices obtained. In order to carry out a financial analysis of the farm business, total gross output of the various different farm products is evaluated in money terms, using current market prices. Hence price data are an essential part of a farm business survey. Where some produce is marketed through a co-operative or a marketing board whilst other produce is sold in local markets, it is useful to record this too.

Measurement of capital assets

On practically every farm there will be certain capital assets which must be taken into account in farm business analysis. These may include livestock, standing crops, irrigation works, drainage and other land improvements, buildings, machinery and equipment, as well as stocks of food, seed and agricultural chemicals both purchased and home produced. Increases in value of certain assets such as growing livestock and tree crops or stocks of food and seed represent a part of the total farm gross output, whereas decreases in value (depreciation) of machinery and equipment represent costs of production.

Generally information on a farmer's capital assets can be collected in a single visit or preferably two visits, one at the beginning of the production period (opening valuation) and one at the end (closing valuation).

The first task in assessing capital assets is to make a list or inventory. This should be fairly straightforward except possibly for recording the numbers of free-ranging livestock or the quantities of grain and other produce on hand.

Valuation of capital assets can raise problems. For items which are commonly bought and sold, such as stocks of food, seed and chemicals, livestock and some tools and equipment the current market prices can be used, *but* where there is no established secondhand market, as is probably the case for permanent crops, irrigation works, other land improvements and some kinds of machinery and equipment, this is not possible. In theory, the present value of such assets should be based on estimates of their future productivity, but, since such estimates would be largely guesswork, the normal practice is to take the original purchase price or cost of establishment and subtract a depreciation allowance for the age of the asset. This is not entirely satisfactory, since prices and costs may change over time and the estimation of depreciation rates is rather arbitrary. It is therefore advisable to use standardized average prices, costs and depreciation rates on all the survey farms when valuing capital assets.

It may be desirable to collect information on the farmer's cash assets, his credit and his indebtedness, but farmers may be reluctant to provide such 'sensitive' information unless there is very good rapport between enumerator and farmer. However, such information although valuable and interesting is not essential for analysis of the farm business. If it is to be collected the following suggestions should be borne in mind:

(i) such information is best collected towards the end of field work;
(ii) questionnaires on those items should be short and simple;
(iii) it is better to interview the farmer in private (Spencer 1972).

Measurement of other inputs and expenditures

Although stocks of seeds, fertilizers and other agricultural chemicals may be included in the capital valuations, it is necessary to record their use and levels of application for purposes of farm business analysis. Where such inputs are purchased their source and price should be recorded. Similar considerations apply to livestock feeds and medicines.

In order to assess the inputs used on individual enterprises, detailed recording is needed. Local measures, such as bowls or even handfuls may be used in distributing seed, fertilizer or chemicals while livestock feeds may be measured in bundles for instance. Average weights must be estimated, by sample weighing, for all these local measures to convert the quantities into more widely recognized units.

Records of hours worked by oxen, power tillers or tractors, irrigation pumps and other equipment may be desirable for farm planning purposes but are not essential for farm business analysis. However, purchased inputs of spares and materials such as fuel or lubricating oil must be recorded.

Information on other sources of income, household expenditure and food consumption is valuable as a cross check on other information collected, besides being interesting and useful in itself. However, such information is not necessary for analysis of the farm business and may be costly and difficult to collect. A decision must be reached before the survey begins, whether the advantages of having these data outweigh the additional costs.

Summary

1 Formal and informal surveys are conducted for FSR and other purposes. The information gathered relates to: description of the farming system, resource endowments, input–output data, income and expenditure, attitudes and objectives.

2 Detailed records are rarely kept by farmers, so data are gathered by interviewing farmers or by direct observation. Approaches vary from the informal group, or key-informant, interviews of rapid rural appraisal, to detailed data gathering with regular visits on case-study farms or a full-scale sample survey.

3 Summary statistics may include the proportion (for binary), the mean or the mode (for continuous or grouped data) and the variance (a measure of spread). Sometimes a 'modal farm' is described, but generally mean values are more useful.

4 The precision of an estimate of a proportion or mean depends directly on the size of the sample and whether it is randomly selected, and indirectly on the population variance and the level of measurement error.

5 Random sampling is the best method of avoiding bias. For a simple random sample every individual has an equal chance of being selected. This requires a sampling frame, or list, from which the sample is drawn. A close second-best method is systematic sampling where every nth individual is chosen.

6 Stratification involves dividing the population into strata, a simple random sample of individuals being selected from each stratum. Precision is generally greater than with simple random sampling for a given total sample size.

7 Cluster sampling involves selecting a random sample of groups, or

clusters, and recording every individual within each selected cluster. Precision may be lower than for simple random sampling, but travel costs are reduced.

8 Multistage sampling involves drawing a random sample at each stage (e.g. ecological/agricultural zone, villages within zones, farm households within villages). It is widely used for formal surveys.

9 Schedules are used for recording factual information, questionnaires for collecting opinions, attitudes and aptitudes. Pre-testing is highly desirable.

10 The organization of a survey is a major administrative task involving formulation of objectives, delineating the study area, choosing a sample, designing and testing questionnaires, selecting and training enumerators, preparing for their support and back-up services and conducting a pilot survey. Sufficient time must be allowed.

11 Enumerators must be carefully selected, given adequate training and a programme of visits planned.

12 The number of visits per farm household may range from a single one to regular and frequent visits over a year or longer. In the latter case there is less reliance on farmer recall, which is desirable the more complex the farming system and the more continuous and non-registered data, such as family labour inputs, are being investigated.

13 The farmer may not be able to provide a precise estimate of the area farmed. Direct measurement (e.g. by triangulation) may be necessary. Land areas may be difficult to measure because of land fragmentation, boundary error, mixed cropping and communal tenure.

14 Accurate labour-input data are obtained by regular recording of hours worked at different tasks by different family members and hired workers. This allows assessment of division of labour by age, gender etc.

15 Crop yields include both sales and home consumption which should be recorded. Accurate measurement may involve crop cutting.

16 For estimates of livestock production, detailed records are needed of births, deaths, purchases, sales, gifts and offtake.

17 Values of capital assets, such as tree crops, machinery, buildings and land improvements may be difficult to estimate. Use of draught animals and machinery should be recorded. Farmers may be unwilling to declare the level of cash savings.

References

Ancey, G. (1975). *Niveaux de decision et functions objectif en milieu Africain*, Paris, INSEE, AMIRA Note de Travail No. 3

Bessell, J. E., R. A. J. Roberts & N. Vanzetti (1968). *Survey Field Work*, Universities of Nottingham and Zambia, Agricultural Labour Productivity Investigation. (UNZALPI) Report No. 1

Byerlee, D., M. P. Collinson, R. Perrin, D. Winkekmann, S. Biggs, E. Mozcardi, J. C. Marinez, L. Harrington & A. Benjamin (1980). *Planning Technologies Appropriate to Farmers: Concepts and Procedures*, El Batan, Mexico, CIMMYT

Casley, D. J. & D. A. Lury (1981). *Data Collection in Developing Countries*, Oxford, Clarendon Press

Clayton, E. S. (1961). 'Economic and Technological Optima in Peasant Agriculture', *Journal of Agricultural Economics*, **14**(3), 337

Collinson, M. P. (1979). 'Micro-level accomplishments and challenges for the less developed world', in Johnson, G. L. & A. Maunder (eds.) *Rural Change: the Challenge for Agricultural Economists*, Proceedings, Seventeenth International Conference of Agricultural Economists, Banff, Canada; England, Westmead

Collinson, M. P. (1982). *Farming Systems Research in Eastern Africa: The Experience of CIMMYT and Some National Agricultural Research Services 1976–1981*, East Lansing, Michigan, Michigan State University, Department of Agricultural Economics Development Paper No. 3

Farrington, J. (1975). *Farm Surveys in Malawi*, University of Reading, Department of Agricultural Economics and Management, Development Study No. 16

Freund, J. E. (1979). *Modern Elementary Statistics*, 5th edn London, Prentice-Hall

Friedrich, K. H. (1977). *Farm Management Data Collection and Analysis*, Rome, FAO

Gastellu, J. M. (1980). 'Mais où sont donc ces unités économiques que nos amis cherchent tant en Afrique?', *Cahiers ORSTOM, Series Sciences Humaines*, **27**(1–2), 3

Hoyoux, J. M. (1979). *A Manual: Measuring Size of Small Farms*, Ibadan, IITA, Discussion Paper 6/79

Kearl, B. (ed.) (1976). *Field Data Collection in the Social Sciences: Experiences in Africa and the Middle East*, New York, Agricultural Development Council

MacArthur, J. D. (1968). 'The economic study of African small farms: some Kenya experiences', *Journal of Agricultural Economics*, **19**(2), 193

Norman, D. W. (1973). *Methodology and Problems of Farm Management Investigations: Experiences from Northern Nigeria*, African Rural Employment Paper No. 8, Department of Agricultural Economics, East Lansing, Michigan State University

Spencer, D. S. C. (1972). *Micro-level Farm Management and Production Economics Research among Traditional African Farmers: Lessons from Sierra Leone*, Africa Rural Employment Paper No. 3, Department of Agricultural Economics, East Lansing, Michigan State University

Stuart, A. (1964). *Basic Ideas of Scientific Sampling*, London, Griffin

Upton, M. & Anthonio, Q. B. O. (1965). *Farming as a Business*, Oxford University Press

Yates, F. (1981). *Sampling Methods for Censuses and Surveys*, 4th edn, London, Griffin

Zarcovich, S. S. (1965). *Sampling Methods and Censuses*, Rome, FAO

12

Analysis

Coding and processing data

At an early stage in the planning of a survey a decision should be reached on how the results are to be analysed in terms of both (i) the types of analysis that will be made, and (ii) the data handling methods to be used, including whether or not to use a computer.

Whatever methods of analysis are to be used, data coding is recommended. For quantitative, numerical information this simply means setting out the figures collected on the farm in a convenient layout for further summary and analysis. In the case of qualitative data such as sex of family head, soil type or statements of opinion, coding consists of allocating numbers to each of the alternative possible answers and using these numbers in further analysis rather than the written answers (e.g. a male head might be coded as 1 and a female head as 2). The reason is simply that it is quicker and more convenient to manipulate numbers rather than written answers. Coding tables may be incorporated in schedules and questionnaires, or enumerators may be required to transfer their records to coding sheets daily when they return from field work.

Use of a computer must depend upon whether computing facilities are available. Even where these facilities are available it is by no means certain that the use of a computer is justified. Against the advantages of high-speed calculations must be set the costs not only of the use of computer facilities, but also of learning how to prepare data for entry to the computer and how to write instructions regarding the analyses to be carried out. These preparatory stages can be very time consuming. Many software packages are now available, on both micro- and main-frame computers. Of particular relevance is the 'Farm Analysis Package' (FARMAP) developed at FAO (FAO 1983) and the Statistical Package for the Social Sciences

(SPSS) (Nie *et al*. 1975) which is designed for the analysis of farm and other surveys. Although the former is specifically designed for farm survey analysis the latter may be more attractive because of its greater flexibility if additional analysis including statistical calculations are intended.

Whether all the analysis is carried out by hand with pocket calculators, or whether a computer is used, analysis and summary of results, together with the writing up, are very time-consuming. Experience suggests that these final stages take at least as long as the survey itself. Frequently inadequate resources of time and funds are allowed. The number and type of staff needed depend upon the data-handling methods chosen. Hand analysis requires clerical and calculating assistants while use of the computer requires computer operators for data entry and analysis.

Initial crosstabulations

There are two broad categories of information that may be obtained from a farm study: simple variables and composite variables. The first category includes those items which are recorded directly in the field. It clearly includes farmers' statements about their attitudes and objectives, but may apply to estimates of total land area, labour use or farm income. The other category refers to those items which are the result of certain calculations applied to the basic data, for instance, when separate labour records are aggregated to arrive at total labour input or accounting methods are used to estimate household income. We deal first with methods of summary and presentation of survey data in an informative way. The same principles may be applied to the presentation of composite variables, such as household income per capita, once they are estimated. Accounting methods used to estimate such variables are dealt with later in the chapter. The following discussion on the summary of survey statistics is, of course, irrelevant when a case-study approach is used. None the less, accounting methods are needed to analyse the case-study system.

Coded responses for any single variable can be grouped into classes and represented as a frequency distribution of the number of observations or households in each class. For binary data there are, of course, only two classes, while for continuous data it is necessary to first identify the classes by defining their limits. In defining class limits the following rules are usually observed: (i) the entire range of values is divided into, generally fewer than, 15 classes, (ii) the classes are mutually exclusive so that each observation can appear in one and one class only, (iii) where possible the classes cover equal ranges of values although this may conflict with the last rule and (iv) the number of observations in each class should be sufficient to justify showing that class separately.

It is a useful first step, in the analysis of any data item, to determine the frequency distribution of the responses. This is not too onerous a task when analyzing data by hand, and is very easily achieved with a survey analysis package such as SPSS on a computer. Having determined the frequencies, it is but a simple step to express the results as relative frequencies, or percentages of the total. This, in effect, gives the probability distribution of the responses. For ease of interpretation it may be useful to plot the frequency histogram as in Figure 12.1.

A tabulation or plot of the frequency distribution of observations is useful in several ways:

(i) in data checking and validation since values lying outside the feasible range are readily identified,

(ii) in examining the form of the distribution, its spread and whether it has more than one modal class or peak (the latter case might suggest that the data come from more than one distinct population),

(iii) in identifying the modal class.

Figure 12.1 shows the frequency distribution of responses, of a sample of Zambian maize growers, as to which is the busiest month. The approach of

Figure 12.1   Distribution of busy months

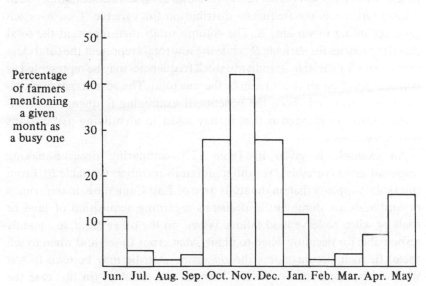

Table 12.1. *Percentage distribution of decision-makers on various activities connected with food crop production*

Activities	Decision-makers				
	Wife	Husband	Both	N.A.[a]	Total
Which crop to grow	44.0	45.8	9.3	0.9	100.0
Acquisition of land	12.0	85.6	2.3	—	100.0
When to plant crops	59.3	33.8	6.0	0.9	100.0
Use of fertilizers	1.9	23.1	1.4	73.7	100.0
Increase farm size	40.3	55.6	4.2	—	100.0
Leave land under fallow	44.4	50.9	3.2	1.4	100.0
Which crops to sell	56.5	35.2	6.0	2.4	100.0
When to sell crops	55.6	39.4	2.8	2.4	100.0
To whom to sell crops	44.9	46.8	5.1	3.3	100.0
Purchase of farm tools	7.4	86.6	5.6	0.5	100.0

[a] N.A. = No answer.

simply asking farmers to indentify critical constraints in this way is clearly cheaper than using detailed records and accounts of the whole farm system for the same purpose as described below.

A useful additional step is to prepare 'cross-tabulations' which present results for two (or sometimes more) variables at once. Each column of such a table represents the frequency distribution for variable A, *within* each class according to variable B. The column totals then represent the total class frequencies for variable B, while the row totals represent the total class frequencies for variable A. Individual cell frequencies may be represented as percentages of either the column or the row total. The advantages of cross-tabulation over and above the benefits of examining frequency distributions already mentioned is that it may assist in identifying associations between variables.

An example is given in Table 12.1 comparing decision-making responsibilities (variable A) of different family members (variable B). From this table it appears that, in the study area of East Cameroon, male farmers or husbands are dominant in decisions regarding acquisition of land or tools or when to leave land fallow. Wives, on the other hand, are mainly responsible for deciding when to plant, what crops to sell and when to sell them. In such circumstances the *chi-square* statistic may be used to test whether the apparent association between the variables (in this case the difference between the sexes) is statistically significant, meaning it is unlikely to be a chance effect (for more details see Freund 1979).

Where the objective is on-farm testing of new technology and a comparison of innovators with a control group, then the binary variable, adopter/non-adopter might be used as one of the variables to classify the data. The cross-tabulation by another variable, say farm income, would allow comparison of the two groups.

Analysis of the farming system

The cross-tabulation of responses and interpretation of the distributions is generally the only analysis that is needed for data on attitudes and objectives collected by interview. For most other variables used in describing a farming system

(a) some analysis or manipulation of the data is needed within each farm household to arrive at the desired measures;
(b) the results obtained from a sample of households are summarized by estimating the mean and perhaps the variance (see last chapter).

It is desirable to carry out these operations in this order; that is to analyse the system for each of the sample households before summarizing by calculating the means. This is the only way in which variation between farms can be assessed. For instance, the mean yield of maize could be estimated by dividing the total output of maize from all farms in the sample by the total area of maize; but this would provide no measure of the variation in yields between farms. Furthermore, it would provide a measure of mean yield averaged over all hectares, whereas we are here concerned to estimate the mean yield averaged over households. Only in this way can we be sure that the mean quantity of maize produced per household is equal to the mean quantity sold plus the mean quantity consumed, stored or wasted. In short, every item in the analysis must be averaged across households for the accounts of the average household to be internally consistent.

Estimates of the variance between households may be used to establish confidence intervals for the main variables measured. However, as we have seen, such estimates are themselves unreliable if the sample was not drawn randomly and the results might be biassed. The other main use of variance measures is in risk analysis. Unfortunately, the variance between farm households within one season may be a very poor and unrepresentative measure of the variance between seasons. The latter is likely to be the main concern of the risk-averse farmer. None the less, having collected data from a sample of farms, the estimation of the variance is relatively easy and is probably justified.

Having considered the presentation of summary data we turn now to the logically prior question of analysis of the individual farming system. The types of data that are needed were discussed in the previous chapter. Apart from the assessment of farmers attitudes and objectives, these consist broadly of (i) descriptive data on the farming system; the resource base, cropping patterns and livestock numbers and (ii) measures of inputs, outputs, costs and returns. Variables in this last group may be estimated for individual plots of land, for specific enterprises and activities or for the whole household.

Descriptive data

The description of available resources and the combination of crop, livestock and off-farm activities may be set out in a series of tables under the headings of land, labour and capital.

(i)   *Land*

There are three different ways in which the total area of land under the control of the farm family may be analysed: (a) by land-use category, (b) by tenure and (c) by crops grown. The different land-use categories may include rainfed arable, irrigated arable, permanent crops, permanent pasture or rangeland and fallow. Further distinctions may be drawn according to soil type or topography. The sum of the areas in all these categories should equal the total farm area.

Categorization by tenure involves separation of common land from that held by individual family members. Land which is pledged or rented in is separated from land which is owned or held under customary tenure. It is useful to supplement this with information on the relative ease of acquiring additional land.

Finally the pattern of land use should be detailed in terms of the areas of different crops grown. Where there is only one crop season per year and sole-cropping is practised, description is straightforward. The sum of the areas of individual crops plus grassland and fallow should add up to the total area of land available to the household. Where two or more crops can be grown sequentially within a year, the area of each crop should be recorded. The total area of crops (and fallow) then exceeds the total farm area. The ratio of these two totals may be calculated, as a measure of the intensity of land use (see Chapter 8).

More serious problems arise in dealing with crop mixtures, when it is difficult to assess whether the component crops are competitive or supplementary. Judgement is needed in deciding whether to treat each component crop as covering the whole area or to assume each crop covers a fraction of the area. In some cases, especially for complicated mixtures of many different crops, it may be most appropriate to treat each mixture as a separate and distinct crop. None of these methods is wholly satisfactory, and special methods of assessment based on relative crop cover may be needed for detailed analysis of mixed cropping.

(ii)   *Labour*
            The basic regular labour force is usually made up of family members. Even hired labourers frequently live in as members of the household. Hence, an analysis of the household composition may give an assessment of the regular labour force available. Household composition is analysed by age and sex categories. Conversion factors may then be used to estimate the total labour-force in standard adult male equivalents. Due account must be taken of other off-farm commitments in calculating the residual labour available for work on the farm. Household composition data may also be used to estimate total food consumption requirements. The data should be supplemented by information on the ease of hiring more labour, and the normal wage rates.

(iii)   *Capital*
            Capital invested in permanent crops is recorded under the cropping pattern. The remaining capital items to be mentioned now are livestock and physical assets of machinery and equipment. Livestock numbers are obviously separated by species, and sometimes by age and sex categories, to give flock or herd structures. For purposes of aggregation, livestock unit conversion factors may be used to arrive at (a) total livestock units of each species, (b) total grazing livestock units for ruminant cattle, sheep and goats or (c) grand total of all livestock units owned by the household.

Separate records may be presented by individual items of machinery and equipment used on the farm or elsewhere. However, it may be thought desirable to estimate the total value of capital assets in money terms. The total value of physical assets plus permanent crops, livestock, stored products and cash in hand minus any outstanding debts gives a measure of the farmer's 'net worth'. Given that some assets are rarely bought and sold so that estimating their value is essentially arbitrary, and given that farmers are often unwilling to disclose their financial position, the measurement of net worth may prove difficult in practice. In any case, the measure is of limited value to a semi-subsistence farmer except as a guide to his creditworthiness.

Input–output data

The objective here is to calculate the quantities of inputs used and of outputs produced per hectare of each crop or per head of each class of livestock. Crop input–output data may be estimated from individual plot records, while, for permanent crops such as oil-palms, it might be appropriate to calculate the amounts per tree.

Let us consider the measurement of inputs. Some, such as agricultural chemicals or tractor services, may be purchased or hired, while others, such as family labour, are supplied from household resources. Inputs of both kinds should be recorded for each plot or enterprise and converted to a per hectare or head of livestock basis.

An alternative distinction may be drawn between stock and flow resource inputs. Resources which are available in the form of stocks, such as seeds, fertilizers and other chemicals or concentrate feeds for livestock, can be stored. If they are not used at a particular point in time, they can be kept for future use. Hence, it is generally not necessary to record the timing of stock resource inputs. Such inputs are generally associated with variable costs.

Resources such as regular labour, or draft animals and equipment provide a continuous flow of man-hours or oxen-hours which cannot be stored for future use in the way that seeds can. Unused labour in January will not add to the labour supply in August. The cost of the flow is fixed and unavoidable, whether the labour is actually used at a particular time of the year or not. If such resources are likely to be limiting constraints, it is highly desirable that the seasonal distribution of inputs should be estimated.

Labour inputs may be recorded separately, not only for different dates, but also by age and sex of the worker, by plot or livestock enterprise and by operation. Some aggregation may be desirable in order to present the seasonal labour profile. Labour inputs for different age and sex groups may be aggregated by converting them all to standard man-days. If the labour profile is to be based on monthly intervals, then labour inputs on different dates and for different operations within the month may be aggregated to give total monthly labour input. Finally, labour inputs on different plots of the same crop may be aggregated to give the total monthly input to that enterprise. The ultimate objective is to determine the seasonal profile of labour inputs per hectare of each crop and per head

Table 12.2. *Estimating total number of goats produced*

	Number of goats
Number sold	3
Number consumed (or given away)	2
Number on hand at end of year	5
Total I	10
Number on hand at start of year	4
Number purchased (or received as gifts)	2
Total II	6
Number produced	
(Total I) − (Total II)	4

of each class of livestock. Similar profiles of inputs may be calculated for draft animals or machines such as tractors.

In measuring the output of each enterprise (or plot) it is important to include both marketed and home-consumed produce. Where yields have been recorded directly, the problem does not arise, but where yield data are not available, then they must be estimated by combining quantities sold with quantities used in the household. Furthermore, in the case of live-stock, and possible some crops, there may be a change in the quantity on hand between the start and end of the year; and some may have been purchased or received as gifts. These items must all be taken into account in estimating the total yield. Losses due to animal mortality or crop wastage are generally excluded from the output measure.

For illustration, the total number of goats produced in a household flock in one year is estimated in Table 12.2. In practice, it might be more useful to separate different age and sex cohorts (see Chapter 7). Transfers into, and out of, different age classes would then have to be taken into account.

Having estimated the total output or yield it is normally expressed on a per hectare basis for crops and per head of livestock.

Farm business analysis

For accounting purposes, in order to compare returns from different enterprises with their costs of production we need a common unit of value. Nutritional measures such as grain equivalents (see Clark & Haswell 1964) or megajoules (MJ) of energy (see Bayliss–Smith 1982) have been used, but, clearly, there are difficulties in evaluating non-food items such as cotton or rubber in this way. Money values, on the other hand, can usually be estimated for all commodities including those produced mainly for subsistence. In most African situations, subsistence crops surplus to household requirements are sold, and the prices received may be recorded.

With data on yields and prices for each enterprise we can calculate the enterprise gross output as follows:

$$\text{gross output} = \text{yield} \times \text{price}$$

Where there is more than one product such as grain and straw, or calves and milk, the total gross output is the sum of the value of the joint products. Also, if permanent crops or livestock change in value between the start and end of the year, the gross output measure must be adjusted accordingly. Crop gross outputs are usually expressed on a per hectare basis or for some permanent crops per tree. Livestock gross outputs are expressed per head or per livestock unit. The whole farm gross output is simply the sum of the gross outputs obtained from the individual enterprises.

Costs of production are usually separated into (a) variable or direct costs and (b) fixed costs or overheads. In earlier chapters on the theory of production we assumed that any input may be varied; the distinction between fixed and variable costs then depends upon which inputs are assumed to vary. However, in farm business analysis, it is convenient to standardize the classification in the following way:

Variable costs	Fixed costs
Crops	
Seeds	Rent or costs of land use;
Fertilizers	wages or costs of labour use;
Sprays	interest on capital invested;
	depreciation of machinery,
Livestock	draft animals, equipment
Livestock feeds	and buildings; maintenance
Veterinary medicines	and repairs

There is no general agreement regarding machinery fuel and running costs or temporary hired labour. Although machinery running costs clearly do vary with the amount of use, it is convenient to treat them as fixed costs for general farm business analysis. Temporary hired labour is also a variable cost, but if only a few farms employ casual workers it may be more appropriate to treat the labour costs as being fixed on all farms. However, where casual hiring is normal practice, say for cotton harvesting, then the cost may be treated as variable.

The distribution between variable and fixed costs has traditionally been drawn on the basis of the difficulty of allocating fixed costs to individual enterprises. However, in African agricultural, the distinction might be based on the difficulty of evaluating the fixed costs. It may be noted that the variable costs generally correspond with stock inputs, most of which have a market price. Fixed costs relate to flow inputs, often provided from household resources and hence free of charge. Their opportunity costs are not easily assessed.

Variable costs can usually be allocated fairly easily, to individual enterprises, except where there is mixed cropping. Just as there are various alternative ways of allocating inputs to components of mixed crops, none of them wholly satisfactory, so, too, is there a choice of methods of allocating variable costs. For any given enterprise the gross margin is the difference between gross output and variable cost.

> Enterprise gross margin = enterprise gross output − enterprise variable costs

Once again crop gross margins are usually presented on a per hectare (or per tree) basis while livestock gross margins are presented per head or per livestock unit. The total sum of all the enterprise gross margins gives the total farm gross margin.

If fixed costs do not alter much with changes in production, then where total gross margin can be increased, farm profit or surplus will rise. If the increase in gross margin can be achieved with the existing supply of fixed resources and hence the existing level of fixed costs, profit will be raised by exactly the same amount as the gross margin. For this reason it is possible to plan changes in the farm system in terms of gross margins alone and leave fixed costs out of the calculation. In fact, in many parts of Africa, the family farmer does not incur explicit fixed costs. He pays no rent, nor wages to his family who make up his regular labour force, he has hardly any buildings and equipment and does not borrow much capital. Practically all the African farmers' costs are variable. This means that practically the whole of the total gross margin represents family or social income.

Thus one useful method of completing the farm business analysis is to compute the enterprise gross margins per unit of limiting resource. In some cases, where land of a certain type (e.g. irrigated land) is limited, comparisons of gross margin per hectare are useful. In other cases, comparisons of gross margins per man-day of peak labour may be more appropriate.

Alternatively, given that there is some expenditure on fixed costs, of wages for instance, land rents or machinery operating costs, these, together with an estimate of the depreciation of machinery and equipment, may be subtracted from the total farm gross margin to estimate net farm income; thus

Net farm income = total gross margin − explicit fixed costs

If income from off-farm activities, including remittances and wages earned from off-farm employment, can be estimated, it is useful to add these to the net farm income to give an estimate of *total household income*. This estimate of the household income from all sources may be divided by the household size (measured in standard consumption units) to arrive at the income per consumption unit.

Other analyses

(i)   *Financial analysis*

It may be useful to carry out a separate analysis to investigate the financial position of the farm household. Such an analysis is concerned solely with cash receipts and expenditure. The total of farm receipts from crop and livestock sales, minus total expenditure on the purchase of farm inputs gives the farm cash surplus.

Farm cash surplus = Total farm receipts − total farm expenditure

Where credit is used, the results may be further adjusted to allow for loans received and debts repaid, thus

Farm cash surplus after financing = Farm cash surplus + farm
loans received − repayment of principal and interest

Finally cash income from off-farm activities may be added to give the *household net cash income*. This is a measure of the amount of cash available for meeting all payments not relating to the farm. It is a less comprehensive measure of welfare than the total household income. None the less, it may be useful to consider the financial position separately from income in kind which is consumed within the household.

(ii)   *Cash flow analysis*

For long-term investments such as permanent crops, there are obvious problems in obtaining the long series of costs and returns data needed for a comprehensive evaluation. The only possible sources of records, over the lifetime of cocoa or oil-palms, are research station reports or long-established plantations. However, information may be obtained from a farm survey on the annual costs and benefits at different stages of the life cycle, from different plots. Thus, it may be possible to build up or synthesize a lifetime profile of costs and returns by combining data from different aged plots.

For purposes of evaluation it is necessary to calculate the annual cash flow, meaning the difference between total revenue and total cost for the enterprise in each year. Cash flows differ from gross margins in that no attempt is made to estimate annual depreciation or appreciation of assets. Instead, the full cost of any capital investment is recorded in the year when it occurs. Similarly, if assets are sold, the sale price is recorded in the year of sale. Costs of labour, even family labour, must be estimated and subtracted in estimating cash flows. Discussion of methods of evaluating the resultant stream of cash flows is deferred until Chapter 15 on Investment Appraisal.

(iii)   *Livestock productivity*

In addition to the estimates of gross margins per head or per livestock unit, already discussed, further livestock productivity measures are desirable. More specifically it is useful for problem diagnosis, and herd or flock growth modelling purposes to estimate

(a) reproduction rates, which may, in turn, depend upon age at first parturition, parturition interval or parturition rate and average litter size,

(b) age-specific mortality rates, and

(c) daily liveweight gain.

Calculation of these measures is, of course, only possible if the necessary data have been recorded. The crude reproduction rate may be estimated as the total number of live births during the year divided by the average number of breeding females in the herd or flock. If the number of parturitions (P) is recorded then the parturition rate (R) is given by dividing by the average number of breeding females (N).

$$R = P/N$$

The mean parturition interval (I) in days is obtained as

$$I = 365/R$$

268   *Field investigations*

while average litter size (*L*) is the number of live births per parturition

$$L = B/P$$

where *B* = total number of live births

The crude mortality rate is simply the ratio of the number of mortalities to the mean number of animals. Age-specific mortality rates are calculated in the same way for specific age cohorts.

Two general points may be noted. First, given that numbers of animals are constantly changing over time, frequent recording is needed to arrive at accurate estimates of average numbers used in estimating reproduction and mortality rate. The second point is that, since individual household flocks and herds are relatively small, there may be many gaps in the estimates of age-specific mortalities and the variation between households in all these measures is likely to be large.

Comparative analysis

The need for comparing adopters with a control group of non-adopters has already been emphasized. However, much may be learned in the diagnosis of constraints and identification of improvements by comparing performance on different farms, given that some farmers are more innovative and successful than their neighbours. Comparisons of the farming systems of the more successful with those of the less successful may help to identify where the critical difference lies. For an example of detailed analysis of this kind see Upton & Petu (1966), and Upton (1964).

Differences may lie in the inherent abilities of the household decision-makers or in their resource endowments; in which case the less successful family may be unable to emulate its more successful neighbours. Nevertheless, it is useful for the researcher to discover whether this is the case. Indeed, it may be possible to promote institutional change which will improve the resource base of poorer households. In other cases, useful indigenous innovations may be identified as a result of comparative analysis.

Summary

1 The analysis of farm survey data is increasingly carried out by computer, using packages such as FARMAP or SPSS. Even if computers are not used, field data should be transferred to coding sheets, using numbers, as codes, in place of qualitative information.

2 Tabulation of data in frequency distributions is a useful first step for checking and validation of data, besides providing an initial summary.

3 Results of a survey of the farm household economy are best analysed first for each household individually, then summarized to measure means and variances.

4 Description of the household resource-base includes tables of land area, by type tenancy and cropping, labour-force, by age, gender and whether hired or family, capital assets including livestock, machinery and equipment.

5 Input–output data relate the quantities of inputs used to the outputs produced per hectare of each crop and per head (often per breeding female) of livestock. Quantities of 'stock resource inputs' (e.g. fertilizer) and seasonal use of 'flow resource inputs' (e.g. labour) are related to output, measured as sales plus home consumption, adjusted for inventory changes, for each enterprise.

6 For each enterprise, gross margin equals enterprise gross output minus variable costs. This gives a useful measure of its contribution to net farm income, which is measured as total gross margin minus explicit fixed costs. Net farm income plus income from off-farm activities, including remittances equals total household income.

7 Financial analysis involves only market sales and expenditure, but may be adjusted for loans received and debts repaid with interest. Cash-flow analysis concerns the difference between total revenue (including sales of capital assets) and total cost (including purchases of capital assets) for the enterprise in each year.

8 Livestock productivity assessment requires analysis based on measures of fertility, mortality, growth and production.

9 Comparative analysis of performance on different farms may provide useful guidance on options for improvement.

References

Bayliss-Smith, T. P. (1982). *The Ecology of Agricultural Systems*, Cambridge University Press

Clark, C. & Haswell, M. (1964). *The Economics of Subsistence Agriculture*, London, MacMillan

Dillon, J. L. & J. B. Hardaker (1980). *Farm Management Research for Small Farmer Development*, Rome, FAO, Agricultural Services Bulletin 41

FAO (Food and Agriculture Organisation of the United Nations) (1983). *The FAO Farm Analysis Package: A General Introduction*, Rome, FAO

Freund, J. C. (1979). *Modern Elementary Statistics*, 5th edn, London, Prentice-Hall

Nie, N. H., C. H. Hull, J. G. Jenkins, K. Steinbrenner & D. H. Bent (1975). *Statistical Package for the Social Sciences*, 2nd edn, McGraw-Hill

Upton, M. (1964). 'A development of gross margin analysis', *Journal of Agricultural Economics*, **16**(1), 111

Upton, M. & D. A. Petu (1966). 'A study of farming in two villages in the middle belt of Nigeria', *Tropical Agriculture*, Trinidad, **43**(3), 179

13

Production functions

Data for production function analysis

The production standards discussed in the last chapter are useful for comparing *average* products of specific resources on different farms or in different enterprises. However, in theory we would expect *marginal* products to be more important in determining the economic optimum level of production, combination of resources and of enterprises. If we are to use the marginal approach to decision-making we must first establish the production function relating output to different levels of inputs. Hence we need a series of observations at different levels of input.

Several observations are needed even in the simplest case where there is one single variable input and one single product and the relationship is assumed to be linear (a straight line). This is illustrated graphically in Figure 13.1 showing hypothetical data relating nitrogen fertilizer input to maize yield. In Figure 13.1(a) we have only one single observation of input and output; there is only a single point on the graph. Obviously, any number of straight lines, all with different slopes, could be made to pass through this single point. The marginal product cannot be estimated. It should be noted, however, that the average product is easily obtained by dividing output by input.

In Figure 13.1(b), where there are two observations and hence two points, there is only one straight line which will pass through both. The slope and hence the marginal product per unit of nitrogen fertilizer on maize can be estimated. However, with only two points, we have no way of assessing the reliability of our estimate of the slope. If there are errors of measurement of either inputs or outputs or if there are other factors influencing output which we have not taken into account, any further observations which are made may not lie close to the line at all. In order to make a more reliable estimate and to assess its reliability, many observations are needed, as in Figure 13.1(c). Generally speaking, the more points that are available, the greater the reliance that can be placed on the estimated relationship. In practice, the problem is further complicated where there are several variable inputs and curved relationships. More observations are needed where there are several inputs which can be varied and where various different curved relationships are considered possible.

A suitable series of observations may be obtained from controlled experiments if they were designed with this object in mind. To fit a function to experimental data, several levels of each input treatment must be included in the experiment. This is often not the case, many experiments having been designed to test whether a particular treatment, sometimes at a single level, has a 'significant effect'. However, more and more researchers in crop and livestock production are realizing the benefits of designing their experiments to measure the slope of the production response curve.

A production function may be fitted to survey data, the results for each farm representing a single observation. Various problems arise with this approach, since none of the variables are controlled as they are in an experiment. In particular, environmental conditions and managerial ability vary from one farm to another. Furthermore, since practically all inputs may vary from farm to farm, some aggregation of both inputs and outputs may be needed.

A production function can only be fitted to data for a single farm, such as a unit farm, if results for several years' operation at different input levels are available. These would then represent the series of observations, in this case a time-series. Such a set of time-series data is unlikely to extend over many years so the scope for production function analysis of single farm data is limited.

Methods of estimating the slope

The production function may be described, as it has been in earlier chapters, by a set of tabulations of specific inputs and the related outputs. However, this is a rather clumsy method and no information is given regarding intermediate points. The economic optimum cannot be estimated precisely, but only to the nearest unit of input. It is therefore customary to attempt to relate inputs and outputs by means of a smooth curve.

Where only one input and one output is involved, the observations can be plotted on a graph as in Figure 13.1(c) and a curve fitted to these points by freehand drawing. Some subjective judgement is involved in drawing the

Figure 13.1 Fitting a straight line; (a) Single observation, (b) Two observations, (c) Many observations

(a)

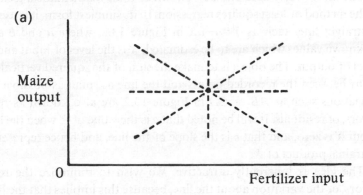

Maize output

0   Fertilizer input

(b)

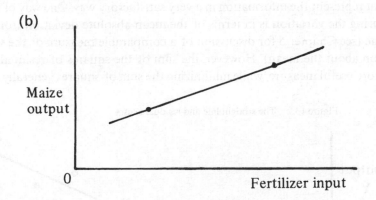

Maize output

0   Fertilizer input

(c)

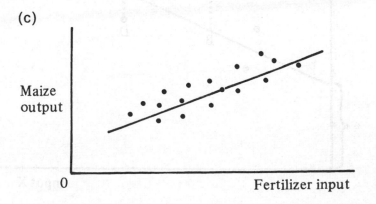

Maize output

0   Fertilizer input

shape and slope of the curve, but the accuracy must depend upon how widely the points are scattered. Alternatively any one of a variety of more systematic mathematical methods can be used.

The most widely used and best known of these mathematical techniques is the method of least squares regression. In its simplest form, it is used to fit a straight line, such as $Y=a+bX$ in Figure 13.2, where a and b are the unknown values which are to be estimated, X is the level of input and Y the level of output. The object is to make the sum of the squared vertical deviations between the recorded points and the line as small as possible. These deviations such as AB or CD in Figure 13.2 are also known as residual errors, or residuals. It will be noted that a is the value of Y when the level of input X is zero, and that b is the slope of the line, and hence represents the marginal product of X.

The idea is inherently attractive. We wish to minimize the residual errors, or the variation about the line, because this implies that the line is a good fit to our points. If the residual variation were large, the line would not represent the information in a very satisfactory way. One way of measuring the variation is in terms of the mean absolute deviation from the line (see Chapter 5 for discussion of a comparable measure of the variation about the mean). However, the sum of the squares of residuals is a more useful measure, while minimizing the sum of squares generally gives

Figure 13.2   The straight line and residual errors

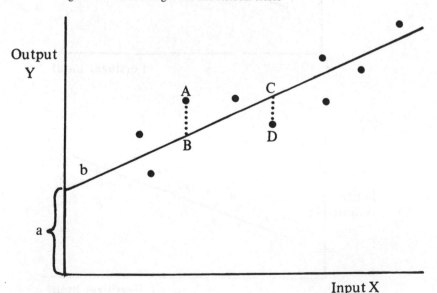

a better fit to all the data points than does minimizing the sum of absolute deviations.

It is possible to compare different lines, which have been fitted freehand, by comparing the sums of squares of residuals, *but* the mathematical technique of least squares regression enables us to estimate the specific values of a and b which minimize the sum of squared residuals. The formulae are

$$b = \Sigma x_i y_i / \Sigma x_i^2$$

and

$$a = \overline{Y} - b\overline{X}$$

where $\overline{X}$ and $\overline{Y}$ represent the means of the two variables and x_i and y_i represent the deviations from these means. Thus, once we have decided on the general shape of the relationship between X and Y, least squares regression enables us to find the line of best fit objectively without having to rely on our personal judgement.

The output Y is referred to as the dependent variable, while the input X is called the independent variable. Multiple regression is the extension of this analysis to include cases where there is more than one independent variable. Thus more than one variable input may be taken into account.

The simplest case of multiple regression is that of multiple linear regression with two independent variables. In that case the equation is of the form

$$Y = a + b_1 X_1 + b_2 X_2$$

which represent a plane in three dimensions. The coefficient b_1 is the slope in the X_1 direction, or in other words the effect of varying X_1 when the other independent variable X_2 is held constant. Similarly, b_2 measures the effect of varying X_2 when X_1 is held constant. Estimation of the values of b_1 and b_2 requires solution of a set of simultaneous equations (known as the Normal Equations)

$$\Sigma x_{1i} y_i = b_1 \Sigma x_{1i}^2 + b_2 \Sigma x_{1i} x_{2i}$$
$$\Sigma x_{2i} y_i = b_1 \Sigma x_{1i} x_{2i} + b_2 \Sigma x_{2i}^2$$
$$\overline{Y} = a + b_1 \overline{X}_1 + b_2 \overline{X}_2$$

(e.g. see Wonnacott & Wonnacott 1970).

Where there are more than two independent variables, the relationship cannot be imagined in three dimensions. Although the methods of estimation are based on the same principles, they are, of course, more complicated and use of a computer is recommended.

Regression analysis

The method of least squares enables us, not only to find the line of best fit, but also to measure how good a fit it is. Let us first note that the variation about the mean of Y, can be measured by the variance, which we may write as

$$y_i^2/(n-1)$$

But each deviation y_i consists of two parts, the deviation of the *predicted* value of Y_i from the mean, written as $\hat{y}_i$, and the residual e_i (see Figure 13.3). If, as is normally assumed, there is no correlation between y and e, then

$$y_i^2 = \hat{y}_i^2 + e_i^2$$

(the variation in Y)=(the variation 'explained' by the regression)+(the residual variation).

These values may be calculated and used to derive the coefficient of determination (R^2)

Figure 13.3   Illustration that $y_i = \hat{y}_i + e_i$

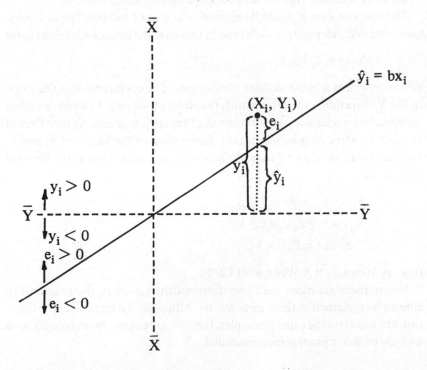

$$R^2 = \frac{\hat{y}_i^2}{y_i^2} = \frac{\text{proportion of the total variation}}{\text{explained by the regression.}}$$

This clearly is a measure of goodness of fit. A value of 1 for R^2 means that all the variation is explained, or that the regression predicts the Y values exactly. A value of zero means there is no association.

The analysis can be taken further by assuming that each predicted value of Y and indeed the value of 'a' and each of the 'b' coefficients, is an 'expected value'. Thus a standard error can be estimated in each case and used to construct a confidence interval or to test hypotheses. It is usual practice, for instance, to test the hypothesis that the true value of each coefficient is zero; there is *no* association. If the hypothesis can be rejected we say the coefficient is 'significant'.

A word of warning is needed, however. Strictly speaking, the estimation of confidence intervals and hypothesis testing is only valid when appropriate random sampling methods have been used. Furthermore, if the sample is small, say less than 30 cases, we have to assume that the sample is drawn from a normally distributed population.

Forms of function

I.   *The linear function*
So far we have been discussing the linear function, which is based on the assumption that the inputs and outputs are all related by straight lines. This means that the slope of each relationship is constant and hence that the marginal product is constant. It makes no allowance for diminishing marginal returns so there can be no economic optimum. The total and marginal product graphs for this function are shown in Figure 13.4. It is assumed that the relationships between inputs are constant (see isoquants illustrated in Figure 13.5), which means that all inputs are perfect substitutes for each other with constant rates of technical substitution. This is obviously nonsense since it would mean that the least-cost combination of resources would consist of one *single* resource input, namely the cheapest per unit of output.

Clearly, the linear function is not satisfactory on theoretical grounds and its use can only be justified on the basis of the ease of fitting it by least squares regression and as an approximation over a limited range of values.

Fortunately, our standard regression procedure can be applied to curved relationships, provided that the variables can be redefined, or the equation transformed to make it linear. The two functional forms most commonly used in this way are the quadratic, or second degree polynomial, and the Cobb–Douglas or power function.

II.   *The quadratic function*

The equation for the quadratic function, in the case of two variable inputs, is:

$$Y = a + b_1 X_1 + b_2 X_2 - b_3 X_1^2 - b_4 X_2^2 + b_5 X_1 X_2 \tag{1}$$

where Y is the level of output and X_1 and X_2 the level of each of the two variable inputs. Additional variables are formed by squaring the values of X_1 and X_2 and by forming the product of these two. Thus X_1^2 could be

Figure 13.4   The linear function for Y on X_1 with X_2 fixed

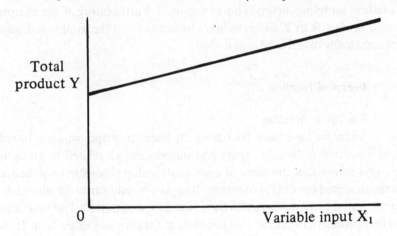

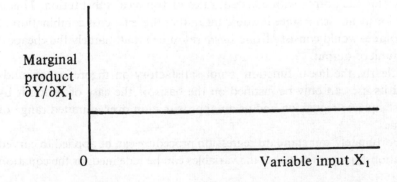

thought of as a new variable X_3, likewise X_2^2 could be thought of as X_4 and X_1X_2 as X_5. For instance, if for a particular observation in a fertilizer trial X_1 is 25 kg of ammonium sulphate and X_2 is 50 kg of superphosphate, then X_3 is $25^2=625$, X_4 is $50^2=2500$ and X_5 is $25\times50=1250$. The values for these new variables are calculated for other observations in the same way. The unknown values of a and all five bs can then be estimated by multiple regression of Y on the five X variables.

In the quadratic equation (1) above, b_1 and b_2 measure the slope of the curve at zero input. They are normally positive, showing a positive production response to increasing inputs of variable factor from zero upwards. On the other hand b_3 and b_4 measure the rate of change in the slope of the response curve. Thus if there are diminishing marginal returns, b_3 and b_4 should have negative signs as shown in equation (1). The interaction between the two variable inputs occurs in the last term of the equation. It is usually positive, meaning that the two inputs are more productive when used in combination, but negative or zero interaction may exist where diminishing marginal returns hold true for both factors. The constant a is the output obtained when X_1 and X_2 are both zero. It therefore represents the output from the mix of fixed resources and may sometimes be zero.

The marginal products are obtained by differentiation so

$$MP_1 = dY/dX_1 = b_1 - 2b_3X_1 + b_5X_2$$

Figure 13.5   Isoquants for the linear function

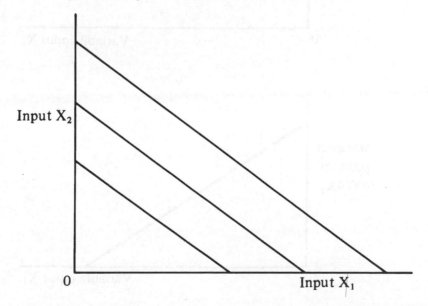

Input X_2

0   Input X_1

$$MP_2 = dY/dX_2 = b_2 - 2b_4X_2 + b_5X_1$$

The typical shapes of the total and marginal product graphs for this function are shown in Figure 13.6. This function can show diminishing marginal returns and even negative ones. There is then a technical optimum beyond which the total product falls. An economic optimum occurs where the marginal value product equals the unit factor cost. A quadratic function can show increasing marginal returns if b_4 and b_5 are positive, but it can never show both increasing marginal products at low levels of input and

Figure 13.6   The quadratic function for Y on X_1 with X_2 fixed

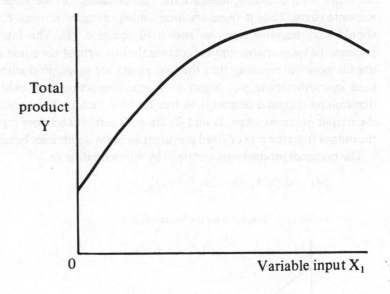

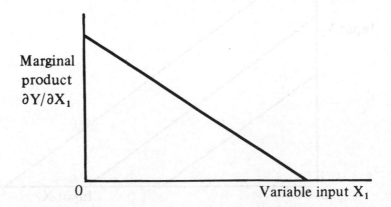

decreasing marginal products at higher levels of input in the same equation. Furthermore, at very high levels of input and possibly for very low ones too, this function may predict negative total products which are clearly impossible. In such a case the function ceases to be meaningful for very high or very low levels of input.

The isoquants and two possible expansion paths are shown in Figure 13.7. The isoquants are generally convex to the origin at low levels of input so they show diminishing rates of technical substitution Thus the least cost method of production is likely to include both variable inputs.

The isoquants may cut the axes of the graph, as is true for the lower output curve in Figure 13.7, which cuts the X_1 axis. It is implied that this level of output can be achieved by using the first variable input alone and none of the second. The expansion paths are straight lines which do not necessarily pass through zero, but converge to the point of maximum physical product. This means that the least-cost combination of resources, that is the optimum ratio of X_1 to X_2, varies according to the level of output.

A possible disadvantage with this form of function is the large number of b values, or regression coefficients, which must be estimated for a given number of variable inputs. Thus, with a linear function the number of regression coefficients is the same as the number of variable inputs, but, for a quadratic function, one variable input involves two regression coefficients, one for the X term and one for the X^2 term. Furthermore, the

Figure 13.7   Isoquants for the quadratic function

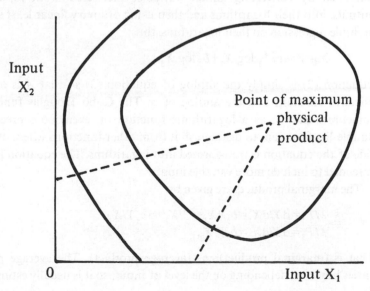

Input X_2

Point of maximum physical product

0   Input X_1

number of coefficients increases more rapidly than the number of variable inputs. In equation (1) with two variable inputs there are five coefficients. With three variable inputs there are ten coefficients if all possible interaction effects are estimated. Hence, if many inputs are allowed to vary in the production function the quadratic function may become very large and cumbersome and may require a very large number of observations for reliable estimation.

In summary, the advantages of this form of function are that it is relatively easy to estimate and that it may show diminishing marginal returns. The possible disadvantages are that it cannot show both increasing and diminishing marginal returns in a single response curve, that it may give negative total products for very high or very low levels of input and that it becomes complex if many variable inputs are included. It is most commonly used for analyzing experimental results where there are few variable inputs but where zero variable inputs do not necessarily yield zero output.

III.   *The Cobb–Douglas function*
         The equation for this function, in the case of two variable inputs, is:

$$Y = A X_1^{b_1} X_2^{b_2}. \tag{2}$$

It is named after two men called Cobb and Douglas who together used it for a production function study in America in 1928! The a and b coefficients are estimated by converting all the variables measured, both inputs and outputs, into their logarithms and then using ordinary linear least squares multiple regression on their logarithms, thus:

$$\log Y = a + b_1 \log X_1 + b_2 \log X_2. \tag{3}$$

Equation (2) is simply the antilog of equation (3) so that A is a multiplicative constant and the antilog of a. The Cobb–Douglas function is sometimes known as a logarithmic function or, even more precisely, a double-log function, to distinguish it from other functions where only one side of the equation is transformed into logarithms. The equation is easily extended to include more variable inputs.

The marginal products are given by

$$MP_1 = dY/dX_1 = b_1 A X_1^{(b_1-1)} X_2^{b_2} = b_1 Y/X_1$$
$$MP_2 = dY/dX_2 = b_2 Y/X_2.$$

That is (marginal product)$= b \times$(average product). The average product varies however, depending on the level of input, so it is usually estimated at the average level. Where there are diminishing marginal returns, b_1 and b_2 are less than 1. A b coefficient of exactly 1 implies constant marginal returns and one greater than 1 implies increasing returns. Since the effect of scale is measured by the sum of elasticities of response for all inputs, the Cobb–Douglas function may be used to estimate returns to scale, *provided that all inputs have been included in the function*. The sum of the b co-efficients then gives an estimate of returns to scale. If the sum is greater than 1 then there are increasing returns, and if the sum is less than 1 there are decreasing returns.

The typical shapes of the total and marginal product curves for the Cobb–Douglas function are shown in Figure 13.8. Provided that the b coefficient is less than 1, the response curve shows diminishing marginal returns. However, negative marginal returns are not possible, so there is no technical optimum or maximum total product. In fact the total and marginal product curves tend to flatten out into an almost straight line at high levels of input. As a result of this, if the economic optimum occurs at a fairly high level of input, the Cobb–Douglas function may give an overestimate of the economic optimum. It will be noted that at zero level of input the output is also zero. This is invariably the case with a Cobb–Douglas function, unlike the quadratic. This is because the variable inputs in equation (2) are multiplied together, so if any one of them is zero, the product must also be zero.

The isoquants shown in Figure 13.9 are again convex to the origin, showing diminishing rates of technical substitution. They never cut the axes however, thus implying some complementarity between resources. It is impossible, according to this function, to produce any product without some of each resource; one can never substitute entirely for another. The expansion paths are straight lines passing through zero. This implies that the least-cost combination (ratio) of resources is the same at all levels of output. Once the optimum combination has been found this can be increased to scale.

The advantages of the Cobb–Douglas function are that it is easy to estimate, it may show diminishing marginal returns and it can also be used to estimate returns to scale. Possible disadvantages are that it cannot show both increasing and diminishing marginal returns in a single response curve, that it does not give a technical optimum and may lead to overestimates of the economic optimum. The implication of zero output at zero input may be unacceptable in some instances. For example, some crop product is usually obtained even when no fertilizer is applied. The implication of a constant elasticity of response at all levels of input may also restrict the usefulness of this function. It is commonly used for analyzing survey data, where many variable inputs are included and it is hoped to measure returns to scale.

IV   *The transcendental logarithmic (translog) function*
      An alternative functional form, widely favoured for production and supply function analysis in many non-agricultural contexts is the

Figure 13.8   The Cobb–Douglas function for Y on X_1 on X_2 fixed

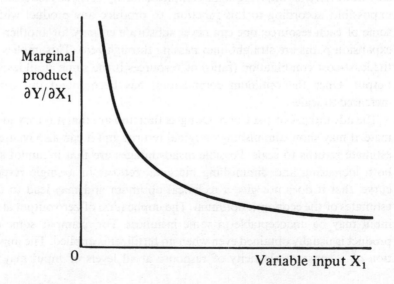

translog function. Its use is now increasing in agriculture also. It is described as a 'flexible functional form' since its shape is less rigidly determined than in those of the Quadratic or Cobb–Douglas functions. In particular, the scale coefficient can vary for different levels of production and different factor proportions. Furthermore, the curvature of the isoquants, measured by the 'elasticity of substitution' can also vary at different points on the production surface, whereas it is fixed at unity (equal to one) for the Cobb–Douglas function. As a result the translog function is consistent with a U-shaped average cost curve like that shown in Figure 5.6.

The formula for a two-variable input translog function is as follows:

$$\log Y = a + b_1 \log X_1 + b_2 \log X_2 + b_3 (\log X_1)^2 + b_4 (\log X_2)^2 + b_5 (\log X_1 \log X_2)$$

The corresponding marginal product equation for the first input is:

$$MP_1 = \frac{\partial Y}{\partial X_1} = \frac{Y}{X_1} (b_1 + 2b_3 \log X_1 + b_5 X_1 \log X_2)$$

Despite its flexibility this functional form has some limitations. As with the Cobb–Douglas function, so too in this case, all input response curves must pass through the origin. This means that if any input is at zero level, then

Figure 13.9   Isoquants for the Cobb–Douglas function

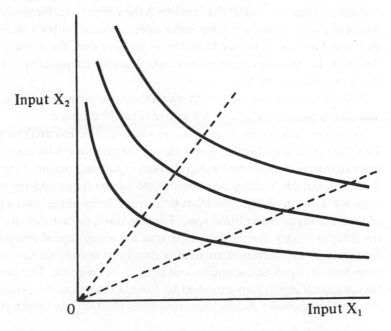

Input X_2

0   Input X_1

the output must also be zero. Also to ensure that the marginal product of input 1 is positive but decreasing, the following inequalities must hold;

$$0<(b_1+2b_3\log X_1+b_5X_1\log X_2)<1$$

and

$$0<(b_1+2b_3(\log X_1-1))$$

These conditions restrict the values of X_2 to quite a narrow range. Similar restrictions apply to X_1 if MP_2 is to be positive but diminishing. None the less this functional form has some clear advantages over the other forms discussed above (see Squires 1987).

Production functions in practice

The mathematical functions which have been discussed are, of course, not the only ones which could have been used to describe production relationships (see Dillon 1977). Nevertheless, they are the ones most commonly met with in practice. The choice of function involves a certain amount of subjective judgement, as does the choice of variable inputs to include in the function. It is possible to compare the values of R^2 obtained or use statistical tests of whether one model is an improvement on another, but since there is always some residual variation in output we cannot prove conclusively that one particular function is the correct one. Economic data do not obey exact laws; hence it is impossible to predict output exactly for a given combination of inputs. However, as we have seen, the quadratic and the Cobb–Douglas functions have certain desirable characteristics from a theoretical point of view.

Nevertheless, the frequency with which these two forms are used is probably due, in part, to the ease with which they can be estimated.

Various problems arise in applying production function analysis to any data. One general problem is that in theory the production function represents an instantaneous relationship between inputs and output. In practice there is invariably a delay between the use of the input and the output response. Thus, in practice, the relationship must be measured over a period of time, usually an agricultural year. However, this is not satisfactory where the delay is longer than a year, as is true for many capital investments. Furthermore, capital inputs are usually chunky or indivisible, so a smooth mathematical function cannot be used to describe response. The introduction of capital inputs into a production function therefore raises considerable problems which have not been completely resolved (see Upton 1979).

An associated problem is that of allowing for risk and uncertainty. The economic optimum represents the level of output which will yield the highest profit *on average*, but there must be considerable uncertainty about the outcome of any productive activity in a particular season on a particular farm. In fact, as we have seen, most farmers make some efforts to avoid risks and are willing to give up some profit for this purpose. Thus the most attractive level of output for most farmers is likely to be somewhere below the economic optimum, since they will discount the potential marginal returns for risk. Furthermore, since farmers vary in their aversion to risk, then the 'most attractive level of output' will vary between farmers. This problem also has not been completely resolved. Other problems are associated with particular studies, whether they are 'experimental' or 'survey', so one example of each type of production function study will be discussed in more detail.

On farm experiments: fertilizer use efficiency in Indian agriculture

A recent study published by the Institute of Development Studies of Jaipur, Rajasthan was aimed at testing the efficiency of fertilizer use in India (Sagar 1995). The conventional wisdom is that the unit cost of food-grain production is rising fast due to the declining marginal productivity of fertilizers. This is supposedly due to (i) extending fertilizer use into inferior, unirrigated production environments and (ii) over use of fertilizers in the better endowed areas, such as the Punjab. This conventional wisdom is tested for wheat and rice using cross-sectional farm level data for several periods in the 1970s and 1980s, from various sources. In particular data were obtained from:

(i) experiments on cultivator's fields (ECF data) from the 'All India Coordinated Agronomic Project',
(ii) uncontrolled field data from the 'High Yielding Varieties Programme' evaluation survey,
(iii) the 'Cost of Cultivation Surveys' which are conducted annually in all States of India.

Linear and quadratic functions are fitted to farm level or district aggregates of kg of fertilizer use, treated as a single variable input, and the yield of wheat or rice also measured in kg. Separate functions are estimated and compared for different time periods. The general findings are that response to fertilizers is rather low in the less well-endowed regions, but that in the more favoured areas response is much higher and is rising over time. For the period 1980–4, the economic optimum level of fertilizer use, estimated from the production function analyses, was 274 kg per ha in the Punjab, but only 45 kg in the Middle Gangetic region.

The increasing response to fertilizers, over time in the more productive areas, is illustrated by data on wheat yields, and fertilizer ($N + P_2O_5$) use in the Punjab over the periods 1981–2, 1985–6 and 1987–8 (Singh et al. 1992). The equations fitted to these data are as follows:

$$1981\text{--}2 \quad Y = 16.78 + 10.73F \quad 1.87F^2 \quad R^2 - 0.80$$
$$(4.86) \quad (1.55)$$

$$1985\text{--}6 \quad Y = 21.22 + 9.29F - 1.00F^2 \quad R^2 = 0.83$$
$$(5.39) \quad (1.71)$$

$$1987\text{--}8 \quad Y = 25.00 + 8.18F - 0.89F^2 \quad R^2 = 0.93$$
$$(2.89) \quad (0.93)$$

Standard errors of the coefficients are given in parentheses. All variables are measured in quintals (1 quintal = 100 kg). These equations show that the response curves are not only shifting, but also rotating upwards (see Figure 13.10). Thus the marginal product of fertilizer is rising over time and so too is the economic optimum use of fertilizer.

This study illustrates the use of simple response curve analysis using the quadratic function, to determine the efficiency of resource allocation by farmers. Since the data are derived from field trials, the levels of input use cannot be as tightly controlled as under experimental conditions, and variable inputs not included in the analysis are not held constant. None the less, the results obtained are more likely to be applicable on farms than those derived from experiments.

The exclusion of other variable inputs from the analysis, as in this study, clearly limits the information derived. For instance, it is likely that investment in research and development of high-yielding variety seeds and irrigation water both have a significant impact on crop yield, which is not measured. Furthermore estimates of the marginal product of fertilizer may be biased by the omission of these other variables.

Farm survey analysis: smallholder farming in Zimbabwe

This analysis is based on a survey of small farms on what was the Chiweshe Reserve in Zimbabwe. Although production function analyses of farm surveys have been made in other parts of Africa, this one has been described and discussed in particular detail (see Johnson 1969 & Massell 1967).

The sample survey was originally conducted during the 1960–1 cropping season and included 118 farms in all. It is claimed that 'in terms of crop production, the 1960–61 season was approximately average for Chiweshe [and] the area sampled appears to be reasonably representative of the reserve as a whole'. A large variety of crops are grown and some livestock are kept, but the analysis was restricted to the three main crops of maize (corn), millet and groundnuts (peanuts). For the production function analysis all farms that had incomplete crop production data or that did not grow all three crops were deleted, leaving a final sample of fifty-six farms in the analysis.

A Cobb–Douglas function was used to relate the output of each crop to the set of observed inuts used in producing the crop. The function can be written, using our notation,

$$\log Y = a + b_1 \log X_1 + b_2 \log X_2 + b_3 \log X_3 + b_4 \log X_4 + b_5 \log X_5 \\ + b_6 X_6 + b_7 X_7 + b_8 X_8$$

where

$Y=$ physical output of the particular crop (maize, millet or groundnuts),

$X_1=$ area of land used for that crop,

$X_2=$ man-hours of labour used in weeding that crop,

$X_3=$ weight of chemical fertilizer applied to that crop (plus a constant),

Figure 13.10 Wheat yield in relation to fertilizer

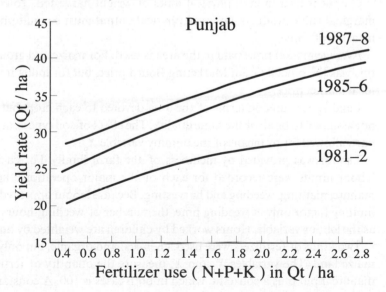

X_4= weight of organic manure applied to that crop (plus a
constant),

X_5= value of farm implements owned, at undepreciated initial
cost,

X_6= soil type, red loam or sandy soil,

X_7= skilled farmer, yes or no,

X_8= semi-skilled farmer, yes or no.

An extra term was added to represent the residual error, but, since we assume that on average the residual error is zero, we can omit it from the equation.

This equation differs from the simple Cobb–Douglas function described earlier in that more variable inputs are included. Furthermore, some of the X variables do not represent quantities of a particular input, but simply take one of two values. For instance X_6 representing soil type takes the value of 1 for red loam or 0 for sandy soil. Variable X_7 takes the value of 1 for a skilled farmer or 0 for a semi-skilled or unskilled farmer. Likewise variable X_8 takes the value of 1 for a semi-skilled farmer or 0 for any other. Such variables are known as 'dummy variables' and are used to estimate the effects of factors which are not easily measured as physical quantities. These dummy variables are not converted into logarithms.

Before discussing the results, the variables included in the function will be considered in a little more detail.

Output is measured in physical units of weight harvested. To compare marginal value products, however, physical output must be multiplied by a measure of value.

Average market price paid in the area is used. For maize and groundnuts this was the official Grain Marketing Board price, but for millet it was the local market price.

Land is measured in terms of the area devoted to each crop, but land is not assumed to be all of the same quality. The effect of soil type is, at least in part, allowed for by means of the dummy variable X_6.

Labour was provided by members of the farm family. For each crop, labour inputs were recorded for each of the major operations: applying manure, planting, weeding and harvesting. Because labour appeared to be a limiting factor only at weeding time, the number of weeding-hours is used as the labour variable. Hours worked by children are weighted by one-half.

Two kinds of fertilizers were used, chemical and organic, but only on the maize land. The variables X_3 and X_4 measure the quantity of fertilizer or manure input plus a constant, which in both cases is 100. A constant must be added before converting to logs since some farmers did not use any on their maize and yet still obtained some output. (Note that log 0 does not exist.) This implies that fertilizers are not essential inputs, as there is some natural fertility in the soil. The constant may be assumed to represent the natural fertility, but the choice of its value is quite arbitrary.

Fixed capital consisted of relatively simple farm implements such as an ox-drawn plough or cultivator. As an index of a farmer's fixed capital inputs, the value of farm implements at undepreciated initial cost is used. This index omits the services of draft animals and investment in the land, neither of which was recorded in the survey. Furthermore, no account is taken of the current condition of the implements.

Managerial inputs are included in the function by means of the dummy variables X_7 and X_8 which are based on a rating of farmers by the government agricultural extension service. Thus farmers who receive advice from the extension service are classified into three categories: co-operators, plot holders and master farmers. A co-operator is any farmer who uses fertilizer, carries out some crop rotation and plants his crops in rows. A plot holder is a farmer who is under tuition by an extension worker to become a master farmer. A master farmer is one who has gone through the plot holder stage and has reached specified higher standards of crop and animal husbandry as laid down by the agricultural department. Of the fifty-six farms in the final sample there were three master farmers, four plot holders and fourteen co-operators. Owing to the small numbers, master farmers and plot holders are combined into a single group of 'skilled' farmers. The co-operators are referred to as 'semi-skilled' and the remaining thirty-five farmers as 'unskilled'. The coefficients b_7 and b_8 are a measure of the contribution to output of 'skill' and 'semi-skill' relative to lack of skill.

The results of the analysis show that there is considerable variation in output which is not explained by the production function. For groundnuts and millet less than half the total variation in output is explained by the analysis, so the authors rightly warn that the results must be interpreted with caution ($R^2 < 0.5$). The only coefficients significantly different from zero were:

for maize – land, soil type, chemical fertilizer & organic manure,
for groundnuts – fixed capital and skilled management,
for millet – land and weeding labour.

The sum of the elasticities of response is nearly 1 for maize and millet, thus suggesting constant returns to scale for these two enterprises.

Table 13.1. *Estimated marginal value products*

	£ per unit of measure		
Input	Maize	Groundnuts	Millet
Land per hectare	3.13	3.04	4.40
Labour per weeding hour	0.005	0.012	0.015
Chemical fertilizer per £ cost	1.69	—	—
Organic manure per metric ton	1.31	—	—
Fixed capital per £ cost	—	0.087	0.025
Soil type per hectare (advantage of red loam over sandy soil)	0.88	0.21	1.07
Skilled farmer	1.35	1.52	−1.05
Semi-skilled farmer	−0.35	0.81	0.29

From Massell (1967). *Farm Management in Peasant Agriculture: An Empirical Study*. They differ slightly from those given in some of the other reports of this research.

However, the sum of elasticities is only 0.753 for groundnuts, which implies decreasing returns to scale. This may be due to the omission of some important factor, such as labour quality, that should enter the groundnut production function.

The estimated marginal value products of the variable inputs from each of the three crops are given in Table 13.1, converted from the original units into £ sterling and metric system physical measures.

These results suggest which variable inputs are most profitable to expand. There is no possibility to bring more land under cultivation, as farmers use all the arable land. Land appears to be a limiting factor. The marginal value product of labour is low in relation to the hourly wage rate in paid employment. Because of the low return to labour on the farm, many farmers spend a considerable part of the year away from the reserve working for wages. The return to chemical fertilizer does not appear adequate to justify much increase in its use. On the other hand it is suggested that the unit factor cost of organic manure is very low, virtually only the labour cost, so the marginal product is a return to labour. As an average of 16 hours was spent applying a ton of organic manure, the return to this labour is about 8p per hour as against only just over 1p per hour for weeding. However, livestock numbers may be an effective constraint on the amount of manure available. The return to capital is low and the results suggest that the area is overcapitalized with respect to implements.

With regard to soil type, the benefit from farming on the red loam soils rather than sandy soils appears greatest for millet and lowest for ground-nuts. The estimates for managerial skill measure technical efficiency only and do not reflect differences between farmers in allocative efficiency. For instance, the figure for skilled farmers in the maize production function is £1.35; this means that, on average for a given level of all other inputs, skilled farmers obtained £1.35 more maize output than unskilled farmers. There are some unexpected results in that skilled farmers obtained *lower* returns from millet production than unskilled farmers, and the same is true for semi-skilled farmers in maize production. It is suggested that this may reflect possible shortcomings in the government rating scheme which tended to focus on maize and groundnuts, or it may be the result of small sample size. The study showed that the quantities of all other resources used are related to managerial skill. Skilled farmers use more land, labour, fertilizer, manure and fixed capital than the semi-skilled, who in turn use more of all these resources than the unskilled.

The analysis is also useful in suggesting how profits may be increased by reallocation of resources. The marginal value productivities of both land and labour are highest in growing millet, suggesting that profits would be raised by shifting resources from maize and groundnuts into millet produc-tion. However the resulting gain is estimated to be relatively small. In so far as the farmers may have objectives other than profit maximizing, such as self-sufficiency, the existing allocation of resources may be satisfactory. This, of course, is only true *on average*. Some individual farmers might benefit considerably from reallocation of resources.

The problems of applying production function analysis to farm survey data arise from the fact that it is impossible for the researcher to control any of the variable inputs. At least, he may restrict his study to farms of a certain size range or type, but he cannot set any inputs at selected fixed levels, or arrange that the inputs are varied independently of each other. This still need not create serious problems if it could be assumed that the quantities of inputs used on different farms varied at random. Unfortunately this is not the case, since the quantities of resources used are largely the result of conscious human decisions. For instance, if the sample of farmers all operate on the same production function, all pay the same prices for inputs and all operate at the economic optimum, then they would all use exactly the same quantity of each input and produce exactly the same output. Although there would be a large number of farms in the sample, they would all be operating at the same point on the production function. It would be impossible to draw or estimate the form of the func-tion as in Figure 13.1a.

In fact the problem need not arise in this extreme form since some inputs are fixed at different levels on different farms, such as the supply of land, the family size or the managerial ability of the farmer. Alternatively, there may be variation between farms in the prices paid for resources. However, it still remains true that the inputs do not vary between farms at random, but are chosen by farmers or allocated by the society according to some set of decision rules. Indeed it is likely that all inputs will vary together, as was found to be the case in the study of Chiweshe farmers just described. The skilled farmers use more land, labour, fertilizer, manure and fixed capital than the semi-skilled, who in turn use more of all these resources than the unskilled. Where, as in this case, the levels of variable inputs are closely related between themselves, we speak of 'multicollinearity'. Its presence means that it is very difficult, if not impossible, to disentangle the influences of the variable inputs and obtain a reasonably precise estimate of their separate effects.

Take, for instance, the case of just two variable inputs, labour and land, which tend to vary together, more labour being employed on larger farms. It is then very difficult to say whether the larger output obtained on the larger farms is the result of the increased inputs of land or the increased inputs of labour, or how the extra output should be apportioned between the two inputs. We could only *safely* do this if there were some farmers who used extra land without using any more labour, that is if the inputs varied independently of each other and there was no multicollinearity present.

Where there is multicollinearity, it is particularly dangerous to omit one of the interrelated variable inputs from the function, because then the marginal product of this input will be attributed to those left in the function. For example, imagine a situation where each extra hectare of land cultivated uses an extra unit of labour and yields an additional output of £26. Now this £26 represents the joint marginal product of both land and labour, but if land is left out of the production function it will appear that the £26 (or at least most of it) is the marginal product of labour alone. The omission of one of the interrelated variable inputs from the production function will therefore give overestimates of the marginal productivities of the other inputs. It will give biased results. Because of this danger it is important that *all* variable inputs should be measured and included in the production function analysis. One input which is frequently omitted, because it is difficult to measure, is the input of management, but its omission gives rise to so-called 'management bias' in the estimated marginal products of the other resources used. In the Chiweshe study, management inputs are included, but only at the three levels of skill, semi-skilled and unskilled, and this ranking is based, at least to some extent, on the subjective judgement of the extension officers. If a more precise ranking of managerial inputs was possible, the estimates of marginal products for other inputs would probably be more accurate.

In summary it would appear that, provided there is some independent variation between inputs, there is not 'exact multicollinearity' and it may be possible to estimate separate marginal products for all inputs. However, the reliability of the estimates may not be very good. Furthermore, it is important that all relevant variable inputs should be included in the function to avoid bias. It may be difficult to measure some inputs such as soil quality and management, and large numbers of input variables may be involved. To reduce the number of variables some attempt at grouping inputs together may be necessary. For instance, child labour is grouped together with adult labour, and different kinds of fixed capital are grouped together. Such grouping must involve some arbitrary choice of which variables to group together and what relative weightings to use.

Recent production function studies on Zimbabwean agriculture include Khatri, Jayne & Thirtle (1995) and Thirtle et al. (1993).

Summary

1 Given a set of observations, from a cross-section of experimental plots or survey farms (or possibly time-series data) a production function may be estimated, relating inputs to output.

2 The method of least-squares regression is outlined, whereby the sum of squares of residual errors is minimized, to give the line (or pseudo-plane) of best fit.

3 The coefficient of variation (R^2) is a measure of goodness of fit. Estimates of standard errors may be used to test the null hypothesis of no relationship between inputs and output or to calculate confidence intervals for the regression coefficients.

4 The linear function is the simplest to estimate, but does not allow for diminishing marginal returns. The quadratic function allows for diminishing and even negative marginal returns, but involves more than one term (coefficient) per variable input. The Cobb–Douglas (double-log) function does not give a technical optimum (maximum) yield and must pass through zero. The translog (transcendental logarithmic) function, is more flexible than the other forms, but is more complicated to estimate.

5 Examples are given of the use of production function analysis (a) to assess the economics of fertilizer use in the Indian Punjab, using a quadratic form, (b) to suggest managerial improvements on smallholder farms in

Zimbabwe, using Cobb–Douglas functions. In the latter case, problems of lack of experimental control of inputs and of multicollinearity are emphasized.

References

Dillon, J. T. (1977). *The Analysis of Response in Crop and Livestock Production*, 2nd edn, Oxford, Pergammon

Flinn, J. C. & J. Lagemann (1980). 'Evaluating technical innovations under low resource farmer conditions', *Experimental Agriculture*, **16**, 91

Goldsworthy, P. R. (1967). Responses of cereals to fertilizers in Northern Nigeria: 1. Sorghum', *Experimental Agriculture*, **3**(1), 29

Idachaba, F. S. (1973). 'Marketing board crop taxation and input subsidies: a second-best approach', *Nigerian Journal of Economic Social Studies*, **15**, 317

Johnson, R. W. M. (1969). 'The African village economy: an analytical model', *The Farm Economist*, **11**(9), 359

Khatri, Y., T. S. Jayne & C. Thirtle (1994). *A Profit Function Approach to the Efficiency Aspects of Land Reform in Zimbabwe*. Paper presented to the International Conference of Agricultural Economists, Harare, Zimbabwe, August 1994

Massell, B. F. (1967). 'Farm management in peasant agriculture: an empirical study', *Food Research Institute Studies*, **7**(2), 205

Norman, D. W., J. A. Hayward & H. R. Hallam (1975). 'Factors affecting cotton yields obtained by Nigerian farmers'. *Cotton Growing Review*, **52**(1), 30

Norman, D. W., D. H. Pryor & C. J. N. Gibbs (1979). *Technical Change and the Small Farmer in Hausaland, Northern Nigeria*. East Lansing, Michigan State University, Department of Agricultural Economics, African Rural Economy Paper 21

Osuntogun, A. (1978). 'The impact of co-operative credit on farm income and the efficiency of resource use in peasant agriculture: a case-study from three States in Nigeria', *African Journal of Agricultural Science*, **5**(2), 1

Sagar, V. (1995). *Fertilizer Use Efficiency in Indian Agriculture*, Institute of Development Studies, Jaipur.

Saylor, R. G. (1974). 'Farm level cotton yields and the research and extension services in Tanzania', *Eastern Africa Journal of Rural Development*, **7**, 46

Singh, I. P., S. S. Grewal & P. L. Sankhayan (1992). 'Input use efficiency in areas of intensive agriculture: a case of Punjab State', *Indian Journal of Agricultural Economics*, **47**(3)

Squires, D. (1987). 'Long-run profit functions for multiproduct firms', *American Journal of Agricultural Economics*, **69**(3), 558–69

Thirtle, C., J. Atkins, P. Bottomley, N. Gonese, J. Govereh & Y. Khatri (1993). 'Agricultural productivity in Zimbabwe, 1970–89', *Economic Journal*, **103**, 474–80

Upton, M. (1979). 'The Unproductive production function', *Journal of Agricultural Economics*, **30**(2), 179

Wonnacott, R. J. & T. H. Wonnacott (1970). *Econometrics*, New York, Wiley

Part IV

Farm planning

14

Budgeting

The need for farm planning

Farm planning means assessing the implications of allocating resources in a particular way before deciding whether to act. It is an essential part of rational decision-making, and we have assumed in earlier chapters that farmers actually do plan what to produce and how to produce it. Thus planning is part of the day-to-day activity of running a farm; but it is particularly important when changes in the farm system are being considered. Few farmers would be willing to adopt an innovation without first evaluating the consequences.

However, for many farmers, planning is subjective and informal. Only on larger, commercial farms, where records and accounts are kept is it likely that formal procedures, such as budgeting are used. None the less, these practices are useful, not only in allowing closer control of the farm system, but also in persuading credit agents to provide loans. Thus there are good reasons for encouraging more farmers to keep records and accounts and to prepare budgets for proposed changes in their farming activities.

Farm planning techniques are also used by researchers, advisors and development planners, in two different ways. On the one hand, farming systems researchers and farm advisors are concerned to *prescribe* what farmers ought to do in order to advise on how systems can be improved. Development planners, on the other hand, may wish to *predict* how farmers will respond to changes in prices, institutions or technology. In either case the reliability of the results depends on how well the planner has identified farmer objectives and constraints. If the planner mistakenly assumes that the sole objective is profit maximization, his prescriptions may be unacceptable to farmers and his predictions will be wrong.

Farm planning techniques are designed for use on individual farms, taking account of the resource endowment, constraints and objectives peculiar to each household. However, given the large number of small farm households, the cost of providing individual advice and assistance would be prohibitive. A more feasible alternative is to prepare plans for one or more 'representative' case-study farms and to generalize from them to the whole target population. Thus Farming Systems Research involves assessing the impact of innovations throughout the recommendation domain, using plans for representative farm households. General guide-lines for farmer advice and extension may be obtained in the same way. Similarly development planning may involve aggregation of budgets from representative case studies to predict the overall performance of a develop-ment project.

For planning purposes the 'representative' farm need not exist as a real farm. Plans can be drawn up for a model farm based on typical or average conditions. However, if the plans are then subjected to on farm testing it is clearly necessary to identify actual case study or unit farms.

The budgeting procedure

A budget is simply an attempt to quantify the effects of a proposed plan. The prediction of inputs and outputs is an exercise in forecasting the future and there is obvious scope for error. Forecasts must, of course, be based on past experience under similar conditions. Budgets may be pre-pared at two different levels. Whole farm budgets are estimates of the overall impact of a proposed plan on the whole system. Partial budgets, on the other hand, are used where the plan only affects a particular enterprise or sub-system, which can then be considered separately. Only those items likely to change are included in the partial budget.

Budgeting involves three main steps:

(1) preparing a description and specification of the proposed plan, in terms of the area of each crop and number of each class of live-stock to be produced and the methods of production;
(2) testing the feasibility of the proposed plan in terms of the resource requirements relative to what are available and to other institu-tional, social and cultural constraints;
(3) evaluation of the plan.

In budgeting, the specification of farm plans depends on the planner's intuitive judgement, although it must be influenced by technical knowledge of what crop varieties, types of livestock and methods of production are suited to the environment. Where it is part of a Farming Systems Research programme, however, it may be based on the diagnosis of farmer problems and limiting constraints. The specification is then designed to remove or overcome the constraints, where promising new technology is available. This stage is best achieved by active collaboration between the farm planner, crop and livestock specialists and, if possible, representative farmers.

The second stage involves estimation of whether sufficient land is available to allow the planned crops to be incorporated in a rotation which will maintain soil fertility. Seasonal labour requirements are compared with labour availability. Where appropriate, animal or machine power and cash constraints may also be considered. The plan may be tested to determine whether sufficient food will be produced to meet family needs.

The final evaluation involves assessing costs and benefits to the farm family. These are usually estimated in money terms, which may place undue emphasis on financial profits. However, as we have argued elsewhere, provided that other objectives are treated as constraints which must be satisfied, farmers may well prefer to choose the most profitable alternative. Nevertheless, if it is thought more appropriate, evaluation might be based on nutritional values for instance. Sensitivity analysis, in which the calculations are repeated for different values of key variables, may be used to give some guidance as to the risk involved.

Sources of planning data

In order to prepare a budget, estimates are needed of the resource input requirements, the yields, costs and benefits of each enterprise included in the plan. These are then compared with the resource base of the representative farm and used in evaluating the outcome. For ease of calculation it is assumed that each enterprise (a) uses inputs in fixed proportions and (b) is subject to constant returns to scale. This means that data on the average input and output per hectare of a crop can simply be multiplied by the number of hectares of that crop to arrive at the corresponding totals. Similarly, inputs and outputs per head of livestock may be multiplied by the number of animals. Planning data needs are thereby limited to information on the characteristics of the representative farm household plus average, per unit input and output for the relevant enterprises. These are known as 'input–output data', or 'coefficients'.

This approach does not necessarily imply that the law of diminishing returns and possibilities of input substitution have been ignored. Rather it is assumed that the least-cost combination of inputs has been found and is represented by the input–output coefficients used.

For crops and animals which have already been raised in the past, input–output data may be derived from farm records and accounts. Such information may have been collected during the description and diagnosis phase of Farming Systems Research. Where an innovation is proposed which has not previously been tested on farms, however, planning data must be derived from research experiments. Field studies have shown that farmers are rarely able to achieve the level of performance obtained on research stations. This is probably due to the much higher level of management that can be afforded on research stations. In any case, it means that the experimental results should be adjusted to allow for this difference before they are used for farm planning.

Input–output data for the main crop and livestock enterprises may be obtained from earlier studies and published sources, if more recent local data are not available. Indeed attempts have been made to provide standard, input–output data for general use (e.g. see Phillips 1964). Official agencies engaged in regular farm survey work, could provide a useful service in producing and updating standard planning data.

Crop mixtures raise special problems since it cannot be assumed that the total input or output for the mixture is simply the sum of the parts. The total monthly labour requirements of a mixture of yams and maize will differ from that of the two crops grown separately. Some operations such as clearing and weeding are shared, while others such as harvesting are not. Thus there may be a case for treating the more common crop mixtures as single enterprises with input–output coefficients specific to them.

An example

The technique of whole farm budgeting will be illustrated with an example from Kenya (Clayton 1961). The plan was devised by agricultural advisors for a representative smallholding of 4.30 hectares in the Star/Kikuyu grass ecological zone. It was intended that the proposed plan, ʼif technically and economically feasible, would be recommended to other farmers in the areas. Although prices and technical input–output coefficients may have changed since this study was reported, it is nevertheless useful in illustrating the principles.

The plan as specified is set out in Table 14.1. It consists essentially of coffee, English potatoes, maize and bean production, together with dairying for cash and some subsistence production.

Table 14.1. *Plan for smallholding in Kenya: Kagere Sub-location, Othaya Division, Nyeri District, Central Province*

(a) Land use

(b) Livestock: Dairy cows to be kept on available fodder area at a stocking rate of one adult beast per 0.4 hectares

	Hectares		Hectares
Homesteads and paths	0.26	Napier grass (fodder)	0.36
Arable rotation	1.54	Vegetables	
Coffee	0.40	(home consumption)	0.23
Napier grass (mulch)	0.42	Bananas	
Cassava (home consumption)	0.26	(home consumption)	0.23
Permanent grass and trees	0.60	Total	4.30

Types of fodder	Hectares
Rotational grass	0.66
Napier grass (fodder)	0.36
Permanent grass and trees	0.60
Total area of fodder	1.62

Hence the farm can carry 1.62/0.4=4 dairy cows.

(i)   *Land use*

The first step in feasibility testing is to plan the pattern of land use. This involves comparing the area of each type of land required with the area available and determining sustainable crop rotations. In this case the area of coffee and of permanent grass had already been established, so the remaining task was to plan the allocation of arable land. It was further assumed that the area allocated to cassava, bananas and vegetables for home consumption should remain unchanged, as should the area of Napier grass for mulch and fodder. The land area remaining for arable crop rotation was 1.54 hectares.

The choice of crop rotation, meaning the sequence of crops, the planting dates and the duration of each, also determines the area of each crop which can be grown. In this ecological zone there are two cropping seasons, the long rains and the short rains, so effectively the proposed seven year rotation involves 14 courses, as shown in Figure 14.1. To maintain a steady-state system, equal areas of land should be allocated initially to each 'year' of the rotation. This is, of course, assuming that the rotation allows fertility to be restored so the system can continue. Thus, in this case, the available area of 1.54 hectares should be divided into seven equal areas of 0.22 hectares. Of these, three are under grass initially, one is planted with beans, one with English potatoes and two with early maize. The resulting crop areas are:

Grass ley	0.66 hectares
English potatoes	0.66 hectares
Beans	0.44 hectares
Early maize	0.44 hectares
Late maize	0.22 hectares

In this example the choice of rotation also determines the area of grazing available and hence the number of cows which can be carried.

(ii)   *Labour requirements*
        In comparing labour requirements of the plan with labour availability it is necessary to take account of the seasonality of farm work, the time needed for off-farm and household activities and possibly differences between men, women and children. Where there is strict division of labour, for instance, where men take sole responsibility for food crops, it may be necessary to treat male and female labour as separate categories. However, where work is shared, labour resources are pooled and should be treated as

Figure 14.1   The planned crop rotation

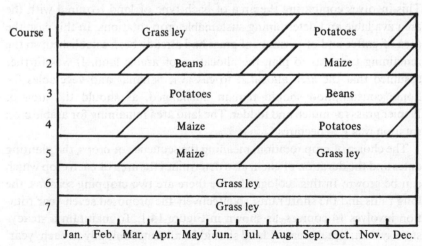

such. There may then be a case for using conversion factors to convert available female and child labour into standard man-days (see Chapter 4).

To allow for seasonality we need to estimate labour requirements and availability month by month (or week by week or at some other suitable interval). For this purpose standard monthly labour requirements per hectare of crops and per head of livestock are needed. The monthly total requirements can then be plotted on a graph as in Figure 4.9 to show the labour profile. From such a profile it is easy to identify where labour deficits and surpluses are likely to occur. This may suggest modifications of the plan to take up slack or to ease labour bottlenecks.

Preparation of a labour profile for the Kenyan farm showed that the plan was only feasible if oxen were hired for seed-bed cultivations, given a family work force of three full-time adult male equivalents. Assuming 300 working days annually, the monthly supply was estimated at 75 man-days. Although in no month did the needs of the plan exceed this, the total was approached in 8 of the 12 months.

(iii)   *Livestock feed*

Here again, it is necessary to compare the livestock feed requirement, with the amount available, allowing for seasonal variations. Of course supplementary foods may be purchased, but it is desirable to estimate the likely quantities and costs. Where, as in this example, animals are dependent on fodder grown on the farm, it may be necessary to adjust the numbers carried to match available supplies. Thus it was estimated that one cow required 0.4 hectares of grazing. Given a total of 1.62 hectares (0.66 of rotational ley, 0.36 of Napier grass and 0.60 of permanent grass), four cows could be carried.

In many situations, more complicated calculations would be needed. First, if there were alternative competing classes of livestock, for instance cattle or sheep, or even different age categories, it would be necessary to convert numbers into standard grazing livestock units for comparison with the carrying capacity of the grazed area. Second, if there were alternative feed sources available, supplies could only be aggregated in terms of nutritional measures such as MJ of metabolizable energy.

(iv)   *Evaluation*

Having estimated whether the proposed plan is feasible it may then be evaluated. The Kenyan farm plan was evaluated in money terms using estimates of the gross margin per hectare of crops and the gross margin per head of dairy cattle. The results are presented in Table 14.2. No charge was

Table 14.2. *Estimated returns and costs in East African shillings* (s)

Enterprise	Number of units	Price of product	Yield	Gross output	Costs	Gross margin	Total gross margin
	hectares	s per bag	*per unit* bags	s	s	s	s
English potatoes	0.66	13	98	1274	189	1085	716
Beans	0.44	43.25	15	648.75	32.75	616	271
Early maize	0.44	25	25	625	15	610	268
Late maize	0.22	25	20	500	14	486	107
		s per kg	cherry parchment kg				
Coffee[a]	0.40	1.1	1253	9511	11	9500	3800
	cows	s per litre	*per cow* litres	s	s	s	
Milk	4	0.33	910	300	50	250	1000
Total							6162
Less cost of oxen hire							140
Net income (return on capital, management and labour)							6022

[a] Parchment: cherry ratio 1:6.9.
After Clayton (1961).

made for capital costs of investment in coffee trees, dairy cows and land improvements. Thus the estimated net income represents the overall cash return on land, labour and capital.

Comment

Unlike production function analysis, or linear programming to be discussed in Chapter 16, budgeting does not lead in a systematic way to an optimal, or most profitable, solution. It can be used to find the most profitable of a set of alternative plans, but it does not guide the original choice of plans for evaluation. Production function analysis or linear programming, on the other hand, yield results in terms of the specific combinations of enterprises and levels of resource use which will yield the maximum profit.

None the less, budgeting will always have a place in practical farm planning because of its simplicity and flexibility. Budgets can be used to explore other aspects of farm plans than those discussed in our example. For instance, where irrigation is practised, water budgets may be used to assess seasonal crop water requirements for comparison with amounts available from precipitation and storage. Such analysis not only allows the feasibility of the proposed irrigation plan to be tested, but also may suggest ways of economizing in water use.

Similarly, budgets may be used to assess seasonal requirements for animal draft power, machinery or equipment. As for labour, requirements and availability may be estimated in terms of working hours or days. Monthly cash-flow budgets may be used to assess working-capital requirements. In this case it should be noted that revenues from sales of produce or off-farm earnings contribute to the supply of working capital, so the total supply is given by the cumulative *net* flow of cash into the household. Such an analysis will suggest where short-term credit may be needed, and whether borrowing can be justified.

Nutritional budgets are used to compare planned subsistence production with household food needs. Quantities are usually measured in MJ of gross energy, but checks may also be made as to whether sufficient protein or other essential nutrients will be available. Table 14.3 shows a simple energy budget for a typical Borana pastoralist household (Cossins & Upton 1986).

Partial budgets

Where only a relatively minor change in the pattern of farming is proposed it is not necessary to prepare a complete farm budget to estimate the

Table 14.3. *Annual energy budget for an eight-cow Borana household*

Source	Gross energy value MJ per year
Energy directly produced	
Milk offtake 18021 at 3.73 MJ	6720
Slaughtered meat 84 kg liveweight at 5.34 MJ	449
Fallen meat (consumable mortalities) 140 kg at 4 MJ	560
Sub-total	7729
Energy purchased	
Cereals 200 kg at 15 MJ	3000
Sugar 31 kg at 14 MJ	434
Other foods	1 140
Sub-total	4574
Total annual energy available	12 303
Basic annual energy requirement for three active adult male equivalents	12 000

(After Cossins & Upton 1986).

result. Instead, a partial budget can be used to arrive at the expected change in profits. This takes into account only those changes in costs and returns that result directly from the proposed modification. Farm costs or returns which are unaffected by the proposal are excluded from the calculation.

The simplest form of partial budget, applicable where a new enterprise or a new process such as the use of herbicides is introduced, involves the following questions:

(*a*) what extra returns (gains) can be expected?
(*b*) what extra costs will be incurred?

Where the proposed new activity substitutes for something already existing, as when one crop substitutes for another or a machine substitutes for labour, we must also ask:

(*c*) what present costs will no longer be incurred?
(*d*) what present income will be sacrificed?

Hence the total gain will be (*a*)+(*c*), the extra returns plus the saved costs, and the total cost will be (*b*)+(*d*), the extra costs plus the present income foregone. The total gain minus the total cost then represents the net gain or expected increase in profit.

As with complete budgets, the first step in partial budgeting should be a description of the proposed change stating clearly what is involved and when it occurs. Information should be included on the stock numbers, the areas of crops and the methods of production to be used. As a second step in partial budgeting it is useful to list those items in the existing system likely to be changed when the new policy is introduced This reduces the likelihood of omitting possible indirect effects of the change. Appropriate values can then be used to predict extra returns, savings in present costs, extra costs and income sacrificed to arrive at the expected change in profit.

A partial budget can be compiled more quickly and easily than a complete budget, since it is only concerned with the costs and returns that are to be changed. The items of cost and income unaffected by the change need not be estimated.

There are obvious dangers in using partial budgeting since, as was argued in Chapter 10, even quite small changes in one enterprise may have repercussions throughout the whole farm system. The dangers are that some of these effects will be forgotten in making a partial analysis of the effects of the change. None the less, partial budgeting is generally preferred to whole farm budgeting, even for planning substantial changes, because fewer items must be estimated.

The example given in Table 14.4 is a partial budget for the adoption of a two-wheel tractor with a trailer and tool bar, injection planter and sprayer, developed at IITA and known as a 'farmobile'. For comparison a partial budget for a small but conventional four-wheel tractor is included. These are clearly major items, likely to have a substantial impact on a smallholder farming system. None the less, it is possible to leave other enterprises such as permanent crops and livestock out of the calculations and prepare partial budgets solely for the impact on arable crops. Those items left out of the budget are treated as being fixed. There is a possible advantage in that the results may be applicable to a wider range of different holdings than would a whole farm budget.

It may be noted that this example involves capital investment in machinery. The extra costs therefore include an allowance for depreciation. A similar approach is used in the partial budget for grain storage presented in Table 14.5. Although these analyses provide a useful assessment of the economic returns, it would, in theory, be more appropriate to use investment appraisal since capital investments are involved. We return to this topic in the next chapter.

Table 14.4. *Partial budget for farm mechanization*

	IITA farmobile 2-wheel tractor	Low horsepower 4-wheel tractor
	Dollars	Dollars
Costs		
Fixed costs		
Depreciation	2040	5610
Interest	1122	3085
Operational costs	1448	4515
Variable costs of farm inputs	10 531	16 555
Total costs	15 141	29 765
Revenue from maize harvest	15 038	25 050
Revenue from cowpea harvest	7555	12 705
Total revenue	22 593	37 755
Net benefit	7452	7990
Net benefit per hectare	857	555

(After IITA 1983).

Use of gross margins

In partial budgeting we are concerned only with those costs and returns which are expected to change. Other items, which are assumed to remain fixed are left out of the calculation. When the proposed change simply involves substituting one enterprise for another, the only costs that are likely to be affected are the variable or direct costs of each enterprise. Thus we may estimate the effect of substituting one hectare of cotton for one hectare of groundnuts by comparing the gross margins of the two crops. We are, of course, assuming that no extra land, labour or equipment is needed as a result of the change. Then

net gain = (extra returns + saved costs) − (extra costs + income foregone)

= (gross output of cotton + variable costs of groundnuts) − (variable costs of cotton + gross output of groundnuts)

= (gross margin of cotton) − (gross margin of groundnuts).

This means that if we know the gross margins of the two enterprises it is a very quick and easy exercise to estimate the result of substituting a hectare

Table 14.5. *Partial budget to estimate extra profit from storage*

---

1 Specification
Proposal to store 10 tons (10 000 kg) sorghum per year. Cost of small concrete bin of 10 tons capacity £100. Expected life of bin ten years. No maintenance or repair cost. Grain to be fumigated, so losses due to insect damage and drying in the bin negligible.

2 Items in present system likely to be changed
Sorghum no longer available for sale at harvest time. No reduction in existing costs.

3 Estimated gains and cost (£)

Gains		Costs	
(a) Extra returns		(b) Extra costs	
Sales of stored grain		Cleaning bin	0.25
10 tons at £24.25	242.50	Fumigation of bin	
		15p per ton	1.50
		Depreciation of bin	
		£100/10	10
(c) Saved costs	nil	(d) Present income sacrificed	
		Sales of grain at harvest-	
		time (10 tons at £20)	200
Total	242.50		211.75

Net gain=242.50−211.75=30.75

	£
Fixed capital	
Initial cost of bin	100
Working capital	
Income foregone by not selling sorghum at harvest-time	200
Cost of cleaning bin	0.25
Cost of fumigation	1.50
Total initial capital	301.75

Return on initial capital=30.75/301.75×100=10%

---

of cotton for a hectare of groundnuts or even of substituting 0.6 hectares of cotton for 1.1 hectares of groundnuts or any other relative change that might be feasible.

Consideration of the feasibility of the change now suggests a way in which to plan on a more rational basis. If we can discover which resource is the most limiting constraint on production, we can select the enterprise which yields the highest gross margin per unit of that limiting constraint. Furthermore, we can decide objectively how far to expand that enterprise. In fact, we should expand it as far as possible until all the limiting resource is used up.

To illustrate, let us assume that the gross margins of cotton and groundnuts are £150 and £120 per hectare respectively and that labour is the

Table 14.6. *Monthly labour requirements per hectare of cotton and groundnuts*

	Man-days	
	Cotton	Groundnuts
January	10	14
February	8	—
March	—	—
April	12	—
May	22	—
June	24	16
July	17	12
August	17	8
September	—	7
October	—	8
November	15	15
December	25	20
Total	150	100

resource which limits production. Hypothetical labour requirements per hectare of the two crops budgeted are set out in Table 14.6.

If labour is only available on a regular basis throughout the year, as is probably true of family labour, then the peak requirement must limit the area of crop that can be grown. In this case the peak requirement for both crops occurs in December, when cotton requires 25 man-days per hectare and groundnuts 20 man-days. Hence we should choose the crop which yields the highest gross margin per man-day of labour in December. For cotton the gross margin per hectare is £150 so the gross margin per man-day of December labour is £150/25=£6. For groundnuts the comparable figure is £120/20=£6. Hence there is nothing to choose between the two crops. However, if we assume that some of the December work might be carried out in November, to spread the peak a little, then we should compare the gross margin per man-day required in November and December together. For cotton the total labour requirement for the two months is 40 man-days and for groundnuts it is 35. Now the gross margin per man-day over the two months is for cotton £150/40=£3.75 and for groundnuts £120/35=£3.43. Hence cotton is the more attractive alternative. The same is true if we take the December and January labour requirements together.

If we know just how much labour will be available in each month we can calculate the amount of cotton that may be grown. Let us say that a surplus of 20 man-days is available in each month for growing either cotton or groundnuts. If the December work load could not be spread into November then the maximum possible area of cotton would be 20/25=0.8 hectares. This would yield a gross margin of £150×0.8=£120. However if we assume that it can be spread equally between the two months the labour available would be 40 man-days and the labour requirement per hectare 15+25=40. Hence a whole hectare could be grown, yielding a gross margin of £150.

This approach of selecting enterprises to introduce or expand according to the gross margin per unit of limiting resource is systematic and logical. So, too, is the policy of expanding that enterprise until the limiting resource is all used up.

However, in practice, several constraints may effectively limit the farmer's choice at the same time. A combination of enterprises may be needed to make best use of these limited resources as we saw in Chapter 4.

If the most limiting constraint could be clearly identified, a logical step-wise procedure might be adopted for planning based on (i) choosing the enterprise which yields the highest return to this constraint, (ii) observing which other constraints become effective (iii) introducing a second enterprise to make better use of the second limiting resource and so on. Such techniques are generally referred to as 'programme planning'.

Programme planning is tedious and difficult to use, and, although it has advantages over budgeting in moving in a logical sequence towards more profitable plans, the economic optimum will not necessarily be found. For this purpose the more formal techniques of linear programming are needed (see Chapter 16).

Summary

1 Planning is an important activity in managing a farming system. Although generally subjective and informal, planning can be improved by using formal budgeting procedures. Budgets are used to design future strategies, for budgetary control, for prescribing and predicting the farmer's decision-making.

2 Budgeting involves three main steps; specifying a plan, testing its feasibility, in terms of resource requirements and availability and evaluating the expected outcome.

3 The necessary input–output data may be obtained from farm survey or case-study records, for new technologies from experimental results (with some adjustment for poorer performance expected on the farm) or from published standards.

4 Whole farm budgeting is illustrated with an example from Kenya. Feasibility tests compared requirements and availability of land, labour and animal feed. Net income was estimated as the total gross margin from arable crops, coffee and milk, less the cost of oxen hire. Net income represents a return on household land, labour and capital resources.

5 Although budgeting does not lead directly to an optimal farm plan, it is a flexible and simple tool for comparing alternative plans. Water budgets (for irrigation), seasonal draught power budgets, working capital budgets and nutritional budgets are also useful.

6 Where a relatively minor change is planned, a partial budget, which compares additional benefits with additional costs, is appropriate. Note that additional costs include revenue foregone, while benefits include cost savings. Partial budgets are simpler and easier to complete than whole farm budgets, but some of the system interactions may be missed.

7 Gross margins may be used for partial budgeting of enterprise substitution. Indeed if the critical constraint on production is identified, then enterprises can be selected objectively in terms of the gross margin per unit of the most limiting resource. Once this enterprise is expanded to the maximum feasible level, other supplementary enterprises may be introduced to use up other unused resources. This technique, called programme planning, is less computationally efficient than linear programming.

References

Clayton, E. S. (1961). 'Economic and technical optima in peasant agriculture', *Journal of Agricultural Economics*, **14**(3), 337

Collinson, M. P. (1972). *Farm Management in Peasant Agriculture: A Handbook for Rural Development Planning in Africa*, New York, Praeger

Cossins, N. & Upton, M. (1986). *The Productivity and Potential of the Southern Rangelands of Ethiopia*, Addis Ababa, International Livestock Centre for Africa

Dalton, G. E. (1973). 'Adaption of farm management theory to the problems of the small-scale farmer in West Africa', in Ofori, T. M. (ed.), *Factors of Agricultural Growth in West Africa*. Proceedings of an International Conference, Legon, University of Ghana, Institute of Statistics, Social and Economic Research

Dillon, J. L. & J. B. Hardaker (1980). *Farm Management Research for Small Farmer Development*, Rome, FAO Agricultural Services Bulletin No. 41

IITA (1983). *Annual Report for 1982*, Ibadan, Nigeria, International Institute of Tropical Agriculture

Phillips, T. A. (1964). *An Agricultural Notebook*, 2nd edn, Ikeja, Nigeria, Longmans

15

Investment appraisal

Capital investment and time horizons

Many technological improvements are embodied in new forms of durable capital. This clearly applies to machinery and equipment innovations and to new varieties of permanent crops and livestock. Land improvements in destumping, terracing or irrigation works also represent long-term investments. In all such cases an ordinary, single-period budget is inadequate for estimating resource needs and evaluating the investment.

Investment appraisal, or to use its other name, capital budgeting involves estimating resource inputs, costs and benefits over the whole lifetime of a medium- or long-term investment. Discounting techniques are then used to provide a single measure of the desirability of the investment. Costs and benefits are almost always measured in money terms, and this planning tool is most relevant to investments made for commercial gain. When a loan is sought from a formal credit agency, it is normal practice to submit a capital budget for the proposed investment in support of the application. Many credit banks require such a budget as proof of the viability of the investment before a loan is considered.

The purposes of investment appraisal are

   (i) assessment of cash requirements for funding the investment;
   (ii) provision of a financial plan to determine credit needs and the schedule of repayments;
   (iii) evaluation of the investment, to determine whether it is financially viable and worth undertaking.

The method is closely similar to that of 'project appraisal' or 'cost-benefit analysis', used by economic planners to evaluate projects from the national point of view. The only difference lies in the prices used for evaluation. Whereas the national planner uses estimates of opportunity costs to the nation in 'economic analysis', or modifies these measures to allow for income distributional impact of the project in 'social analysis', we are here concerned with 'financial analysis' based mainly on market prices. (For further details of project appraisal see Gittinger 1982.)

The three main stages of an investment appraisal are

(i) specification of the investment plan, including its size, timing, pro ductive life and sources of finance;
(ii) estimation of the series of costs, and benefits, over the lifetime of the investment;
(iii) evaluation of the investment using discounting techniques.

In practice, the first two stages may overlap since the size and timing of the project is likely to be influenced by the estimated costs. As a specific example, consider a plan to introduce dairy cows on a farm. The number of cows that can be kept, that is the size of the dairy enterprise, must depend upon the fodder and cash requirements per cow, in relation to the amounts available. If resources are particularly scarce and credit lacking, cow numbers may be built up gradually over several years, rather than the whole herd being purchased together at the outset.

An early decision must be made as to the planning horizon, or length of life of the project. This is clearly linked with the choice of replacement policy; how long to keep each capital asset before its disposal and possible replacement. Let us assume, for present purposes, that a replacement policy has been chosen, and the economic 'optimum' life of each asset is known. In determining the planning horizon, three main cases may be distinguished.

Case 1 Short- or medium-term investment

Short-term investments in working capital such as seeds, fertilizers, stored produce or labour hire and medium-term investment in machinery and equipment, generally have a clearly defined, finite life. Whilst working capital is replaced every year, machines and equipment last several years. Investments in pigs and poultry are sometimes treated under this heading. Not only is the livestock replaced each year, but also the housing may only last a limited number of years. In such a case we may treat the life of the investment as the planning horizon. It really does not matter whether the investment will be replaced, it is treated as a 'one-off' case.

Case II Continuous replacement/upkeep and infinite planning horizon

Long-term investments include such crops as cocoa, coffee, tea, oil-palm and rubber, breeding livestock and irrigation and other land improvements. In these cases a policy of continuous replacement or upkeep may be adopted to maintain a steady-state system. Thus if oil-palms have an estimated productive life of 30 years, then $\frac{1}{30}$ of the area may be replanted annually. Similarly 20 per cent of the beef breeding herd may be replaced each year. Careful annual upkeep and repair of irrigation works and land improvements is intended to maintain productive capacity permanently. Following this approach of continuous maintenance of the original investment, the project should continue indefinitely; it has an infinite life.

In this case, once the project reaches maturity, the annual cost and benefits may be expected to remain constant indefinitely. Such a constant and infinite stream of costs or benefits is known as a perpetuity, and is very easily discounted to give the present value (V) as follows

$$V = A/i \quad \text{where } A = \text{annual cost or benefit}$$
$$i = \text{discount rate.}$$

Thus, if the project is expected to reach maturity in year five from which point on it will earn an annual net benefit of £A, as a perpetuity, this infinite stream can be replaced by a net benefit of £V in year five. In this way an infinite planning horizon is reduced to a five-year horizon.

Case III Long-term investment with irregular replacement

For some long-term investments it may be inappropriate to assume a continuous replacement so net benefits do not form a perpetuity. It may then be necessary to decide arbitrarily on a planning horizon of say 20 or 30 years. Strictly speaking the value of the terminal assets, remaining at the end of the period, should be included in the stream of benefits. However the precise estimation of costs and benefits beyond about 20 years ahead is relatively unimportant. When discounting, even at fairly low rates, the more distant future costs and benefits have a relatively low weighting. For instance, when discounted at 10 per cent, £1 expected in 20 year's time is worth only 15p now. Thus it makes little difference whether a 20-year or a 30-year horizon is chosen.

Cash-flow budgets

As in the case of simple budgeting, it is important to test the feasibility of the proposed plan by comparing expected resource requirements with resource availability. It may be appropriate to prepare budgets for land, labour, irrigation water, livestock feed or household diets. However, the development over time of resource requirements must now be considered. Several land use, labour or dictary budgets may now be needed for different stages of the proposed investment. Such feasibility testing may suggest modifications or improvements to the original plan.

The estimates used in any planning exercise are necessarily subject to uncertainty, which is greater the further ahead we try to plan. Decisions made now about productive activities several years hence are unlikely to be implemented in exactly the way, and with the precise results presently foreseen. However, since capital investment involves a commitment to a particular set of activities in the future, there is a strong case for attempting to predict the outcome as accurately as possible.

Detailed estimates of future resource inputs and product outputs, combined with forecasts of future prices are used in preparing the cash-flow budget. This is the profile or sequence of cash flows (extra income minus extra costs) over the life of the investment project. They are usually estimated on an annual basis, although shorter intervals might be used. Thus when evaluating crop storage it might be more appropriate to work with quarterly or even monthly cash flows. However, since interest is generally charged at an annual rate, medium and long term investments are best divided into yearly intervals. Most investments start with negative cash flows associated with the costs of establishing the project. Positive cash flows come later as the annual returns increase (see Figure 15.1).

Although money values are used in estimating cash flows, non-marketed items are included. For instance, increases in home-consumed produce resulting from the planned investment should be included as benefits, while the opportunity costs of family labour or land form part of the total cost. The estimation of these opportunity costs raises particular problems; and may require whole farm budgeting (see below) or Linear Programming (see Chapter 16).

The essential feature of cash-flow budgeting is that costs and benefits are accounted for *at the time they are expected to occur* (see Chapter 12). Thus if the plan involves purchase of an ox plough in the third year of the project, the whole cost of the plough is subtracted from the cash flow for that year. If it is resold three years later, the cash flow is increased accordingly in the sixth year of the project. Naturally no depreciation allowance is made as this would involve double counting of the replacement cost.

We are, of course, only concerned with the *extra* costs and *extra* benefits associated with the planned investment, and the differences between them which measure the extra or incremental cash flows. Thus the incremental cash flow in a particular year may be measured either as extra benefit due to project minus extra cost or as cash flow with project minus cash flow without the project.

In discounting we implicitly assume that transactions occur at yearly intervals, rather than continuously. The cost and benefits which arise in year 1 are assumed to occur at the end of the year. This means that the cash flow for year 1 is discounted one year in estimating the net present value. Similarly the cash flow for year 2 is discounted by two years and so on. The only exception to the rule that transactions are assumed to fall at the end of the year, is the initial investment. If the project is planned to start with the purchase of an item of capital, the purchase is assumed to occur at the *start* of year 1. To distinguish this date from the *end* of year 1, it is generally referred to as year 0.

Given that transactions are supposed to fall at the end of each year, it is necessary to make allowance for seasonal working-capital requirements. If there is any increase in operating expenses between one year and the next, at least a part of the extra cost must be met in advance and this requires working capital. The allowance for additional working capital is included

Figure 15.1 Cash flows over time

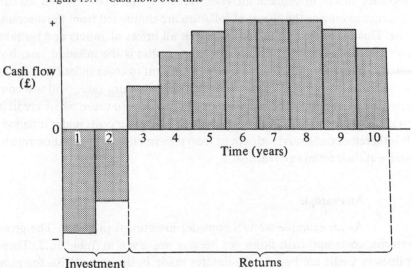

Table 15.1. *Estimating working-capital requirements*

	Year 1	Year 2	Year 3
Operating cost without working capital	£100	£150	£180
Operating cost with working capital, assuming two crops per year	£125	£165	

with the costs for the previous year in estimating cash flows. The ratio of working capital to operating costs depends upon the farming system. If only one crop is taken per year then the entire operating cost must be met before the crop is harvested. Working capital then represents 100 per cent of operating cost. If two crops are taken per year, only half the annual operating cost must be met before the first harvest, so working capital is around 50 per cent of operating cost (see Table 15.1). At the end of the project life, the total of these additional working-capital requirements is added to the terminal benefits, to allow for the fact that it is recovered eventually.

If credit is needed to finance the project, its impact may be measured by estimating cash flows after financing. This involves adding loan receipts to the cash flows for the relevant years and subtracting debt service payments. Two evaluations may then be made, one 'before financing' to give an overall assessment of the feasibility of the project and one 'after financing' to assess the effect on the farmer's income.

Where prices are rising due to inflation, the question arises of how to allow for this in investment analysis. Generally the answer is that we can ignore it so long as the effects of inflation are eliminated from the discount rate. This is justified on the grounds that all prices of inputs and outputs rise together at, say 15 per cent per year, if that is the inflation rate. But interest rates too will be increased by 15 per cent to cover inflation. Thus, if we subtract 15 per cent from all interest and discount rates, and use constant prices, the effects of inflation are eliminated. However, where credit is used, the repayments do not increase along with other costs under inflation. It is therefore necessary to discount loan repayments at the inflation rate to arrive at their estimated real cost.

An example

As an example we will consider investment in cocoa. The gross returns, costs and cash flows per hectare are given in Table 15.2. These values in Cedis are based on estimates made in the early 1970s for pure

Table 15.2. *Annual cash flows from cocoa* (Cedis per hectare.)

	Year 0	Year 1	Year 2	Year 3	Year 4	Year 5	Year 6	Years 7 to 30
Gross returns	—	—	—	—	75	125	200	250
Costs	198	35	47	47	45	43	53	55
Cash flows	−198	−35	−47	−47	30	82	147	195
Loan disbursement and repayment	250	—	—	—	—	−45	−45	−45
Cash flows after financing	52	−35	−47	−47	30	37	102	150

(Adapted from Rourke 1974).

stand cocoa, at the lower yield limit. With higher cocoa yields or with inter-cropping the returns would be greater. Note that the initial negative cash flows are followed later by positive ones, and that from year 7 to year 30 the cash flows represent an annuity.

In Table 15.2 we also illustrate a possible disbursement and repayment schedule for a cocoa loan. The whole loan, sufficient to cover the establishment costs to the end of year 1 is paid at the outset. There is a five-year grace period, then the principal plus interest at 10 per cent are to be repaid by a series of 25 equal annual instalments. As a supplementary exercise, the reader may care to check that a 25-year annuity of 45 Cedis, discounted at 10 per cent is worth 408 Cedis. This, discounted a further 5 years for the grace period, has a present value of 254 Cedis which with a slight margin covers the loan. By adding in the loan, and subtracting the repayments when due, we arrive at the net cash flows after financing.

The discounting exercise is carried out in Table 15.3; assuming a discount rate of 18 per cent. Discount factors are taken from Appendix Table 1. However the annual flow of 195 Cedis from year 7 to year 30 is an annuity. Thus it must be multiplied by the annuity factor for 23 years at 18 per cent which is 5.432 (Appendix Table II).

The resultant present value of the annuity in year 7 is further multiplied by the discount factor for 7 years at 18 per cent, of 0.314 to give the present value at year zero. The sum of the discounted cash flows gives the Net Present Value (NPV) of 147 Cedis, per hectare of cocoa.

A similar discounting exercise is used to arrive at the NPV after financing. As might be expected, since the interest rate of the loan is only 10 per cent while the discount rate is 18 per cent, the NPV is increased by taking the loan.

Table 15.3. *Discounted cash flows from cocoa* (at 18 per cent)

Year number	Cash flow	Discount factor	Discounted cash flow	After financing	
				Cash flow	Discounted cash flow
0	−198	–	−198	52	52
1	−35	0.848	−30	35	−30
2	−47	0.718	−34	−47	−34
3	−47	0.609	−29	−47	−29
4	30	0.516	15	30	15
5	82	0.437	36	37	16
6	147	0.370	54	102	38
7–30	195	0.314×5.432	333	150	256
Net present value			147		284

We may also estimate the internal rate of return (*IRR*) for the investment (before financing). As suggested in Chapter 7, this involves a trial and error procedure. One approach is to estimate the *NPV* for various different discount rates and to plot the graph of *NPV* against the discount rate. This is shown in Figure 15.2 from which it is clear that the *IRR* (that is the discount rate where *NPV* is zero) is approximately 23 per cent.

Alternatively, given just two estimates of the *NPV*, one positive (at the lower discount rate) and one negative (at the higher discount rate) the following formula may be used (see Gittinger 1982).

IRR=lower discount rate+Difference between discount rates
×(*NPV* at lower discount rate/Sum of absolute values of
*NPV*s at the two discount rates)

We have seen that the *NPV* at 18 per cent discount rate is 147 Cedis (Table 15.3). At a discount rate of 24 per cent, the *NPV* is calculated as −21 Cedis. Hence the estimated *IRR* is found approximately to be

IRR=18+6(147/168)=23.25 per cent

If we attempt to estimate the *IRR* after financing we run into problems. As we have seen, the *NPV* at a discount rate of 18 per cent is 284 Cedis. Even at much higher discount rates the *NPV* is still positive. For instance at a discount rate of 50 per cent the *NPV* is 31 Cedis, at 100 per cent it is 23 Cedis, at 200 per cent 34 Cedis and so on. In fact, if we plot *NPV* of the investment after financing against discount rate, as shown by the broken line in Figure 15.2, it is clear that the *NPV* never falls to zero. This means that no *IRR* exists.

Alternative measures

The possibility that an *IRR* may not exist is one reason why some authorities discourage the use of this measure in evaluating projects. However, for most standard projects of the type represented in Figure 15.1, where negative cash flows are followed by positive ones (i.e. there is only one change of sign in the sequence), an *IRR* does exist. It is particular useful in comparing investments of different size and duration, where the *NPV* would be less meaningful.

There is another alternative approach to comparing investments of

Figure 15.2   The internal rate of return for cocoa

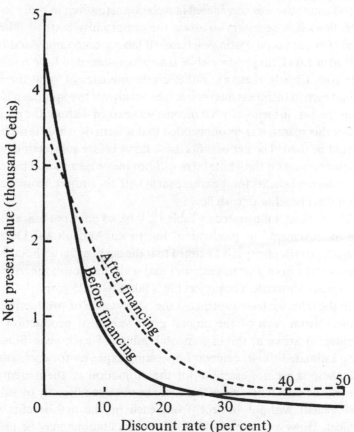

different duration, which is to estimate the equivalent annuity. This would enable us to compare different permanent crops. To illustrate, let us return to the cocoa crop (before financing) which at a discount rate of 18 per cent yields an *NPV* of 147 Cedis. This applies to a 30-year life. Now an annuity of 1 Cedi for 30 years discounted at 18 per cent gives a present value of 5.517 Cedis (see Appendix Table II). Hence the equivalent annual annuity, yielding an *NPV* of 147 Cedis is

147/5.517 = 26.64 Cedis per year.

This figure may now be compared with the return from annual crops, or the equivalent annual annuity for any other perennial crop.

Whole farm comparisons

The above example represented a form of partial budgeting. The cocoa enterprise was considered in isolation. However, in order to estimate cash flows it is necessary to assess the opportunity costs of all resources used. For the cocoa costing exercise, all labour both family and hired was valued at 1.00 Cedi per day, while land was assumed to have zero opportunity cost. Clearly, these are rather crude estimates of what the resources would earn in their best alternative use. An alternative approach is to determine the cost in terms of what income was earned without the project.

For this reason it is recommended that a form of whole farm budgeting should be used. The net benefits (cash flows before subtracting household resource costs) for the whole farm without the project should be subtracted from the net benefits for the whole farm with the project, to arrive at incremental net benefits, or cash flows.

The method is illustrated in Table 15.4, based on hypothetical figures for the improvements in production due to an Agricultural Development Project. For simplicity it is assumed that the net benefits without the project are constant from year to year, and that with the project they are constant from year 4 onwards. The project life is taken to be 25 years.

In the table we have subtracted the 'gross value of production without project' from each of the annual gross values of production with the project, to arrive at the incremental values of each year. Similarly, we have estimated the incremental operating expenses for each year. These calculations are not essential for the estimation of the incremental net benefits or cash flows, since these can be obtained directly by subtracting 'net benefit without project' from each of the net benefits with the project. However, a cross-check of the calculations may be useful. The

Table 15.4. *Farm level cash flow budget* (£)

	Without project	With project				
		Year 0	Year 1	Year 2	Year 3	Years 4 to 25
Gross value of production	170	170	170	190	250	300
Incremental value of production	—	0	0	20	80	130
Operating expenses	20	220	50	50	50	50
Incremental operating expenses		200	30	30	30	30
Net benefit	150	−50	120	140	200	250
Incremental net benefit or cash flow		−200	−30	−10	50	100

incremental net benefits are then used in the discounting exercise to arrive at *NPV* or *IRR*.

Sensitivity analysis

For a given set of cash flows, discounted at a given rate, we obtain a single estimate of the *NPV*. In some unusual cases, more than one *IRR* may be found, or no *IRR* may be found as we have seen. However, in normal cases, a single estimate of the *IRR* is obtained. Clearly, when planning an investment for the future we cannot be sure that the precise estimate of *NPV* or *IRR* will be achieved. Some allowance should be made for risk.

The simplest method of allowing for the uncertainty associated with investment planning is sensitivity analysis. This involves:

(i) Identifying key variables which first are likely to have a major impact on project performance and second are variable or uncertain;

(ii) repeating the discounting analysis for high and low values for each of the key variables.

As a result we obtain a set of estimates of the *NPV* or *IRR*. The whole exercise may prove a little tedious if done by hand, but it is very easily carried out by computer.

There are two possible weaknesses associated with sensitivity analysis. One is that the number of possible combinations of different levels for each of the key variables may prove very large. For instance, if there are six key variables, each with high, average and low values, the number of possible combinations is:

$$3^6 = 729.$$

Possibly some of these combinations are so unlikely as to be not worth testing. The probability of achieving low yields, low prices, and high costs of inputs together may be very small indeed. However, since no attempt is made to estimate probabilities, the choice of which combinations of key variables to test becomes purely a matter of judgement. The analyst may judge that it is not worth considering the more favourable combinations of key variables. If the project looks viable on average, it will appear even more so when optimistic values are used for the key variables.

The other weakness is that sensitivity analysis gives no clear guidance as to whether a project should be accepted or not. For instance, suppose we have a project for which the expected NPV is positive, but that after sensitivity analysis, eight out of twenty estimates of the NPV are negative. We have no clear guidance as to whether the project is acceptable. Despite these weaknesses, sensitivity analysis does provide some measure of the risk attached to a particular project. It also gives guidance as to where careful management will be needed because the final result is sensitive to the variable concerned. (For a more elaborate method of risk analysis, see Reutlinger 1970.)

Summary

1 Investment appraisal, or capital budgeting, is necessary for assessing future cash requirements, providing a financial plan and evaluation of the project. The stages are specifying the plan, estimating costs and benefits (cash flows) and appraisal using discounting.

2 Three types of time profile are considered, a one-off short- or medium-term investment, continuous replacement to yield a perpetuity or a long-term investment with a finite life.

3 In all cases it is advisable to test the feasibility (or profitability) of the proposed plan by preparing a cash-flow budget. This consists of predictions of the profile of annual incremental costs and benefits (incomes) over the life of the investment project, including capital items recorded at the time they are expected to occur.

4 If credit is used, analysis of cash flows after financing may be useful. The effects of inflation are usually excluded from cash-flow analysis.

5 An example, of investment in a cocoa plantation, is used to illustrate a

cash-flow budget and the calculation of the net present value (NPV) and the internal rate of return (IRR). Since the former is estimated to be positive, and the latter greater than the market rate of interest, the investment is considered feasible.

6 Some problems relate to the use of the IRR (e.g. it may not exist), but in most cases the two measures rank investments in the same way. The equivalent annual annuity for a long-term investment may be compared with the annual return from short-term projects.

7 Whole farm capital budgeting may be based on comparisons of cash flows with and without the project. The differences represent the incremental cash flows, which may be discounted as before.

8 Sensitivity analysis (repeated analyses with alternative values of key variables) may be used to assess the riskiness of a project. It gives little guidance as to the probabilities of different outcomes or on whether to invest, but draws attention to risky elements of the plan.

References

Brown, M. L. (1979). *Farm Budgets: From Farm Income Analysis to Agricultural Project Analysis*, Baltimore, Maryland, Johns Hopkins

Gittinger, J. P. (1982). *Economic Analysis of Agricultural Projects*, 2nd edn, Baltimore, Maryland, Johns Hopkins

Reutlinger, S. (1970). *Techniques for Project Appraisal under Uncertainty*, Baltimore, Maryland, Johns Hopkins

Rourke, B. E. (1974). 'Profitability of cocoa and alternative crops in Eastern Region. Ghana', in Kotey, R. A., C. Okali & B. E. Rourke (eds.), *Economics of Cocoa Production and Marketing*, University of Ghana, Legon Institute of Statistical, Social and Economic Research

Upton, M. (1966). 'Tree crops: a long term investment', *Journal of Agricultural Economics*, **17**(1), 82

16

Linear programming

The assumptions

Linear programming (LP) is a systematic, mathematical procedure for finding the optimal plan, or programme, for a given set of conditions. To use this method the conditions must be presented in the following form:

(1) a limited choice of several activities;
(2) certain fixed constraints affecting the choice;
(3) straight-line (linear) relationships.

These basic assumptions made in linear programming need further explanation.

The alternative activities may correspond with the crops and animals which could be produced on the farm being planned, but the word 'activity' as used in linear programming does not necessarily mean the same as the word 'enterprise'. Thus buying activities may be considered in drawing up the plan. Furthermore, several different activities might be associated with the same enterprise, where several alternative methods of production are possible. Yams grown in a mixture represent a different activity from yams grown alone; irrigated cotton represents a different activity from rainfed cotton. In some cases it may be appropriate to treat a particular crop mixture as a single activity. The choice must be limited to a suitable number of activities for calculation. For the simple examples to be worked out in this chapter, the number of activities is limited to two or three. However, larger problems only differ in the amount of arithmetic involved; the nature of the arithmetic is the same. For this reason most real linear programming problems are solved on computers which can deal with hundreds of alternative activities. Even so there is still a limit on the number of activities which can be considered.

The fixed constraints restrict the combinations of activities which are feasible. A plan which violates any constraint is assumed not to be feasible, which means that the constraint is assumed to be rigidly fixed. Thus, if July labour, limited to 28 man-days, is a constraint, then a plan requiring 30 man-days of July labour would be rejected as not feasible in linear programming, although in practice it might be possible to manage the extra work. The constraints may be physical quantities of productive resources, they may be technical requirements such as that cotton cannot be grown more than 2 years in direct succession, or they may be conditions which the farmer insists on for personal reasons. Many constraints are open-ended, which means that they need not be met exactly, but are either maximum or minimum limits. For instance, although the total use of July labour cannot exceed 28 man-days, it may be less than this; the requirement for July labour must be equal to, or less than, the quantity available.

The assumption of linearity means that no matter how many units of a particular activity are included in the plan, the cost and return per unit remains the same. Thus if 1 hectare of maize needs 8 man-days of July labour and yields a gross margin of £100 then 3 hectares of maize are assumed to need $3 \times 8 = 24$ man-days of July labour and to yield a gross margin of $3 \times £100 = £300$. Likewise a quarter of an hectare is assumed to need $8/4 = 2$ man-days of July labour and to yield £100/4 = £25. The relationships between inputs and outputs are assumed to be straight lines. This can result in linear-programmed plans which include unrealistic fractions, particularly where livestock enterprises are involved. In a wide variety of problems the precision lost in rounding fractions to whole numbers is not sufficient to invalidate the solution. However, many linear programming packages for the computer now include an option for specifying that certain variables can only take on integer, or whole-number, values. This 'integer programming' option is clearly an advance on ordinary LP, but it does involve more computations. For the present we ignore this alternative.

The data needed for linear programming consist of a specification of the alternative activities to be considered and the return or gross margin per unit of each activity. The constraints must also be identified and the total capacity of each estimated, together with the demands of each activity on each constraint. These demands for inputs per unit of output are sometimes known as 'input–output coefficients'.

An example

We will take, as an example, a highly simplified farm planning problem with just two alternative activities, maize production and

Table 16.1. *Data for linear programming problem*

	Activities		Constraint level
	Maize	Groundnut	
Gross margin	£100	£320	
Constraints			
Land (hectares)	1	1	3
July labour (man-days)	8	16	28
November labour (man-days)	4	16	24
Total labour (man-days)	50	100	250

groundnut production, and four constraints. The objective is to maximize total gross margin. The constraints are land area, limited to 3 hectares, labour in the peak requirement months of July and November limited to 28 man-days and 24 man-days respectively, and total labour limited to 250 man-days. Each hectare of maize requires 8 man-days of labour in July, 4 man-days of labour in November and 50 man-days of labour in total and yields a gross margin of £100. Each hectare of groundnuts requires 16 man-days of labour in each of the peak months and 100 man-days of labour in total to yield a gross margin of £320. These data are set out in Table 16.1.

If we use the symbols X_1 and X_2 to represent the number of units (hectares in this case) of maize and groundnuts in a plan and Z to represent the total gross margin, we can express the planning problem by a set of mathematical relationships as follows. Note that the symbol $\leq$ means 'is less than or equal to' and $\geq$ 'is greater than or equal to'.

Maximize total gross margin Z where

$$Z = 100X_1 + 320X_2 \tag{1.1}$$

Subject to (ST) the constraints,

$$1X_1 + 1X_2 \quad \leq 3 \text{ (hectares of land)}$$
$$8X_1 + 16X_2 \quad \leq 28 \text{ (man-days of July labour)}$$
$$4X_1 + 16X_2 \quad \leq 24 \text{ (man-days of November labour)} \tag{1.2}$$
$$50X_1 + 100X_2 \leq 250 \text{ (man-days of total labour)}$$

and the non-negativity constraints

$$X_1 \geq 0, \ X_2 \geq 0. \tag{1.3}$$

$$\left.\begin{array}{c} \\ \\ \\ \\ \\ \\ \\ \\ \\ \end{array}\right\} \quad (1)$$

This is the standard form for a linear programming problem. It consists of three parts, (1.1) the function (e.g. profit or total gross margin) to be maximized, which is called 'the objective function', (1.2) the ordinary structural constraints and (1.3) the non-negative conditions on the variables. These need to be specified since a negative activity would have no acceptable meaning within the framework of the model. The structural constraints are expressed as inequalities, to allow for the possibility of leaving land fallow or of leaving labour unemployed at certain times of the year. It may be noted that if these had been expressed as exact equalities, implying that all available resources had to be used up in production, the problem would have *no* solution. The four constraint equations could not be satisfied simultaneously, with only two variables, X_1 and X_2. Thus we allow for non-use or disposal of the constraining resources.

This problem is a specific example of the general LP maximizing model which may be written as follows:

$$\left. \begin{array}{ll} \text{maximize } Z = \sum c_i \times x_j & (2.1) \\ \quad \sum a_{ij} \times x_j \leqslant b_i & (2.2) \\ \quad (i = 1 \text{ to } n) & \\ \text{and} \quad x_j \geqslant 0 (j = 1 \text{ to } m) & (2.3) \end{array} \right\} \quad (2)$$

or even more concisely using matrix and vector notation as:

$$\left. \begin{array}{ll} \text{maximize } \mathbf{Z} = \mathbf{c'x} & (3.1) \\ \quad \mathbf{Ax} \leqslant \mathbf{b} & (3.2) \\ \quad \mathbf{x} \geqslant \mathbf{0} & (3.3) \end{array} \right\} \quad (3)$$

where the x_j are the m activity levels,
  the c_j are the m per unit revenues or gross margins,
  the a_{ij} are the $(n \times m)$ input–output coefficients,
  and the b_i are the n constraint levels.

Thus LP is simply a formal method of maximizing returns subject to a set of constraints. It deals with the economic problem of allocating scarce resources (constraints) among alternative competing uses (activities) to achieve desired ends (the objective function). Two methods of solution will be illustrated using our simple example. First a graphical method, based on plotting the production possibility boundary as in Chapter 3, is used. Then a more general, formal procedure, known as the 'simplex method' will be described.

A graphical approach

Feasible combinations of maize and groundnut production are plotted in Figure 16.1. Note that each of the constraint lines represents full use of the resource, so there is none in disposal. For instance, consider the land constraint line *AB*. The equation of this line is $1X_1 + 1X_2 = 3$, which means that the area of maize plus the area of groundnuts is equal to the total area of 3 hectares. On this line, the land constraint is said to be

Figure 16.1   The feasible region

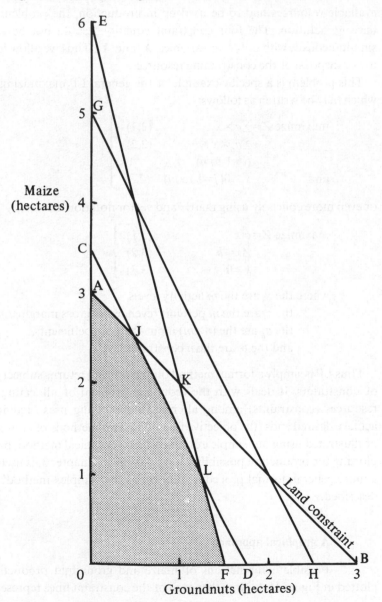

'binding' or 'effective'. Points below and to the left of this line, however such as *L* or *F*, represent plans which leave some land in disposal, so this constraint is not effective.

Similarly, line *CD* represents combinations of the two activities, for which the July labour constraint is binding, so none of this resource is in disposal. Line *EF* represents combinations of maize and groundnut production which would exhaust all the available labour in November, so there would be none of this resource in disposal, and the constraint would be binding. Finally, line *GH* represents the total labour constraint.

It should now be apparent that all feasible combinations of maize and groundnut production are represented by the area *OAJLF*, which is shaded. Points outside this area such as *K*, *G* or *H* are infeasible. Thus the total labour constraint line *GH* lies entirely outside the feasible area, so this constraint can never be effective. There will always be some labour in disposal or unemployed at certain times of the year. The total labour constraint is said to be 'dominated' by other constraints and it could be omitted from the rest of the analysis.

Figure 16.2 shows the production possibility boundary from Figure 16.1, with isorevenue lines for total gross margins (*Z*) of £300, £400 and £500. Clearly the maximum feasible gross margin is £500 obtained from a combination of 1.25 hectares of groundnuts and 1 hectare of maize (point *L*). This then is the optimum solution.

Some useful general conclusions may be drawn from further consideration of this illustration. First, it may be noted that, since the aim is to produce more rather than less, the optimal solution must always lie on the boundary of the feasible area; no matter what the relative product prices or gross margins are. Secondly, because the boundary is made up of straight-line segments, the optimum must always occur at a corner, which is an extreme point of the feasible area.

This important result represents the fundamental principle of linear programming (LP), namely that in seeking an optimum solution we need only consider the combinations represented by extreme points of the feasible region. In this way LP greatly simplifies the problem of finding the optimum. Even in this very simple example with only two alternative activities of maize growing and groundnut growing, the number of feasible combinations is infinite. Any combination of the two, represented by a point inside the area *OAJLF*, would be feasible. Using simple budgeting we could estimate the total gross margin from even hundreds of these combinations and still never find the optimum, but the LP principle tells us we need only consider the extreme points of which, in this case, there are just five.

The same rule applies even when we have many activities and constraints, so the graphical method cannot be used. At each extreme point we are, in effect, setting the number of real activities in the plan equal to the number of binding constraints. Thus the number of variables (activity levels) is equal to

Figure 16.2   The optimal solution

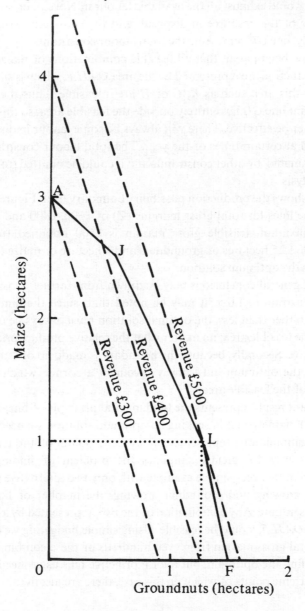

Table 16.2. *The basic feasible solutions*

| Extreme point | Real activities | | Amount of resource unused (man-days) | | | | |
	Maize X_1	Groundnut X_2	Land (ha)	July labour	November labour	Total labour	Total gross margin
0	0	0	3	28	24	250	0
A	3	0	0	4	12	100	300
J	$2\frac{1}{2}$	$\frac{1}{2}$	0	0	6	75	410
L	1	$1\frac{1}{4}$	$\frac{3}{4}$	0	0	75	500
F	0	$1\frac{1}{2}$	$1\frac{1}{2}$	4	0	100	480

the number of equations (effective constraints) and an exact solution can be found. Such a solution is known as a 'basic feasible solution' (BFS). The fundamental principle of LP may therefore be restated as 'the optimum solution will always be found from among the basic feasible solutions'.

These ideas may be illustrated by Figures 16.1 and 16.2. Points A, J, L and F represent BFSs. The levels of each activity in each of these BFSs are given in Table 16.2. Other points such as G and K represent basic solutions, but, of course, they are not feasible. Point A represents one activity, maize production, and one binding constraint, land. Points J and L represent combinations of the two activities with two effective constraints, land and July labour at J, and July and November labour at L. Point F again represents only one activity, groundnut production and one constraint, November labour. As we have seen, the optimum occurs at one of these BFSs, namely point L.

The fact that, in the optimum solution, the number of real activities equals the number of effective constraints is of some practical importance. Although a farmer may be faced with many different constraints, if he is limited to say five alternative activities, he will only be able to satisfy five constraints. Other scarce resources will have to remain unused. Conversely, if there are few critical constraints, few activities are needed and a simple system will be adequate. The apparent complexity of many African farms may reflect an attempt to make best use of a multitude of different constraints.

Shadow prices

For each BFS of an LP problem there is a corresponding set of shadow prices. These are the opportunity costs of the resources used, and reflect their relative scarcity. For a resource which is in disposal, and the constraint is not effective, the shadow price is zero. There is no opportunity cost of using an extra unit of such a resource because there is a surplus already available. For resources which are effective constraints the opportunity cost is the revenue foregone when one unit of the resource is released. It represents the value of the marginal product, and this in turn is the maximum amount it is worth paying to hire in an extra unit of the resource. In summary, there are three alternative views of a shadow price:

  (i) the opportunity cost per unit
 (ii) the marginal value product per unit
(iii) the maximum amount it is worth paying to hire the resource.

Again the shadow price may be illustrated using our example. At point A, where 3 hectares of maize are produced, land is the only effective constraint. There is surplus labour at all periods, so the shadow price of labour is zero. However each hectare of maize yields a return of £100, so the cost of releasing one unit of land is £100. This is the shadow price. At point F, November labour is the only effective constraint. Each man-day used in growing groundnuts produces £320/16=£20. Hence this is the shadow price of November labour.

The calculation of shadow prices is more complicated where there is more than one effective constraint. Let us consider the optimum solution at point L, representing a total revenue of £500. Here there are two effective constraints, July labour and November labour, and we need to separate their effects. Consider, first, a reduction in July labour from 28 to 24 man-days. This would cause the optimum solution to move from point L to point F, as the reader may check from Figure 16.2. Note that the line segment JL represents the July labour constraint, and that the assumed reduction would cause this line to move to a parallel position through A to F. Hence the optimum would move to F, which represents 1.5 hectares of ground-nuts, yielding £320×1.5=£480. The reduction of July labour by 4 man-days results in a reduction of total revenue by £20 (£500–£480). The shadow price per man-day of July labour is therefore £20/4=£5.

To calculate the shadow price of November labour, it is somewhat easier to assume an *increase* in availability to 28 man-days. This would then allow the optimum solution to move to point D, representing 1.75 hectares of groundnuts. The total revenue would then be £320×1.75=£560. Thus an increase of 4 man-days of November labour allows an increase in revenue of £60 (£560–£500). The shadow price per man-day of November labour is therefore £60/4=£15. Note that this is different from the shadow price at point F. Land and total labour are in disposal so their shadow price is zero. We could calculate the shadow price of land and July labour at point J in a similar fashion.

Two further important points should be noted in relation to shadow prices. The first is that if the cost of each unit of resource inputs is assumed to be the same as the shadow price, the total revenue is exactly equal to the total cost. There is then no profit or loss. This applies to both the whole plan and to individual activities included in the plan.

For instance, at point F, 1.5 hectares of groundnuts yield a total return of £480. At this point the shadow price of November labour is £20 for 24 man-days whilst it is zero for all other resources. Thus the total cost is £20×24=£480, which is equal to total return. Clearly, the same result obtains if calculated on a per hectare basis.

At point L, the results are as follows:

	July labour cost		November labour cost		Total revenue
Whole plan	(£5×28)	+	(£15×24)	=	£500
per hectare maize	(£5× 8)	+	(£15× 4)	=	£100 (4)
per hectare groundnuts	(£5×16)	+	(£15×16)	=	£320

In fact, this provides another way of calculating shadow prices. They are those values for limited resources which account for the total return from activities in the plan exactly. The determination of shadow prices is sometimes described as the 'dual problem' in relation to the 'primal problem' which concerns the determination of an optimal plan. In practice, a knowledge of shadow prices may be as useful as or even more useful than the estimated best plan.

The second important point to note is that shadow prices obey the law of diminishing marginal returns. To illustrate, let us assume that inputs of July labour are gradually increased, whilst the other resources are held fixed at their constraint levels. The effect on total revenue (gross margin) is shown in Figure 16.3. The first 24 man-days of July labour may be used in groundnut production which yields the highest marginal value product of £20, per man-day. This takes us to point F on Figure 16.2. Other constraints prevent the expansion of groundnut production beyond this point.

However, total revenue can be increased still further and more July labour can be employed by introducing maize production into the plan.

Between point *F* and point *L* in Figure 16.2, some maize is substituted for groundnuts. As we have seen, the marginal value product (shadow price) is now £15. This decline of the marginal (value) product of July labour from £20 to £15 therefore reflects the operation of the law of diminishing marginal returns. None the less, if all inputs are increased together, that is to scale, there are constant returns because of the linearity assumption.

The simplex method

We turn now to a formal mathematical approach to linear programming. By following the procedures described here it should be possible to solve larger, more complicated problems than our present example. In principle, the method is applicable to problems with any numbers of activities and constraints, and forms the basis of most computer programs for LP such as LINDO.

All formal methods of LP, involve a step-by-step approach which moves from one basic feasible solution to another; each move being known as an 'iteration'. It is not normally possible to move directly to an optimum solution in one iteration, except in the very simplest cases. The idea of the simplex method is to start from an initial BFS and then calculate whether the value of the objective function can be increased by moving to a neighbouring BFS. If so, the move is made (an iteration is completed) and again

Figure 16.3   Diminishing marginal returns in linear programming

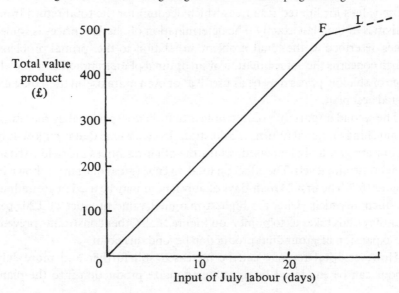

Input of July labour (days)

calculations are applied to determine whether further improvement is possible by a subsequent move. When finally a BFS is attained that does not admit of further improvement, this constitutes the optimum solution.

Thus there are two key features of the method:

(i) the calculations lead from one BFS to a neighbouring BFS at each iteration;

(ii) each movement is in the direction which increases the value of the objective function.

It may be viewed as a 'hill-climbing technique' for scaling the hill of increasing returns. If there is an optimum, it must eventually be reached. The method is efficient in that only a limited subset of BFSs are calculated in moving to the optimum. We shall illustrate the technique using the example from Table 16.1.

There are three preliminary steps to be carried out which will make the calculations easier.

Preliminary step 1: Introduce slack variables

Slack variables are used to represent the non-use or disposal of resources. Their use enables us to convert the constraint inequalities of the LP problem into equalities. In our example we will introduce four slack variables S_1 to S_4 to allow for disposal of each of the constraining variables. Variable S_1 represents non-use or fallowing land. It is measured in hectares, adds nothing to total gross margin and requires no labour. Similarly S_2, S_3 and S_4 represent leisure or non-use of labour and are measured in mandays. Our illustrative example, equations (1), may now be written as follows:

Maximize:

$$Z = 100X_1 + 320X_2 + 0S_1 + 0S_2 + 0S_3 + 0S_4 \quad (5.1)$$

S.T.

$$1X_1 + 1X_2 + 1S_1 + 0S_2 + 0S_3 + 0S_4 = 3$$
$$8X_1 + 16X_2 + 0S_1 + 1S_2 + 0S_3 + 0S_4 = 28$$
$$4X_1 + 16X_2 + 0S_1 + 0S_2 + 1S_3 + 0S_4 = 24 \quad (5.2)$$
$$50X_1 + 100X_2 + 0S_1 + 0S_2 + 0S_3 + 1S_4 = 250$$

and

$$X_1 \geqslant 0,\ X_2 \geqslant 0,\ S_1 \geqslant 0,\ S_2 \geqslant 0,\ S_3 \geqslant 0,\ S_4 \geqslant 0 \quad (5.3)$$

(5)

The zeros are included to complete the rectangular matrix of values.

Table 16.3. *Simplex tableau: Tableau I*

	Z	X_1	X_2	S_1	S_2	S_3	S_4	Constant b
Row 0	1	-100	-320	0	0	0	0	0
Row 1	0	1	1	1	0	0	0	3
Row 2	0	8	16	0	1	0	0	28
Row 3	0	4	<u>16</u>	0	0	1	0	24
Row 4	0	50	100	0	0	0	1	250

Preliminary step 2: Rearrange the objective function

Although the purpose may not be immediately obvious, it is convenient to treat Z as yet another variable in the analysis and to move the right-hand side of the objective function over to the left as follows:

$$Z = 100X_1 + 320X_2 + 0S_1 + 0S_2 + 0S_3 + 0S_4$$
implies
$$Z - 100X_1 - 320X_2 - 0S_1 - 0S_2 - 0S_3 - 0S_4 = 0$$

Of course, the sign of the zero terms does not really matter; zero is neither positive nor negative.

Preliminary step 3: Set up the simplex tableau

This simply involves rearranging the data of equations (4) in the tidier form of a tableau, as shown in Table 16.3. A column is reserved for each variable, for real activities and slacks. In addition there is a column for Z and another on the right for the b-values or constraint levels. The corresponding coefficients are set out in the rows below, representing the original equations. The vertical line between the S_4 column and the b column is where the equal sign should be in the various equations. It is advisable to compare Table 16.3 with Table 16.1 to see how one is derived from the other.

It should be noted that this Simplex tableau actually represents a basic feasible solution, albeit a rather unattractive one, since the value of the objective function is zero. This particular solution is to produce nothing and leave all the resources in disposal. It may be read-off from the tableau by concentrating on those columns which consist only of ones and zeros. They are known as 'identity vectors'. These vectors form the, so-called, 'basis' and from them we can identify the corresponding BFS. The X_1 and X_2 columns are not in the current basis and may be ignored temporarily. In effect we assume $X_1 = X_2 = 0$. The BFS is thus

$$Z = 0$$
$$S_1 = 3$$
$$S_2 = 28$$
$$S_3 = 24$$
$$S_4 = 250$$

The numbers in row 0, represent the costs, per unit, of introducing non-basic variables into the basis. As they are negative in this case, it means the costs are negative: that is there are positive gains to be made by introducing maize or groundnuts into the plan.

We are now ready to start the iterations which will lead to the optimum solution.

The iterations

Essentially, each iteration consists in substituting one activity from outside the basis for one that is already in the basis. Thus in the first iteration we will substitute a real activity for a disposal activity. The incoming activity is identified with a particular column, called the 'pivot column'. Each basis activity is associated with a particular row; for instance S_1 with Row 1, S_2 with Row 2 and so on in Tableau 1. Thus the outgoing activity is associated with a particular 'pivot row'. The element which occurs where the selected column and row intersect is known as the 'pivot'. We can now describe the calculations involved in each iteration by a series of simple rules.

Rule 1. Choice of pivot column

Scan Row 0, and select the element with the highest negative value. The corresponding column is the pivot column. This rule ensures that the incoming activity is the one which adds most to the value of the objective function. In Table 16.3 the pivot column is the one for groundnuts (X_2) since 320 is the largest negative value in Row 0.

Rule 2. Choice of pivot row

For this purpose, we must divide each (positive) element in the pivot column into the corresponding element in the *b* column. The element for which the resulting quotient is smallest is in fact the pivot. (For our example these ratios are

Row 1   3/1   =3
Row 2   28/16   =1.75

Table 16.4. *Tableau II*

	Z	X_1	X_2	S_1	S_2	S_3	S_4	Constant b	R
Row 0	1	-20	0	0	0	20	0	480	
Row 1	0	$\frac{3}{4}$	0	1	0	$-\frac{1}{16}$	0	$1\frac{1}{2}$	2
Row 2	0	4	0	0	1	-1	0	4	1
Row 3	0	$\frac{1}{4}$	1	0	0	$\frac{1}{16}$	0	$1\frac{1}{2}$	6
Row 4	0	25	0	0	0	$-6\frac{1}{4}$	1	100	4

Row 3   24/16   =1.5
Row 4   250/100 =2.5

Clearly the quotient 1.5 in Row 3 is the smallest, so this is the *pivot row*, and the number 16 in Row 3 of the groundnut activity column is the pivot. It is underlined in Table 16.3.)

The objective of this procedure is to ensure that the next basic solution will be feasible. By choosing the smallest ratio we ensure that all the constraints can be satisfied.

Rule 3. Derive the new pivot row

This is achieved by dividing every element in the row by the pivot element. In our example this means dividing each element in Row 3 by 16, to give the results shown in Row 3 of the new tableau in Table 16.4.

Rule 4. Derive other rows

The objective here is to replace all elements in the pivot column, other than the pivot itself, with zeros. This is achieved by subtracting (or adding) a suitable multiple of the pivot from (or to) the old element. Thus if the old element is 'a' then 'a/b' times 'b' must be subtracted from 'a' to yield zero.

However, to be consistent, the same operation must be applied to every element of the row. Thus each element of the pivot row must be multiplied by 'a/b' before subtracting it from the corresponding element of the old 'a' row.

The elements of the new Row 0 shown in Table 16.4 are derived as follows. Note first that to reduce -320 to zero requires *adding* 320/16=20 times the pivot element. Thus the whole Row 0 becomes

$$1, -100+(20\times4), -320+(20\times16), 0, 0, +(20\times1), 0, +(20\times24)$$

Similarly, the new Row 1 is obtained from the old Row 1 by subtracting 1/16 times the pivot row to give

$$0, 1-4/16, 1-16/16, 1, 0, -1/16, 0, 3-24/16.$$

The results of similar calculations for each of the rows are given in the new tableau of Table 16.4.

Rule 5. *Inspect the new tableau*

In particular Row 0 should be scanned. If there are no negative elements, the optimum has been found. If, on the other hand, there are negative elements, then a further iteration is required, for which we return to rule 1 and repeat the cycle. However, the calculations are now all based on the new tableau. The process is repeated until an optimum is found.

From Table 16.4, Tableau II we see that the result of the first iteration is a plan to grow $1\frac{1}{2}$ hectares of groundnuts. From the set of identity vectors we see that the whole plan is

$Z=480$ (total gross margin)

$X_2=1\frac{1}{2}$ (hectares of groundnuts)

$S_1=1\frac{1}{2}$ (hectares of land unused)

$S_2=4$ (man-days of July labour unused)

$S_4=100$ (man-days of total labour unused)

However, it is clear that this plan can be improved upon by introducing the maize growing activity X_1, (coefficient of -20 in Row 0). In Table 16.4 an extra R column has been added to show the outcome of dividing elements of the X_1 column into the corresponding elements of the b column. Clearly, Row 2 is the pivot row, and unused July labour S_2 leaves the basis. In other words July labour will be fully employed.

The results of the second iteration are shown in Table 16.5, Tableau III. It is clear that this is the optimal solution since no negative values appear in Row 0. As we have already seen it represents 1 hectare of maize and $1\frac{1}{4}$ hectares of groundnuts. This leaves $\frac{3}{4}$ hectare of land in disposal and 75 man-days of labour unused over the whole year.

The BFSs represented by each of these three tableaux are represented by extreme points in Figure 16.2. Thus the origin represents Tableau I, point F represents Tableau II and point L, the optimum, represents Tableau III. The Simplex method has allowed us to find an optimum without even considering the BFSs represented by points A and J.

Table 16.5. *Tableau III: The optimum*

	Z	X_1	X_2	S_1	S_2	S_3	S_4	Constant b
Row 0	1	0	0	0	5	15	0	500
Row 1	0	0	0	1	$-\frac{3}{16}$	$\frac{1}{8}$	0	$\frac{3}{4}$
Row 2	0	1	0	0	$\frac{1}{4}$	$-\frac{1}{4}$	0	1
Row 3	0	0	1	0	$-\frac{1}{16}$	$\frac{1}{8}$	0	$1\frac{1}{4}$
Row 4	0	0	0	0	$-6\frac{1}{4}$	0	1	75

Interpreting a tableau

As we have seen, the identity vectors, together with the right-hand side (**b**) vector, allow us to read off the current farm plan at each iteration. At the same time Row 0 gives the current values of the shadow prices. Thus the Simplex method provides both a primal and a dual solution for each basis.

The two are optimized together. This means that the *true* opportunity costs of scarce resources are given by the shadow prices at the optimal solution.

The figures in the remaining columns, for variables not in the basis, are the rates at which they substitute for activities which *are* in the basis. For instance the (S_3) November labour column in Table 16.5, tells us first that the shadow price is £15. This arises because one man-day of November labour substitutes for $\frac{1}{8}$ hectare of land (row 1) and $\frac{1}{8}$ hectare of groundnuts (row 3). However it would result in an *increase* of $\frac{1}{4}$ hectare of maize (row 2) shown by a negative rate of subsitution. In fact, these numbers are incidental to the main calculations and need not concern us further.

From Row 0 of Table 16.5 we see that shadow prices for the four resource constraints are zero for land, £5 per man-day for July labour, £15 per man-day for November labour and zero for total labour. These shadow prices can be used for partial budgeting to estimate the desirability of introducing a new activity on to the farm. For instance, suppose our farmer could grow cotton as an alternative to maize and groundnuts. The gross margin for cotton is £400 per hectare, but the labour requirements are 32 man-days and 20 man-days in July and November respectively. We can calculate the net cost of introducing this crop into the farm plan as follows:

Opportunity costs of resources minus revenue equals net cost
£(32×5)   +   (20×15)   −400   =   £60
July labour   November labour

Clearly, although cotton returns a higher gross margin per hectare than either maize or groundnuts, the high labour cost makes cotton an unattractive alternative. Total farm gross margin would be reduced by £60 for each hectare of cotton introduced.

Readers may find it instructive to include this cotton-growing activity in the initial tableau and to repeat the calculations to find the optimal solution. Although cotton will enter the basis at the outset because of the high return per hectare, it will then be forced out again because of the high labour requirement. The optimal solution will be no different from that shown in Table 16.5. Cotton production will end up as a non-basis activity with a 'shadow price' of £60 which represents the cost of introducing one hectare of the activity into the optimal plan.

In fact, a general conclusion may be drawn: of the alternative productive activities considered, those which are included in the optimal plan have zero net cost (cost of resources valued at their shadow prices exactly equals revenue as shown in equations (4)), while those which are excluded have a positive net cost. This mirrors the result for resource constraints, that, if some of the resource is in disposal, the shadow price is zero, whereas, if the constraint is effective, a positive shadow price applies. Note that negative shadow prices must imply that the optimum has not been found. There are rare cases, of so-called 'degeneracy', in which these conclusions do not apply, but otherwise they are generally true.

Some extensions

LP is a much more flexible tool than is apparent from the discussion so far. In practice, many more complicated relationships may be modelled, but skill is needed in building the initial Tableau. Some useful extensions will now be outlined.

(i)   *Parametric programming*

This is simply ordinary LP in which either (a) one or more of the values in the objective function or (b) one or more of the resource constraints are allowed to vary. The effects of these changes on the optimal plan can then be estimated. Many computer programms for LP allow for these options within a single programming run. However, the range of alternatives compared can be extended to include new activities or changes in the input–output coefficients simply by rerunning the programme.

Parametric programming may be used in various ways:

(a) sensitivity analysis, to test the stability of the optimal solution in view of possible errors in estimating the data used;

(b) risk analysis, to test the effect of chance variations in the data (e.g. see Heyer 1972; Farrington 1976);

(c) prediction of farmer supply (or input demand) response to changing prices. This of course depends on the assumptions that farmers are maximizers and that the model farm is representative of the whole population of farms (see Ogunfowora 1972, or Ogunfowora & Norman 1974.)

(d) Evaluation of the impact of alternative technologies on farming systems and farmer incomes. Again the model farm is assumed to represent a larger population, while coefficients for new technologies are based on research station trials. This application of LP clearly relates to farming systems research. Mixed cropping (Ogunfowora & Norman, 1974), zero tillage systems (Knipscheer, Menz & Verinumbe 1983) and mechanization practices (Ahmed & Kinsey 1984) have been evaluated in this way.

(ii)   *Buying activities and tie rows*

    The purchase or hire of inputs is easily incorporated in an LP problem. Each buying activity has a positive cost in row 0 and contributes to the relevant constraints row. It therefore has a negative coefficient. Thus we might incorporate a labour hiring activity, at £2 per day, for the month of July (X_3) into our model of Table 16.3 by adding the following column of coefficients:

row 0	Cost	2
row 1	Land	0
row 2	July labour	−1
row 3	November labour	0
row 4	Total labour	−1

Note that labour hire in July also contributes to total annual labour availability. The effect on the optimal plan is as follows, as the reader may readily check by repeating the analysis.

Total gross margin: Z	=	£520
*Labour hire in July: X_3	=	4 man-days
Maize production: X_1	=	2 hectares
Groundnut production: X_2	=	1 hectare
Total labour in disposal: S_4	=	54 man-days

The shadow prices are now

Land, £16; July labour, £2; November labour, £17.

In some cases an extra constraint should be added to limit the level of hiring or buying. A limit may be imposed by shortage of funds for instance.

In this example, the July labour constraint row becomes a 'tie-row'; since it ties the labour hiring activity to the labour-using activities of maize and groundnut production. Indeed, a situation might arise in which no family labour was available in July, so labour would have to be hired. The tie row would then read

$$8X_1 + 16X_2 - 1X_3 + 1S_2 = 0$$

with all variables as already defined. Thus the labour hiring activity (X_3) yields a 'permit' (represented by the negative coefficient) to introduce other labour-using activities.

A similar technique may be used to tie a bush-clearing activity to subsequent cropping activities, through a tie row for cleared land. A livestock producing activity may be tied to a fodder-producing activity through the fodder tie row. Furthermore, rotational constraints, on the maximum proportion devoted to certain crops, may be imposed in the same way. For instance, in an early LP study of mixed farming in Nyeri district of Kenya, a constraint was imposed which required that at least four years of grass ley are included for each three years of cropping (Clayton 1961). The rotational tie-line is

$$3X_1 + 3X_2 + 3X_3 - 4X_4 \leqslant 0$$

where X_1, X_2 and X_3 are hectares of arable-crop activities and X_4 represents hectares of ley.

(iii)   *Minimum target constraints*

Let us now return to the original problem of Table 16.1, but introduce the additional constraint that the farmer needs to produce, *at least*, 15 000 MJ of food energy for family subsistence. Maize yields 7500 MJ per hectare and groundnuts 5000 MJ per hectare. This dietary constraint may be written in GJ (1GJ=1000 MJ) as follows:

$$7.5X_1 + 5X_2 \geqslant 15$$

Note that the inequality is the reverse of those dealt with so far; total energy production may exceed 15 GJ but must not fall below this level. If a slack variable (S_5) is introduced, it must have a negative coefficient. This means

Table 16.6. *Finding an initial BFS*

	Z	X_1	X_2	S_1	S_2	S_3	S_4	S_5	Q_1	Constant b
Tableau I										
0 Objective	1	−100	−320						1000	
1 Land		1	1	1						3
2 July labour		8	16		1					28
3 November labour		4	16			1				24
4 Total labour		50	100				1			250
5 Diet		7.5	5					−1	1	15
Tableau II										
0 Objective	1	−7600	−5320					1000	0	−15 000
1 Land		1	1	1						3
2 July labour		8	16		1					28
3 November labour		4	16			1				24
4 Total labour		50	100				1			250
5 Diet		7.5	5					−1	1	15

that the origin, where nothing is produced, cannot form the initial BFS since it is not feasible. At least 15 GJ of energy must be produced to prevent S_5 from taking a negative (i.e. infeasible) value.

The problem of finding a starting-point may be overcome by introducing an artificial variable Q_1, which represents an imaginary supply of pure, but very costly energy. Thus each unit of this activity is assumed to supply one GJ of energy and to cost, say, £1000, as shown in Table 16.6, Tableau I. Then 1000 times each element of the dietary constraint row must be subtracted from row 0, to give the initial BFS as shown in Tableau II. The problem can then be solved in the usual way. In this case the graphical method can be used as shown in Figure 16.4. The new constraint has caused a slight reduction in the optimal area of groundnuts and a small increase in the area of maize. Total gross margin is reduced to £485, and each GJ of energy has a shadow price of £12.

Of course, the actual cash earning at this point is zero, because all the produce is consumed. The objective of maximizing *total* gross margin is perhaps inappropriate given the subsistence constraint. If, instead, the objective were to maximize the *surplus* gross margin over subsistence needs, the optimal solution would be to grow two hectares of maize for subsistence, and to use the remaining July labour to produce $\frac{3}{4}$ hectare of groundnuts for sale (point N in Figure 16.4). For solution by the Simplex method, separate maize and groundnut selling activities would have to be incorporated with tie rows linking them to maize and groundnut production.

A useful extension of this approach, to allow for risk, is based on the inclusion of minimum survival constraints for each state of nature. To illustrate, let us assume that there are only two possible states of nature: maize yields 7.5 GJ of food energy per hectare in wet years but only 6 GJ in dry years. Groundnuts, on the other hand, yield 5 GJ in wet years but 10 in dry years. The constraint equations are then

$$7.5X_1 + 5X_2 \geqslant 15 \text{ for wet years}$$

Figure 16.4   Meeting minimum dietary constraints

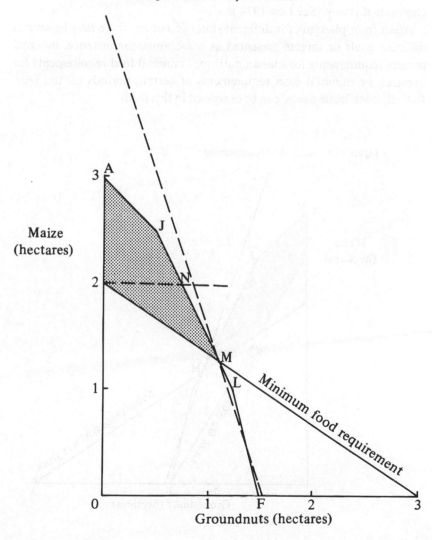

and

$$6X_1 + 10X_2 \geqslant 15 \text{ for dry years}$$

Slack and artificial variables can be added and the problem solved in the usual way. Also see the feasible area shown in Figure 16.5. It is a 'safety-first' model in that the programme ensures that subsistence needs are met under all states of nature, before an optimum is sought (see Chapter 6). This method was used to analyse farm systems in South East Ghana. The resulting farm plan was closely similar to actual farming systems in the area, which was interpreted as evidence that farmers actually do make choices in this way. (See Low 1974.)

Apart from planning for different states of nature, there may be several different goals or targets presented as constraints, for instance, minimal protein requirements for human nutrition, minimal feed requirements for livestock or minimal cash requirements at certain periods of the year. Indeed, most 'basic needs' can be expressed in this form.

Figure 16.5   Safety-first programming

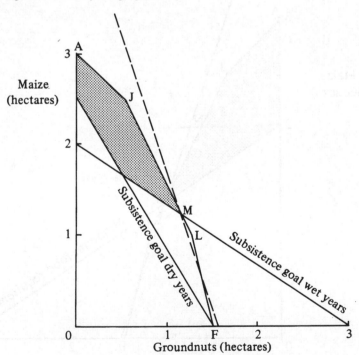

Table 16.7. *Data for LP problem: example 2*

| | Activities | | |
	Good land cropping (ha)	Poor land cropping (ha)	Constraint level
Yield of grain (quintals)	8	4	
Constraints			
Good land (hectares)	1	0	2
Poor land (hectares)	0	1	2
Total labour (man-days)	80	80	240

This leads on to the possibility of using LP to minimize the cost of meeting a given set of targets, rather than maximizing the return. A cost minimization problem can easily be converted into a maximization problem by changing the signs of the coefficients in the objective function. Minimizing C is just the same as maximizing minus C.

(iv)   *Distinguishing between land types*

The example used above to illustrate LP includes separate constraints for labour at different periods of the year. Where there is division of labour between hired and family workers or between men and women, each category should be represented by a separate constraint for each peak work period.

In just the same way, where there are two cropping seasons, early season land should be treated as a separate constraint from late season land. Thus a 3 hectare farm has 3 hectares of early land and 3 hectares of late season land (see Clayton 1961). Also, if there are different land types with different cropping alternatives for each, for example upland and river valley land, these should be treated as separate constraints.

Consideration of an alternative simple LP problem with just two types of land, good and poor, reinforces the arguments of Chapter 8, regarding intensity of land use. Example 2 is set out in Table 16.7. Note that we have assumed that both land types require the same labour input per hectare, but that the poor land produces half the yield of the good land.

The problem is easily solved, as shown graphically in Figure 16.6. At the optimum, all the good land is in use but one hectare of the poor (marginal) land is unused. Twenty quintals of grain are produced. The shadow price of labour is 1/20 quintals or 5 kg, while the shadow price, or rents, of good and poor land are 4 quintals and zero respectively. Any increase in labour availability would increase the cultivated area of poor land, or extend the margin of cultivation.

Figure 16.6   Linear programming land use

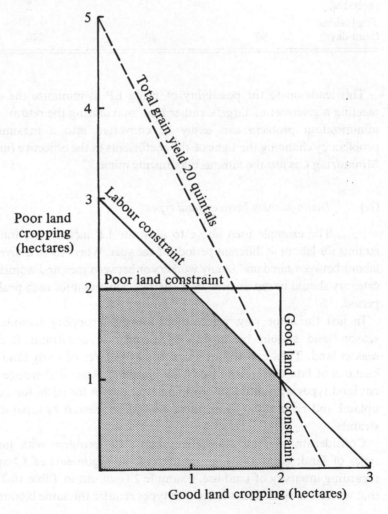

Poor land cropping (hectares)

Good land cropping (hectares)

(v)   *Multiperiod programming*

LP is readily extended to allow for investment of either circulating or durable capital. If we treat time as being divided up into a series of discrete periods, e.g. cropping seasons, investment simply means that produce or purchases in one period are carried forward for use in a subsequent time period. Thus separate sets of activities and constraints are needed for each time period within the plan, while tie rows are used to represent investments, linking the various time periods together. The resultant 'block-diagonal' structure of the initial LP tableau is shown in Figure 16.7.

The only other consideration is the treatment of the objective function. Clearly produce which is invested in a given period cannot also be sold or consumed in that period. Hence consumption or sales activities in each period must compete with investment for the future. This is represented by the tie rows into which the current productive activities supply funds, and from which the consumption activities and future production activities draw funds. The objective function then includes the values of current consumption activities *plus* the total value of what is produced in the terminal period.

We may illustrate with a simple, two period example (3) with two productive activities, maize and groundnuts, and three constraints in each period, land, labour and working capital. The data are set out in Table 16.8 and the initial tableau is shown in Table 16.9. Note that X_1 and X_2 now represent the areas of maize and groundnuts planned for year 1, while X_4 and X_5 represent the areas of maize and groundnuts planned for year 2. Activity X_3 simply allows for current consumption. Similar land and labour constraints apply in both years, but, whereas in year 1, cash needs are met from reserves of £200, in year 2 they must be met from year 1 income.

Figure 16.7 Multiperiod programming

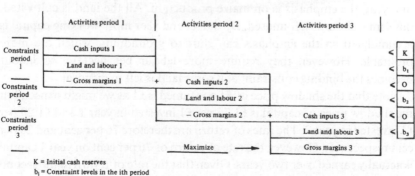

K = Initial cash reserves
b_i = Constraint levels in the ith period

Table 16.8. *Data for LP problem: example 3*

	Activities		
	Maize	Groundnut	Constraint level
Annual gross margin	100	320	
Constraints			
Land (hectares)	1	1	3
Labour (man-days)	60	120	240
Capital (£)	50	200	200 (year 1)
			0 (year 2)

The optimal solution is obtained after four iterations as follows:

Total gross margin in second year	£608
year 1: maize	$2\frac{2}{3}$ hectares
groundnuts	$\frac{1}{3}$ hectare
unused labour	40 man-days
year 2: maize	8/15 hectare
groundnuts	$1\frac{11}{15}$ hectare
unused land	$\frac{11}{15}$ hectare

The corresponding shadow prices are:

year 1:	Land (per ha)	£32.00
	Working Capital (per £)	£ 1.76
	Consumption (per £)	£ 1.00
year 2:	Labour (per man-day)	£ 0.67
	Working capital (per £)	£ 1.20

Thus we have a situation where, through shortage of working capital in the first year, the emphasis is on maize production. All the land is cultivated, but some labour is left unused. By the second year more working capital is accumulated so the emphasis can shift to groundnuts, which are more profitable. However, they require more labour per hectare, so labour becomes the binding constraint and some land is left in disposal.

Note that the shadow price of £1 consumed is £1 as we might expect, but the shadow price of capital is £1.76 per £1 invested in year 1 and £1.20 per £1 invested in year 2. The rates of return are therefore 76 per cent and 20 per cent respectively. However, the rate of return of 76 per cent on year 1 capital is actually earned over two years. Given that the rate of return in the second year is 20 per cent, the rate of return in the first year is obtained as follows:

Table 16.9. Initial tableau for 2 period LP

		Z	X_1	X_2	X_3	S_1	S_2	S_3	X_4	X_5	S_4	S_5	S_6	Constant b
Row 0	Objective	1	0	0	-1	0	0	0	-100	-320	0	0	0	0
Row 1	Capital year 1	0	50	200	1	1	0	0	0	0	0	0	0	200
Row 2	land 1	0	1	1	0	0	1	0	0	0	0	0	0	3
Row 3	labour 1	0	60	120	0	0	0	1	0	0	0	0	0	240
Row 4	Capital year 2	0	-100	-320	0	0	0	0	50	200	1	0	0	0
Row 5	land 2	0	0	0	0	0	0	0	1	1	0	1	0	3
Row 6	labour 2	0	0	0	0	0	0	0	60	120	0	0	1	240

$$(1+r_1)(1+r_2)=1.76$$
$$1.2(1+r_1)=1.76$$
$$1+r_1=1.76/1.2=1.467$$

IIence $r_1=46.7$ per cent.

This method of analysis can be applied to any multi-period planning problem. The number of periods may be increased, using the same approach, while a 'period' may be less than or more than a year.

Furthermore, the 'working capital' transferred through the tie rows may be in cash or in kind. Thus maize storage might be represented by the transfer of grain from one seasonal period to the next.

Investment in durable capital, such as oxen and a plough, is represented by an investment activity. Such an activity is illustrated by the first column of Table 16.10 which is adapted from Table 16.9 by adding durable capital investment, borrowing and lending activities and omitting the disposal activities for ease of presentation. Of course, slack variables would have to be added to arrive at a solution. We assume that the durable capital investment can be treated as an integer variable, that it costs £150 initially, depreciates by 20 per cent to £120 over two years and saves 80 man-days of labour each year. The initial cost is set against cash funds in year 1, the terminal value appears in the objective function and the services it provides (in this case labour savings) appear in tie rows for each year of the plan. For the set of coefficients given, the investment is unlikely to be attractive since the costs of £1.76×150=£264 far exceed the benefits of £0.67×80+£120=£173.33. However, if credit is available the picture changes.

Borrowing and lending activities are also included in Table 16.10. A borrowing activity contributes to cash funds in one period, but involves a cost of the loan plus interest (assumed to be 10 per cent here) in the following period. It may be necessary to include a constraint to reflect the limits on borrowing likely to apply in practice. A lending activity, on the other hand, has a cost in one period but yields a return of the principal plus interest in the next period. At 10 per cent interest, borrowing is clearly attractive and the optimal solution is to borrow £483.33 for the purchase of the durable asset and expansion of the groundnut area in year 1 to $2\frac{2}{3}$ hectares.

Thus we have a method of dynamic planning which can, in principle, allow for all the complexities of intertemporal choice. Alternative investment opportunities with different productive lives and different starting dates may be considered, together with a range of alternative borrowing

Table 16.10. *Initial tableau example 4: Durable capital, borrowing and lending*

		Activities								
	Z	Durable capital investment [a]	Maize year 1	G'nuts year 1	Consume year 1	Borrow year 1	Maize year 2	G'nuts year 2	Lend year 2	Constant b
Objective	1	-120	0	0	-1	0	-100	-320	-1.10	0
Cash year 1	0	150	50	200	1	-1	0	0	0	200
Land year 1	0	0	1	1	0	0	0	0	0	3
Labour year 1	0	-80	60	120	0	0	0	0	0	240
Cash year 2	0	0	-100	-320	0	1.10	50	200	1	0
Land year 2	0	0	0	0	0	0	1	1	0	3
Labour year 2	0	-80	0	0	0	0	60	120	0	240

[a] Integer variable; 20 per cent depreciation over two years; saves 80 man-days per year.

and lending activities. The main limitation is that of scale. Since a matrix of coefficients is included for each period of the plan, the whole multiperiod problem may become very large indeed. Clearly, the choice of time horizon, affects the size of the problem, but some reduction may be achieved by including activities for, say, every fifth year, rather than for all years. Skill and judgement are involved in deciding the amount of detail and complexity needed to provide an adequate representation of the real world problem.

(vi)   *Choice of objectives*

It may have been noted in the previous section that first-year consumption did not appear in the optimum solution; the entire gross margin from the first year was allocated to productive investment for the second year. This is the inevitable result of the way the objective function was formulated, giving equal weightings to current and future consumption. Thus lending even at very low interest rates yields more than consumption. The total consumption is then maximized by maximizing growth. Greater realism might be achieved by imposing minimum subsistence consumption constraints for each year of the plan, to allow for basic needs. However, growth would still be maximized subject to these constraints.

If, as seems more likely, farmers are willing to forego some growth in exchange for somewhat higher current consumption, we must discount future returns in the objective function. The appropriate discount rate to use is the estimated personal discount rate of the farmer. This choice is important because it establishes the threshold rate of return for the inclusion of productive activities in the plan. In our example, given a personal discount rate of 25 per cent, the value for consumption in the first year becomes $-1/1.25$, while all the returns in the second year must be divided by 1.25^2. This current consumption becomes more attractive relative to investment for the future.

The objective is now to maximize net present value of annual consumption flows plus the terminal assets. Investment appraisal is effectively incorporated within an LP framework. This approach was used to plan tree-crop investment in East and West Cameroon by Abalu (1975).

Further refinements are possible, in specifying the objective function. For instance, the value or utility per unit of consumption may decline with increasing consumption in a particular year. This is easily represented by including more than one consumption activity in each year.

For illustration, each £1 of consumption of the first £100 might be valued at 1 unit of utility. Beyond this each £1 is valued at 0.5 units. Apart from the three activities, in each year, two additional constraints would be needed, limiting each of the first two activities to a maximum of £100 consumption.

A broadly similar approach has been proposed to deal with risk rather than multiperiod planning. In this method, known as discrete stochastic programming, each 'block' of the tableau relates to a particular state of nature, and the values in the objective function are 'expected utilities' obtained as the product of the probability of a particular state of nature and the utility of the consumption on a diminishing scale as described above.

However, as discussed earlier in Chapter 3, rather than attempting to combine multiple objectives into a single utility function, it might be more practical simply to rank goals in order of priority. High-priority goals may then be treated as targets or constraints. A more sophisticated approach, which allows deviations from the target levels of achievement of various objectives, is known as 'goal programming' (see Romero & Rehman 1984; 1985). One application of goal programming to farm planning in Senegal gives results which only differ slightly from those of ordinary linear programming (Barnett, Blake & McCarl 1982).

Practical application of LP

It should be clear from this discussion that LP is a very flexible tool. Many different on- and off-farm activities can be included, physical and social constraints can be imposed and it can be adapted to deal with multiple objectives, risk and planning over time. However, its most valuable feature is that it is a whole farm planning tool, particularly suited to handling the interactions of a complex system. In contrast, partial-budgeting is concerned only with one activity or sub-system.

The main disadvantage of LP is its complexity and the need to use a computer for all but the simplest problems. As already remarked, skill and judgement are needed to assess how complex the model should be in order to provide useful insights. However, even very simple versions, such as those described in this chapter, can help our understanding of the general problem of optimization subject to constraints. The increasing availability of computers and LP packages for microcomputers allows wider use of this tool by researchers and farm advisers.

Nevertheless, the use of LP is too costly for individual farm planning, except perhaps for very large-scale units such as state farms. The main applications are based on analysis of a typical, average or model farm which is supposed to represent the whole population. Thus it is used either to predict how the majority of these farmers will respond to technical and economic changes, or to prescribe how their farming systems might be improved. Clearly, this raises problems of defining the target population and identifying a representative case study. Furthermore, the value of the results depends upon the accuracy and reliability of the data. But these probems arise with any objective approach to farming systems research, as discussed in Chapter 10.

Another problem that arises with any kind of model building, or indeed theorizing about farming systems, is that of validation. We start with assumptions or hypotheses about farmer objectives and subjective constraints, and base our predictions and prescriptions on these. But it is very difficult to test whether our initial assumptions are valid. Validation procedures are generally based on comparing the model predictions with what farmers are actually doing. If the predictions differ from reality, we conclude the initial assumptions were wrong and need modifying, but it could alternatively be concluded that the assumptions were right and farm management practices should be changed. If the predictions are accurate, on the other hand, we cannot be sure that the assumptions were correct. However, if the model is tested and validated over a range of circumstances, our confidence in its use is strengthened. Farmers may, of course, be asked what their objectives and constraints are, but their replies may be too vague and ill-formed for inclusion in quantitative models.

The criticism has been made that LP, even multiperiod LP, is suited only to planning at a specific point in time, whereas farmers are sequential decision-makers who continuously adapt to changing circumstances (see Chapter 6). However, this is hardly a valid criticism. After all, sequential decision-making simply involves a sequence of plans made at specific points in time. In view of this, farmers maintain flexibility, for instance by leaving some land uncleared until the rains are well established. Suitable constraints could be included in an LP model to represent this practice. However, the main point is that at the start of the season the farmer must make a comprehensive plan for the whole season, possibly including some sequential clearing and planting. Later, perhaps only a few days later, he may revise the plan in the light of the weather and other external variables, but that does not alter the fact that he started with a comprehensive plan, which can be modelled using LP. Used intelligently, this planning tool can yield valuable insights into the structure and possible improvements of farming systems.

Summary

1 Linear programming (LP) is a systematic, mathematical procedure for finding the optimal plan, where there is a limited choice of activities subject to fixed constraints and all relationships are linear (straight lines). Unrealistic fractional activity levels may result but can be avoided by using 'integer programming'.

2 A typical farm planning problem includes three components; the objective function (to be maximized), the constraint inequalities (ensuring that resource use is less than or equal to the quantities available) and non-negativity constraints on all the variables.

3 With two activities (or two constraints) the optimal plan may be identified from a simple two-dimensional graph, showing the feasible region, the corners of which represent extreme points or basic feasible solutions (BFS). The optimum is found at the BFS which yields the highest return.

4 The shadow price (dual value) of a resource constraint may be calculated as the effect of relaxing the constraint by one unit. If the constraint is non-binding, the shadow price is zero. The sum of products of the constraint levels and their corresponding shadow prices equals the total value of the objective function.

5 The simplex method is a formal procedure leading step-by-step from one BFS to another until the optimal solution is reached. Each step, or iteration, is taken in the direction of increasing the value of the objective function.

6 Rules are given to ensure that, at each iteration, the total return is increased without exceeding any constraint limits. The final tableau gives both the optimal combination of activities (the primal solution) and the shadow prices of the constraining resources (the dual solution).

7 Parametric programming allows testing of the effects of varying the return per unit of an activity, or the level of a resource constraint. Thus the supply response for a product or the demand for a resource input can be plotted.

8 A labour-hiring activity supplements the available supply or constraint level, and permits extra production. Thus the extra labour hired must be subtracted from the total labour requirements of the production activities, in a tie row. Similarly a bush-clearing activity permits subsequent cropping activities, or fodder production permits ruminant livestock production. Rotational constraints can be represented in this way.

9 Minimum target constraints, such as household food requirements, require outcomes which are greater than, or equal to, the target level. Such

constraints, imposed for each state of nature, provide for 'safety first' programming. LP can also be used for cost minimization subject to target constraints.

10 Good land (yielding a higher return per hectare) may be distinguished from poor land, for productive activity and as a constraint. This analysis demonstrates that good land is used more intensively and yields a higher rent than poor land.

11 Multiperiod programming involves linking a series of annual input–output matrices, through working capital tie rows, in a 'block-diagonal' structure. The objective function may include both current consumption and the total value of production and invested capital in the terminal period. The shadow price of working capital gives a measure of the rate of return. Durable capital investment, borrowing and lending activities may be included.

12 Because capital investment earns a positive return, the optimal solution is always to invest all income and maximize growth, unless current consumption is forced into the plan. This may be achieved by including target constraints for annual consumption levels and discounting income to be received in later years. Discrete stochastic programming is a similar approach which allows for risk.

13 Linear programming is a very flexible tool that can be adapted to deal with multiple objectives, risk and planning over time. It normally requires careful data preparation and use of a computer, so is unsuited to the analysis and planning of individual smallholder farms. However, used intelligently, this planning tool can yield valuable insights into the structure and possible improvements of farming systems.

References

Abalu, G. O. I. (1975). 'Optimal investment decisions in perennial crop production: a dynamic linear programming approach', *Journal of Agricultural Economics*, **26**(3), 383

Ahmed, I. & B. H. Kinsey (eds) (1984). *Farm Equipment Innovations in Eastern and Central Southern Africa*, Aldershot, Hants. Gower for ILO

Barnett, D., B. Blake & B. A. McCarl (1982). 'Goal programming via multidimensional scaling applied to Senegalese subsistence farms', *American Journal of Agricultural Economics*, **64**(4), 720–7

Clayton, E. S. (1961). 'Technical and economic optima in peasant agriculture', *Journal of Agricultural Economics*, **14**(3), 337

Farrington, J. (1976). 'A note on planned versus actual farmer performance under uncertainty in underdeveloped agriculture', *Journal of Agricultural Economics*, **27**(2), 257

Hardaker, J. B. (1979). 'A review of some farm management research methods for small farm development in LDCs', *Journal of Agricultural Economics*, **30**(3), 315

Heyer, J. (1972). 'An analysis of peasant farm production under conditions of uncertainty', *Journal of Agricultural Economics*, **23**(2), 135

Knipscheer, H. C., K. M. Menz & I. Verinumbe (1983). 'The evaluation of preliminary FS technologies: zero tillage systems in W. Africa', *Agricultural Systems*, **11**, 95–103

Low, A. R. C. (1974). 'Decision taking under uncertainty: a linear programming model of peasant farmer behaviour', *Journal of Agricultural Economics*, **25**(3), 311

Ogunfowora, O. (1972). 'Conceptualizing increased resource demand and product supply inducing policies in peasant agriculture', *Nigerian Journal of Economic and Social Studies*, **14**, 191

Ogunfowora, O. & D. W. Norman (1974). *An Optimization Model for Evaluating the Stability of Sole Cropping and Mixed Cropping Systems under Changing Resource and Technology levels*, Zaria, Nigeria, Ahmadu Bello University, IAR. Research Bulletin No. 217

Olayide, S. O. & S. O. Olowude (1972). 'Optimum combination of farm enterprises in W. Nigeria: a LP analysis', *Nigerian Journal of Economic and Social Studies*, **14**(1), 63

Romero, C. & T. Rehman (1984). 'Goal programming and multiple criteria decision making in farm planning', *Journal of Agricultural Economics*, **35**(2), 177

Romero, C. & T. Rehman (1985). 'Goal programming and multiple criteria decision making in farm planning: some extensions'. *Journal of Agricultural Economics*, **36**(2), 171

Vail, D. J. (1973). 'Induced farm innovation and derived scientific research strategy', *East African Journal of Rural Development*, **6**(1)

Index

ability, managerial, 291
  see also management
accounting, 256, 263–4, 299
activity, linear programming, 111, 328–38
  productive, 110–11
  substitution, 112
administrative costs, 160
adopters, 235, 259
adverse selection, 136
aerial survey, 245
aggregation (of labour), 262
agriculture
  development, 4–18
  population, 3–4, 28
  sector, 3
  trade, 6–10
agro-ecological zone, 219
aims, farmer's, 49, 127–8
  see also objectives
allocation
  resources, 34–5, 293–4
  water, 197–201
animal draught, 87–8
  see also bullocks, oxen
annuity, 321
  factors, 321, 365
aquifer, 190, 198, 206, 208–9
arable cultivation, 171
area measurement, 244–7
arithmetic mean, 233
artificial variable, 348
assets, 141–3, 250–1
  see also capital
association between variables, 258
  see also correlation
attitudes, farmers', 230
average cost, 99 104, 228
average product, 70, 73, 271, 282
averaging out and folding back,
  131–4

background information, 219
backward-bending supply curve, 80
  see also negative response
bank loan, 151
banks, 160–1
basic feasible solution (BFS), 335, 339–40,
  343–4, 348
  food needs, 53
  see also survival
basis, 340–1
bent-stick response, 108–9
bias, statistical, 235, 239, 259, 294
biased innovations, 98
binary data, 233, 256, 259
binding constraints, 52, 331–8
  see also effective constraints
biological resources, 166–70
biomass, 166–70
block-diagonal structure, 353
borrowing, 156–60, 356
boundaries
  farm or plot, 245
  system, 218
budgeting, 299–313, 318–20
bullocks, 143
  see also draught animals, oxen
bureaucratic allocation, 198, 200–3
bush fallow, 27, 171
buying activities, 346–7

calorie intake, 5
canals, 191, 200–2
  lining, 202
capital, 19–22, 141–63, 165, 250–1, 261–2
  budgeting, 315–27
  circulating (working), 142, 148–50, 161,
  354–6
  in production functions, 286
  investment, 142–3, 145–54, 190, 309–10,
  315–26, 353